T0181290

Lecture Notes in Information Systems and Organisation

Volume 19

More information about this series at http://www.springer.com/series/11237

Fabrizio D'Ascenzo · Massimo Magni
Alessandra Lazazzara · Stefano Za
Editors

Blurring the Boundaries Through Digital Innovation

Individual, Organizational, and Societal Challenges

 Springer

Editors

Fabrizio D'Ascenzo
Department of Management
Sapienza Universitá di Roma
Rome
Italy

Alessandra Lazazzara
Department of Human Sciences "R. Massa"
University of Milan Bicocca
Milan
Italy

Massimo Magni
Department of Management and Technology
Bocconi University
Milan
Italy

Stefano Za
Faculty of Law
eCampus University
Novedrate
Italy

ISSN 2195-4968   ISSN 2195-4976   (electronic)
Lecture Notes in Information Systems and Organisation
ISBN 978-3-319-38973-8   ISBN 978-3-319-38974-5   (eBook)
DOI 10.1007/978-3-319-38974-5

Library of Congress Control Number: 2016939569

Printed on acid-free paper

This Springer imprint is published by Springer Nature
The registered company is Springer International Publishing AG Switzerland

Preface

The recursive interaction between Information and Communication Technology (ICT) and behaviour in organizational contexts is widely recognized. However, the digital revolution is breaking traditional levels of analysis (i.e. individuals, organizations, and society) and blurring internal and external organizational environment boundaries. This book contains a collection of research papers focusing on the interaction between ICT and behaviour with a threefold perspective. First, analysing individual behaviour in terms of specific organizational practices (e.g. learning, collaboration, knowledge transfer) or use of ICT within organizations. Second, exploring dynamics occurring at the border between the internal and the external environments by analysing the organizational impact of ICT usage outside the company (e.g. employer branding, consumer behaviour, organizational image). Third, investigating the adoption of ICT in order to face societal challenges outside the company (e.g. waste and pollution, smart cities, e-government). The plurality of views offered makes this book particularly relevant for users, companies, scientists and governments. The content of the book is mainly based on a selection of the best papers (original double-blind peer-reviewed contributions) presented at the annual conference of the Italian chapter of AIS which took place in Rome, Italy, in October 2015 but also at other reputable international peer-refereed information systems conferences.

Milan
March 2016

Fabrizio D'Ascenzo
Massimo Magni
Alessandra Lazazzara
Stefano Za

Contents

Introduction

**Fabrizio D'Ascenzo, Massimo Magni, Alessandra Lazazzara
and Stefano Za**

The XII ItAIS Conference has been held in Rome and it represents the main source of papers for this volume. The conference theme: "Reshaping Organizations through Digital and Social Innovation" embraces the need of information systems to develop a stronger connection between the organizational dimensions, the technical perspective and the dialogue with the social community. The interconnections within and across organizational boundaries have been outlined in several studies both in organization and IS literature (e.g. [1, 2]). According to this perspective, the role of technology can be seen through a wider lens which increases the magnitude of the impact that IS research may provide to the social community [3, 4].

The rigorous research that have been presented to ItAIS and other conferences, which is reported in this volume, can be considered as a further step to make the IS research valuable for the managerial community and for the society in general, thus helping to face the challenges outlined by European and other International Institutions for the XXI century [5]. Indeed, the digital revolution is breaking

F. D'Ascenzo
Department of Management, Sapienza University, Rome, Italy
e-mail: fabrizio.dascenzo@uniroma1.it

M. Magni
Department of Management and Technology, Bocconi University, Milan, Italy
e-mail: massimo.magni@unibocconi.it

A. Lazazzara (✉)
Department of Human Sciences, University of Milan Bicocca, Milan, Italy
e-mail: alessandra.lazazzara@unimib.it

S. Za
eCampus University, Novedrate (CO), Italy
e-mail: stefano.za@uniecampus.it; sza@luiss.it

S. Za
CeRSI – LUISS Guido Carli University, Rome, Italy

F. D'Ascenzo et al. (eds.), *Blurring the Boundaries Through Digital Innovation*,
Lecture Notes in Information Systems and Organisation 19,
DOI 10.1007/978-3-319-38974-5_1

traditional levels of analysis (i.e. individuals, organizations, and society) and blurring internal and external organizational environment boundaries [6].

Besides undertaking a perspective within and across organizational boundaries, the present volume embraces also a perspective that spans across levels of analysis, thus taking into account the single individual, the interaction among individuals, the organization as a whole, as well as the interaction between organization and social community. Such point of view is consistent with Johns [7] who called for taking a multilevel perspective in studying organizations, noting that strictly macro-level approaches ignore the individual mental processes and behaviors, while strictly micro-level approaches ignore how macro-level context shapes the interaction among different organizational and institutional actors. This perspective emphasizes the recursive interaction between Information and Communication Technology (ICT) and behaviour in organizational contexts.

With the idea of spanning across levels and across organizational boundaries, the volume collects 23 contributions that were selected from the ItAIS Conference papers (16) and from other conferences (7), namely the 23rd European Conference on Information Systems (ECIS) and the 28th BLED e-conference. All the selected papers have been evaluated through a standard blind review process in order to ensure theoretical and methodological rigor. The threefold structure of the volume reflects three main pillars that have been explored by the included papers. The first part is focused on analysing individual behaviour in terms of specific organizational practices (e.g. learning, collaboration, knowledge transfer) or use of ICT within organizations. The second part focuses on the exploration of dynamics occurring at the border between the internal and the external environments by analysing the organizational impact of ICT usage outside the company (e.g. employer branding, consumer behaviour, organizational image). The third part investigates the adoption of ICT in order to face societal challenges outside the company (e.g. waste and pollution, smart cities, e-government).

This publication is the result of a team work where many people have actively contributed. We are grateful to the Authors, the Conference Chairs and Committee members, to the members of the Editorial Board, and to the Reviewers for their competence and commitment.

1 Part I: Individual Behavior and ICT Adoption Within Organizational Boundaries

If we ask managers what is the most important asset of their organization, we have high chances that they will answer "people". This sentence is particularly true in the domain of ICT, where individuals play a pivotal role in shaping the support of technology in reaching the organizational goals by embracing behaviors that support the alignment between the ICT deployment and use with the strategic objectives. Take the case of few years ago when employees of a well known airline carrier decided to neither support or being an obstacle for the introduction of a new information system. In particular, employees did not explicitly disclosed all the critical aspects of their job, but at the same time they allowed the team of the developers to observe them and to implement the system without raising any objections. Their neutral behavior did not allow to properly match the system characteristics with the organizational processes and goals: after few months the system has been dismissed with an approximate loss of 40 million of dollars.

The first part of the book takes into account the pivotal role of the individual through different lenses, and it provides a wide overview of the relationship between individuals' behavior and ICT. In particular, four main streams can be outlined in this first part (i.e. networks, learning, design, and trust,). From a network perspective, Augier and Mola take into account the role of social networks in shaping organizations. In particular, they provide a theoretical perspective on how collaboration tools can support organizations that are striving toward more decentralized and flat configurations. On this vein, Ghiringhelli and Lazazzara point out the training needs that should be taken into account in order to effectively manage the integration of geographically dispersed knowledge, thus allowing organizations that implement decentralized structures to be better poised to leverage on virtual teams advantages. In so doing they underscore the critical role played by the HR function in sustaining and supporting the need for specific training in setting where individuals mainly interact through ICT.

The challenge of preparing individuals to face the networked and dispersed context is recognized both by organizations and educational institutions. One the one hand, Iannotta, Gatti and D'Ascenzo explore the diffusion of ICT in the landscape of Italian corporate universities. Their study underscores that, despite the incumbent learning by technology revolution, just few corporate universities make extensive use of ICT, tracing back such issue to the culture and organizational characteristics. By taking a different angle, Caporarello and Iñesta look at how educational institutions may play a pivotal role in accelerating the spread of technology-based learning approaches. Specifically, they try to frame a better understanding of what universities are doing to implement programs that are based on advanced technologies, thus enhancing the awareness of such tools for educational and training purposes.

However, as outlined in the study conducted by Za and Scornavacca, the cultural and organizational dimension is not enough for gaining competitive advantage through technology. In particular, the authors outline the importance of the design dimension. Indeed, by adopting a design science approach it is more likely to foster and facilitate a learning process through ubiquitous technology. The importance of design is also underscored by Bohanec, Kljajić Borštnar and Robnik-Šikonja who take an organizational learning perspective in the design process and explore the gap between expected and actual performance. By taking a case on B2B forecasting they illustrate how machine learning techniques can be related to organizational learning. Finally, two papers outline the importance of trust in all the processes that are related to the relationship between ICT and individual attitudes and behaviors. Pistilli and Pennarola point out the role of trust in the technology adoption process.

From a complementary perspective, Braccini and Marzo, by relying on experimental settings, outline how trust and control dynamics are different across digital native individuals and digital immigrants. Such findings outline new and potential pathways to develop research at the individual levels that takes into account how attitudes and behaviors toward technology are rapidly changing across different cohorts of the population.

2 Part II: Crossing the Organizational Boundaries

Organizations are not entities that live in the vacuum. Individuals and organizational actors are constantly interacting within and across the boundaries of the organization, making the role of communication technology particularly relevant for developing and sustaining the connection with the external environment. Nowadays, the relationship between the organization and the external environment is characterized by two main challenges: the ethical approach to the relationship, and the reputational and social image dimension while interacting outside the organizational boundaries.

From an ethical standpoint Vassio, Metwalley and Giordano underscore the issue related to the use of personal data and users' information that are now spread all over the web. Indeed, firms can take advantage of such data and information without the acknowledgement of the interested individuals, thus posing an ethical dilemma on the redefinition of the boundaries of individual privacy. From such standpoint, a particularly sensitive set of data is represented by citizens' health information. Kenny and Connolly urge us to reflect about the trade off related to the benefits of collecting healthcare information through ICT, and the potential liabilities for patients' privacy. In order to investigate the tendency to embrace unethical behaviors, Jafarkarimi, Sim, Saadatdoost and Hee proposed a method for designing a scenario-based assessment for better understanding individuals' behavior in facing ethical dilemmas.

Other studies took the perspective of the firm, rather than considering the single individuals. For example the study conducted by Karjaluoto, Mäkinen and Järvinen stimulates the debate on the firms activity in social media. Specifically, the study provides a better understanding on the relationship between media activity, performance and reputation of the company. In another study, conducted by Karjaluoto, Munnukka and Tiensuu is evident the effect of the community in developing brand engagement, thus pointing out the influence of the community in shaping individuals' attitude toward firms' brand and reputation. Another study outlined the factors concerning the social image of the firm and their influence on individuals' behaviors. Harfouche, Ezzeddine and Asmar by studying the adoption of a banking system in Lebanon found that both intrinsic and extrinsic religiosity may affect individual adoption of an e-banking system. The relationship with the customers through ICT has been also investigated by the study of Mladenow, Bauer and Strauss which provides further insights into the emerging collective buying domain. By adopting a SWOT analysis approach the paper offers insights to improve business models in the field of collective buying through ICT.

3 Part III: Societal Challenges and ICT Adoption Outside the Organizational Boundaries

Recent research outlined the critical role of ICT to face the social challenges of the XXI century. For example, a longitudinal study that lasted 7 years conducted by Venkatesh et al. (forthcoming) aims at providing a better understanding on how ICT can support the diffusion of medical information in rural areas, thus diminishing infant mortality. Following this vein, the third part of the book focuses on the challenges related to the importance of ICT outside the organizational boundaries. In particular, there are three main domains that can be outlined in this third part: social issues and impact, communities, and government and institution.

The paper by Herrmann, Prilla and Nolte takes a socio-technical perspective to analyze a case related to the services that can be provided by elderly people. On the same topic, the paper by De Paoli uses contextual analysis to investigate the role of e-service for elderly people and outline the pivotal role of inclusion policies and co-production. The study outlines the importance of taking blended perspective by taking into account the organizational and technical standpoint. The importance of ICT for society and the challenges of the XXI century is taken into account by Bonomi, Ricciardi and Rossignoli who investigate the impact that ICT may have on food waste reduction. Specifically, the authors take into account a longitudinal case of smart organization in facing this challenge. The research developed by Cocchia and Dameri explore the emerging phenomenon of smart cities. In particular, they take into account and analyze the perspectives of the different stakeholders involved.

The attention toward the issues that cross organizational boundaries is also taken into account by those papers which are more keen to investigate the role of the online communities. In particular, the work by Braccini, Federici and Sæbø considers the concept of affordance to better understand the relationship among technology, people and organizational structures. Nguyen, Tahmasbi, de Vreede, de Vreede, Oh and Reiter-Palmon take into account the emergent phenomenon of crowdsourcing by investigating the engagement of individuals in such phenomenon. In so doing, they develop the Participant Engagement Index that quantifies behavioral aspects of engagement in crowdsourcing communities.

A third stream of research looked at the institutions and government. In particular, the paper by Gesuele, Metallo and Agrifoglio explores the use of social media in Italian municipalities by investigating the way through which nine Italian cities use Facebook. Langley, Wijn, Epskamp and Van Bork investigate how social media can be used as a tool to support and encourage the vaccination. They undertake an experiment to demonstrate that the decision of vaccination does not occur into a vacuum but is tied to the social interactions among individuals.

References

1. Brass, D.J., Galaskiewicz, J., Greve, H.R., Tsai, W.: Taking stock of networks and organizations: a multilevel perspective. Acad. Manag. J. **47**(6), 795–817 (2004)
2. Sasidharan, S., Santhanam, R., Brass, D.J., Sambamurthy, V.: The effects of social network structure on enterprise systems success: a longitudinal multilevel analysis. Inf. Syst. Res. **23**(3), 658–678 (2012)
3. Venkatesh, V., Rai, A., Sykes, T.A., Aljafari, R.: Combating infant mortality in rural india: evidence from a field study of ehealth kiosk implementations. MIS Q. (forthcoming)
4. Ahuja, M.K., Chudoba, K.M., Kacmar, C.J., McKnight, D.H., George, J.F.: IT road warriors: balancing work-family conflict, job autonomy, and work overload to mitigate turnover intentions. MIS Q. 1–17 (2007)
5. Venkatesh, V., Sykes, T.A.: Digital divide initiative success in developing countries: a longitudinal field study in a village in India. Inf. Syst. Res. **24**(2), 239–260 (2013)
6. Markus, M.L., Robey, D.: Information technology and organizational change: causal structure in theory and research. Manage. Sci. **34**(5), 583–598 (1988)
7. Johns, G.: The essential impact of context on organizational behavior. Acad. Manag. Rev. **31**(2), 386–408 (2006)

Part I
Individual Behavior and ICT
Adoption Within Organizational
Boundaries

Reshaping Organizations with Social Networks and Collaboration

Marc Augier and Lapo Mola

1 Introduction

According to the coordination mechanism chosen and used, organizations can adopt different structures, business processes, and relations between actors. For instance, coordination could help to harmonize the various activities that a company pursues and the interdependencies among its members, which should contribute to the competitiveness of the organization [1]. The ability of organizations to create coordination mechanisms that can sustain and increase the efficiency and effectiveness of relationships across business units is particularly critical in a competitive context [2–4].

With greater support for decision-making and its decentralization, as well as greater communication and knowledge sharing, coordination mechanisms should be more efficient, allowing the actors in the organization to better perform their tasks and complete their processes.

The digital revolution is impacting many aspects of the society and organizations are not the least. This is a time for a stronger pressure from both the competition and the consumers because of pervasive computers, connected devices and collaboration tools that give to anyone anywhere almost the same opportunities for business development. Definitely, in order to take advantage and to adapt to this new situation, the enterprise needs to switch and set up new business and management processes, activity that we want to refer to as *"Organization Design and Engineering"* (ODE). Interestingly, the same acronym can be used for *"Organization for the*

M. Augier (✉) · L. Mola
SKEMA Business School, BP 85, 06902 Sophia Antipolis Cedex, France
e-mail: marc.augier@skema.edu

L. Mola
e-mail: lapo.mola@skema.edu

© Springer International Publishing Switzerland 2016
F. D'Ascenzo et al. (eds.), *Blurring the Boundaries Through Digital Innovation*,
Lecture Notes in Information Systems and Organisation 19,
DOI 10.1007/978-3-319-38974-5_2

Digital Enterprise" and this is the proposition for a new organization that we would like to propose in this study.

We already mentioned the competition and the customers, but the employees are also taking advantage of this new digital environment and the traditional hierarchical model is challenged by new organization designs that we will develop further.

> The CEO of 2022 will have to manage a complex business of far-flung inputs from customers' and employees' tweets (or the 2022 equivalent) to all kinds of data persistently emitted from billions of phones, sensors, and other connected machines. Companies that can manage and mine all those bits and bytes stand to make a killing [5].

In most situations, organizations operate in a changing environment that adds complexity to an already tense competition environment. In such situation, organization design can be an essential element for success because it allows to improve the way the organizations operate by providing an holistic thinking about the organization and the way the whole operates, and the rules of interaction by defining the relationships among people who assume the roles prescribed by the organization and the relationships of organizational groups or units to which they belong [6, 7].

2 Challenges and Opportunities for Digital Transformation

Organizations today are facing unprecedented challenges, the most important being rapidly accelerating pace of change and complexity. These new challenges are the result of the extensive usage of digital devices and shared resources linked together on the Web 2.0, the people-centric Web or participative Web [8]. Web 2.0 technologies provide a more interactive and collaborative environment, emphasizing peers' social interaction and collective intelligence, allowing users to engage more effectively [9].

Combining the progresses made on the hardware with the progresses made in software development, the Web is one of the many examples of disruptive technologies that are also pervasive, allowing mass collaboration across the planet and letting some people think it is flat [10], a view that is may be exaggerated [11] because much of this connectivity occurs inside the borders of a country. But what is not yet true for globalization is already true for the organizations and they require to take advantage of this new level of connectivity and agility in order to become Enterprise 2.0 [12–14]. The corporations are both trying to take advantage of the vast amount of information at their disposition, now referred as "Big Data" [15] and at the same time build more efficient infrastructures by using "Cloud services" [16–18].

The effort to improve human cognition started by collecting knowledge (Encyclopedists) and developing classification [19, 20] to reproduce the way our brain is working by creating associations and linking ideas together. With the introduction of Digital Technology, this progressed a big step further by reshaping the way we work and live, moving from a single user perspective to improve their cognitive capacity to a group perspective and thus allow the development of collective intelligence. This journey started with an article in The Atlantic monthly "*As we may think*" [21] where Vanevar Bush describes a mechanical apparatus ("MemEx" for Memory Expander) designed to help scientists collect and share information. This article was an inspiring source to many, like Theodor Holm (Ted) Nelson who coined the word "hypertext" in an article for Dream Machine and started the "Xanadu project" in order to investigate and develop an hypertext system to link not only documents but ideas [22–24]. This was the beginning of a long quest to develop tools to augment human intellectual capacity, and even if the MemEx as designed by Bush was never built, it is still a source of creativeness and even recently a research project at Microsoft "MyLifeBits" [25] started to develop a system that could manage and store all the digital documents individuals are now producing.

To summarize, hypertext systems are used to improve collaboration with a human-machine interface tailored to our way of thinking and part of their success comes from a dumb device that is also the symbol of the pervasive computer era, the mouse that appeared for the first time at the Stanford Research Institute in Menlo Park, California when Douglas Engelbart ran the "*mother of all presentations*" [26]. That was the first appearance of a new pointing device, the mouse and also of a personal working environment where the documents are displayed in different windows and can be shared with several persons connected on the same local network. Because the main ambition of Douglas Engelbart was augmenting the human intellect, and if we consider all that was developed from his inventions, that goal is more than achieved. The hypertext can really be taken as a foundation from which we can develop a cognitive model for different situations. Because it works with a single person and it works also between different brains, when people work together, their brains not only create links inside themselves but also from one to another. It is perhaps too easy to see the correlation with the links in a hypertext system and the links between neurons, but this allows to think that the more brains you are able to link together, the more ideas you get, creating a common single super brain, a collective brain [27] of people connected together via their computers on the internet.

The combination of these technologies leads to a future where corporations will have virtually unlimited capacity, both in storage and in computing power. This cannot be done following the old hierarchical ways of organizing and executing work, "*the old hardwired 'plan and push' mentality is rapidly giving way to a new, dynamic engage and co-create' economy*" [28]. Instead, with the help of information systems they can build new forms of organizational design through a host of new capabilities in the coordination and control of organizational processes [29–31], competence management [32, 33] strategic alignment [34] or boundary spanning mechanisms [35, 36].

The importance for the organizations to change and develop new relationships with their partners and employees is displayed in a recent study from IBM (IBM Global CEO, Leading Through Connections, produced through interviews with almost 2,000 CEOs across the globe and from multiple industry sectors). It also indicates that the most effective enterprises are able to access and use customer data through a collaborative organization, making them what we already called *"Enterprises 2.0"* to refer to their capability at managing their business via the collaborative platforms offered by the Web 2.0. To take advantage of this new business environment, it is not enough to use new tools inside old fashioned organization models, a more complex deep transformation based on innovation is required and for over 50 % of CEO's from the IBM Global CEO study this remains a top priority. Because sometimes it is not about creating new services or products, it is in fact about creating new industries or moving into existing ones. Still according to the same study, CEO's are placing greater focus on open and collaborative business, responding to the phenomenal growth of our networked society, 75 % of CEO's see developing an open and collaborative culture as critical to matching the complexity of business today. Collaboration and social learning are seen as the key traits for adapting to change. More than half of them expect that social channels will become the primary method of communicating with customers.

For the first time since 2004, technology is the top priority for CEO's and seen as key to future success, more precisely they are planning investment in internal social technologies to facilitate grater and broader collaboration with partners and between employees. These CEO should however take into account that technology is not the only answer, it is the main driver and the foundation on top of which to build the change. The main challenge is not to implement technology but to adapt our management practices, because a fundamental change of traditional practices is needed. If we only look to communication, there have been dramatic improvements. In the last 20 years we saw appear and almost totally disappear the fax, made obsolete by the email, which is now an ubiquitous communication tool. But the email may now suffer from its success and this is why some are already thinking about replacing that with social services. Our mailboxes are bloated with hundred of messages everyday, some are just a couple of lines, some are essentials for our business and some are spam. Each and every message falls into the same bucket and we spend a lot of time, too much time, to read and sort those out. The younger generations have understood the email is no longer an efficient communication tool and prefer to use instant messaging and social networks, were their messages keep sorted in different "conversations". Several companies are already thinking to move in this direction, some are giving more importance to their social network, some ask their employees to refrain for a systematic usage of the mail and prefer phone calls or instant messaging for simple messages and some are taking a step further and have announced their decision to forbid the usage of email for internal communication, as for instance did Thierry Breton, CEO of Atos Origin in February 2011. The email may follow the same path as the fax or the regular mail, disappear or kept for very formal communication.

3 Digital Revolution

During the industrial revolution, muscle power from animals or men was replaced by technology: steam power, then gas or electrical engines, in order to produce goods and cultivate more efficiently. We are at the beginning of a big change, that can be summarized through its name "digital revolution" or "knowledge revolution" [37], we can now increase our brainpower by using computers, databases, networks, etc. Improving the brainpower is not enough; it leaves apart the great advantages that can be unleashed by using it more efficiently. To use a new device does not make a revolution and in order to better understand the transformation to overcome we can make a parallel with the evolution of the transportation industry. Obviously we don't use a plane like a car but there is more than that because the invention of the plane did not make the car obsolete. We continue to use them, upgrading the roads infrastructure and improving the traffic code, to take full advantage of the benefits of using them. In the same way, in order to make the digital devices more efficient we need to improve the communication links, that same image was used by the then-senator Al Gore in the 80s calling for an "information superhighway" in order to foster education in America for all citizens regardless of their income. With the digital revolution, we have developed new cars (computers) and new roads (Internet) to communicate faster, but we are still in the process of learning how to drive and developing new rules for driving faster and better. There is much more than technology, it is another way to understand the world, which leads to a new paradigm for doing business.

Translated in management opportunities, we have to develop new organization models that take advantage of the new opportunities offered by worldwide omnipresent connected computers. At this point, realizing we are in the middle of the digital revolution, with many connected devices available to enhance the way human beings think, we should see enterprises taking advantage of the new situation and develop innovative and more effective organization [38].

It may be exaggerated to talk about a revolution, because during the evolution of the devices created across the time in order to manage information or knowledge, there are few technological disruptions. We can identify clearly only two: the introduction of electric power and the invention of the semiconductor microchip. In fact, the disruption initiated by the transition from an analog world to a digital one does not come from technology but from a switch of mindset, from closed hierarchical structures to more open ones. Technology was not enough to create digital knowledge as we know it today. For that, we had to have the Internet and the spirit of knowledge sharing behind it that supported its development. It is important to notice for instance that more than 50 % of the Web servers in service all around the world are using the Apache software,[1] those development is performed as an open source project managed by a not for profit foundation. If we add to this figure the

---

[1]The NetCraft services company provides a monthly review of the different Web Server softwares in use around the world at http://www.netcraft.com/internet-data-mining/hosting-analysis/.

15 % using the nginx server, another Open Source server, we will figure out that quite 70 % of world wide web sites are relying on an Open Source engine, in other words by a software developed collaboratively by thousands, may be million of programmers dispatched around the globe and that barely meet each others.

Nothing would have been possible if young MIT programmer Richard Stallman upset by a bad printer and the collapse of his community of programmers [39], decided to start the GNU project in 1985 with the aim to maintain the freedom of sharing software and ideas about software. That was the first step for the Free Software Foundation that developed the legal infrastructure to host thousands of software development projects, the most famous being the Apache web server already mentioned, the Mozilla Firefox web browser and the GNU/Linux operating system.

Because in the digital world the tools and the documents they manipulate are closely bound, the same rules had to be set in order to provide the community with open standards for storing and retrieving information, like for instance the extensible markup language (XML) [40] that is part of the technical roots of the semantic Web [41]. When using the appropriate open standards, digital documents, like the source code of the program allow remixing: copy, adapt, improve and publish again. From technical documents to any sort of digital document, the step was easily crossed, and the sharing philosophy developed by the FSF was extended to other types of documents, text, music, pictures, video, etc. In 1995 Ward Cunningham created the Portland Pattern Wiki [42] in order to help people share their best practices in software development, he coined the name Wiki from the Hawaiian words that mean "fast", because he was looking for something fast and easy to use. The wiki technology was reused eventually by others to create much more ambitious knowledge sharing projects like the Wikimedia foundation and its collection of encyclopedias and dictionaries, it started from the Wikipedia encyclopedia launched in 2001 by Jimmy Wales and Larry Sanger. At the same time, with the same spirit but a different background Lawrence Lessig, Stanford University Law School professor, applied the same philosophy to cultural goods and started the Free Culture movement [43, 44] and created the Creative Commons to provide a legal framework for this new way of working and help artists share and remix their work on the Internet.

Today all these different projects are used together and for instance the Wikipedia encyclopedia technology is based on the MediaWiki free software and the contents are contributed via a Creative Commons License.

4 From Digital to Open in Organization Design

We can think that we have arrived at the end of our digital journey, but we could also think that the move from software to culture is only the first step. The digital revolution or the simple evolution our society is actually living through widespread usage of Web 2.0 technologies and initiatives like the free culture movement, crowdsourcing could have deeper implication in the way it is organized and structured. This is more or less what the Free Culture movement started while different organizations worked out on creating new models, like the Creative Commons one which aim is to give a legal framework to the new economy that is now developing online, most of it being based on the "remix".

The remix means that you can take one's work and replay it adding your own interpretation, like it was possible with the oral tradition. But there is a problem with this model. The intellectual property rights are very difficult to maintain in a world where every act on the Web is a copy and at the same time the laws are expecting to regulate copies [45]. Before we use digital documents and the Web, things where very clear. There were authors going through publishers to address their audience or readers, which was at the same time customers of the publishers. Now anyone can be author and self-publish her work on the Web.

With the industrial revolution, the manufacturing industry was able to move from muscle to engine powered machines, which gave huge improvements and benefits. Then, slowly these businesses realized that they need to get more from their machines and they developed industrialization processes in order to be more efficient. The utmost benefits where achieved during the second part of the XXth century, when performance improvements were still made possible through automation and mechanization. But since then, it was difficult to get great benefits and the industry concerns moved from the manual worker in manufacturing to the knowledge worker [46], because this is where the biggest paybacks can be achieved now. In fact, it seems that their productivity remained steady for different reasons, the most important one being that the knowledge workers should not be managed, in any way, like the manual worker.

They have to have autonomy and motivation, continuing innovation, learning and teaching, developing and assimilating knowledge management practices. Then, if their productivity is not as good as expected, the main reason to blame is outdated management practices from the XXth century based on a strong hierarchical structure with control mindset, bureaucratic processes and standardization. This approach worked well for driving productivity in manufacturing but is harmful for innovation and engagement, which are the key ingredients for success of modern organizations. Knowledge workers needs are very similar to those of the Y generation, and we will not debate who originated them, but there is an obvious link between the two because most students from the Y generation and after will become knowledge workers. They tend to ignore or even challenge corporate hierarchy and instead give respect to skilled people, whatever is their rank in the corporation. For them "the world is flat" [10], they have a global mindset and they are very mobile, always connected to their social network. They expect to be treated as peers rather than subordinates. When managed inappropriately, in an organization designed to automate and optimize work, they become less engaged and will collaborate less, leading them to operate below their full potential [47–51]. The traditional organizations no longer provide them with the proper tools to perform their task and usually most of the solutions they develop daily come from their social network outside the entity, sometimes even using their own devices usually smartphones or

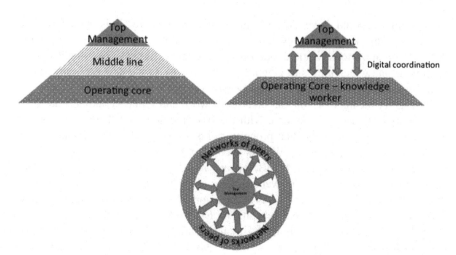

Fig. 1 Three steps evolution process

tablets they bring in the workplace contributing to put the organization infrastructure under pressure [52]. As a result, conventional organizations are increasingly suboptimal, because these do not really own what creates value but they only rent it from their knowledge workers.

We need agile corporations that can adapt easily to new markets and customers, this involves to achieve several engagements, concerning the enterprise infrastructure, the management processes and that may go up to rethinking the nature of employment in an increasingly automated, borderless and highly mobile global economy. To summarize the situation we depicted from different perspectives, we can say that we are in the middle of a great shift from industrial to cultural production. Figure 1 shows three main steps from the hierarchical organization to a flat organization using ICT as main coordination mechanism and then to social network based organization, where top management becomes the focal point rather than the top of the organization.

This evolution is reinforced by the diffusion of cloud computing [17, 18], the most advanced representation of the commoditization of ICT, even if it is far from being the only one. Many IS services are more and more externalized in the form of subscribed online services also known as software as a service, SaaS [53]. It is interesting to note that once the organization ICT is externalized and accessible anywhere, it is much easier to break the physical borders of the enterprise to allow workers to access the corporate data from anywhere. This is not only necessary to take advantage of teleworking in some specific situations but compulsory in order to create a new organization framework. The *office* is wherever the knowledge worker is sitting, be it a formal space like the physical office at the company's building or informal spaces, at home, at the coffee shop or even commuting, in the train, at the airport, etc. We need to redefine what is attached to the office concept.

This is no longer an image, a building owned by someone else where you wear a suit and smile at the boss's jokes, today, the office has to be understood in terms of service, it is a place where the knowledge worker is able to perform his job, and mainly that means wherever she or he is online [54, 55].

The loss of boundaries has positive factors because we can now work without constraints about time, location [56, 57] but on the negative side the fuzzy line between professional and private life can also generate problems. Another concern is the alteration of human interaction because they engage with devices, less and less computers since the rise of the smart phone and tablets, but that makes even easier to engage in a conversation online rather than in real life.

All these factors make the enterprise 2.0 a place where people sharing the same project would work together, as independent workers. The only thing that would make people prefer working in large corporations would be stability and security, but as far as business is concerned, they no longer need to have these large hierarchical based organizations. This is the second evolution transforming deeply our enterprises, it is preparing on top of the increasing role of social networks. These allow implementing totally new ways of distributing roles within an organization and we may see this evolve until the hierarchical systems we used to see in the past totally disappear. The information is able to flow more easily between people, from different departments, and even from different companies, because more and more deep expertise is needed in very heterogeneous disciplines, organization are requesting experts to manage these areas.

5 Conclusion

For several reasons, the current system of corporate governance is under pressure, ICT and the Web 2.0 have empowered employees and customers, those can communicate faster and better, sharing ideas and information. In order to face competition enterprises are focusing on innovation, research and development, and they take advantage of ICT to help employees extend their traditional function to a wide-ranging role of experts participating in communities of practice. Moreover, the digital economy made distribution and marginal costs disappear, thus allowing producers to get direct access to billions of customers; open source communities and free culture are showing that flattened hierarchies are possible; and last but not least, the Y Generation is expecting these changes. The traditional corporations, with hierarchies that are exceedingly wasteful of human talent and energies are losing ground and a form of post-capitalist, decentralized corporation is about to emerge. The prolongation of this evolution would be to imagine an organization where the employees are no longer employees but freelance specialists, sharing their expertise between several companies, according to the projects they find interesting and in which they want to participate. This would definitely pose several problems such as the trade-off between hierarchical control and peer-to-peer collaboration.

Currently a first pattern of organization for the digital enterprise can be proposed with the employees freely organized in communities of practice according to their personal skills and objectives. Even if it is difficult to conceive that workers on a production line can participate or not to the different steps of the assembly of the products, we can imagine for instance a quota of required time for production and some allocated "creative" time where the workers can experiment different roles and positions. Looking backward, the implementation of quality circles in the late 80s looks like a small experiment in this direction, but they were set up according to the traditional formal structure, the communities of practice at the end of the 90s were another step towards giving more autonomy to the employees but these were still lacking the complete autonomy. These examples demonstrated limitations after several years of experimentation. However, some organizations are now experimenting positive effects of this transformation, like FAVI in France and Steam in the USA. Therefore, we are aiming at investigating the mechanisms that enable such evolution. So far, the most challenging phase of this new organization model seems to be the absolute "let it go" from management. It requires to demonstrate a strong trust-behavior relationship between the various components of the organization and also to put in place recollection processes that do not interfere with their autonomy but allow harmonizing the different contributions in order to achieve the organization objectives.

References

1. Thompson, J.D.: Organization in Action. Social Science Based of Administrative Theory. McGraw-Hill, New York (1967)
2. Markus, M.L., Robey, D.: Information technology and organizational change: causal structure in theory and research. Manage. Sci. **34**(5), 583–598 (1988)
3. Lucas, H.C., Baroudi, J.: The role of information technology in organization design. In: Journal of Management Information Systems 10.4, pp. 9–23. ISSN: 07421222. http://www.jstor.org/stable/40398092 (1994)
4. Bailey, D.E., Leonardi, P.M., Chong, J.: Minding the gaps: understanding technology interdependence and coordination in knowledge work. Organ. Sci. **21**(3), 713–730 (2010)
5. Tapscott, D., Williams, A.D.: Macrowikinomics: Rebooting Business and the World, vol. BIF-5, p. 336. ISBN: 1591843561 (2010)
6. Hatch, M.J., Cunliffe, A.L.: Organization Theory: Modern, Symbolic and Postmodern Perspectives. Oxford University Press, Oxford (2006)
7. Stanford, N.: Guide to Organisation Design: Creating High Performing and Adaptable Enterprises, vol. 10. Wiley (2007)
8. O'Reilly, T.: What Is Web 2.0. O'Reilly Media (2005)
9. Murugesan, S.: Understanding Web 2.0. IT Professional, vol. 9 (2007)
10. Freidman, T.: The World is Flat. Farrar, Straus and Giroux, New York (2005)
11. Ghemawat, P.: Why the world isn't flat. Foreign Policy, 54–60 (2007)
12. Sambamurthy, V., Bharadwaj, A., Grover, V.: Shaping agility through digital options: reconceptualizing the role of information technology in contemporary firms. MIS quarterly, 237–263 (2003)
13. McAfee, A.P.: Enterprise 2.0: the dawn of emergent collaboration. Manage. Technol. Innov. **47**(3) (2006)

14. McAfee, A.: Enterprise 2.0: New Collaborative Tools for Your Organization's Toughest Challenges. Harvard Business Press (2009)
15. Manyika, J. et al.: Big data: the next frontier for innovation, competition, and productivity (2011)
16. Vaquero, L.M., et al.: A break in the clouds: towards a cloud definition. ACM SIGCOMM Comput. Commun. Rev. **39**(1), 50–55 (2008)
17. Armbrust, M., et al.: A view of cloud computing. Commun. ACM **53**(4), 50–58 (2010)
18. Mell, P., Grance, T.: The NIST definition of cloud computing (draft). NIST Spec. Publ. **800** (145), 7 (2011)
19. Dewey, J.: How We Think. Courier Dover Publications (1997)
20. Otlet, P.: Traité de documentation: le livre sur le livre, théorie et pratique. Editiones Mundaneum (1934)
21. Bush, V.: As we may think. Atlantic Monthly (1945)
22. Nelson, T.H.: Complex information processing: a file structure for the complex, the changing and the indeterminate.In: Proceedings of the 1965 20th National Conference, pp. 84–100. ACM, New York, NY, USA (1965)
23. Nelson, T.H.: As we will think. In: From Memex to hypertext, pp. 245–260. Academic Press Professional, Inc. (1991)
24. Lowes, J.L., Coleridge, S.T.: The Road to Xanadu: A Study in the Ways of the Imagination. Houghton Mifflin (1964)
25. Gemmell, J. et al.: MyLifeBits: fulfilling the Memex vision. In Proceedings of the Tenth ACM International Conference on Multimedia, pp. 235–238. ACM (2002)
26. Engelbart, D.C.: Augmenting human intellect: a conceptual framework (1962). (2001)
27. Levy, P.: L'intelligence collective (1994)
28. Tapscott, D., Williams, A.D.: Wikinomics. Atlantic Books, London (2008)
29. De Sanctis, G., Fulk, J.: Shaping Organization Form: Communication, Connection and Community. Sage, Thousand Oaks, CA (1999)
30. Weick, K.E.: Making Sense of the Organization. Blackwell Publishing, Malden, MA (2001)
31. Malone, T.W., Crowston, K., Herman, G.A. (eds): Organizing Business Knowledge: The MIT Process Handbook. MIT Press, Cambridge, MA (2003)
32. Hoogervorst, J., Koopman, P.L., Van Der Flier, H.: Human resource strategy for the new ICT-driven business context. Int. J. Hum. Resour. Manage. **13**(8), 1245–1265 (2002)
33. Lindgren, R., Henfridsson, O., Schultz, U.: Design principles for competence management systems: a synthesis of an action research study. MIS Q. **28**(3), 435–472 (2004)
34. Chan, Y.E.: Why haven't we mastered alignment? The importance of informal organizational structure. MIS Q. Executive **1**(2), 97–112 (2002)
35. Pawlowski, S.D., Robey, D.: Bridging user organizations: knowledge brokering and the work of information technology professionals. MIS Q. **28**(4), 645–672 (2004)
36. Levina, N., Vaast, E.: The emergence of boundary spanning competence in practice: implications for implementation and use of information systems. MIS Q. **29**(2), 335–363 (2005)
37. Kotkin, J.: The New Geography: How the Digital Revolution is Reshaping the American Landscape. Random House Digital, Inc (2002)
38. Orlikowski, W.J., Barley, W.R.: Technology and institutions: what can research on information technology and research on organizations learn from each other? MIS Q. **25**(2), 145–165 (2001)
39. Stallman, R.: Free software, free society (2002)
40. Bray, T., et al.: Extensible markup language (XML). World Wide Web J. **2**(4), 27–66 (1997)
41. Decker, S., et al.: The semantic web: the roles of XML and RDF. Internet Comput. IEEE **4**(5), 63–73 (2000)
42. Leuf, B., Cunningham, W.: The Wiki way: quick collaboration on the Web (2001)
43. Lessig, L.: The future of ideas, the fate of the commons in a connected world (2001)
44. Lessig, L.: Free Culture (2004a)
45. Lessig, L.: Free (ing) culture for remix. Utah Law Rev. 961 (2004b)

46. Drucker, P.F.: Management Challenges for the 21st Century. Butterworth-Heinemann, Oxford (1999)
47. Armour, S.: Generation Y: they've arrived at work with a new attitude. USA Today, **6** (2005)
48. Eisner, S.P.: Managing generation Y. IEEE Eng. Manage. Rev. **39**(2), 6–18 (2005)
49. Rothwell, J.D.: In mixed company: communicating in small groups and teams. CengageBrain. com (2011)
50. Shaw, S., Fairhurst, D.: Engaging a new generation of graduates. In: Education + Training 50.5, pp. 366–378 (2008)
51. Weiler, A.: Information-seeking behavior in Generation Y students: motivation, critical thinking, and learning theory. J. Acad. Librarianship **31**(1) 46–53 (2005)
52. Thomson, G.: BYOD: enabling the chaos. Netw. Secur. **2012**(2), 5–8 (2012)
53. Benlian, A., Hess, T., Buxmann, P.: Drivers of SaaS-adoption–an empirical study of different application types. Bus. Inf. Syst. Eng. **1**(5), 357–369 (2009)
54. Hiltz, S.R.: Online Communities: A Case Study of the Office of the Future, vol. 2. Intellect Books (1985)
55. Ramírez, Y.W., Nembhard, D.A.: Measuring knowledge worker productivity: a taxonomy. J. Intellect. capital **5**(4), 602–628 (2004)
56. Barrett, S., Konsynski, B.: Inter-organization information sharing systems. MIS Q. 93–105 (1982)
57. Johnston, H.R., Vitale, M.R.: Creating competitive advantage with interorganizational information systems. MIS Q. 153–165 (1988)

Perceived Training Needs for Effective Virtual Teams: An Exploratory Study

Cristiano Ghiringhelli and Alessandra Lazazzara

1 Introduction

New developments in Information and Communication Technology have fostered the collaborative and social dimensions of work, leading to the widespread adoption of the virtual team format within organizations. In information-oriented and geographically distributed organizations in particular, virtual teams facilitate collaboration, learning and the accomplishment of complex tasks, in groups of people working together over long distances. More in general, numerous studies have highlighted the ongoing shift from physical to virtual workplaces that many organizations are currently experiencing (see [1]). Given this background, academic research has increasingly focused on the factors that affect the success of virtual teams. Aspects such as trust, organizational culture, HR policies and practices, the tasks assigned to the team, team design and the features of the technology used to support teamwork have been investigated in relation to the social processes enabled by virtual teams and with a view to identifying the conditions required to make a virtual team effective [2–4]. Another crucial factor affecting the efficacy of the virtual team is leadership style, which can enhance both team performance and the quality of learning and development experienced by team members [5–9].

Despite the growing interest in virtual teams and in understanding the factors that can affect their success, surprisingly few studies have examined the training and development initiatives needed to form an effective and successful virtual team. Similarly, little attention has been paid to how the human resource function can

C. Ghiringhelli (✉) · A. Lazazzara (✉)
Department of Educational Human Sciences, University of Milano-Bicocca, Milan, Italy
e-mail: cristiano.ghiringhelli@unimib.it

A. Lazazzara
e-mail: alessandra.lazazzara@unimib.it

© Springer International Publishing Switzerland 2016
F. D'Ascenzo et al. (eds.), *Blurring the Boundaries Through Digital Innovation*,
Lecture Notes in Information Systems and Organisation 19,
DOI 10.1007/978-3-319-38974-5_3

promote the learning and development of the knowledge and skills required by a virtual team for optimum performance [1, 5].

In order to address these gaps in the existing research, we conducted an exploratory study with the aim of identifying the specific training needs of virtual teams whose members do not have prior experience of virtual teamwork, and consequently defining the role of the HR function in supporting them. The study comprised three levels of analysis: first, the needs and challenges associated with the early stages of virtual team membership; second, the factors likely to influence the effectiveness of a virtual team, with a particular focus on training needs; third, the role of the human resources function in helping virtual teams to develop the knowledge and skills they require to be effective and successful. More specifically, our research questions were: What are the perceived benefits at the early stages of virtual collaboration? What do novice virtual team members perceive to be their training needs? What factors must be configured and carefully managed when implementing a virtual team? Finally, how can the HR department contribute to making virtual teams more effective?

In light of these aims, we adopted a qualitative research method, interviewing five employees of Nielsen TAM Italy who had recently been appointed to global virtual teams. The goals of this phase of our research were to build up an account of the complexity involved in providing the optimum conditions for effective virtual teams and to identify the most salient issues requiring further in-depth investigation.

2 Theoretical Framework

The scientific literature offers multiple definitions of virtual team. Most of these state that a virtual team is a group of people who use computer-mediated technologies to work interdependently across space, time and organizational boundaries [10, 11]. Although virtual teams engage in technology-supported working across a wide range of activities and contexts [12], the use of technology in itself does not make a team virtual. Indeed, for a team to be identified as virtual, it must have six attributes [13]: (a) definable team membership; (b) interdependence among team members; (c) joint responsibility for outcomes among team members; (d) relationships among team members across organizational boundaries; (e) geographical dispersion of team members; (f) predominance of computer-mediated communication rather than face-to-face communication among members for the joint accomplishment of tasks. The first of these four attributes are shared by all forms of team; the last two are more specific to virtual teams. Overall, one of the most comprehensive yet economical definitions to date has been provided by Towsend, DeMarie and Hendrickson, who describe virtual teams as "groups of geographically and/or organizationally dispersed coworkers that are assembled using a combination of telecommunications and information technologies to accomplish an organizational task" [14: 18].

Numerous studies have shown that effective virtual teams can generate a wide range of organizational advantages, especially in terms of enhanced productivity, communication, mutual sharing of inter-organizational resources and innovation [15].

First, effective virtual teams can enable organizations to respond faster to increased competition [8, 16], reduce time-to-market [17], generate greater client satisfaction [18] and enhance productivity [19, 20]. In addition, virtual teams can "follow the sun" and implement 24 h work schedules [21], make it easier for team performance to be documented, assessed and reviewed [22, 23] and, of course, help the organization to save on the time and costs of relocation as well as on travel expenses. Other key benefits associated with the effective implementation of virtual teams concern the internal organizational environment and culture. Virtual teams can yield superior outcomes in terms of quality, productivity, and satisfaction [24, 25], enhance communication and coordination, encourage the mutual sharing of inter-organizational resources and competencies [5, 10, 26–28], as well as promoting a sense of responsibility in their members [29, 30]. Virtual teams can also foster innovation processes by linking up experts in highly specialized fields working at great distances from one other [26], enabling the creation of centers of excellence in which talents can collaborate regardless of location [16, 28, 31–37], and encouraging and managing creativity [34, 38, 39].

Nevertheless, when dealing with virtual teams, there are also drawbacks to be taken into account and managed. For example, the lack of physical interaction can make it more difficult for team members to develop a conceptual understanding of complex tasks [32, 40–42], while the distance factor can be challenging from a project management perspective [34, 43, 44]. Other disadvantages that have been observed include difficulties in managing conflict [25, 43, 45–47], mistrust, breakdowns in communication, and power struggles [26, 32, 48].

These weaknesses of virtual teams prompt researchers to address the challenges of online collaboration by exploring the conditions required to be effective and the specific training needed by those joining or managing a virtual team. Scholars have identified a wide range of factors influencing the effectiveness and success of virtual teams, which include issues related to trust [2–4, 49, 50], reward strategies and performance measurement [51], conflict management [4, 49, 52], team empowerment/decision making [49, 51], the design of task, roles and responsibilities, as well as the definition of team goals and clear success criteria [4, 49], socio-emotional cues and cultural differences [4, 49, 51, 52]. Special attention has also been paid to team members' needs for specific training and encouragement [53], mainly in relation to project management, the deployment of technology and networking skills, self-management, as well as cultural and interpersonal awareness [54]. Furthermore, appropriate leadership is a fundamental requirement for a successful and effective virtual team, as a number of studies have shown [5, 6, 8, 9, 46].

A holistic approach to analyzing the effectiveness of virtual teams is provided by Bal and Gundry's model of the factors involved in effective team working [51, 55].

Fig. 1 Factors for effective
team working [55]

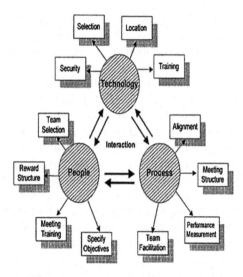

In this model, the authors divided a broad set of factors required for effective teaming into three main areas: People, Processes and Technology (Fig. 1).

As noted by Bal and Foster [51], this model includes factors that are not taken into account by other models. In other words, the key strength of this model is that it provides a comprehensive and holistic overview of the factors affecting virtual teaming, as identified in studies previously conducted by other scholars.

For this reason, in designing our qualitative interview protocol we drew on the Bal and Gundry model to identify the areas to be investigated: in relation to people factors, we explored dimensions such as virtual team objectives (motivation), meeting behavior (trust), reward structure (motivation and goal setting) and team selection (support, culture). In relation to technology factors, in line with the model, we examined system selection (appropriate technology), security (team effectiveness), location (open-plan offices or separate virtual team rooms) and training (skills and competence). In relation to process factors, we set out to assess process alignment (integration), meeting structure (order), performance measurement (feedback, encouragement, direction) and team facilitation (resource allocation, support).

3   Methodology

We conducted our study in a specific information-oriented organizational context, namely Nielsen Television Audience Measurement (TAM) Italy. Nielsen is an American global information and measurement company. TAM is its specialised media research branch, dedicated to quantifying and qualifying detailed television audience information. Analysing the adoption of virtual teams in Nielsen TAM Italy is of particular interest because of its unique features. First, the use of virtual teams has only recently been extended to Italian employees, as part of a broader integration phase following the launching of a joint venture between Nielsen and its European competitor, the AGB Group. The reorganization of the group has increased the need for global virtual teams of highly skilled specialists to accomplish complex tasks—e.g., identifying new solutions to business problems or developing new products. This scenario allowed us to analyse training needs in the early stages of virtual team membership. In addition, the Italian employees joining virtual teams had received little or no prior training in skills related to collaborative behaviour or project management. Therefore, the outcome of our analysis was not influenced by any prior training in virtual collaboration received by the participants. Third, although the Italian virtual team members were new to online collaboration, internationally Nielsen has a long history of virtual team adoption and working together virtually. This meant that the Italian members were immediately exposed to the working practices and styles of more experienced colleagues and challenged to develop virtual team skills quickly. Finally, although the scope of this exploratory study was limited to the Italian subsidiary, other Nielsen companies around the world present the same conditions (integration phase, newly appointed virtual team members, no prior training in virtual team skills), so the next step of the study is to extend the research to other local units with similar characteristics.

Given the exploratory nature of our research question, we conducted semi-structured interviews with five virtual team members at Nielsen TAM Italy. The interviews began with a brief description of the research project by the researcher and some questions about the informant's organizational setting. We next used Bal and Gundry's model [55] as a guide to asking for information about the three dimensions of people, processes and technology and how they can affect the efficacy of virtual teams. Finally, we asked interviewees about the training they felt they required to equip them for participating in virtual teams, potential benefits arising from virtual collaboration, and existing or planned HRM practices supporting the development of virtual teaming skills. The interviews were tape recorded and transcribed, and averaged approximately 1 h in length.

In order to identify success factors, training needs and other issues related to virtual team membership, we subjected the interview data to thematic analysis, adopting the approach developed by Strauss and Corbin [56]. We engaged in multiple iterations of coding and discussion: first, we identified and grouped preliminary concepts (open coding); second, we made connections between the emergent themes and grouped them into higher-order conceptual categories (axial coding); third, we selected and discussed core categories emerging from the analysis [56, 57]. The results are presented in the next section.

4 Results and Discussion

4.1 Factors Influencing the Efficacy of Virtual Teams

We have organized our presentation of the interview findings around the categories listed in Bal and Gundry's model [55].

Process issues. In this area, Bal and Gundry identified four key aspects: alignment, meeting structure, performance measurement and team facilitation. Among these, team facilitation and alignment were the issues most frequently referred to by the interviewees, who placed less (albeit significant) emphasis on meeting structure and rarely mentioned performance issues.

In relation to team facilitation, the role of the team leader (often described as a project manager) emerged as the main factor facilitating the work of the team. This appeared to be related to the lack of face-to-face communication characterizing the virtual team, perceived by the interviewees as extremely challenging. The team leader is required to manage the team, recognize who needs advice, drive the decision-making process, and create and sustain commitment. Team facilitation is particularly crucial when something goes wrong. The interviewees described in depth several aspects of the leader's contribution to the effectiveness and success of the virtual team. For example, they observed that the leader must contribute in different ways at different stages of the team life cycle: goal setting (technical and organizational) should be the priority focus for the virtual leader at the initial stages of team functioning. At the intermediate stage, he or she is required to provide social and psychological support, as well as delegating technical tasks to team members, leveraging on their growing knowledge and confidence. At the final stage of the virtual team cycle, the leader is once again required to switch focus, now concentrating on managing project wrap-up, and especially on pointing up the task and results achieved by the team, the role played by the various members and the main learning outcomes attained. Interestingly, there were similarities between our participants' perspective on the responsibilities of the virtual team leader and Hersey and Blanchard's situation leadership theory [58]. Furthermore, the interviewees emphasized the role of the leader in developing trust, solidarity, shared objectives and tasks, mutual interests, and internal legitimacy. In sum, a virtual team leader is not only required to invest in technical and social skills and competencies, but also to recognize that members' needs evolve in line with the evolution of the team itself and adapt his/her role accordingly. In sum, we might say that the leader's role in facilitating team activities and dynamics (technical as well as social) emerged as a highly critical factor determining the success of the virtual team from the interviewees' point of view.

A similar picture emerged in relation to alignment, showing that the participants had developed a clear awareness of virtual team functioning. Indeed, the interviewees essentially agreed on the fact that the need for alignment and communication tools may also vary over time, as a function of developments in team members' skills and competencies as well as of the complexity of the task to be accomplished.

Most of our informants stressed the importance of creating forms, feedback processes, repositories and cloud solutions, so that team members can track one another's progress and coordinate their efforts. The facility to check what actions have been completed by other team members promotes integration, and is critical to retaining an overview of the entire process, sustaining problem solving, building and maintaining trust, and reinforcing the social contract. Clearly, this is not only of value to the formal team leader, but also to individual team members. Ensuring alignment by these means can also counteract the fact that team members rarely have the opportunity to integrate via face-to-face meetings.

With regard to meeting structure, the interviewees noted the importance of planning a meetings schedule, in order to create a "rhythm" for the virtual team and sustain commitment over time. They also suggested that meetings should be conducted following a fixed format, to optimize meeting preparation, participation and follow up on the part of all team members. Surprisingly, very few interviewees spoke about performance measurement. It seems that the only performance criteria assumed by interviewees was the overall success/failure of the project. A possible explanation for this is that none of our informants had played the role of team leader during their first virtual team experience and the projects they were involved in were still ongoing.

People issues. In this area, Bal and Gundry's model comprises four key aspects: team selection, reward structure, meeting training and specification of objectives. The interviewees emphasized all of these aspects, reflecting their overall perception that managing people issues is critical to the success of virtual teams. In particular, team selection emerged as a critical factor to be taken into account when assembling and managing a virtual team. More specifically, participants stressed the need to identify optimum team size, by carefully evaluating the trade-off between the need for resources (having many members may increase skills, knowledge, experience, viewpoints, etc.) and the need for neatness (too many team members may increase complexity and make decision making, coordination, communication and strategic direction processes more challenging). It is critical to identify the criteria on which team selection should be based: clearly, team members must hold skills and competencies related to the task assigned to the team, but the interviewees claimed that other factors are also important, including training, culture, language, time orientation and expertise. That is to say, in relation to the task assigned, specific combinations of these non-task related dimensions can make the virtual team more or less effective. Participants also identified reward structure as a critical aspect of virtual teaming. Interestingly however, most of the reward options mentioned as necessary for sustaining virtual team membership, commitment and motivation were not financial: approval from the team leader and other team members, enhanced reputation, endorsement and acknowledgment were those listed, at least by our informants who were at the early stages of virtual team membership, as good practices for virtual teams. This was the view put forward unanimously by all five participants, who also displayed a high level of agreement in relation to the specification of objectives, the third area mentioned by almost all the interviewees. Specifically, they discussed the specification of personal objectives (in terms of goal

setting, role clarity and transparency about responsibility) as well as the specification of objectives for the team, which are usually defined in the course of preliminary discussions among team members. The final aspect of people issues is
meeting training. Contrary to our expectations, only two interviewees out of five
cited this as a priority, pointing out the need to leverage on specific skills,
knowledge and organizational choices to ensure effective meetings on ICT platforms. Thus, on the whole, participants did not perceive meeting training to be as
salient as other issues.

Technology issues. Technology issues were far less critical in the interviewees'
opinion than people and process issues. During the interviews, very few concerns
were raised about security and selection, and none at all in relation to location and
training. With regard to security, interviewees highlighted the need for the data
shared among team members to be stored in a protected area. This is compulsory,
considering the kind of data produced and analyzed by Nielsen. Furthermore, the
Nielsen virtual teams apply technologies already used within the organization,
explaining why interviewees did not discuss specific security challenges or issues
with selection or adoption. In sum, the interview data supported the idea that
success in implementing virtual team working is more about processes and people
than about technology.

4.2   The Role of Training in Sustaining Effective Virtual Teams

Perceived Training Needs and Formal Learning Initiatives

When asked to identify—based on their initial experience of virtual teams—the
kind of training and development programmes required for successful participation
in virtual teams, the interviewees answered as follows. Overall, they viewed the
development of a specific set of skills and competencies as essential to effective
virtual teaming. To this end, they recommended ad hoc training courses aimed at
providing participants with a strong background in the key knowledge and best
practices associated with virtual teams. In particular, they identified four areas of
knowledge and skills, which they felt should be developed urgently.

The first area mentioned by our informants was the need to develop English
language skills. This training requirement is not specifically connected with virtual
teams, but arises from the history of the Italian unit, which has only recently entered
the multinational environment that characterizes Nielsen worldwide. Nonetheless, it
is clear that virtual teams exacerbate this training need because of their global
nature.

Interviewees identified cross-cultural knowledge and skills as a second crucial
area of required training in light of their initial virtual team experience. They
recognized that, in order to interact and contribute successfully within their virtual

teams, it was indispensable to be familiar with the other members' cultural behaviors, social rules and habits. Obviously, this need is heightened by the lack of physical interaction and face-to-face communication among virtual team members.

The third area addressed in the interviews was project management. Interviewees felt that it was very important to develop the specific competencies and skills required to act effectively and successfully as a leader but also as a member of a virtual team. They recognized that traditional competencies and skills are inadequate in a virtual environment, which is a different context governed by different rules.

Leadership was the final area of knowledge and skills in which participants wished to receive training, in light of their virtual teaming experience to date. They appeared to view leading a virtual team as a huge challenge. Some of the interviewees came across as highly concerned at the thought that the organization might ask them to lead a virtual team in the future. Interestingly, when discussing this issue, the participants referred once again to the all key people and process issues reported in paragraph 4.1. This indicates that their initial experience had made them fully aware of the complexity involved in implementing virtual teams.

Cross-Cultural and Social Leadership Issues: The Role of Informal Learning

Overall, participants clearly perceived informal learning as playing a key role in their experience of virtual teaming. They reported that their involvement in virtual teams had allowed them to develop a wide range of skills and knowledge: not only of a technical nature, but also in terms of conflict management, motivation, decision-making processes, and leadership. In short, working on virtual teams offers the opportunity to enhance one' personal professionalism across a wide range of skills and competencies, which may be reinforced and sustained by appropriate formal training, as discussed above.

From this perspective, among the most interesting and unexpected results emerging from the interviews was the participants' evaluation of the learning and benefits they had acquired from their virtual teaming experience, which may be divided into two main areas.

First, interviewees perceived changes in their global identity and cultural intelligence. Global identity reflects a sense of belonging to a global multicultural team [59, 60]. Specifically, interviewees reported experiencing a greater feeling of inclusion and a lesser sense of national identity due to their perception of belonging to a group composed of culturally diverse members and, more in general, they felt that they had acquired a more holistic view of organizational functioning. This is consistent with studies indicating that multicultural work experience positively influences the development of a global identity [61]. The organization also stands to benefit given that the development of a global identity is positively related to multicultural team effectiveness [61], positive emotions [62], and global leadership effectiveness [61]. Interviewees also perceived themselves as having become more skilled and professional at operating in a multicultural context. This outcome may be interpreted in light of the construct of cultural intelligence, defined as the specific form of intelligence underpinning an individual's ability to understand and reason correctly in situations of cultural diversity [63, 64]. All the interviewees reported an increase in their ability to function effectively within the multicultural environment of the virtual team.

Second, and surprisingly, a social dimension of leadership emerged as a consequence of joining virtual teams. This comprised three main aspects: (1) team members frequently emerged as leaders when they had the skills, knowledge, expertise that the team needed; (2) members were able to access information that in previous traditional team experiences had been exclusively available to leader; (3) the leader's influence was affected by followers' greater opportunity—with respect to traditional teams—to be aware of and contribute to the decision-making process [65]. These three points are consistent with an emergentist account of leadership, framed as an outcome of group dynamics [66] and interpreted as shared among team members [67]. In short, leadership "entails a simultaneous, ongoing, mutual influence process within a team that is characterized by the "serial emergence" of official as well as unofficial leaders" [68]. Interestingly, this implies that leadership is both an individual trait and an organizational trait [69]. In short, this finding suggests the value of exploring leadership issues within virtual teams in greater depth, in light of the e-leadership, shared leadership and social leadership concepts that have recently been put forward in the literature. Specifically, e-leadership is defined as a process of social influence mediated by technology that leads to changes in attitudes, feelings, thinking, behavior, and/or performance on the part of individuals, groups and/or organizations [70]. Shared leadership on other hand, is defined as "a dynamic, interactive influence process among individuals in groups for which the objective is to lead one another to the achievement of group or organizational goals or both" [71: 1]. Join on both the e-leadership and shared leadership concepts, in an earlier publication we proposed the construct of social leadership, defining it as "a social process of mutual influence among the members of a group/organization who, by interacting through social media, share the responsibility of leadership in order to achieve group/organizational goals" [72: 3].

5   Discussion and Conclusion

This paper reports the initial findings of an ongoing research project aimed at identifying the specific training needs of novice virtual teams. Based on the results of this preliminary stage, we are developing a research model to be used in a future study on the role of the HR function in supporting virtual teams. In the current exploratory phase, we investigated three main aspects: the needs and challenges associated with the early stages of virtual team membership; the factors likely to influence the effectiveness of virtual teams, with a specific focus on training requirements; the role of the HR function in helping virtual teams to develop the knowledge and skills they require to be effective.

We interviewed five employees of an information-oriented organization who had been allocated to global virtual teams in the context of an integration project. Interviews were based on the Bal and Gundry's model of effective team working [51, 55], which divides the factors contributing to effective teaming into three main areas: people, processes and technology. We obtained four main results.

First, the issues perceived as most critical for the successful functioning of virtual teams are those that concern processes and people. In contrast, technology is perceived as posing little or no challenge to virtual team members. This may be due to the fact that Nielsen has adopted user-friendly technological solutions and tools that are easy for its employees to implement.

Second, the interviewees stress the vital importance of good leadership for virtual teams. The many facets of virtual leadership described include generating trust and solidarity, setting shared objectives and tasks, promoting shared interests, and strengthening internal legitimacy. The leader is also required to drive the decision-making process, create and sustain commitment, and provide technical and social guidance in line with team members' changing needs, skills, competencies and behaviors, which in turn are a function of the life stage of the team itself. However, leadership processes are not the sole key factor believed to influence the effectiveness and success of virtual teams. Unexpectedly, our interview data also points up a social dimension of leadership as a characteristic of virtual teams. This is in line with emergentist perspectives framing leadership as an outcome of group dynamics [66], and as a function that does not depend on a single formal leader, but is shared among team members [67]. Consequently, our results suggest that leadership is not only an individual, but also an organizational, trait [69]. Following our earlier work within the emergentist paradigm, we believe that the construct of social leadership [72] emerges particularly strongly in this exploratory study and requires further investigation.

Third, the HR department is called on to play a dual role in sustaining the development of the skills and competencies needed to contribute to virtual teams. First, it is required to deliver formal training programs designed to support and refine the informal learning acquired through hands-on involvement in a virtual team. This applies to both leaders and regular team members. The main areas of competence (both technical and relational) to be developed are English language skills, project management, leadership and cross-cultural skills for virtual contexts specifically. Second, the HR department should support, promote and reward the informal learning acquired through practical experience of virtual teaming, as well appropriately linking formal and informal learning opportunities. In short, on-the-job training should be coordinated with the formal training and development programs provided by the HR department.

Fourth, this exploratory study suggests that the multicultural aspect of working on global virtual teams has key implications. Interviewees reported experiencing a greater feeling of inclusion and a lesser sense of national identity due to their perception of belonging to a group composed of culturally diverse members. More generally, they felt that being on a virtual team had allowed them to acquire a more holistic view of organizational functioning. Setting up a global team breaks down boundaries and provides members with the opportunity to work collaboratively in an international environment, fostering a multicultural outlook.

This qualitative study is a starting point for a larger-scale project aimed at assessing a HR training and development strategy for enhancing the efficacy of virtual teams. Although this preliminary study presents a number of limitations such as small sample size and the adoption of a convenience sampling method, its goal was to gain new insights from which to develop new hypotheses to be tested at a further confirmatory phase. Therefore, we plan to implement a new research project that on the one hand measures the effect of social leadership and cultural intelligence on the efficacy of virtual teams, and on the other, further tests the effects of formal and informal training. Indeed, this exploratory study not only reveals the importance of social leadership skills and cross-cultural competence for the positive functioning of virtual teams, but also points up specific non-technical training needs and suggests that virtual teams provide particularly learning-inducing environments. As the social learning perspective [73] suggests, it seems that by observing and interacting with colleagues who are more experienced in virtual teaming, newcomers develop the knowledge and skills they need to contribute effectively to their teams. Therefore, we expect social leadership and cultural intelligence to positively influence virtual team efficacy (H1). Furthermore, we expect social leadership and cultural intelligence skills to increase as a consequence of virtual team membership (H2). Finally, we expect that receiving additional formal training in social leadership and cross-cultural issues will foster the development of these skills in virtual team members more than experiencing informal learning only (H3). In order to test these hypotheses, the future study will employ a quasi-experimental longitudinal design. At T1, during the early stages of functioning of a virtual team, members' social leadership and cross-cultural skills, as well as the efficacy of the virtual team, will be measured. At T2, the organization, assisted by the researchers, will provide specific training in social leadership and cross-cultural issues to a group of virtual team members. At T3, the initial measurements will be repeated. The effect of changes in social leadership and cross-cultural skills on virtual team efficacy will be examined, while controlling for the effects of pre-formal and informal training and relevant demographic variables. The study will be conducted among Nielsen TAM employees working in units which have only recently begun to take part in virtual teams following on their acquisition by Nielsen.

Acknowledgments The authors thank the study participants for their generous contributions and insights and Rosalinda Sinatra for her invaluable assistance.

References

1. SHRM.org.: Virtual teams used most by global organizations, survey says (2013)
2. Lipnack, J., Stamps, J.: Virtual Teams: Reaching Across Space, Time and Organizations with Technology. Wiley, New York (1997)
3. Lipnack, J., Stamps J.: Virtual teams: the new way to work'. Strategy Leadersh. **27** (1999)
4. Jarvenpaa, S.L., Leidner, D.E.: Communication and trust in global virtual teams. Organ. Sci. **10** (1999)
5. Chen, C.C., Wu, J., Ma, M., Knight, M.B.: Enhancing virtual learning team performance: a leadership perspective. Hum. Syst. Manag. **30**, 215–228 (2011)
6. DeRosa, D.M., Hantula, D.A., Kock, N., D'Arcy, J.: Trust and leadership in virtual teamwork: a media naturalness perspective. Hum. Resource Manag. **43**, 219–232 (2004)
7. Kayworth, T., Leidner, D.: Leadership effectiveness in global virtual teams. J. Manag. Inf. Syst. **18**, 7–40 (2001)
8. Pauleen, D.J.: An inductively derived model of leader-initiated relationship building with virtual team members. J. Manag. Inf. Syst. **20**, 227–256 (2003)
9. Thomas, D.M., Bostrom, R.P.: Vital signs for virtual teams: an empirically developed trigger model for technology adaptation interventions. MIS Q. **34**, 115–142 (2010)
10. Lipnack, J.S., Stamps, J.: Virtual Teams: People Working Across Boundaries with Technology. Wiley, New York (2000)
11. Bell, B.S., Kozlowski, S.W.: A typology of virtual teams. Group Org. Manag. **27**, 14–49 (2002)
12. Anderson, A.H., Mcewan, R., Bal, J., Carletta, J.: Virtual team meetings: an analysis of communication and context. Comput. Hum. Behav. **23**, 2558–2580 (2007)
13. Berry, G.R.: Enhancing effectiveness on virtual teams. understanding why traditional team skills are insufficient. J. Bus. Commun. **48**, 186–206 (2011)
14. Townsend, A.M., DeMarie, S.M., Hendrickson, A.R.: Virtual teams: technology and the workplace of the future. Acad. Manag. Executive. **12**, 17–29 (1998)
15. Ebrahim, N.A., Ahmed, S., Taha, Z.: Virtual Teams: a literature review. Aust. J. Basic Appl. Sci. **3**, 2653–2669 (2009)
16. Hunsaker, P.L., Hunsaker, J.S.: Virtual teams: a leader's guide. Team Perform. Manag. **14**, 86–101 (2008)
17. May, A., Carter, C.: A case study of virtual team working in the European automotive industry. Int. J. Ind. Ergon. **27**, 171–186 (2001)
18. Jain, V.K., Sobek, D.K.: Linking design process to customer satisfaction through virtual design of experiments. Res. Eng. Design **17**, 59–71 (2006)
19. Mcdonough, E.F., Kahn, K.B., Barczak, G.: An investigation of the use of global, virtual, and collocated new product development teams. J. Prod. Innov. Manag. **18**, 110–120 (2001)
20. Mulebeke, J.A.W., Zheng, L.: Incorporating integrated product development with technology road mapping for dynamism and innovation. Int. J. Prod. Dev. **3**, 56–76 (2006)
21. Solomon, C.M.: Managing virtual teams. Workforce **80**, 60–64 (2001)
22. Gibson, C.B., Cohen, S.G. (eds.): Virtual Teams That Work: Creating Conditions for Virtual Team Effectiveness. Jossey-Bass, San Francisco (2003)
23. Chudoba, K.M., Wynn, E., Lu, M., Watson-Manheim, M.B.: How virtual are we? Measuring virtuality and understanding its impact in a global organization. Inform. Syst. J. **15**, 279–306 (2005)
24. Gaudes, A., Hamilton-Bogart, B., Marsh, S., Robinson, H.: A framework for constructing effective virtual teams. J. E-working **1**, 83–97 (2007)
25. Piccoli, G., Powell, A., Ives, B.: Virtual teams: team control structure, work processes, and team effectiveness. Inf. Technol. People **17**, 359–379 (2004)
26. Rosen, B., Furst, S., Blackburn, R.: Overcoming barriers to knowledge sharing in virtual teams. Org. Dyn. **36**, 259–273 (2007)

27. Zakaria, N., Amelinckx, A., Wilemon, D.: Working together apart? building a knowledge-sharing culture for global virtual teams. Creativity Innov. Manag. **13**, 15–29 (2004)
28. Furst, S.A., Reeves, M., Rosen, B., Blackburn, R.S.: Managing the life cycle of virtual teams. Acad. Manag. Executive **18**, 6–20 (2004)
29. Johnson, P., Heimann, V., O'Neill, K.: The "wonderland" of virtual teams. J. Workplace Learn. **13**, 24–30 (2001)
30. Precup, L., O'Sullivan, D., Cormican, K., Dooley, L.: Virtual team environment for collaborative research projects. Int. J. Innov. Learn. **3**, 77–94 (2006)
31. Criscuolo, P.: On the road again: researcher mobility inside the R&D network. Res. Policy **34**, 1350–1365 (2005)
32. Cascio, W.F.: Managing a virtual workplace. Acad. Manag. Executive **14**, 81–90 (2000)
33. Fuller, M.A., Hardin, A.M., Davison, R.M.: Efficacy in technology-mediated distributed team. J. Manag. Inf. Syst. **23**, 209–235 (2006)
34. Badrinarayanan, V., Arnett, D.B.: Effective virtual new product development teams: an integrated framework. J. Bus. Ind. Mark. **23**, 242–248 (2008)
35. Prasad, K., Akhilesh, K.B.: Global virtual teams: what impacts their design and performance? Team Perform. Manag. **8**, 102–112 (2002)
36. Boudreau, M.C., Loch, K.D., Robey, D., Straub, D.: Going global: using information technology to advance the competitiveness of the virtual transnational organization. Acad. Manag. Executive **12**, 120–128 (1998)
37. Boutellier, R., Gassmann, O., Macho, H., Roux, M.: Management of dispersed product development teams: the role of information technologies. R&D Manag. **28** (1998)
38. Leenders, R.T.A.J., Engelen, J.M.L.V., Kratzer, J.: Virtuality, communication, and new product team creativity: a social network perspective. J. Eng. Tech. Manag. **20**, 69–92 (2003)
39. Atuahene-Gima, K.: The effects of centrifugal and centripetal forces on product development speed and quality: how does problem solving matter? Acad. Manag. J. **46**, 359–373 (2003)
40. Hossain, L., Wigand, R.T.: ICT enabled virtual collaboration through trust. J. Comput. Mediated Commun. **10** (2004)
41. Kankanhalli, A., Tan, B.C.Y., Wei, K.K.: Conflict and performance in global virtual teams. J. Manag. Inf. Syst. **23**, 237–274 (2006)
42. Rice, D.J., Davidson, B.D., Dannenhoffer, J.F., Gay, G.K.: Improving the effectiveness of virtual teams by adapting team processes. Comput. Support. Coop. Work **16**, 567–594 (2007)
43. Wong, S.S., Burton, R.M.: Virtual teams: what are their characteristics, and impact on team performance? Comput. Math. Organ. Theory. **6**, 339–360 (2000)
44. Martinez-Sanchez, A., Perez-Perez, M., De-Luis-Carnicer, P., Vela-Jimenez, M.J.: Teleworking and new product development. Eur. J. Innov. Manag. **9**, 202–214 (2006)
45. Hinds, P.J., Mortensen, M.: Understanding conflict in geographically distributed teams: the moderating effects of shared identity, shared context, and spontaneous communication. Organ. Sci. **16**, 290–307 (2005)
46. Kayworth, T.R., Leidner, D.E.: Leadership effectiveness in global virtual teams. Manag. Inf. Syst. **18**, 7–40 (2002)
47. Ramayah, T., Muhamad, J., Aizzat, M.N., Koay, P.L.: Internal group dynamics, team characteristics and team effectiveness: a preliminary study of virtual teams. Int. J. Knowl. Culture Change Manag. **3**, 415–435 (2003)
48. Kirkman, B.L., Rosen, B., Gibson, C.B., Tesluk, P.E., Mcpherson, S.O.: Five challenges to virtual team success: lessons from Sabre Inc. Acad. Manag. Executive **16**, 67–79 (2002)
49. Horwitz, F.M., Bravington, D., Silvas, U.: The promise of virtual teams: identifying key factors in effectiveness and failure. J. Eur. Ind. Train. **30**, 472–494 (2006)
50. Kelley, E.: Keys to effective virtual global teams. Acad. Manag. Perspect. **15**, 132–133 (2001)
51. Bal, J., Foster, P.: Managing the virtual team and controlling effectiveness. Int. J. Prod. Res. **38**, 4019–4032 (2000)
52. Hertel, G., Geister, S., Konradt, U.: Managing virtual teams: a review of current empirical research. Hum. Resour. Manag. Rev. **15**, 69–95 (2005)

53. Ryssen, S.V., Godar, S.H.: Going international without going international: multinational virtual teams. J. Int. Manag. **6**, 49–60 (2000)
54. Lee-Kelley, L., Sankey, T.: Global virtual teams for value creation and project success: a case study. Int. J. Proj. Manag. **26**, 51–62 (2008)
55. Bal, J., Gundry, J.: Virtual teaming in the automotive supply chain. Int. J. Team Perform. Manag. **5**, 174–193 (1999)
56. Strauss, A., Corbin, J.: Basics of Qualitative Research, Grounded Theory Procedures and Techniques. Sage, Newbury Park (1998)
57. Miles, M.B., Huberman, A.M.: Qualitative data analysis: An expanded sourcebook. Sage, Beverly Hills (1994)
58. Hersey, P., Blanchard, K.H.: Life cycle theory of leadership. Train. Dev. J. **23**, 26–34 (1969)
59. Arnett, J.J.: The psychology of globalization. Am. Psychol. **57**, 774–783 (2002)
60. Erez, M., Gati, E.: A dynamic, multi-level model of culture: from the micro-level of the individual to the macro-level of a global culture. Appl. Psychol. Int. Rev. **53**, 583–598 (2004)
61. Erez, M., Lisak, A., Harusch, R., Glickson, E., Nouri, R., Shokef, E.: Going global: developing management students' cultural intelligence and global identity in culturally diverse virtual teams. Acad. Manag. Learn. Educ. **12**, 330–355 (2013)
62. Glikson, E., Erez, M.: Emotion display norms in virtual teams. J. Pers. Psychol. **12**, 22–32 (2013)
63. Ang, S., Van Dyne, L.: Conceptualization of cultural intelligence: definition, distinctiveness, and nomological network. In: Ang, S., Van Dyne, L. (eds.) Handbook of cultural intelligence: theory, measurement, and applications, pp. 3–15. M.E. Sharpe, New York (2008)
64. Earley, P.C., Ang, S.: Cultural Intelligence: Individual Interactions Across Cultures. Stanford Business Books, CA (2003)
65. Avolio, B.J., Kahai, S.: Adding the "e" to e-leadership: how it may impact your leadership. Org. Dyn. **31**, 325–338 (2003)
66. Day, D.V., Gronn, P., Salas, E.: Leadership capacity in teams. Leadersh. Q. **15**, 857–880 (2004)
67. Grint, K.: The sacred in leadership: separation, Sacrifice and Silence. Organ. Stud. **31**, 89–107 (2010)
68. Pearce, C.L.: The future of leadership: combining vertical and shared leadership to transform knowledge work. Acad. Manag. Executive **18**, 47–57 (2004)
69. O'Connor, P.M.G., Quinn, L.: Organizational capacity for leadership. In: McCauley, C. D., Van Velsor, E. (eds.) The Center for Creative Leadership Handbook of Leadership Development, pp. 417–437, 2nd edn. Jossey-Bass, San Francisco, CA (2004)
70. Avolio, B.J., Kahai, S., Dodge, G.E.: E-leadership: implication for theory, research, and practice. Leadersh. Q. **11**, 615–668 (2000)
71. Pearce, C.L., Conger, J.A.: All those years ago: the historical underpinnings of shared leadership. In: Pearce, C.L., Conger, J.A. (eds.) Shared Leadership: Reframing the Hows and Whys of Leadership, pp. 1–18. Sage Publications, Thousand Oaks, CA (2003)
72. Lazazzara, A., Ghiringhelli, C.: Developing social leadership: cultural and technological influences. In: Mola, L., Pennarola, F., Za, S. (eds.) From Information to Smart Society, pp. 31–47. Springer International Publishing (2015)
73. Bandura, A.: Social Learning Theory. Prentice Hall, Englewood Cliffs, NJ (1977)

The Diffusion of ICT Across Italian Corporate Universities: An Exploratory Study

Michela Iannotta, Mauro Gatti and Fabrizio D'Ascenzo

1 Introduction

Developing human capital is fundamental for the intellectual viability of both employees and organizations. Over the last decades, the necessity of matching the creation of distinctive organizational skills with the opportunities of workers' employability has made the phenomenon of Corporate Universities increasingly widespread [1]. Nowadays, these training centres have achieved high levels of sophistication, to the extent that the extensive use of IC technologies represents a distinctive characteristic of the so called "third generation" of Corporate Universities (CUs) [2]. This is mainly due to multiple advantages of employing technologies in business education, such as cost and time savings, flexibility in time and space of learning, and the adoption of more social and collaborative learning methods [2–6]. By and large, thanks to the extension of the Internet and Information Technology, Corporate Universities have found new opportunities for improving their training processes and programs [5, 7, 8]. As a result, traditional training tools have been often joined to or progressively replaced by technology-based instruments (e.g., e-learning, net-learning, mobile devices, self-portal). At the same time, both the organization's context and culture have influence on the actual implementation of ICT in business education, as well as in knowledge management systems [2, 9].

M. Iannotta (✉) · M. Gatti (✉) · F. D'Ascenzo
Department of Management, Sapienza University of Rome,
Via Del Castro Laurenziano 9, 00161 Rome, Italy
e-mail: michela.iannotta@uniroma1.it

M. Gatti
e-mail: mauro.gatti@uniroma1.it

F. D'Ascenzo
e-mail: fabrizio.dascenzo@uniroma1.it

© Springer International Publishing Switzerland 2016
F. D'Ascenzo et al. (eds.), *Blurring the Boundaries Through Digital Innovation*,
Lecture Notes in Information Systems and Organisation 19,
DOI 10.1007/978-3-319-38974-5_4

Starting from this state of art, our study explores the most recent trends about the diffusion of ICTs within the Italian CUs. We report and comment the results of a survey conducted in 2014 and involving 20 Italian Corporate Universities. This exploratory moment aims to describe the common characteristics of the phenomenon (the "What" question) and it is a part of a broader research project aimed to address the more important explanatory question, i.e. why and when IC technologies are not very pervasive in business education.

The paper is structured as follows. The second section provides a review of the literature, which samples the main ICTs employed in business education. After presenting our research methodology in the third section, we report and discuss the main findings of the survey (Sect. 4). Discussion and conclusions are provided in the last sections.

2 Literature Review and Research Questions

2.1 Formal Learning and the Emergence of Corporate Universities

The knowledge-based economy, along with the development of international labor markets, has marked learning as a strategic factor for both businesses and workers [1, 10, 11]. On the one hand, by increasing skills and expertise, learning enables workers to enrich their professional career and to achieve work-related goals [12]. Moreover, it guarantees workers' lifelong employability in the labor market [10], especially when learning involves some general skills that can be transplanted into different organizational contexts [1]. On the other hand, by continuously empowering individual skills and competencies [13], learning improves corporate competitiveness, since "continuous learning is essential for surviving in dynamic and competitive environments" [14: 186].

Learning in a company can generally occur into two ways: (1) formal learning; and (2) informal learning. The former refers to all training activities and programs where learning is generally highly planned and structured [10, 15]. Typically, it takes place off the job, based on formal classroom, and it aims to provide employees with job-related knowledge and skills [15, 16]. Conversely, informal learning methods include natural learning that is neither planned nor organized [17], such as experimenting, daily routines, interacting with others, team working [16]. Despite the latter can be effective and quite inexpensive, formal training ensures the same learning for everyone and, when it is well designed and implemented, can foster the employees' commitment [18, 19] and the overall productivity of the firm [20]. Therefore, formal training is a key factor to attain the strategic objectives of companies and to sustain their competitive advantage [17].

Generally, Corporate Universities (CUs) have been instituted by companies to connect learning initiatives with organizational objectives [21]. They are defined as overarching designations for the formal learning activities of the organization [22].

Although their debut has occurred in the 1950s, CUs have had a pervasive diffusion since the 1990s; nowadays, the necessity of matching the creation of distinctive organizational skills with the opportunities of workers' employability has made the phenomenon of CUs increasingly widespread [1].

Many definitions have been provided for corporate universities, but what is most important to underline is their role as entities that are strategically devoted and oriented to develop individual and organizational learning [23: 9]. In line with Fresina [24], CUs have three main strategic roles: (1) reinforcing and perpetuating behaviours and values of organizations; (2) managing organizational change; and (3) driving and shaping the future direction of organizations. In a similar vein, Walton [25] classifies three generations of CUs. In particular, the first generation (e.g., the Disney University) includes those initiatives aiming to the adoption of organizational culture and based on traditional classroom attendance. A similar setting is shown by the second generation of CUs (e.g. Motorola); however the second generation is characterized by more strategic initiatives with regard to the organizational learning, such as partnerships with other institutions or with the broader community [2, 22]. The third generation includes those CUs that: (1) make the best use of technology for learning; (2) likely possess virtual elements in their learning processes; and (3) have a great strategic importance in integrating individual training with the strategic objectives of the organization [2, 22]. This generation of Corporate Universities has achieved high levels of sophistication.

In the next section we will describe the role of the Information Technology in improving both processes and training programs of corporate universities. Moreover, we will analyze the most recent trends about the diffusion of ICTs in business education.

2.2   Learning Methods and Technologies in Business Education

With the concept of technology-mediated learning, Alavi and Gallupe [5] refer to the significant use of information and communication technology in a learning experience. Generally, employing technologies in formal and informal learning ensures multiple advantages [4, 6]. First of all, Internet and Information technology provide a higher cost effectiveness, since they allow companies to reduce expenses for classroom-based training and to reach a larger audience. Moreover, employees can learn at their workplace without travelling, instead of the traditional 'off the job' training [5, 8, 17]. Secondly, technologies enables flexibility in time and space of learning, in a sort of 'just in time' formula [5, 8]. They provide more efficient and customizable tools for training, in a way that employees can learn whenever and wherever they want and obtain more specific learning programs [17]. Furthermore, technologies such as online intranet, corporate portals, podcasts or webcasts, facilitate the access to learning content and materials [5]. Lastly, information technologies can foster the adoption of learning methods that are more social and collaborative, especially with the advent of social media and virtual community. Thus, traditional training tools have been often joined to or progressively replaced by technology-based instruments (e.g., e-learning, net-learning, mobile devices, self-portal).

The concept of e-learning refers to training activities that are delivered online through the use of ICTs [17]. To that regard, it certainly calls for action to revisit and transform the traditional teaching and learning models [26, 27]. While the benefits of e-learning are well known (cost advantages, flexibility, training customization), its main drawbacks arise from the problem of low interaction among peers and from the fact that learning mainly depends on the action of learners, rather than teachers [17]. Moreover, according to Stewart and Kenneth [17], it can lead teachers to simply put written material on computer without any interaction with students.

A further step in distance learning consists of net-learning or Asynchronous Learning Networks (ALNs) which emphasize the role of the net in enhancing collaborative and personalized learning through people-to-people communication and interaction [1, 28]. The main ALN components are computer-based training (lab simulations, authorware, macromedia constructed systems), self-learning (reading, browsing, test taking), asynchronous interacting (e-mail, news group, threaded conferencing systems), and synchronous interacting between people (chat systems, telephone, video systems) [28]. Alternatively, blended learning offers the opportunity of integrating classroom face-to-face learning with online learning experiences [29]. Its major advantage is to simultaneously exploit the benefits of technology with the high quality of the face-to-face classroom, ensuring a continuous learning [1]. Finally, two of the most recent trends in distance learning are mobile learning and MOOCs (Massive Open Online Courses). The former refers to learning "delivered or supported solely or mainly by handheld and mobile technologies such as personal digital assistants (PDAs), smartphones or wireless laptop PCs" [30: 13]. In this way information and learning materials are available anywhere and at anytime. The latter consists of open online courses that bring together thousands of learners into a common event of free training [31]. For this reason, generally MOOCs are deployed in service platforms for managing the massive amount of learners (community) [32].

Distance learning is enabled by several technologies, depending on the environment in which they are implemented [26]. While CD-ROM media represent the earliest technological tools to support employees' learning, more innovative technological infrastructures, such as Learning Management Systems (LMS), Content Management Systems (CMS) and Learning Content Management Systems (LCMS), provide both tracking and administration support to learning processes [8, 26]. It is widely acknowledged that information systems have a great importance in supporting internal processes (e.g. [33]). In business education, they are particularly valuable in keeping track of employees' training pathways, by allowing companies to monitor and evaluate their effectiveness. Alongside, a new type of e-learning platform, called Sharable Object Content Reference Model (SCORM), offers a different way of reusing content and functionalities and it makes content objects interoperable across multiple e-learning platforms [34]. Lastly, Multimedia Communities and Virtual Worlds have transformed significantly distance learning, by allowing e-learning environments to incorporate multimedia content and to stimulate learning through simulations, games, and interactions [26].

2.3 The Role of Technologies in the Third Generation of CUs

As suggested by the academic literature, Internet and Information Technology revolution has dramatically changed teaching and learning methods. As a consequence, Corporate Universities have got new opportunities for improving their training processes and programs [8]. Clearly, beyond its strategic aims, one of the essential purposes for instituting a CU is the need for centralizing resources to reduce expenses of training activities [35]. In such cases, new technology, and especially e-learning are seen to play the most relevant role [2]. However, as noted by Allen [36], technology should be used to facilitate, and not replace, traditional classroom-based learning, because learning, instead of technology, is the goal of CUs. Moreover, in order to be really effective, information technology should be implemented along with significant changes in teaching approaches and learning processes, rather than merely used for automating training activities provided in physical classrooms [3].

At the same time, the actual implementation of ICTs in business education may be influenced by corporate culture, as well as by organizational contexts. Although they were referring to the use of knowledge management (KM) techniques and technologies, Davel and Snyman [9] underline that KM technologies are significantly dependent on organizational culture. More in depth, the authors show that task-driven culture (generally consultancy organizations, that focus on value expertise rather than position, on creativity and variety, flexibility and high employee autonomy), and character-driven culture (e.g. specialist groups such as lawyer partnerships, with focus on the individual and equal opportunities) are associated to a more extensive use of KM technologies, including e-learning, web-based file sharing, tele- and video-conferencing software. Conversely, this does not occur in the case of power-driven culture (typically small entrepreneurial organizations with autocracy, without many rules and regulations, where employee learn by trial and error), and role-driven culture (generally large and bureaucratic organizations, with focus on long-term careers, stability and predictability). Moreover, while Abel and Li [8] find that the majority of CUs utilize technologies in CUs' operations, especially distance learning technologies and comprehensive Learning Management System (LMS), Homan and Macpherson [2] uncover that the e-learning strategy is not always the most popular in CUs. According to the authors, this circumstance is due to the influence of organizational contexts, with particular regard to their technological sophistication and to the need of integrating e-learning approaches with corporate and HR objectives. In this perspective, the focus should be on the strategic potential of e-learning tools, rather than only on their flexibility and cost-efficiency [2]. It is clear that technology needs to have a strategic relevance in business education.

Overall, the role of new technologies in CUs emerges unclearly from the arguments reviewed, and this sounds quite unusual if it is true that technology plays the most relevant role in the third generation of CUs. Unfortunately, very little research has addressed these aspects, e.g. [2, 8]. It is in this gap that we place our study. The challenge is to add knowledge about the actual adoption and diffusion of Information and Communication Technologies in Corporate Universities and seek to know the characteristics that make companies more or less involved in employing the new frontiers of technology in their CUs. In order to reach our research objectives, we surveyed a number of Italian companies. Italy is a particularly suitable scenario, for our aims. Firstly, Italian CUs have shown a great interest in e-learning initiatives to improve the delivering of training program and reduce costs, but their diffusion has been rather limited in time [37], resulting in an asymmetrical development of e-learning strategies [38]. Unfortunately, national literature has neglected to monitor and deepen this phenomenon, with very few exceptions (e.g. [29]). Furthermore, Italy is one of the European countries that present a large number of CUs, and the simultaneous presence of both "historical" and younger CUs [29] is really interesting to explore their heterogeneity with regard to the diffusion of ITs and e-learning initiatives.

3 Research Methodology

In order to explore the role of ICT in supporting training processes within the Italian Corporate Universities, we employed an empirical analysis, based on the collection of questionnaires completed by CU's managers and heads that are engaged in training and development processes. The sample consisted of 35 Italian companies, recruited according to their participation, affiliation, and formal membership to Assoknowledge (n = 35), which is the Italian Association of the Education and Knowledge of Confindustria, an employers' collective association. Questionnaires were administered through the online survey platform 'Qualtrics', and they were collected from February to April 2015. Of all the surveyed companies, 22 completed the questionnaire, with a response rate of 63 %. From collected questionnaires, 2 were excluded due to partial responses. Therefore, a total of 20 complete responses were coded for descriptive data analysis, particularly useful for exploring the profile of companies that employ or not ICTs in their CUs. The questionnaire (developed in Italian) was implemented in collaboration with Assoknowledge, with the aim to carry out the annual survey (2014) on the Italian CUs. It consisted of 10 sections, including some aspects not directly relevant to our investigation. For this reason, our data analysis was performed mainly on Section 8, which investigates the typology of the provided training (i.e., "How many learning models are generally available and what are the most frequently employed ones?") and Section 10, which aimed to collected information about the role of ITs in the CUs, with a particular focus on the adoption and diffusion of innovative technologies to support employees' training and development (e.g., "Which of the following processes of the CU are supported by an information system?", "What are the areas where the e-learning is more frequently used?"). The main learning methods and technologies which respondents were inquired about, were primarily based on, but not limited to, the existing literature. Indeed, since the aim of this study was to investigate the most recent trends, we have included some items with the choice "Other (to be specified)".

Generally, companies are distributed almost heterogeneously by industry, size and type of company setting. While 40 % of companies employ from 50 to 1000 workers, the majority of them employ 1001–5000 workers (35 % of respondents), or over 5000 employees (25 %). Moreover, a good percentage of companies (45 %) are unlisted multinational companies; the remaining is divided into: listed national companies (15 %), unlisted national companies (20 %), and listed multinational companies (20 %).

4 Main Findings

4.1 Descriptive Analysis

By investigating the learning models that are generally activated in the Italian CUs (multiple choice questions) and their importance for interviewees, respondents show a clear inclination for traditional training methods. The results reveal that the most important learning models are considered face-to-face lessons (N = 12), exercises (e.g., incident or case study, N = 13), while the remaining gets less attention, such as simulations (i.e., role playing, behavioural modelling or business game) (N = 8), experiential methods (i.e., outdoor training or action learning) (N = 7), and social methods (N = 5). A smaller percentage of informants considers very important e-learning (N = 7), one-to-one methods (N = 4), and net-learning (N = 2). Very little relevance is given to MOOC and this is probably due to their recent development.

In order to analyze the level of technological sophistication of companies, we included some items about the implementation of corporate portals for training processes. Only half of the surveyed companies states they have implemented self-service portals that allow managers and employees to interact with training processes. These portals consist of several functionalities that are currently available, such as social tools, accessing to individual training plan/programs/materials/e-learning courses, and training accounting. Conversely, the majority of companies do not hold a corporate portal aiming at to managing the internal faculty (47 %) or they plan to implement it in the next future (47 %).

Regarding e-learning strategies, the results show that 38 % of the respondents employ online training in very low percentages (from 5 to 10 %). Only in very few companies (6 %), e-learning initiatives provide more than 50 % of the total training. Generally speaking, compliance is the main area in which companies employ e-learning tools (e.g., legal, health safety environment), while training initiatives for commercial expertise or change management experiences make very little use of e-learning instruments. However, in these few cases, the most common e-learning methods that are adopted by CUs are e-learning SCORM based (93 %). In the future, companies would like to implement other e-learning methods, such as business game ($N = 7$), gamification ($N = 8$), social learning ($N = 7$), and MOOC ($N = 9$). To that regard, they are very interested in MOOC platforms, with the aim to support training content and processes. Moreover, we have explored the use of mobile devices for business education. We note that a very small portion is taken by those technologies. About 76 % of respondents affirm they do not use mobile devices to support classroom-based learning (47 %) or they plan to use them in the next future (29 %). Mobile devices are currently employed for learning initiatives only from 24 % of companies.

Interestingly, by analyzing the suitability of technological infrastructures across CUs, we find that in 59 % of companies, ICT support is considered to be not appropriate to meet the total amount of activities carried out by CUs (35 %) or it is only partially appropriate (24 %). On the contrary, just under half of companies (41 %) is satisfied.

5 Discussion, Conclusions and Future Research

In contrast to the distinctly technological features of the third generation of CUs, the analysis reveals that Italian Corporate Universities do not make extensive use of ICTs. Compared to the dominant literature, this appears as a rather "deviant" behaviour and we would offer some insights and interpretations of this phenomenon. After highlighting some key factors which could affect the adoption and diffusion of ICTs in the Italian CUs, we propose the future steps of our research to better investigate their actual influence.

Essentially, three main aspects of interest emerge. First, Italian CUs make primary use of traditional learning methods. Second, since technological infrastructures are very limited in training activities, they do not show high levels of technological sophistication. Taken together, these results are enough consistent, because if companies mainly prefer traditional learning methods, we expect that they do not make great investment in innovative ITs. Indeed, Information Technology should be implemented along with significant changes in teaching approaches and learning processes, rather than merely used for automating the information delivery function in classrooms [3]. However, it is interesting to note that the majority of respondents considers inappropriate the technological support to CU activities. This circumstance may suggest that, despite the need for improving IC technologies in CUs, the new technologies are not considered really strategic for their success.

As suggested by the academic literature, these technological choices could be related to a number of organizational features, such as technological sophistication and the need for integrating e-learning approach with corporate and HR objectives [2]. Moreover, the HR readiness and familiarity with technology could be other possible hindrances.

Finally, the deviant behaviour of the Italian CUs could be associated to the organizational culture of companies. In line with Davel and Snyman [9], our sample mainly consists of large organizations, which probably incorporate a role-driven culture (focus on long-term careers, stability and predictability). These might be some of the possible reasons why Italian CUs pay less attention on the implementation of innovative technologies in managing their training processes, or why they prefer mostly traditional technologies.

Trough this research in progress paper, we contribute to the debate about the actual role of ICTs in CUs and the possible reasons that make companies more or less involved in employing the new frontiers of technology in their CUs. Moreover, we contribute to national literature by exploring the Italian market of CUs and monitoring its evolution. However, this work represents a first stage of a larger research project aimed to address the research questions arising from the theoretical section (why and when IC technologies are not very pervasive in business education). Clearly, our first insights require further investigations to address the explanatory reasons of the phenomenon. The next step of the research project concerns the implementation of a comparative case study [39–41]. To that end, the present work allows us to select cases to be included in our future analysis, particularly those which show a not extensive use of ICT in training processes. Moreover, compared to the high level of sophistication of the third generation of CUs, it gives evidence for the existence of a number of deviant cases among the Italian companies and for the importance to analyze why and how companies are more o less prone to make an extensive use of IC Technologies. This is particularly relevant from a managerial perspective, since companies should implement and invest much more in technological infrastructures in order to: (1) support the increasing activities of their CUs; (2) to increase their competitiveness at international level; and (3) to make their learning models more dynamic and more effective.

Therefore, the selected cases will be included in the further stages of the research. We will employ semi-structured interviews to CUs' heads, HR manager and employee. In this way, we can ensure the triangulation of data and we could also analyze the perception of the use of ICT in CUs from the perspective of employees. Finally, we will provide aggregate measures of the organizational culture at CU level and we will take into account several organizational features that could have an impact on the adoption and diffusion of ICT in the Italian CUs.

References

1. Costa, G., Gianecchini, M.: Risorse Umane. Persone, Relazioni e Valore. McGraw-Hill, Milano (2009)
2. Homan, G., Macpherson, A.: E-learning in the corporate university. J. Eur. Ind. Train. **29**(1), 75–90 (2005)
3. Leidner, D., Jarvenpaa, S.: The use of information technology to enhance management school education: a theoretical view. MIS Q. **19**(3), 265–291 (1995) [Special Issue on IS Curricula and Pedagogy]
4. Robey, D., Boudreau, M.C., Rose, G.M.: Information technology and organizational learning: a review and assessment of research. Account. Manag. Inf. Technol. **10**, 125–155 (2000)
5. Alavi, M., Gallupe, B.: Using information technology in learning: case studies in business and management education programs. Acad. Manag. Learn. Edu. **2**(2), 139–153 (2003)
6. Lockyer, L., Patterson, J.: Integrating social networking technologies in education: a case study of a formal learning environment. In: Diaz, P., Kinshuk, I. Aedo, Mora, E. (eds.) Eighth IEEE International Conference on Advanced Learning Technologies, pp.529–533. IEEE Cmputer Society, Los Alamitos, California (2008)
7. El Tannir, A.A.: The corporate university model for continuous learning, training and development. Educ. Train. **44**(2), 76–81 (2002)
8. Abel, A.L., Li, J.: Exploring the corporate university phenomenon: development and implementation of a comprehensive survey. Hum. Resour. Dev. Q. **23**(1), 103–128 (2012)
9. Davel, R., Snyman, M.M.M.: Influence of corporate culture on the use of knowledge management techniques and technologies. S. Afr. J. Inf. Manag. **7**(2) (2005)
10. Manuti, A., Pastore, S., Scardigno, A.F., Giancaspro, M.L., Morciano, D.: Formal and informal learning in the workplace a research review. Int. J. Train. Dev. **9**(1), 1–17 (2005)
11. Szoboszlai, V.: Current Shifts in corporate learning meet 'Enabler Competencies'. In: Proceedings of FIKUSZ'12 Symposium for Young Researchers, pp. 97–108 (2013)
12. Muhamad, M., Idris, K.: Workplace learning in Malaysia: the learner's perspective. Int. J. Train. Dev. **9**(1), 62–78 (2005)
13. Lytras, M., Sicilia, M.: The knowledge society: a manifesto for knowledge and learning. Int. J. Knowl. Learn. **1**(2), 1–11 (2005)
14. Popper, M., Lipshitz, R.: Organizational learning. mechanisms, culture, and feasibility. Manag. Learn. **31**(2), 181–196 (2000)
15. Stevens, J., Ashton, D., Kelleher, M.: The developing contribution of workplace learning to organisational performance. In: CIPD and the European Consortium of Learning Organisations, Workplace Learning in Europe, pp. 13–19. London, Chartered Institute of Personnel and Development (2001)
16. Marsick, V.J., Watkins, K.E.: Informal and incidental learning. New Dir. Adult Continuing Educ. (Spring) **2001**(89), 25–34 (2001)
17. Stewart, G.L., Kenneth, G.B.: Human Resource Management. Linking Strategy to Practice. Wiley, Hoboken, NJ (2008)
18. Barlett, K.R.: The relationship between training and organizational commitment: a study in health care field. Hum. Resour. Dev. Q. **12**(4), 335–352 (2002)
19. Allen, D.G., Shoe, L.M., Griffeth, R.W.: The role of perceived organizational support and supportive human resource practices in the turnover process. J. Manag. **29**(1), 99–118 (2003)
20. Zwick, T.: the impact of training intensity on establishment productivity. Ind. Relat. **45**(1), 26–46 (2006)
21. Rademakers, M.: Corporate universities: driving force of knowledge innovation. J. Workplace Learn. **17**(1/2), 130–136 (2005)
22. Prince, C., Beaver, G.: The rise and rise of the corporate university: the emerging corporate learning agenda. Int. J. Manag. Educ. **1**(3), 17–26 (2001)
23. Allen, M.: The Corporate University Handbook: Designing, Managing, and Growing a Successful Program. AMACOM, New York, NY (2002)

24. Fresina, A.: The three prototypes of corporate universities. Corp. Univ. Rev. **5**(1), 3–6 (1997)
25. Walton, J.: Strategic Human Resource Development. Pitman, London (1999)
26. Kahiigi, E.K., Ekenberg, L., Danielson, M., Hansson, H.: Exploring the E-learning state of art. In: Proceedings of the ECEL 2007: 6th European Conference on E-Learning, Copenhagen Business School, Denmark, Academic Conference Limited Reading, UK (2007)
27. Sambrook, S.: E-learning in small organizations. Educ. Train. **45**(8/9), 506–516 (2003)
28. Bourne, J.R.: Net-learning: strategies for on-campus and off-campus network-enabled learning. J. Asynchron. Learn. Netw. **2**(2), 70–88 (1998)
29. Garrison, D.R., Kanuka, H.: Blended learning: uncovering its transformative potential in higher education. Internet High. Educ. **7**(2), 95–105 (2004)
30. Ally, M.: Mobile Learning Transforming the Delivery of Education and Training. AU Press, Athabasca University, Edmonton (2009)
31. Grünewald, F., Meinel, C., Totschnig, M., Willems, C.: Designing MOOCs for the support of multiple learning styles. In: Scaling up learning for sustained impact, pp. 371–382. Springer, Heidelberg (2013)
32. Alario-Hoyos, C., Pérez-Sanagustín, M., Delgado-Kloos, C., Parada, G.H.A., Muñoz-Organero, M., Rodríguez-de-las-Heras, A.: Analysing the impact of built-in and external social tools in a MOOC on educational technologies. In: D. Hernàndez-Leo et al. (eds.) EC-TEL 2013, LNCS 8095, pp. 5–18. Springer, Heidelberg (2013)
33. Martinez, M., De Marco, M.: I criteri di scelta delle metodologie di IS Development: un contributo dalle teorie di progettazione organizzativa. Sinergie **19**, 133–147 (2005)
34. Vossen, G., Westerkamp, P.: Towards the next generation of E-learning standards: SCORM for service-oriented environments. In: Proceedings of the Sixth International Conference on Advanced Learning Technologies (ICALT), pp. 1031–1035, IEEE Computer Society (2006)
35. Arnone, M.: Corporate universities: a viewpoint on the challenges and best practices. Career Dev. Int. **3**(5), 199–205 (1998)
36. Allen, M.: Corporate universities 2010: globalization and greater sophistication. J. Int. Manag. Stud. **5**(1), 48–53 (2010)
37. Asfor: *Le Corporate University in Italia*, In: 2ª Giornata della Formazione Manageriale Asfor, Milano (2004)
38. Cappiello, G., Pedrini, G.: Le corporate university italiane. L'industria **XXXIV**(2), 295–328 (2013)
39. Yin, R.K.: Case Study Research: Design and Methods. Sage Publications, Beverly Hills, CA (1984)
40. Eisenhardt, K.M.: Building theories from case study research. Acad. Manag. Rev. **14**(4), 532–550 (1989)
41. Kaarbo, J., Beasley, R.K.: A Practical Guide to the comparative case study method in political psychology. Polit. Psychol. **20**(2), 369–391 (1999)

Blended Learning Approach: How Is the Learning Educational Paradigm Changing? Reflections and a Proposed Framework

Leonardo Caporarello and Anna Iñesta

1 Introduction

The evolution of educational paradigms has been widely discussed in literature.

In this context, as it is well known, the use of technology has influenced a lot the evolution of education paradigms.

Although many studies and researches have investigated the role and influence of technology for educational purposes, its actual effectiveness is still an open issue [1–4].

So, a first question we intend to address is "are the current technology-enabled learning models, i.e. e-learning, effective enough or is there a new paradigm in the learning model evolution path?".

The effective use of a learning model typically requires some enabling conditions. How educational institutions are facing the use of technology for educational purposes? How do they have to change in order to be ready for successfully adopting this kind of learning model?

Leveraging on two bodies of literature, online education and change management, this paper aims at contributing to the managerial debate about the technology-enabled learning models. In particular, based on the online educational model literature, we intend to answer the first two above questions; next, referring

L. Caporarello (✉)
Department of Management and Technology, and SDA Bocconi School of Management, Bocconi University, Milan, Italy
e-mail: leonardo.caporarello@unibocconi.it

A. Iñesta
ESADE Center for Educational Innovation, ESADE Business & Law Schools, Ramon Llull University, Barcelona, Spain
e-mail: ana.inesta@esade.edu

© Springer International Publishing Switzerland 2016
F. D'Ascenzo et al. (eds.), *Blurring the Boundaries Through Digital Innovation*,
Lecture Notes in Information Systems and Organisation 19,
DOI 10.1007/978-3-319-38974-5_5

to the change management literature, we intend to answer the third question, specifically providing some recommendations to educational institutions in order to help them understanding how to make the educational paradigm transition happen.

2   Literature Review

Educational paradigms have continuously evolved over the last 35 years. Analyzing their evolution, we can identify three major shifts. The first shift was in the 1980s. Throughout the 1980s, the educational process was mainly led by teachers [5, 6]. The second shift was in the early 1990s, where the education process focused on the relationship between teachers and learners [7]. The third shift can be traced back to the late 1990s. From then onward the educational process is aiming at fostering the learner-centric focus [8–11].

During this time, the evolution of technology has played an important role in influencing the shift of educational paradigms. The use of technology for educational purposes has created new concepts and models, e.g. online and distance education, web-based learning, computer-mediated learning, e-learning [12].

Online education is defined as any form of learning that takes place via computer network [13]. Among these new ways of learning, the e-learning model has gained lot of attention in literature in the last 15 years [14].

A recent study defines e-learning as "a set of models, methodologies, and processes for the acquisition and use of knowledge distributed and facilitated primarily by electronic means" [1]. Compared to the traditional learning models, e-learning offers the following main advantages: the learning process is flexible and can be self-paced; collaboration and interaction are the two most important characteristics of the learning environment; learning materials and resources can be maintained and updated in a efficient way [15–17].

Although many researchers support the benefits of both online and e-learning models [18], others have identified some relevant pitfalls of this model, particularly in terms of its limited capacity to actively engage learners in the educational process, and to make learners feeling to establish a positive relationship with the teacher [19, 20]. These models seem not able to deliver the expected results [16, 21–25], lacking some of their most important key success factors that are the sense of presence, the feeling of immediacy, and the dynamicity and fluidity of the learning environment [26].

Following the above discussion, a formal shift in the educational paradigm has to be identified and recognized, that is the blended model. This is not just a new educational model, but a new wave in the technology-enhanced educational models.

An overview of the evolution of the learning paradigm, from educational and technological perspective is given in Fig. 1.

The blended model provides a learning experience through the integration of different learning methodologies, including face-to-face with technology-enabled

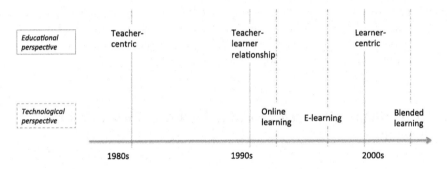

Fig. 1 Evolution of the learning paradigm: an educational and technological perspective

environment [27–30]. In the simplest form, the blended learning model is the thoughtful integration of online and face-to-face-instruction [31].

The blended model is not a new concept in literature, but recently it has received increased attention among academics and practitioners [32–35]. Comparing blended to e-learning models it's possible to identify some relevant differences, as emerge in literature.

Learners in the e-learning model perceive a higher instructional difficulty than those in blended learning model. Moreover, in the e-learning setting, learners experience a significant higher workload for their study than those in the blended learning setting. A third relevant aspect is about the learning support that is perceived higher in the blended learning model than in the e-learning one.

Moreover, a recent study predicts a relevant percentage of learners that will prefer to take courses in blended format respect to courses in face-to-face setting [36]. According to this study, a large part of learners prefers to take courses in blended model. This phenomenon is large as 71 % of learners: from 14.1 million in traditional courses enrollment in 2010 to a 4.1 million in 2015.

Another recent study [37] conducted over one million learners' responses (2008–2011) analyzes the effectiveness of blended learning initiatives with the effectiveness of other ways of learning. The following results emerge: 52 % of respondents rated the blended learning courses they have taken highest as "excellent", while other ways of learning (online and face-to-face courses) were rated as excellent by the 48 % of respondents.

Another important indicator is the withdrawal rate. In the blended courses learners tend to withdraw much lower than they do in other modes of learning.

From a general perspective, learners are positive about the courses that offer flexibility in both time and space. Although this flexibility is maximized with fully online courses, learners do not want to eliminate any face-to-face form of interaction [38, 39]. This challenge is overcome by the use of blended learning model. Moreover, some authors [40] highlight the importance of learning environments to foster interaction, communication, learning enhancements, and constructivism. Blended learning model is expected to enable these elements. Furthermore, this model has potential to create a much more reflective learner population, and to extend learning far beyond the boundaries of traditional classrooms.

So, let us explore in the next paragraph the critical success factors for educational institutions interested in adopting this model.

3 Adopting the Blended Learning Model: Critical Success Factors

Educational institutions that intend to adopt a blended learning model have to carefully consider the following three critical success factors [41]. These are common factors to any level of education (e.g. undergraduate, graduate, executive), and type of educational institution (e.g. private or public).

The first factor is about the alignment of the blended learning model with the institutional goals and objectives. In other words, all the institutions stakeholders must be in alignment if a blended learning program has to be successful.

The second factor refers to the organizational capabilities to effectively execute and deliver a blended learning program. Among the organizational capabilities we can mention: the role of instructional designers of blended learning programs, the preparation of faculty members to develop and structure contents that are aligned with the blended model, the management of technological infrastructure, the support to both learners and teachers.

The third factor is the represented by the communication process. Adopting a blended learning model requires the engagement of many stakeholders. Thus, it's a useful idea to create a specific narrative for each homogeneous group of stakeholders. This narrative allows creating and using a common vocabulary and definitions, which in turn facilitates the acceptance by stakeholders.

4 Change Process

Following the above considerations, the use of technology for educational purposes is pushing educational institutions to rethink and change the traditional way of designing and delivering their learning programs [42]. And the change process involved in switching from a 'classic' institution based on face-to-face faculty-student interaction to an innovative institution capable of making the most out of the potential of blended-learning environments is far from simple. Partly because faculty members not only face the change involved in learning how to use the technology proposed (e.g. moodle, tokbox…) but, perhaps more importantly, they face the challenge of adopting learner-centered practices, something different research has shown to be far from easy [43].

In order to make this transition possible, organizations and institutions interested in adopting blended learning models must have a clear vision and a strong support from the various stakeholders involved in the change process [38], and be ready to exercise what Garrison and Vaughan mention [44], that is sustained collaborative leadership. Going beyond effective and inspirational communication strategies, such leadership involves the design of an adequate action plan which, among others, have the following interconnected dimensions into account: desired change speed and desired change scope, policy-making strategy and characteristics of faculty body.

We start with the last dimension, the characteristics of the school's faculty body, which we consider key. Faculty are of course one of the essential stakeholders in the process since they will be protagonists in their classes and if they are not convinced of the benefits of the new blended learning approach this will never be adequately explained to the learners (a sine qua non condition for learner engagement). Among the aspects playing a key role in the change management process we find faculty talent (i.e., their adjustment to the knowledge and competence profile the School development will need), their stage in their academic career (the more initial in their career the more flexible they may be towards change and the closer they can be to learners' mindset), and of course their disposition towards change, given their history in the institution and their vision of where the institution should head towards in the future.

Secondly, assessing the necessary speed and scope whereby the change needs to be effected will be essential when making decisions as to the ways to go about change implementation: the more urgent the change, the more top-down the leadership for change need to be, and the higher the connection faculty have with the institutional vision, with more ease will the top-down approach be perceived and experienced. Needless to say, and thirdly, if the scope of change focuses on a reduced number of programs (as opposed to all the programs of the institution), a top-down but also a bottom-up approach in change leadership can be applied, as the complexity of the process is reduced, especially if the sense of urgency is decreased.

Finally, the policy-making strategy will need to have all the above in mind to allocate the necessary resources to provide for adequate faculty support and development and to put into effect incentives for blended learning experiences (e.g., ways of providing faculty with the necessary recognition for their willingness to contribute to the institutional change).

5 Make the Change Happen: A Proposed Framework

In this paragraph we intend to propose some recommendations to educational institutions' decision-makers and/or change agents in order to make the above-described change happen. Specifically, we propose the following educational change framework that is based on the Kotter's eight-step framework [45].

Table 1 Steps in the educational change framework

Steps	Actions
1. Make the need for change visible	• Collect data, facts and evidences that demonstrate how and why the blended model can be more effective than the e-learning one • Make the case regarding the what blended learning will bring to the School's value proposition
2. Create a change team	• Identify faculty members with a high level of credibility, who may be open to explore and innovate, and able to influence other stakeholders in the institution (particularly, stakeholders who are resistors)
3. Define the new educational paradigm	• Elaborate and define how the blended model can be successful in their organization by connecting it with the institution's educational strategy, • Consider which tools would be most useful, • Provide a framework of reference regarding the ways in which those tools may be used in particular classroom settings to enhance learners' learning and, not just any kind of learning but that which connects with the exit profile that aligns with the school mission
4. Design and implement the execution plan	• Elaborate a resource plan that will be necessary to equip the institution with the adequate technology • Ensure there is a team of experts in technology-enhanced learning, and blended learning models and methodologies to provide faculty with the necessary support to make the change possible
5. Communicate the new educational paradigm	• Design the communication strategy to present the blended learning model: how it works, advantages and key success factors • Incorporate in this communication examples of the pilot editions of the educational model run with selected faculty

Our framework consists of the following five steps, which are presented in Table 1.

The first step is to make the need for change visible. The more visible the need for change, the higher the sense of urgency [45, 46]. Creating the sense of urgency is extremely relevant for activating the change process. How to create the need for change? The change agent has to collect data, facts and evidences that demonstrate how and why the blended model can be more effective than the e-learning one and s/he needs to make the case regarding the what blended learning will bring to the School's value proposition.

When the need for change has been demonstrated, it is time to elaborate on what the changed educational model should articulate around. In order to do this, the change agent has first to create a change team whose members have a high level of credibility, are open to explore and innovate, and able to influence other stakeholders in the institution (particularly, stakeholders who are resistors). This team needs to elaborate and define how the blended model can be successful in their organization by connecting it with the institution's educational strategy. Such model should not only consider which tools would be most useful, but it should also consider providing a framework of reference regarding the ways in which those tools may be used in particular classroom settings to enhance learners' learning and, not just any kind of learning but that which connects with the exit profile that aligns with the School mission.

Moreover, the change agent and the change team must give execution to the educational change process. Indeed, a great new educational model and an execution plan are keys of a change process since, on too many occasions changes remain at the level of discourse. One of the dimensions to have in mind when designing this execution plan is the resources that will be necessary to equip the institution with the adequate technology but also, perhaps more importantly, to ensure there is a team of experts in technology-enhanced learning, and blended learning models and methodologies to provide faculty with the necessary support to make the change possible.

Then, the change agent along with the change team describes and presents the blended learning model (how it works, advantages and key success factors) to all institutional stakeholders. This is a massive and intensive communication process, which will have begun earlier in the process, when some faculty will have been selected to run pilot editions of the educational change. Communication has to be properly designed according to the different targets, and the possibility of using pilot projects to support and illustrate the tangibility of the alleged value brought by the new model will be key. Underestimating the power of the communication can be the reason why the educational change process fails.

6 Conclusions

This paper has contended that blended learning is increasingly gaining support as the model of the future in higher education. As we have seen, blended learning not only provides a series of advantages as compared to fully e-learning education (decreased learners' perception of instructional difficulty or excessive workload, increased perception of blended learning as excellent learning experiences, decreased withdrawal from learners) but it may also contribute to add value to face-to-face live class sessions, by enhancing learners' preparation for those via online activities and resources.

All these reasons suggest that blended learning will increasingly regarded as an approach to be incorporated in higher education institutions, especially in those international ones in constant quest for excellence and innovation in the learning experiences they propose to their students. And these institutions will no doubt face the challenges outlined when implementing the change management processes necessary for blended learning to bring the necessary value to their programs. As Garrison and Vaughan mention [44], sustained collaborative leadership with the components mentioned above will be necessary to introduce blended learning effectively. Such collaborative leadership should, however, be articulated around a clear and sound change management framework such as the one proposed, which will allow for the educational change brought by the introduction of the blended learning model to become a reality.

References

1. Caporarello, L., Sarchioni, G.: E-learning: the recipe for success. J. E-learning Knowl. Soc. **10** (1), 107–118 (2014)
2. Caporarello, L., Sarchioni, G.: Does technology-mediated learning matter for effective teams? In: Spagnoletti, P. (ed.) Organizational Change and Information Systems. Springer, Heidelberg, Germany (2012)
3. Nemanich, L., Banks, M., Vera, D.: Enhancing knowledge transfer in classroom versus online settings: the interplay among instructor, student, content, and context. Decis. Sci. J. Innovative Educ. **7**(1), 123–148 (2009)
4. Song, L., Singleton, E., Hill, J.R., Koh, M.H.: Improving online learning: Student perceptions of useful and challenging characteristics. Internet High. Educ. **7**(1), 59–70 (2004)
5. Dunken, M.J.: A review of research on lecturing. High. Educ. Res. Dev. **2**(1), 63–78 (1983)
6. Milliken, J., Barnes, L.P.: Teaching and technology in higher education: student perceptions and personal reflections. Comput. Educ. **39**(3), 223–235 (2002)
7. Ramsden, P.: Learning to teach in higher education. Routledge, London (1992)
8. Ong, C.-S., Lai, J.-Y.: Gender differences in perceptions and relationships among dominants of e-learning acceptance. Comput. Hum. Behav. **22**(5), 816–829 (2006)
9. Saade, R., He, X., Kira, D.: Exploring dimensions to online learning. Comput. Hum. Behav. **23**(4), 1721–1739 (2007)
10. Wang, Y.-S., Wang, H.-Y., Shee, D.Y.: Measuring e-learning systems success in an organizational context: Scale development and validation. Comput. Hum. Behav. **23**(4), 1792–1808 (2007)
11. Yang, X., Li, Y., Tan, C.-H., Teo, H.-H.: Students' participation intention in an online discussion forum: why is computer-mediated interaction attractive? Inf. Manag. **44**(5), 456–466 (2007)
12. Guri-Rosenblit, S.: Eight paradoxes in the implementation process of eLearning in higher education. High. Educ. Policy **18**(1), 5–29 (2005)
13. Kearsley, G. A: Guide to Online Education. http://gustavolarriera.tripod.com/doc/tech/online.htm (last access on 16 May 2015) (1998)
14. Liaw, S.S., Huang, H.M., Chen, G.D.: Surveying instructor and learner attitudes toward e-learning. Comput. Educ. **49**, 1066–1080 (2007)
15. Graff, M.: Learning from web-based instructional systems and cognitive style. Br. J. Educ. Technol. **34**(4), 407–418 (2003)
16. Liaw, S.S.: Investigating students' perceived satisfaction, behavioral intention, and effectiveness of e-learning: a case study of the blackboard system. Comput. Educ. **51**, 864–873 (2008)
17. Zhang, D., Zhou, L., Briggs, R.O., Nunamaker Jr, J.F.: Instructional video in e-learning: Assessing the impact of interactive video on learning effectiveness. Inf. Manag. **43**(1), 15–27 (2006)
18. Otte, G., Benke, M.: Online learning: New models for leadership and organization in higher education. J. Asynchronous Learn. Netw. **10**(2), 23–31 (2006)
19. Daniels, H.L., Moore, D.M.: Interaction of cognitive style and learner control in a hypermedia environment. Int. J. Instr. Media **27**(4), 1–15 (2000)

20. Oh, E., Lim, D.H.: Cross relationships between cognitive styles and learner variables in online learning environment. J. Interact. Online Learn. **4**(1), 53–66 (2005)
21. Sitzmann, T., Kraiger, K., Stewart, D., Wisher, R.: The comparative effectiveness of web-based and classroom instruction: a meta-analysis. Pers. Psychol. **59**, 623–664 (2006)
22. Zhang, D.S., Zhao, J.L., Zhou, L., Nunamaker, J.F.: Can e-learning replace classroom learning? Commun. ACM **47**(5), 75–79 (2004)
23. Bruckman, A.: The future of e-learning communities. Commun. ACM **45**(4), 60–63 (2002)
24. Piccoli, G., Ahmad, R., Ives, B.: Web-based virtual learning environments: A research framework and a preliminary assessment of effectiveness in basic IT skills training. MIS Q. **25**(4), 401–426 (2001)
25. Decker, T., Frailey, D., McNell, E., Mould, D.: Forum: debating distance learning. Commun. ACM **43**(2), 11–15 (2000)
26. Fontaine, G.: Presence in "Teleland". In: Rudestam, K.E., Schoenholtz-Read, J. (eds.) Handbook of Online Learning: Innovations in Higher Education and Corporate Training, pp. 21–52. Sage, Thousand Oaks, CA (2002)
27. Martyn, M.: The hybrid online model: good practice. Educause Q. **26**(1), 18–23 (2003)
28. Jennings, A., Mullally, A., O'Connor, C., Dolan, D.: Is the jury still out for "blended learning"?—use of a web-based collaborative teaching platform. In: Fillipe, J., Cordeiro, J., Pedrosa, V. (eds.) Web Information Systems and Technologies, pp. 355–366. Springer, Heidelberg, Germany (2006)
29. So, H., Brush, T.A.: Student perceptions of collaborative learning, social presence and satisfaction in a blended learning environment: relationships and critical factors. Comput. Educ. **51**(1), 318–336 (2008)
30. Reid-Young, A.: The key to e-learning is b-learning. HCi J. Inf. Dev. https://www.hci.com.au/b-learning (last access on 16 May 2015) (2003)
31. Graham, C.R.: Emerging practice and research in blended learning. In: Moore, M.G. (ed.) Handbook of Distance Education, 3rd edn, pp. 333–350. Routledge, New York, NY (2013)
32. Reece, M., Lockee, B.: Improving training outcomes through blended learning. J. Asynchronous Learn. Netw. **9**(4), 49–57 (2005)
33. Picciano, A.G.: Blended learning: implications for growth and access. J. Asynchronous Learn. Netw. **10**(3), 85–91 (2006)
34. Singh, H., Reed, C.: A White Paper: Achieving Success with Blended Learning: ASTD State of the Industry Report. American Society for Training & Development, Alexandria, VA (2001)
35. Thorne, K.: Blended Learning: How to Integrate Online & Traditional Learning. Korgan Page Ltd, London (2003)
36. Insight, A.: 2011 Learning and Performance Technology Research Taxonomy. Ambient Insight, Monroe, WA (2011)
37. Moskal, P., Dziuban, C., Hartmanet, J.: Blended learning: a dangerous idea? Internet High. Educ. **18**, 15–23 (2013)
38. Dziuban, C., Hartman, J., Cavanagh, T., Moskal, P.: Blended courses as drivers of institutional transformation. In: Kitchenham, A. (ed.) Blended Learning Across Disciplines: Models for Implementation. IGI Global, Hershey, PA (2011)
39. Dziuban, C.D., Moskal, P.D., Bradford, G.R., Brophy-Ellison, J., Groff, A.T.: Constructs that impact the net generation's satisfaction with online learning. In: Sharpe, R., Beetham, H., De Freitas (eds.) Rethinking Learning for a Digital Age: How Learners are Shaping Their Own Experiences. Routledge, New York, NY (2010)
40. Norberg, A., Dziuban, C.D., Moskal, P.D.: A time-based blended learning model. On the Horizon **19**(3), 207–216 (2011)
41. Stacey, E., Gerbic, P.: Success factors for blended learning. In: Hello! Where are you in the landscape of educational technology? Proceedings ascilite Melbourne. http://www.ascilite.org.au/conferences/melbourne08/procs/stacey.pdf (last access on 16 May 2015) (2008)
42. Janicki, T., Steinberg, G.: Evaluation of a computer-supported learning system. Decis. Sci. J. Innov. Educ. **1**(2), 203–223 (2003)

43. Hargreaves, A.: The emotions of teaching and educational change. In: Hargreaves, A., Lieberman, A., Fullan, M., Hopkins, D. (eds.) International Handbook of Educational Change. Kluwer, Dordrecht (1998)
44. Garrison, D.R., Vaughan, N.D.: Institutional change and leadership associated with blended learning innovation: two case studies. Internet High. Educ. **18**, 24–28 (2012)
45. Kotter, J.P.: Leading change: why transformation efforts fail. Harvard Bus. Rev. (2007)
46. Ginsberg, A., Venkatraman, N.: Institutional initiatives for technological change: from issue interpretation to strategic choice. Organ. Stud. **16**(3), 425–448 (1995)

Designing a Competence Acquisition Mobile App

Stefano Za and Eusebio Scornavacca

1 Introduction

Organizational learning is an area of increasing concern for businesses seeking to achieve sustainable competitive advantage [1]. In this context, digital technologies play a relevant role in transforming resources into core capabilities—having the potential to become an "active component of the firm's competitive advantages" [2].

These digital tools and their governance models can be used as a platform for fostering diverse learning processes through different learning strategies such as open and flexible learning (autonomous), distributed learning (dependent), and learning communities (collaborative) [3–5]. This can be particularly helpful within business settings as human resources can develop individual competences and skills that could translate into competitive advantages for their organizations [6].

Managers can attain continuous improvements of organizational performance by encouraging the development and strengthening of organizational competences [6, 7]. As a matter of fact, a source of competitive advantage lies in the ability of top management to consolidate technologies and productive capacity into core competences that allow each business to quickly adapt to continuously changing scenarios as well as to capture potential market opportunities [7].

S. Za (✉)
eCampus University, Novedrate, CO, Italy
e-mail: stefano.za@uniecampus.it; sza@luiss.it

S. Za
CeRSI – LUISS Guido Carli University, Rome, Italy

E. Scornavacca
University of Baltimore, Baltimore, MD, USA
e-mail: escornavacca@ubalt.edu

© Springer International Publishing Switzerland 2016   59
F. D'Ascenzo et al. (eds.), *Blurring the Boundaries Through Digital Innovation*,
Lecture Notes in Information Systems and Organisation 19,
DOI 10.1007/978-3-319-38974-5_6

There is no convergent definition of the term "competence" in the literature [8]. It often referred as a combination of different factors such as knowledge, skills, and/or individual characteristics. Delamare-Le Deist and Winterton [8] propose a holistic competence model composed by three fundamental dimensions: cognitive (knowledge and understanding), functional (skills) and social (behavior and attitude). While the distinction of the three fundamental dimensions could be analytically identified, in practice the competence of an individual is the result of the combination of the three fundamental dimensions. In addition, competencies may be learned through training and development [9], aiming to improve the performance of specific tasks. The extent to which the training is effective may be measured on the basis of pre-established criteria [10].

Digital technologies can be a powerful tool for training and development of human resources [11]. The rapid pace of mainstream adoption of new forms of ubiquitous computing devices such as smartphones, tablets and 'phablets' is enabling an ubiquitous learning environment that can be paramount for the development of competence acquisition tools [12, 13]. As users are able to accomplish a multitude of tasks and interact fluidly in a ubiquitous ecosystem, they become empowered of their own individual learning process [14].

It is not surprising that the largest app category within Google Play (the world's largest marketplace for mobile apps[1]) is "Education". It equates to approximately 10 % of Google Play apps, offering more than 135,000 apps focused on a variety of instructional goals.[2] However 18 % of the apps in this category as classified as "unlikely to be useful" and only 4 % reach the 50,000 downloads mark. Apps dedicated to learning a language are the most common type of app among the top 100 "all-time popular apps" in the Education category. This is followed by apps focused on acquiring technical skills (e.g. drawing, playing a musical instrument, passing the driving license exam), brain training, child development and accessing distance learning environments such as Backboard.[3]

Following a Design Science (DS) research methodology, this paper, as research in progress, attempts to describe the design process of a competence acquisition mobile app. The structure of the paper is as follows: after this introduction Sect. 2 describes the DSRM methodology. This is followed by a discussion on core theories related to skill acquisition, the problem to solve and the design of the artefact. Final considerations and brief information on the next steps of the research will conclude the paper.

---

[1]http://uk.businessinsider.com/google-play-vs-apple-app-store-2015-2?r=US&IR=T.

[2]http://www.appbrain.com/stats/android-market-app-categories.

[3]http://www.appbrain.com/apps/popular/education/.

2   The DSRM Process

The main goal of the Design Science research approach is the creation of successful IT artefacts [15]. The design science research methodology (DSRM) proposed by Peffers et al. [15] is a holistic design science process that is robustly anchored on prior IS literature [16–19]. The DSRM is composed by the following six steps:

1. *problem identification and motivation*—including knowledge of the state of the problem and the importance of its solution;
2. *definition of the objectives for a solution*—from the problem definition and knowledge it is necessary to infer the objectives of a solution and what is possible and feasible. Usually, it is needed to take into account the knowledge of the state of problems and current solutions;
3. *design and development*—the creation of the *artefact*, such as technical or social innovation [16, 20], or more in general "new properties of technical, social, and/or informational resources" [21]. This step includes the definition of the artefact functionality and architecture, and its creation;
4. *demonstration*—in this step it is demonstrated the capability of the artefact to solve one or more instances of the problem (e.g. through experimentation, simulation, case study, proof, or other appropriate activity);
5. *evaluation*—the goal of this step is to observe and measure how well the artefact supports a solution to the problem, comparing the objectives of a solution to actual observed results. The evaluation could take many forms, quantitative and qualitative (e.g. a comparison of the artefact's functionality with the solution objectives from step 2, objective performance measures, satisfaction surveys, client feedback, or simulations). At the end it is possible to decide whether to iterate back to step 3 (design and development) attempting to improve the effectiveness of the artefact or to leave further improvement to subsequent projects.
6. *communication*—at the end, it is suggested to communicate the carried out process and the obtained results to researchers and other relevant audiences.

Even though the process described above is structured sequentially, it is important to observe that there is no expectation to always proceed in a consecutive order from step 1 through step 6, as shown in Fig. 1. For example a problem-centred approach should follow the nominal sequence, starting from step 1. An objective-centred solution, could start with step 2, triggered by a research need that can be addressed by developing an artefact, while a design- and development-centred approach would start with step 3.

In the following section we provide the description of our design problem and the first three phases of the DSRM process for developing a competence acquisition mobile app.

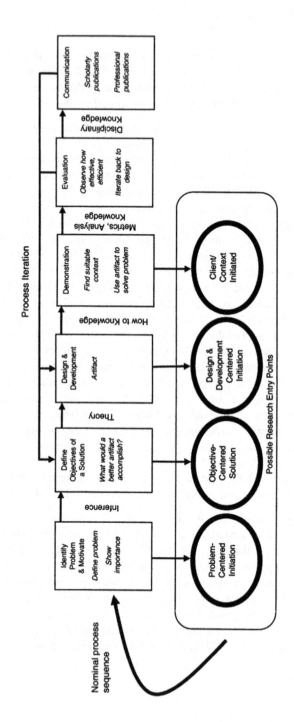

Fig. 1 DSRM process model [15]

3   The Design of a Competence Acquisition Mobile App Through the DSRM

Based on the DSRM process model, this paper follows a Problem-Centered approach. Firms can be viewed as a collection of "unique competences and capabilities" that influence their performance, evolution and strategic growth [22]. In order to achieve competitive advantage, firms need to strategize the management and development of their unique set of competences [23, 24]. In this process, digital technologies could become an "active component" of building or reshaping firms' core competencies [11, 25].

The extinction of mobile phones and the proliferation of fluid multi-device platforms that have blurred the traditional boundaries between stationary and mobile information systems [14, 26], enabling a new digital environment to facilitate organizational learning processes [12]. With this context in mind, the following subsections sequentially describe the first three steps of the DSRM process.

3.1   Step 1: Problem Identification and Motivation

There are several models in the literature focused on developing and measuring competence acquisition—e.g. Russel's [27] five stages for learning a new technology, Bloom's educational objectives [28, 29] and Nonaka's [30] modes of knowledge creation. In this paper we adopt Howell's [31] five-stage competence model (Fig. 2). This learning model is quite comprehensive and could cover a wide variety of competences valuable to a organizational setting—from behaviors related to IS security [32] to skills required for cross-cultural team working [33, 34]. The key assumption underlying the model is that people will respond to training when they are aware of its value and need [32]. The five stage of competence are described below:

1. *Unconscious Incompetence*: At this stage employees are unaware of the existence of a specific competence. Unintentionally, they may possess an undesired behavior regarding a specific task. They do not necessarily perceive a deficiency in their skills set. As a result, there is a need to become conscious about the competence before starting the specific learning process.
2. *Conscious Incompetence*: employees are aware about the missing competence required to carry out a desirable behavior or to perform a specific task correctly. Often this state of awareness occurs when the individual lacks parity with other colleagues competence set.
3. *Conscious Competence*: employees need to make a mental effort (think through) in order to be able to perform a task competently. The desired behavior

is still not spontaneous or "innate". This phase is characterized as being "thoughtful-analytical," where each problem is considered and analyzed at a time.

4. *Unconscious Competence*: the task is performed correctly and spontaneously. The correct behavior is part of the employees' subconscious. In this case, employees could have some difficulty to really explain how the task need to be done since it has become mostly ingrained in their competence set.

5. *Unconscious Super Competence*: in this stage employees have practiced and internalized effective ways to accomplish tasks. They become extremely (or super) competent in accomplishing these tasks.

In this competence acquisition process, once the competence required for improving the level of task performance is identified, it is necessary to specify the duration of the required behavioral change (only once, span of time, or on-going), and the type of change that need to accomplish (whether a new behavior is introduced, a familiar behavior is maintained, increased, decreased, or ceased to occur [35, 36].

Persuasion is known to be an effective the method to imply a voluntary change of behavior in individuals [37]. It differs from coercion or deception since persuasion does not force a change of behavior or stipulate the use of misinformation. In this situation, media technologies (from billboards to television as well as the internet) play a relevant role in "facilitating the delivery of persuasive messages to purchase, donate, vote, concede, or act" [38]. "Persuasive technologies" are interactive computing systems designed to influence people's attitudes and behaviors towards a specific target [39]. Furthermore, the continuous temporospatial availability as well as profound user affinity with these systems could also represent one of its core advantages and translate into greater persuasive power [39]. The process of persuading individuals to perform a target behavior requires the simultaneous presence of three factors: motivation, ability, and triggers [40]. Figure 3 presents Fogg's conceptual framework that illustrates the relationships among these three factors. The green star represents the target behavior to be performed, and its position suggests that high motivation (reason to carry out the target behavior) and high ability (often related to "simplicity" for accomplishing a specific task) are necessary to make it possible. Finally, the third factor is emphasized by the dotted arrow pointing to the target behavior (green star). Triggers are the third fundamental factor: "without an appropriate trigger, behavior will not occur even if motivation and ability are high". A trigger can have different forms, such as an alarm or a

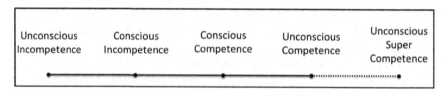

Fig. 2 The five-stage competence model [31]

Fig. 3 The three main factors for persuading people to perform a specific behavior [40]

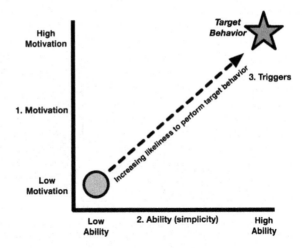

notification. The main objective is to draw the individual's attention to perform a specific task.

As illustrated above, the interactive and persuasive mature of mobile technologies bring new challenges and opportunities for managers to encourage the development and strengthening of organizational competences.

3.2 Step 2: Definition of the Objectives for a Solution

The objective for a solution is to develop a method-based mobile app for supporting acquisition (learning process) of a specific competence—exploiting the ubiquity nature of modern digital technologies.

This mobile app needs to provide tools for individuals to leverage a specific competences from "unconscious incompetent" to "unconscious competent" [31]. During this learning process the three factors suggested by Fogg [40] must be present simultaneously.

3.3 Step 3: Design and Development

The artifact (app) to be designed could be perceived as an instrument for delivering a sequential training method (STM). This method is based on a series of small specific exercises regarding an atomic competence [41]. Atomic competences (also known as micro competences) can be understood as the smallest element of a competence [42, 43]. These exercises are used for training individuals during a pre-defined period of time (e.g. 3 or 4 weeks) by performing one small set of

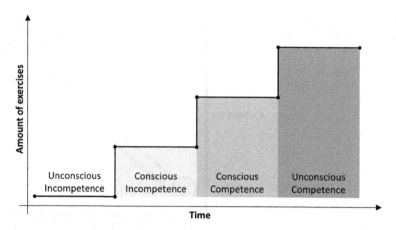

Fig. 4 The sequential training method for acquiring an atomic competence

exercises every day. There is a correspondence between the number of exercises completed successfully and the level of "consciousness" of the specific competence. Users develop the competence following a step by step structure—starting from initially becoming aware of their current incompetence, then acquiring and applying it consciously, to finally executing this competence autonomously (Fig. 4).

The main principles on which this STM is based could be summarized in the following sequence of steps:

(a) Identifying the competence to acquire, verifying if it is an atomic competence [41] or if it is composed by a set of micro competences. If so, each micro competence will require a dedicated training process.
(b) Defining the three intervals of time (phases) in which the individual (phase 1) becomes aware about his/her incompetence, (phase 2) acquires the competence and (phase 3) applies it in an autonomous way.
(c) Building a set of specific exercises (such as multiple choice and true/false questions, matching quiz, etc.) for each of the three phases. These exercises need to be really simple and clear, with an objective understanding, avoiding any form of subjectiveness or interpretation.
(d) In order to attain an unconscious competence level, the individual need to be capable of applying the new skill autonomously. This means that she/he will perform a desirable behavior even though there are "distractions" (e.g. the presence of a count down during an exercise, a random flashing alert or physical vibration of the device).

In order to ensure that the process of persuading individuals to perform a target behavior is robust, the app should also possess the three key factors suggested by Fogg (REF) (ability, motivation and triggers).

Ability (or Simplicity) should be attained by developing very simple, clear and objective exercises that does allow any form of subjectiveness or interpretation by the users. *Motivation can be achieved by* exploiting the hedonic and gamification nature of mobile apps [44, 45]. The app should incorporate typical elements of game playing such as point scoring, competition with others and rules of play. *Triggers* can be incorporated in the mobile app by implementing a notification system. This system could not only be used to remind the user to perform the exercise on a daily basis, but also to notify if there is an invitation for a challenge or to award achievement. Furthermore the notification system could be developed with a multi-channel strategy using email and or SMS messages.

4 Conclusion

Organizational learning and the continuous development and acquisition of competences by a firm's employee are fundamental instruments for achieving sustainable competitive advantage. In this scenario, digital technologies play a relevant role to foster this learning process.

This paper, as research in progress, aimed to define the main design aspects of competence acquisition mobile app. It used as a starting point and theoretical foundation the literature on competence acquisition and was able to elicit the system key components and characteristics.

The mobile app is currently under development. Once completed, it will be tested in a suitable context regarding a specific set of micros-kills (demonstration phase). The results of the test will iterate back to step 3 of the DSRM process (design and development) in order to refine the architecture and functionalities of the mobile application.

Future research should focus on measuring the overall effectiveness and efficiency of the app in a real-life scenario. An experiment will be developed using two groups of employees (e.g. test group and control group) in a partner organization. During four weeks, the test group will use the mobile app (at least five sets of ten exercises per week), while the control group will attend traditional a training session (face to face class). At the beginning and at the end of this period all employees involved in this experiment will perform a test in order to assess the improvement of their competence level and compare group performance. Additional qualitative data should be collected regarding user's experience using the app.

Acknowledgments This research proposal was supported by the *Skilleyd* team (http://www.skilleyd.net). We thank Francesca Battaglino, Stefano Monticelli and Giovanni Tonon who provided insight and expertise that greatly assisted this research.

References

1. Za, S., Spagnoletti, P., North-Samardzic, A.: Organisational learning as an emerging process: the generative role of digital tools in informal learning practices. Br. J. Educ. Technol. **45**, 1023–1035 (2014)
2. Yoo, Y., Henfridsson, O., Lyytinen, K.: Research commentary—the new organizing logic of digital innovation: an agenda for information systems research. Inf. Syst. Res. **21**, 724–735 (2010)
3. North-Samardzic, A., Braccini, A.M., Spagnoletti, P., Za, S.: Applying media synchronicity theory to distance learning in virtual worlds : a design science approach. Int. J. Innov. Learn. **15** (2014)
4. Za, S., Braccini, A.: Designing 3D virtual world platforms for e-learning services. New frontiers of organizational training. In: Snene, M. (ed.) Exploring Services Science, LNBIP 103, pp. 284–296. Springer, London (2012)
5. Za, S.: New frontiers of managerial training: the LiVES project. In: De Marco, M., Te'eni, D., Albano, V., Za, S. (eds.) Information Systems: Crossroads for Organization, Management, Accounting and Engineering, pp. 499–506. Physica-Verlag HD, Heidelberg (2012)
6. Boyatzis, R.E.: Competence and job performance. the competent manager: a model for effective performance, pp. 10–39 (1982)
7. Prahalad, C.K., Hamel, G.: The core competence of the corporation. Harv. Bus. Rev. **68**, 79–91 (1990)
8. Delamare-Le Deist, F., Winterton, J.: What is competence? Hum. Resour. Dev. Int. **8**, 27–46 (2005)
9. McClelland, D.C.: Identifying behavioral event interviews. Psychol. Sci. **9**, 331–339 (1998)
10. Boyatzis, R.E.: The competent manager: a model for effective performance. Wiley, New York (1982)
11. Andreu, R., Ciborra, C.: Organisational learning and core capabilities development: the role of IT. J. Strateg. Inf. Syst. **5**, 111–127 (1996)
12. Lyytinen, K., Yoo, Y., Varshney, U., Ackerman, M., Davis, G., Avital, M., Robey, D., Sawyer, S., Sorensen, C.: Surfing the next wave: design and implementation challenges of ubiquitous computing. Commun. Assoc. Inf. Syst. **13**, 697–716 (2004)
13. Chu, H.N., Lo, Y.H.: The establishment of ubiquitous portfolio management system and learning behaviour analysis scheme. Int. J. Mob. Learn. Organ. **5**, 317 (2011)
14. Carillo, K., Scornavacca, E., Za, S.: An investigation of the role of dependency in predicting continuance intention to use ubiquitous media systems: combining a media system perspective with expectation-confirmation theorie. In: Twenty Second European Conference on Information Systems (ECIS2014), pp. 1–17. Tel Aviv, Istrael (2014)
15. Peffers, K., Tuunanen, T., Rothenberger, M.A., Chatterjee, S.: A design science research methodology for information systems research. J. Manag. Inf. Syst. **24**, 45–77 (2008)
16. Hevner, A.R.A.R., March, S.T.S.T., Park, J., Ram, S.: Design science in information systems research. MIS Q. **28**, 75–105 (2004)
17. Walls, J.G., Widmeyer, G.R., El Sawy, O.A.: Building an information system design theory for vigilant EIS. Inf. Syst. Res. **3**, 36–59 (1992)
18. Walls, J.G., Widmeyer, G.R., Sawy, O.A.El: Assessing information system design theory in perspective: how useful was our 1992 initial rendition? J. Inf. Technol. Theory Appl. **6**, 43–58 (2004)
19. Gregor, S., Jones, D.: The anatomy of a design theory. J. Assoc. Inf. Syst. **8**, 312–335 (2007)
20. van Aken, J.E.: Management research on the basis of the design paradigm: the quest for field-tested and grounded technological rules. J. Manag. Stud. **41**, 219–246 (2004)
21. Järvinen, P.: Action research is similar to design science. Qual. Quant. **41**, 37–54 (2007)
22. Lei, D., Hitt, M.A., Bettis, R.: Dynamic core competences through meta-learning and strategic context (1996)

23. Spender, J.C., Grant, R.M.: Knowledge and the firm: overview. Strateg. Manag. J. **17**, 5–9 (1996)
24. Spender, J.C.: Competitive advantage from tacit knowledge? Unpacking the concept and its strategic implications. Acad. Manag. Proc. **8**, 37–41 (1993)
25. Srivastava, M., Franklin, A., Martinette, L.: Building a sustainable competitive advantage. J. Technol. Manag. Innov. **8**, 47–61 (2013)
26. Vodanovich, S., Sundaram, D., Myers, M.: Research commentary—digital natives and ubiquitous information systems. Inf. Syst. Res. **21**, 711–723 (2010)
27. Russell, A.L.: Stages in learning new technology: naive adult email users. Comput. Educ. **25**, 173–178 (1995)
28. Krathwohl, D.R.: A revision of bloom's taxonomy: an overview. Theory Pract. **41**, 212–217 (2002)
29. Bloom, B.S., Englehard, M.D., Furst, E.J., Hill, W.H., Krathwohl, D.R.: Committee of college and university examiners: taxonomy of educational objectives: the classification of educational goals. New York **16**, 207 (1956)
30. Nonaka, I.: The dynamic theory of organizational knowledge creation. Organ. Sci. **5**, 14–37 (1994)
31. Howell, W.S.: The Empathinc Commmunicator. Wadsworth Pub. Co., Belmont (1982)
32. Thomson, K., Solms, R.Von, Technikon, P.E., Africa, S.: Towards an information security competence. Comput. Fraud Secur. **2006**, 11–15 (2006)
33. Tung, R.L.: Managing cross-national and intra-national diversity. Hum. Resour. Manage. **32**, 461–477 (1993)
34. Barnes, D.M., Craig, K.K., Chambers, K.B.: A review of the concept of culture in holistic nursing literature. J. Holist. Nurs. **18**, 207–221 (2000)
35. Fogg, B.J.: The behavior grid: 35 ways behavior can change. Int. Conf. Persuas. Technol. 1–5 (2009)
36. de Boer, J., Teeuw, W., Heylen, D.: Applying the behavior grid for improving safety in industrial environments. In: Berkovsky, S., Freyne, J. (eds.) 8th International Conference on Persuasive Technology (Adjunct Proceedings), p. 8, Sydney, Australia (2013)
37. Berdichevsky, D., Neuschwander, E.: Toward an ethics of persuasive technology. Commun. ACM. **42**, 51–58 (1999)
38. IJsselsteijn, W., de Kort, Y., Midden, C., Eggen, B., van den Hoven, E.: Persuasive technology for human well-being: setting the scene. In: IJsselsteijn, W., de Kort, Y., Midden, C., Eggen, B., van den Hoven, E. (eds.) Persuasive 2006, LNCS 3962, pp. 1–5. Springer, Berlin (2006)
39. Fogg, B.J.: Persuasive Technology: Using Computers to Change What We Think and Do. Morgan Kaufmann, Amsterdam (2002)
40. Fogg, B.J.: A behavior model for persuasive design. In: Proceedings of the 4th International Conference on Persuasive Technology—Persuasive'09 (2009)
41. Baldoni, M., Baroglio, C., Brunkhorst, I., Henze, N., Marengo, E., Patti, V.: Constraint modeling for curriculum planning and validation. Interact. Learn. Environ. **19**, 81–123 (2011)
42. Pedraza-Jimenez, R., Valverde-Albacete, F., Molina-Bulla, H., Cid-Sueiro, J., Navia-Vázquez, A.: Assessment and reuse of contents in the competence-based educational platform InterMediActor. WSEAS Trans. Comput. **1**, 115–121 (2004)
43. Valverde-Albacete, F.J., Pedraza-Jiménez, R., Molina-Bulla, H., Cid-Sueiro, J., Díaz-Pérez, P., Navia-Vázquez, A.: InterMediActor: an environment for instructional content design based on competences. Educ. Technol. Soc. **6**, 30–47 (2003)
44. Landers, R.N.: Developing a theory of gamified learning: linking serious games and gamification of learning. Simul. Gaming **45**, 752–768 (2015)
45. Shchiglik, C., Barnes, S.J., Scornavacca, E.: The development of an instrument to measure mobile game quality. J. Comput. Inf. Syst (forthcoming)

Integration of Machine Learning Insights into Organizational Learning: A Case of B2B Sales Forecasting

**Marko Bohanec, Mirjana Kljajić Borštnar
and Marko Robnik-Šikonja**

1 Introduction

An organizational ability to grasp and transform knowledge in a continuous learning curve is a multifaceted problem [1, 2]. A learning ability is needed to preserve the capacity to adapt to changes in an environment in order to achieve organizational goals and vision. The learning curve increases from ignorance and converges towards full understanding while approaching a given goal [2]. This logic is rooted in Locke's philosophy [3] postulating that knowledge of the world can only be gained by experience (and its generalization by reflection).

The learning is characterized by the change of behavior as a result of an individual and/or group exposure to experience [2]. Two types of learning are distinguished: a single-loop and a double-loop learning [4–7]. The double-loop learning refers not just to changing the behavior in order to achieve the stated goal (single loop), but changing mental models, vision and beliefs, and therefore organizational knowledge. With the proposed approach we build a foundation to achieve the double-loop learning—as a basis to establish new premises (i.e. paradigms, schemes, mental models, or perspectives), with potential to override existing ones [7]. The same authors are fully aware that an effort to question and rebuild existing perspectives, interpretation of frameworks, or decision premises can be very difficult to implement in organizations; it requires persistent activities. The organiza-

M. Bohanec (✉)
Salvirt ltd., Ljubljana, Slovenia
e-mail: Marko.Bohanec@salvirt.com

M.K. Borštnar
Faculty of Organizational Sciences, University of Maribor, Kranj, Slovenia
e-mail: Mirjana.Kljajic@fov.uni-mb.si

M. Robnik-Šikonja
Faculty of Computer and Information Science, University of Ljubljana, Ljubljana, Slovenia
e-mail: Marko.Robnik@fri.uni-lj.si

© Springer International Publishing Switzerland 2016

71

F. D'Ascenzo et al. (eds.), *Blurring the Boundaries Through Digital Innovation*,
Lecture Notes in Information Systems and Organisation 19,
DOI 10.1007/978-3-319-38974-5_7

tional learning presents ongoing effort of creating organizational knowledge. Team learning, personal mastery and mental models principles [8] are part of organizational knowledge.

In this paper, we propose a classification model and its interpretation, which builds on experience of B2B sales professionals. The human knowledge is presented in a form of sales history described with features reflecting attributes of sales process and B2B relationships [9]. Machine learning techniques are applied to build the classification model, which is capable to classify future, unseen sales opportunities. The classification model represents the organizational knowledge, presented and visualized in a human comprehensible form to support the double-loop learning process within an organization.

Our aim is to develop such a model, based on B2B sales history, and show useful visualization which support forecasting process and transparent reasoning.

2   Literature Review and Methodology

Comprehensive research by [10] reveals that application of data mining techniques is widespread in the field of Customer Relationship management (CRM). Applicants are benefiting from customer data and past purchase behavior. However, in specific field of B2B sales forecasting, which is influenced by dynamics of markets, loosely structured information and possible noise in data, lack of academic approach and modeling is obvious [11]. As Monat concludes, a final step of making the forecast is left to a decision maker. Despite improved statistical and organizational learning capabilities, Rieg [12] identified an environmental uncertainty as a significant reason why there is no evidence about increased forecasting performance. Different approaches and solutions are proposed as forecasting support systems (FSS), however it was reported that they are not delivering on their promise, mostly pointing out low trust in FSS recommendations and suggesting improvements in explanations, work on better perception of FSS systems and more comprehensible format of information delivery [13].

To represent the B2B sales domain knowledge is an important first step in order to build a learning data set. Following Monat [11] conclusions, an overview of attributes (features) was compiled using research articles from academic databases and sales professionals' additions [9]. A selection of attributes, which sales experts can reflect upon for cases from their sales history, defines "descriptive language" of specific sales organization. This creates a foundation to describe sales context of both successful and failed sales opportunities.

To secure a high quality learning data set, literature is outlining different data preparation techniques, e.g., focus on outlier detection, data normalization, handling of missing data, noise detection and reduction, feature enhancements, data reduction or generation, etc. A decision which techniques to use is highly dependent on a particular problem. The approach is guided by a process of data preparation based on insights, created knowledge in the process of building learning data set, and selected machine learning algorithms [14]. Therefore, creators of data set need to pay an extra attention to secure high data quality and enable good performance of machine learning techniques. Lack of attention to data quality can possibly lead to "Garbage In, Garbage Out" problem.

Machine learning (ML) in our context is interpreted as an acquisition of structural descriptions from examples [15]. The fact that it leverages different models and algorithms to approximate complex theories which are difficult to be exactly represented with other mathematical tools, connects it to the field of artificial intelligence. ML has been successfully applied in different fields, e.g., medical diagnostics, spam filtering, OCR, internet browsers, etc. [10, 16, 17]. ML techniques take training data set to learn relationships needed to categorize new, yet unseen, objects to target categories [15, 18]. Some classification models produced are able to explain their decisions, which can help in better adoption of ML techniques in practice due to users' faster understanding of ML insights [18, 19].

2.1 Methodology

Our research methodology is best described as the action design [20]. The selected method supports our goal to create an IT artifact within the context of organization in both development and use phase. The nature of organizational learning requires continuous process to maintain organizational agility as a response to internal and external market dynamics.

In Fig. 1 we present the research framework, combining machine learning methods for model building and introduction of extracted knowledge to the forecasting learning loop. Each cycle of forecasting is evaluated (forecasts, supported by the classification model, are compared to actual results) and the feedback is used twice: first in the machine learning model and second in a decision maker. The process is iterative and each plan-act-reflect cycle is done in a natural setting of the organization.

The proposed approach was presented to selected companies participating in the research. They expressed the interest and some shared their CRM data for an initial review. The practical experience shows that this approach is quite challenging,

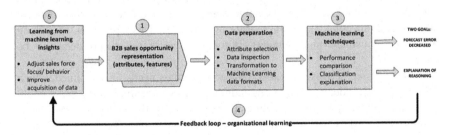

Fig. 1 The research framework

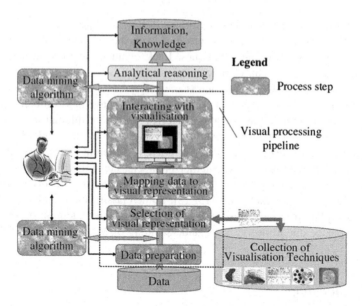

Fig. 2 Visual data mining process—Simoff et al. [30] (originally in color)

because it seems that typical CRM implementations are missing sales opportunity's attributes reflecting relationship dynamics, individual, and organizational attributes [9]. Thus, the context of particular case is not described in a suitable way for machine learning techniques to perform adequately as the existing CRM-based attributes contain low information and cause poor prediction performance. CRM systems should therefore be updated and sellers shall adapt their process of information collection. This created new level of complexity and effectively stalled participation of companies. Therefore, we leveraged anonymized sales history from the company founding the research. We applied R package *semiartificial* [21] to generate sufficient number of instances to allow modeling and development. A full CRISP-DM process [22] was followed in combination with visual data mining as portrayed in Fig. 2. Such approach supports well the modeling presented in this paper, and can serve as a reference for inclusion of new external organizations with their historical B2B sales data in the future.

At the beginning, we have a roughly defined set of real-world sales opportunities historical data with their outcomes, minus sign representing failure to close the deal and plus sign reflecting successful closure of it (Fig. 3). This represents the starting point where business understanding (through expert's reflection) needs to be demonstrated.

In the next step, a subset of most influential features needs to be defined, which at the beginning is determined by the judgment of sales team. Starting point could be (but not limited to) a list of features proposed in [9]. Based on the selection of features, real world cases reflecting the sales history is described with values of

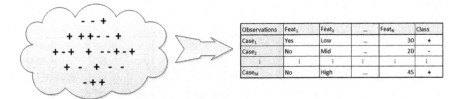

Observations	Feat$_1$	Feat$_2$	...	Feat$_N$	Class
Case$_1$	Yes	Low	...	30	+
Case$_2$	No	Mid	...	20	-
⋮	⋮	⋮	⋮	⋮	⋮
Case$_M$	No	High	...	45	+

Fig. 3 Real-world training cases transformation to learning data set

these features. In Fig. 3, table view reflects selection of N features and M cases, with different types of values illustrating versatility of the approach.

Frequently the question about the number of historical cases needed arises. According to [23] some authors recommend as a rule of thumb ten records for every feature. They are also citing Delmar and Hancock, which propose the number of cases equal to 6 * m * p, where p represents the number of selected features and m represents the number of class values (two in our case). In case of p = 10 and m = 2, we would therefore need 120 past cases, which is practically possible, provided that several experienced sellers participate in the construction of training data set.

It is important to note iterative nature of this process. In case ML ranking and classification techniques will not immediately perform at the expected level, we should "go back" and select additional attributes, not yet part of the subset. In this phase, our goal could be to add new attributes, while keeping existing ones. We might reconsider values of particular attributes with the help and argumentation of participating sales experts.

In this stage of our research, our aim is to build a compact, comprehensible model, intended for source of insight for sales force and sales management. Therefore, the final selection of features should be limited to a number, which can be cognitively handled. According to Miller's recommendation [24], this would be 7 ± 2 features. In this way, the complexity of the model is still cognitively feasible, and overfitting of data set is unlikely. However, the parsimony of the model has to be balanced with the model's performance on real world cases, to prevent excessive elimination of attributes at the expense of model accuracy. Machine learning techniques need sufficient information to expose relationship between attributes and outcome. An efficient way to achieve this goal is by ranking features.

2.2 Ranking Features

Ranking of features helps us to identify which features are the most important in the training data set, by ranking them according to how informative they are. To estimate feature significance several different scoring techniques are available, some

Table 1 Features evaluation—some techniques from Orange suite

Attribute	ReliefF	Inf. gain	Gain Ratio	Gini	RF
Negotiations	0,961	0,819	0,523	0,215	2,078
Reaction	0,913	0,848	0,332	0,223	0,085
Prospect_authority	0,900	0,802	0,802	0,213	11,717
S_A_Pilot	0,822	0,830	0,362	0,220	0,876
Need_defined	0,783	0,775	0,775	0,207	17,405
Product	0,490	0,324	0,137	0,099	0,000
Client_growth	0,323	0,098	0,056	0,032	1,007
Other_solution	0,308	0,110	0,122	0,037	1,041
Source	0,246	0,226	0,156	0,072	0,137
Owned	0,233	0,183	0,110	0,055	0,055
Budget_limits	0,226	0,020	0,018	0,007	0,400
Existing_client	0,146	0,174	0,305	0,047	1,169
Familiary_wVendor	0,132	0,030	0,027	0,009	0,125
External_svcs	0,106	0,026	0,060	0,009	0,191
Competitors	-0,005	0,034	0,089	0,010	0,232
Deal_size	-0,013	0,083	0,041	0,028	0,437

of them are used in Table 1. We use Orange data mining suite [25] for majority of ML techniques applied in this paper.

A scoring technique *ReliefF* measures attributes' ability to separate similar cases with different outcomes. It detects conditional dependencies between attributes and provides a unified view on the attribute estimation in regression and classification. In addition, its attribute importance estimates have a natural interpretation [18]. The *Inf. gain* is measuring information entropy of attributes conditioned upon class with a downside that this measure prefers features with more values. *Gain Ratio* prevents this by normalization with attribute entropy [26]. Similarly, *Gini index* estimates purity of class values conditional to the split by the values of attribute. *RF* represents *Random Forest*, an ensemble learning technique, which can also output attribute importance score estimated on internal set of instances. Random forest method is robust to noise, does not overfit and offers possibilities for explanation and visualization of its output [27].

In our case, looking across all scoring approaches, a general observation from B2B sales domain perspective is that there are approximately 5 informative features out of 16, namely *Negotiations, Reaction, Prospect authority, S_A_Pilot* (how easy was to get a pilot of a solution) and *Need defined* (by a buyer). The rest of the features show lower importance, except for features *Source* and *Existing Client* for which some methods indicate contribution.

We presented the insights into the analysis and discussed the results with a team of experts during preparation of the description of sales history. On one side, it was expected that some features are considered very important; however, it was rather surprising that others produce so low estimates. For example, in presented case it looks that *familiarity with vendor* (seller's company), *Deal size* and *competition* have very little relevance.

The obtained scores shall encourage sales experts to thoroughly analyze each surprising result and eventually update learning data set with additional cases, provide missing values, or introduce new or different features into the training data set. Alternatively, they can accept the insight as a learning opportunity and update their beliefs and mental models. Continuous movement back and forth between phases Analytical Reasoning and Data preparation in Fig. 2 is therefore required. McCarthy Bryne, Moon and Mentzer [28] have shown in their research that inclusion of sales professionals is important; however, they need to be included in such a way to maintain a positive attitude towards the learning potential of the model in the light of the forecasting task.

When sales experts agree that the model seems to be correct and no obvious or hidden flaws are identified, we can proceed to the next step and verify how well machine learning techniques are capable to learn based on the produced data set. The training data set at this stage is considered stable from the point of view of accepted features, number of missing values, and the number of provided training instances.

2.3 Building and Testing Machine Learning Model

Based on the prepared training data set different machine learning techniques can be utilized to build an automated reasoning system. Results of learning are presented in Table 2 and show that three selected classification techniques are exceeding 70 % classification accuracy (CA), which can be considered a good performance taking into account difficulty of this real-world problem. The performance estimates were computed using "Leave-one-out" cross-validation [29]. AUC stands for Area Under the ROC curve, which is a standard machine learning performance measure giving information about the quality of the produced class probabilities [15].

Random Forest technique is performing the best with the CA of 96 %. The case study training set has 133 examples, 73 classified as NO (lost deal), and 60 classified as YES (won deal). Additional analysis of confusion matrix reveals that 5 opportunities which should be classified as the class NO, were incorrectly classified as YES. For the class YES all cases were classified correctly.

Table 2 Performance of some classification techniques, produced by Orange system

Method	CA	AUC
Random Forest	0.9624	0.9934
Naive Bayes	0.9474	0.9764
Classification Tree	0.9398	0.9315

Table 3 Evaluation using only top seven features from Table 1, as ranked by ReliefF

Method	CA	AUC
Random Forest	0.9624	0.9852
Naive Bayes	0.9549	0.9588
Classification Tree	0.9398	0.9311

2.4 Testing Machine Learning Model with a Limited Set of Features

As evident from Table 1, top ranked attributes represent less than a half of all features. We indicated that we would prefer to work with less attributes to maintain simplicity and parsimony of a model in a balance. The question is how ML performance will be affected if selected techniques would use only top seven attributes (as ranked by *ReliefF*). In Table 3, results of this limited feature set are presented. Comparison of CA results in Tables 2 and 3 reveals that performance of random forest and classification tree was not affected by a smaller set of attributes and naïve Bayes has even slightly improved its score, indicating some noise in the excluded features.

3 Results—Representation of B2B Sales Knowledge

In this section, we apply different ML techniques and visualizations to emphasize the insights and to create an input to the double-loop learning within B2B forecasting task. The results are preliminary and are based on conceptual model building, its evaluation and validation. Sales domain interpretations are related to the case study presented in this paper; for a different organization, they could be completely different, reflecting their training data set and context.

3.1 Sieve Multigram Projection

Sieve multigram shows how features are correlated. Solid lines indicate negative correlation and dashed lines indicate positive correlation. Thickness of lines indicates how strong the correlation is. For example, from Fig. 4 we can see that value *Yes* for the feature *Need defined* is negatively correlated to the value *Mid* for the feature *Prospect authority*, however it is positively correlated to the value *High* of the same feature. There are some other interesting relationships revealed, for example, that client stability (value *Stable*) and presence of competitors are positively correlated meaning that stable organizations look for offers from more vendors, compared to organizations in transition.

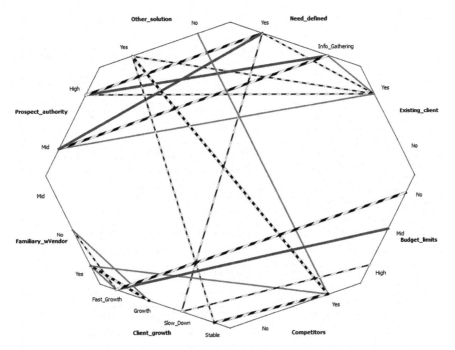

Fig. 4 Sieve multigram showing correlations among selected features (created by Orange, originally in color)

3.2   Generating Association Rules

Using RStudio (www.rstudio.com) and R library *arules*, we created a set of association rules (Table 4). For each rule, we present three standard evaluation metrics: support, confidence and lift. The *support* measures the proportion of transactions in the training data set, which contain the *lhs* items (left side of a rule). The *confidence* reflects the proportion of cases satisfying rule preconditions (i.e., lhs), that also satisfy rule consequences, i.e., *rhs* (right side of a rule). The *lift* reports the ratio of the observed support to that expected if lhs and rhs were independent (Witten et al., 2011). To illustrate: the first rule from Table 4 reveals that *buyer's need* accompanied by *high prospect authority* occurs in 45 % of all cases in training data set (therefore 45 % support), and when this is true, it yields a 95 % confidence for this rule to lead to a contract signature. The lift value of 2.1 reports that support of a rule "lhs implies rhs" (i.e. its confidence) is 2.1 times more likely than support of rhs and lhs estimated independently in the whole population.

This (shortened) list of association rules is transparently revealing "preconditions" for outcome of sales opportunity in the next observational period. The transparent representation of rules creates a solid foundation for an individual or group review of forecasts.

Table 4 The association rules for positive (YES) and negative (NO) outcome (using RStudio, Library arules)

lhs	rhs	support	confidence	lift
1 {Need_defined=Yes,				
Prospect_authority=High}	=> {Signed=YES}	0.4511278	0.9523810	2.111111
2 {Competitors=No,				
Prospect_authority=High}	=> {Signed=YES}	0.4436090	0.9516129	2.109409
3 {Need_defined=Yes,				
Competitors=No,				
Prospect_authority=High}	=> {Signed=YES}	0.4436090	0.9516129	2.109409
4 {External_svcs=Yes,				
Need_defined=Yes,				
Prospect_authority=High}	=> {Signed=YES}	0.3834586	0.9444444	2.093519
a {Need_defined=Info_Gathering,				
Prospect_authority=Mid,				
Negotiations=Not_started}	=> {Signed=NO}	0.4812030	1.0000000	1.821918
b {Existing_client=No,				
Need_defined=Info_Gathering,				
Negotiations=Not_started}	=> {Signed=NO}	0.4962406	1.0000000	1.821918
c {External_svcs=Yes,				
Need_defined=Info_Gathering,				
Negotiations=Not_started}	=> {Signed=NO}	0.4736842	1.0000000	1.821918
d {Existing_client=No,				
Need_defined=Info_Gathering,				
Prospect_authority=Mid}	=> {Signed=NO}	0.4887218	1.0000000	1.821918

3.3 Classification Tree

Based on the case study training data set, the classification tree presented in Fig. 5 was built. It reveals an importance of the attribute *Negotiations*, ranked highest by the *ReliefF* algorithm. The first insight is that it is good to be in some kind of negotiations; when negotiations did "not_start" yet, no deal was closed (quite obvious, though). The second insight reveals that success is high when moderate negotiations take place and there is a possibility of some other solution. Here it is important to make a distinction between competing with other providers and competing with other solutions. In the context of our case study, other solution could be an old solution, which needs to be replaced, or a manual solution, which needs to be upgraded; therefore, a client is not really comparing different external providers competing for the business, but investigating different alternatives within provider's portfolio.

The next insight reveals that when sellers are involved in moderate negotiations and they offer a solution to the existing client, they always win. This insight reflects organizational strength for cross selling and could be recognized as one of the key sales approaches for future growth. However, when sellers offer the same solution

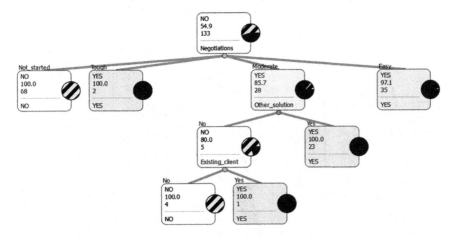

Fig. 5 Decision tree with ReliefF attribute selection criterion (Orange, originally in color)

to a new prospect, they always fail. This indicates importance of client relationship for the analyzed case study.

3.4 Parallel Coordinates—Visualization

When dealing with multiple features, a parallel view of the training data is presented in Fig. 6. Each training instance is presented with one line and we can see frequently occurring patterns. The whole graph reveals a "broader story" of what works and which scenarios should be avoided. Solid lines represent won deals and dashed lines represent lost deals. For our case study, we can learn that selling to existing clients who have some level of dynamics from growth perspective, with their business needs clearly expressed by a person with high enough authority to secure the budget, and who is eager to start negotiations with us only (no competitors), creates a great likelihood for a success. Sellers are used to storytelling practice and such interpretations are compelling to them to position their sales in the context of what need (or can) be changed to fit into the "success story". For different training data set, a different pattern could emerge.

3.5 Scatter Plot

In comparison to parallel coordinates, showing several features at once, the scatter plot shows only two interacting features; however, those are compared against each other and thus may create a new perspective. Figure 7 shows the relationship between *ability to secure a pilot* (or trial) testing (value 0 means failure to secure a

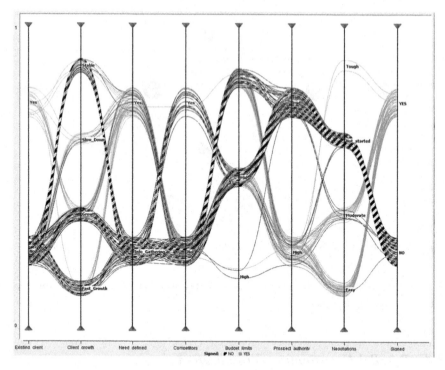

Fig. 6 Parallel coordinates (Orange, originally in color)

pilot, and value 5 means easy to secure a pilot, values between represent graded assessment) of offered solution and a *prospect's authority* to execute the deal. One insight from this visualization is prevailing—sellers should work hard to secure a person with high authority on the other side of the table, who needs to be keen to try the solution. Other scenarios do not close the deals. This is clearly indicated by a distribution of two outcomes (circle—lost, square—won) in Fig. 7, where cases on the top-left side failed and the cases on the bottom-right side of the border succeeded. Circles indicate that sometimes there was a failure even when the pilot was secured.

Such visualizations are important, as they quickly help to assess new sales opportunities; if an opportunity fails in this simple classification, it is safe to go for "No" in the forecasting task. If a positive answer is secured, the opportunity needs to be further analyzed before a conclusion about the forecast is reached, taking into account different models and visualizations. For example, a different scatter plot could compare *familiarity with vendor* and *budget limits*, enriched with what was offered to the prospect (*Product*) and the size of the shape reflecting the relative size (*Deal size*) of an offer. From this perspective our case study offers mixed results. It might indicate low flexibility on price or a possibility that other client's priorities

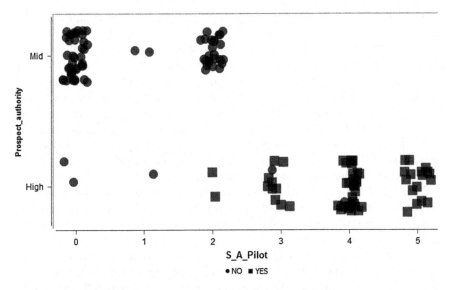

Fig. 7 Scatter plot (Orange)

have higher budgetary attention—the case has to be further researched with sales professionals.

Comparing the conclusions from Figs. 4, 5, 6 and 7, we can see that different insights were presented in a transparent way, revealing an important knowledge for development of broader understanding of sales dynamics. Different views contribute to and stimulate strong, facts based dialog and assessment of sales opportunities. In this way, they improve understanding needed for more realistic B2B forecasting, with the goal to decrease the forecasting error.

4 Discussion and Conclusions

In this paper a novel approach towards organizational learning using machine learning techniques and specific domain knowledge from the field of B2B forecasting is proposed. Our goal is to develop a model supporting decision-makers in the process of forecasting by transparent reasoning, based on real-world data. Insights provided by the ML model must be presented in a comprehensible way, enabling decision-makers to reflect on in the double-loop learning and in this way to update their sales knowledge. New knowledge should give directions to adapt or change behaviors and thereby create new sales opportunities and decrease decision-makers forecasting error. We used transparent ML techniques capable to explain their recommendations, which is essential for the double-loop learning.

The training data set consisting of 133 unique cases was built from anonymized sales history of a company providing services to their clients. Initial list of 16 features (attributes), describing sales history, was assessed by 5 different ML attribute evaluation techniques. Based on the results we selected 7 out of 16 features which contain important information for the development of the prediction model. Using several feature evaluation techniques we reduced the probability of biased and subjective prioritization, frequently observed when working with individual domain experts. From numerous visualizations available within Orange and R data mining environments, we selected a small subset of interesting techniques relevant for our scenario. For a given case study, the selected ML prediction models achieved high classification accuracy. Altogether, the presented methodology reveals several important insights, which encourage modification of seller's behavior and challenge their traditional intuitive forecasts of new opportunities.

The goal of this paper was to investigate the possibility to develop a classification model, based on B2B sales history, which supports forecasting process and provides transparent reasoning. We are convinced that results positively confirm viability of our methodology.

To further develop the model, we need additional companies from different industries to participate with their data. However, getting well-structured tabulated data with attributes describing B2B sales opportunities presents a challenge, mainly because companies and sales personnel currently put no attention to attributes, needed to create domain knowledge reflection framework. Further research also has to address the number of cases needed to create acceptable level of forecasting accuracy, effect of adding new attributes to the training data set, statistical quantification of predictive confidence, etc.

The work presented establishes a basis for a further research in domains other than sales forecasting and stimulates a critical discussion about selection of powerful and insightful visualizations used with machine learning and data mining techniques. This will increase trust in forecasts and bridge the gap between users and technology.

Acknowledgments We are grateful to the company Salvirt ltd. for funding the research and development of the model, presented in this paper. Mirjana Kljajić Borštnar was supported by the Slovenian Research Agency, ARRS, through research programme P5-0018. Marko Robnik-Šikonja was supported by the Slovenian Research Agency, ARRS, through research programme P2-0209 and also received funding from the European Union Seventh Framework Programme (FP7/2007-2013) under grant agreement no. 604102 (HBP).

References

1. Gronhaug, K., Stone, R.: The learning organization. Compet. Rev. Int. Bus. J. **22**(3) (2012)
2. Kljajić Borštnar, M., Kljajić, M., Škraba, A., Kofjač, D., Rajkovič, V.: The relevance of facilitation in group decision making supported by a simulation model. Syst. Dyn. Rev. **27**(3), 270–293 (2011) ISSN 0883–7066
3. Locke, J.: An essay concerning human understanding (Slovenian translation). Slovenska šolska matica, Ljubljana (1924)
4. Argyris, C.: On Organizational Learning. Blackwell, New York (1996)

5. DiBella, A.J., Nevis, E.C.: How Organizations Learn. Jossey-Bass, San Francisco, USA (1998)
6. Gephart, M.A., Marsick, V.J., Mark, E., VanBuren, M.E., Spiro, M.S.: Learning organizations come alive. Training Development **50**(12), 36–41 (1996)
7. Nonaka, I., Takeuchi, H.: The Knowledge Creating Organization. Oxford University Press, New York (1995)
8. Senge, P.: The Fifth discipline: The Art & Practice of the Learning Organization. Doubleday Currency, New York (1990)
9. Bohanec, M., Kljajić Borštnar, M., Robnik-Šikonja, M.: Modeling attributes for forecasting B2B opportunities acquisition. In: Proceedings of 34th Conference of Organizational science development, Portorož, Slovenia (2015)
10. Ngai, E.W.T., Xiu, L., Chau, D.C.K.: Application of data mining techniques in CRM: a literature review and classification. Expert Syst. Appl. **36**, 2592–2602 (2009)
11. Monat, J. P.: Industrial sales lead conversion modeling. Market. Intell. Plan. **29**(2), 178–194 (2011)
12. Rieg, R.: Do forecast improve over time? Int. J. Account. Inform. Manage. **18**(3) (2010)
13. Alvarado-Valencia, J.A., Barrero, L.H.: Reliance, trust and heuristics in judgmental forecasting. Comput. Hum. Behav. **36**, 102–113 (2014)
14. Maaß, D., Spruit, M., Waal, P.D.: Improving short-term demand forecasting for short-lifecycle consumer products with data mining techniques, pp. 1–17. Decision Analytics, Springer (2014)
15. Witten, I.H., Eibe, F., Hall, M.A.: Data mining—practical machine learning tools and techniques, 3rd edn. Elsevier (2011)
16. Liao, S.H., Chu, P.H., Hsiao, P.Y.: Data mining techniques and applications—a decade review from 2000 to 2011. Expert Syst. Appl. **39** (2012)
17. Bose, I., Mahapatra, R.K.: Business data mining—a machine learning perspective. Inf. Manag. **39**(3), 211–225 (2001)
18. Robnik-Šikonja, M., Kononenko, I.: Explaining classification for individual instances. IEEE Trans. Knowl. Data Eng. **20**(5), 589–600 (2008)
19. Collopy F., Adya M., Armstrong, J.S.: Expert systems for forecasting. In: Principles of Forecasting: A Handbook for Researchers and Practitioner. Kluwer (2001)
20. Sein, M.K., Henfridsson, O., Purao, S., Rossi, M., Lindgreen, R.: Action design research. MIS Q. **35**, 37–56 (2011)
21. Robnik-Šikonja, M.: SemiArtificial: generator of semi-artificial data, R package version 1.2.0. http://cran.r-project.org/package=semiArtificial (2014)
22. Chapman, P., Clinton, J., Kerber, R., Khabaza, T., Reinartz, T., Shearer, C., Wirth, R.: CRISP-DM 1.0 Step-by-step data mining guides, ftp://software.ibm.com/software/analytics/ spss/support/Modeler/Documentation/14/UserManual/CRISP-DM.pdf (2000)
23. Shmueli, G., Patel, N.R., Bruce, P.C.: Data mining for business intelligence: concepts, techniques, and applications in microsoft office excel with XLMiner. Wiley (2007)
24. Miller, G.A.: The magical number seven, plus or minus two: some limits on our capacity for processing information. Psychol. Rev. **63**, 81–97 (1956)
25. Demšar, J., Zupan, B.: Orange: Data mining fruitful and fun—a historical perspective. Informatica **37**, 55–60 http://orange.biolab.si (2013)
26. Quinlan, J.R.: C4.5: Programs for Machine Learning. Morgan Kaufmann, San Francisco (1993)
27. McCarthy Byrne, T.M., Moon, M.A., Mentzer, J.T.: Motivating the industrial sales force in the sales forecasting process. Indus. Market. Manage. **40**, 128–138 (2011)
28. Breiman, L.: Random forests. Mach. Learn. J. **45**, 5–32 (2001)
29. Elisseeff, A., Pontil, M.: Leave-one-out error and stability of learning algorithms with applications. In: Suykens, J.A.K. (ed.) Advances in Learning Theory: Methods, Models and Applications. IOS Press (2003)
30. Simoff, S.J., Böhlen, M.H., Mazeika, A. (eds.): Visual Data Mining. Springer, Lecture Notes in Computer Science (2008)

One More Time Trust Matters: A Theoretical Investigation of the Role of Technology Mediated Trust in the UTAUT Model

Luca Pistilli and Ferdinando Pennarola

1 Introduction

It is widely acknowledged, also by practitioners, that the pure act of purchasing any piece of information technology (IT) does not guarantee its diffusion, adoption, and acceptance. These processes are heavily influenced by social factors that compose an intricate interplay of elements, a maze of relationships that can really make the difference between success and failure of many IT related projects. Fortunately, the complexity of the issue has been deeply investigated in more than 20 years of research that has contributed to the whole information systems field significantly, becoming one of its most important pillars. Unfortunately, the most updated debates on the issue contributed only with incremental empirical evidence [1–3] that has returned higher and robust theoretical constructs to what we call the "founding father models" of technology acceptance (TA), but researchers failed to really modernize and contextualize the model to the nowadays' society. To explain this point a date must be unveiled: in 2003 on MISQ the UTAUT (Unified Theory of Acceptance and Use of Technology) model was formulated by [4], as a unifying manifesto of the long stream of previous contributions on TA. In that very original paper, authors acknowledged the need to improve the theory by searching for other moderating factors to explain more insights about adoption, acceptance and use.

We depart from this point to contextualize the role of UTAUT in the modern ages, and we aim at offering a further theoretical development of the TA models. Our argument stands from the role of another moderator in the TA models, namely the technology-mediated trust that we will illustrate in Chap. 3. Our hypothesis has

L. Pistilli (✉) · F. Pennarola
Bocconi University, Milan, Italy
e-mail: luca.pistilli@unibocconi.it

F. Pennarola
e-mail: ferdinando.pennarola@unibocconi.it

© Springer International Publishing Switzerland 2016   87
F. D'Ascenzo et al. (eds.), *Blurring the Boundaries Through Digital Innovation*,
Lecture Notes in Information Systems and Organisation 19,
DOI 10.1007/978-3-319-38974-5_8

to do with the role of trustworthy technologies that today are widely available on the marketplace. For example, the adoption of an ERP solution at firm level can be influenced by its reliability and predictability, as proved by other users. Predictability and reliability are two components of early definitions of trust [5]. Not only organizational decision makers, like CEOs, are sensitive to trustworthy technologies, but also end users are. For example, virus free operating systems—or better, operating systems that are less frequently subject to hack attacks—infuse more trust, and thus they can be more easily adopted and used. We didn't find a place in the UTAUT model for these arguments, and we propose that it would be of great benefit for the advancement of the field to upgrade the model by acknowledging new variables.

Proposing a theory upgrade is a rather challenging endeavor and we asked ourselves if there is room for doing so in the latest versions of the TA theories. We decided to use the UTAUT model, being the one of the most comprehensive and representative. A major upgrade of the UTAUT model, versus the TAM model and further version of the latter, was the acknowledgement of "social influence" as new independent variable, defined as "the degree to which an individual perceives that important others believe he or she should use the new system" [4]. As authors affirm, social influence comes from previous models of TA (TAM, TAM2, TRA, and so on) under different names, such as, for example, "social norms" that are a direct determinant of behavioral intention to adopt, accept and use. "While they have different labels, each of these constructs contains the explicit or implicit notion that the individual's behavior is influenced by the way in which they believe others will view them as a result of having used the technology" [4].

Although social influence, as independent variable, represented a major upgrade in the TA theory, we believe that modern IT penetrate markets, and are successfully used, because of something more. Our proposal, explained below, is to introduce a new moderator in the unified theory of acceptance and use of technologies, to be empirically tested in further research. Before explaining the role of the new moderator, we synthetize the TA debate in the next paragraph.

2 The Founding Fathers: Background Literature on TA

Since the early '90 s, a new literature was written under the major chapter of TA. The Technology Acceptance Model (TAM) is an information systems' theory introduced by Davis in 1989; its major extensions are represented by the TAM2 [6, 7] and the Unified Theory of Acceptance and Use of Technology (from now on UTAUT, [8]). It has also been proposed a TAM3 [9] and a UTAUT2 [10]. The core concept of the TAM is that there are a number of factors influencing how people react to and therefore "accept" a new technology. In the original version of TAM those forces are:

- Perceived Usefulness, described as the perceived job performance enhancement due to the use of a particular system [11];
- Perceived Ease of Use, described as the perceived degree to which a person finds using a particular system free from effort [11];
- External Variables, or "External Stimulus", are system design features and all external variables that may influence user's perception of use.

This theory is widely accepted and consolidated. Many scholars have provided empirical evidence of this model's validity and reliability through replications and re-examinations [12–16]. Because of its reliable foundations, this model triggered the production of many extensions able to explain the effect of other factors in technology acceptance. In TAM2 extended model [7] found that user acceptance was significantly influenced by both social influence and cognitive instrumental processes in mandatory settings. Cognitive instrumental processes determining perceived usefulness are instead: job relevance, output quality, result demonstrability and perceived ease of use. Therefore, the psychological and social components started to gain increasing importance in such technical and technological field. In the proposed unifying theory or UTAUT [8] social influence constructs were found significant in mandatory settings only. Moreover, the determinants of intention varied over time, with some variations from significant to not significant as the level of experience increased. Performance expectancy, effort expectancy, social influence, and facilitating conditions were found to be direct determinants of user acceptance and technology use. In the work of [8], facilitating conditions are described as the perceived support of organizational and technical infrastructure to the use of information systems. This concept of facilitating resources, as perceived existence of resources and support availability, was reapplied by [17].

There have been many real cases where technology adoption in organizations failed because of user resistance due to bad implementation. This suggests that the prerequisite for technological system's acceptance is for organizations to develop effective involvement actions [9].

The UTAUT [8] model is represented in the below Fig. 1.

The key components of the model are the following independent variables:

- Performance expectancy: The degree to which an individual believes that using the system will help him or her to attain gains in job performance.
- Effort expectancy: The degree of ease associated with the use of the system.
- Social influence: The degree to which an individual perceives that important others believe he or she should use the new system.
- Facilitating conditions: The degree to which an individual believes that an organizational and technical infrastructure exists to support use of the system.

The mediating variable is behavioral intention, i.e. the degree to which a person has formulated conscious plans to perform or not perform some specified future behavior. Authors argued that the following variables act as moderator of the relationship between the independent variable and the mediating variable "behavioral intention": (1) age, (2) gender, (3) experience, (4) Voluntariness (the extent to

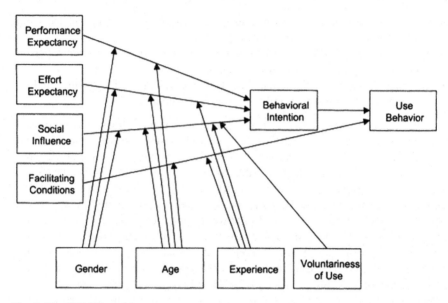

Fig. 1 The UTAUT model

which potential adopters perceive the adoption decision to be non-mandatory). The ultimate result variable is the user behavior in the adoption, acceptance and use of an IT. It's noteworthy to remind that the study where [9] introduced a TAM3 model also focuses on the moderating effect of experience, as the UTAUT model does. In fact, since people attitude and reactions change over time, experience represents an important factor in Information Technology and Information Systems research [18, 19]. In addition, the ultimate success of a new system or technology can be judged only in the medium-long run [20–22].

The UTAUT2 model [10] integrated the original UTAUT with 3 new constructs: hedonic motivation, price value, and habit. The role of enjoyment was also stressed by [17] for increasing behavioral intention to use. Vividness and interactivity were shown to enhance satisfaction and interest. Varying with task complexity, also performance and reduced mental effort were attained [23]. The user acceptance of an information system is also a matter of expectations; [24] discovered that the disconfirmation of expectations reduced system intention to use because users developed lack of trust. Earlier findings by [25] in a related field stated that when unrealistically negative expectations were developed, job applicants' attraction diminished. Following this stream of research, [24] supposed that, despite potentially positive experience, users might still focus on negative aspects of the system. In other words, it is the typical real-life situation where, even though a system does N things, users focus on the N + 1 thing it does not do. Those findings recommend organizations to create realistic expectations, so as to increase the likelihood of acceptance and long-run usage [24].

Venkatesh [7] went further to test for the influence of both internal and external dimensions of control. On the one hand, external control was represented by facilitating conditions in the use of technology [26]. Those include technical support and availability of IT staff, which are especially important in early stages, when the impact with new technology provokes a shock to routine operations [27]. The relevance of such support was confirmed in later empirical studies showing consultant backup to positively affect control perception [28, 29]. On the other hand, internal control was approximated by computer self-efficacy, i.e. the self-assessed ability to perform computer-based actions. Venkatesh and Davis [30] found that, even after substantial experience, internal control perception remains the main determinant of a system's perceived ease of use. Based on this, [7] argues that, despite previous experience, ease of use will be determined by general confidence with the computerized system.

We acknowledged several previous contributions to this stream of research in highlighting and empirically verifying the role that trust plays in the adoption and acceptance behavior. In particular, [31] claim that trusting the vendor is an essential component to achieve a successful e-commerce transaction; the authors argue that purchases accomplished on the net lack the typical human interaction where trust appears in its widely recognized dimensions and peculiarities. Moreover, [32] analyze the role of trust in the setting of consumer adoption of mobile payment systems; their conclusions highlight and remark the key role that trust plays in promoting the adoption of such tool by consumers. Srivastava [33], in a similar vein, perform an exploratory study which empirically supports the idea that trust is a relevant component in technology adoption and acceptance, therefore ignoring trust when technology adoption and acceptance models are conceived could lead to misleading or, at least, incomplete theoretical frameworks; their study focuses mainly on the Technology Acceptance Model (TAM), with little consideration of the UTAUT model, which are instead both our point of departure. Furthermore, [34] propose that technology trust and interpersonal trust, when coupled with planned change initiatives, lead to greater technology adoption and internalization, reinforcing the research interest toward a more comprehensive and representative technology adoption model departing from the well consolidated UTAUT model.

All these contributions make it clear that trust is a component that must not be ignored when antecedents and consequences of technology adoption are taken into account, otherwise there exists the concrete risk of missing an important piece of the puzzle, if not the main one. Starting from this evidence, our article aims at covering such research gap by proposing an extension of the UTAUT model, bearing in mind the crucial role of trust. In the next chapter we formalize and review the different typologies and dimensions of trust, in order to finally define the technology-mediated trust, which will ultimately be our core concept to be used for extending the UTAUT model proposed by [8].

3   Where Trust Comes from

The concepts of Trust and Trustworthiness probably started playing a role since the human beings existence on earth. We have an innate bent that pushes us to act in our own self-interest [35] and in order to improve and maintain better conditions for ourselves we often need to cooperate: in other words, the absence of Trust between two individuals can lead to worse situation for both of them, as in the famous case of "The Prisoner's Dilemma" [36]. According to the previous case, if both of the players cheat, they pull down themselves into a lower payoff scheme; at the same time, being loyal could lead them to higher pay-offs, but this is true for both if and only if no one betrays the other counterpart. Therefore, they need to trust each other to get involved in a win-win situation [37].

Through the centuries, the concept of Trust acquired a progressive stronger importance in the human relations [38]: from the macro events, like wars with the various countries alliances and international treaties, to more personal situations, like marriages. Nowadays Trust can be considered as a key word, a lubricant that allows tons of daily events and agreements to go on. The bills that we all have in our wallet represent a good example: they are no more than small pieces of paper but we can buy very valuable goods just in exchange of these rectangular sheets. Our monetary system started being based on golden and silver coins, which have value themselves, depending on the amount of precious material contained. During a transition period some banks allowed to deposit gold giving back a "certificate" which entitles the owner to repeat the exchange, bringing back his precious element whenever he desires [39]. It is glaring that this structure requires a strong amount of Trust toward the bank. The transitional stage came to an end and now we do not even need to have this possibility to convert the coins and bills into gold, but simply almost everyone trusts the entities which emitted money: it does not have an intrinsic value but thanks to Institutional Trust the system works [40]. Institutional Trust makes people confident toward institutions such as governments or banks that these last are willing to protect the individual's rights without damaging or putting in danger citizens [41].

As anticipated earlier, we take, for the purpose of this paper, the following definition: total Trust is the result of Trust as an attitude (Trustworthiness) and Trust as a choice (Trustfulness), according to [42]. The author highlights that while several academics underline the importance of being trustful, believing that faith and social education nurturing positive expectations are the keys for Trust and cooperation, in reality the crucial component is trustworthiness. In fact, overoptimistic or deceitful promises might disappoint the trustful actor, making him distrustful, while entering in contact with trustworthy partners may promote successive cooperation. He therefore concludes that the trustworthiness rate is actually the key element, which determines whether Trust increases or decreases.

Another interesting point is that intra-cultural and inter-cultural aspects influence the level of Trust and that different cultural backgrounds could lead to incomprehension/misinterpretation; but, if well managed, they can turn into richness [43]. A good research related to this issue is the one carried out by [44], which analyzes Trust among countries. They found that Trust is affected both by the characteristics of the country being trusted and by cultural features of the match between trusting country and trusted country, like their historical paths and their religious, genetic, and somatic traits. This issue is very challenging from an economic point of view because they empirically discovered that a lower level of bilateral trust determines also less trade, less portfolio investment, and less direct investment. Intuitively, the previously mentioned effect accounts more for those goods, which are more Trust intensive.

In addition, conflicts in specific procedures/means could be beneficial and solvable while conflicts in specific goals/procedures cannot be solved and are harmful [45]. This issue is anyway not so clear and it is debatable, since other researchers predicted an always negative relationship between conflicts and team performance/team member satisfaction [46]. Still, the most widely accepted vision assumes that conflicts might be under some circumstances beneficial, and this depends upon the kind of conflict plus the groups' structure in terms of task type, interdependence, and group norms [47]. Switching to the issue of Trust building, this process is also characterized as to be dynamic and continuative [48]. In fact, it is a process, which evolves continuously during the repetitive interactions between the parts.

Some words are also worth to be spent on the relational-based interchange of Trust, an important phenomenon according to which Trust can be spread among different people through the underlying relations' network [49]. This mechanism remarks the importance of the role played by networks of human relationship in the Trust building process, due to the fact that if A trusts B, and B trusts C, it is more likely that A will trust also C, for the above mentioned mechanism. For example, [50] argued that hypertext links from a website to another one raise up the similarity perception of the linked organizations, and this provokes a transfer of Trust between the two firms. Of course, in a similar vein, also distrust might be transferred.

Finally, we highlight the role of target culture's knowledge for the generation of Trust. According to the opinion that Trust can lower transaction costs, facilitate inter-organizational relationships, and enhance manager-subordinate relationships [51], it would be particularly fruitful to be more aware of the cultural traits of the interlocutor, in order to generate mutual Trust in a quicker way [52]. Such an adaptive learning process works if and only if there is the mutual willingness to shortcut the cultural distance and barriers that often exist, especially if the two individuals belong to very different cultural settings [53]; managers operating in very heterogeneous business contexts should therefore sustain the creation of Trust by promoting appreciative learning cultures in the organizations [54]. Travelling, and foreign experiences more in general, are also associated with more Trust toward the society, due to an opening-mind process [55].

3.1 Particularized Versus Generalized Trust

Tonoyan [56] offers a clear description about the difference between particularized and generalized Trust. He claims that generalized Trust is a type of Trust versus anonymous others like political institutions or public services, while particularized Trust is the one directed to friends, kin or a specific individuals more in general; several studies [57–59] evidenced that particularized Trust might be the antecedent of corruption and other distortions of the economy, while generalized Trust is, on average, something beneficial and desirable.

Moreover, [60] specify that generalized and particularized trust cannot be seen as aspects of the same phenomenon, they have different antecedents and different consequences. Rose-Ackerman [61] further refines the classification of Trust, claiming that there are three variants: generalized interpersonal trust, one-sided trust or reliability, and two-sided reciprocal trust. Still, for the sake of this paper, we would consider beneficial to stay on the standard classification of particularized versus generalized trust.

3.2 Institutional Trust

The institutional Trust is a subset of generalized Trust and it is referred mainly to the Trust related to institutions like the government, supranational organizations, schools, universities, regulated markets, and so on [62].

Several studies have been conducted to analyze the impact of institutional Trust on given activities, or also the other way round. For example, [63] evidenced a case where a merger provoked the loss of institutional trust; [64] showed that institutional Trust act as a facilitator for electronic transactions, in other words consumers feel more prone to successfully conclude an on-line purchase if they have a high level of institutional Trust; [65] highlighted that also inter-firm relationships are influenced by institutional Trust.

The previous discussion, for our purpose, serves to clarify that institutional Trust is powerful, able to influence and modify phenomena and relationships; the importance that institutional Trust holds among the research on Information Systems is broadly discussed and analyzed by [66].

3.3 Technology-Mediated Trust

The concept of technology-mediated Trust plays a crucial role in several academic articles; its precise definition is still under debate and it is argued that modern information technologies actually challenged traditional views on Trust [67]. In other words, Trust is not attributable to technology artifacts, but technology-mediated Trust is a representation of trust in social actors such as designers, creators and operators of technology more in general; therefore is the trustworthiness of those agents that mainly determines the trustworthiness level on average enjoyed by the technology itself [68]. This concept is extremely relevant for the sake of our study: it implies that if an individual, or an institution, are trustworthy, there will be also a Trust toward the technological artifact that they use to connect each other. Therefore, if we assume the presence of trustworthiness, we might infer that the relationships proposed in the UTAUT model should be positive reinforced. This issue, which represents the major theoretical contribution of this article, will be more carefully discussed in the next paragraph.

Other researches further confirmed that Trust, when technology mediated, is strongly correlated to the Trust toward the person(s) behind the interface. For example [69] demonstrated that interventions such as self-reported vendor guarantees might increase the overall technology-mediated Trust level and therefore the probability of obtaining successful e-commerce outcomes rises as well. Another important research conducted by [31] revealed that online Trust increases whether users believe that the vendor has nothing to gain by cheating, if they assume that there are safety mechanisms embedded to the Web site, and if the interface is both easy to use and designed in a certain way. This last study confirms that the human component behind the machine (the vendor in this case) plays a determinant role for the formation of technology-mediated Trust. Moreover, [70] further claim that, in online environments, the presence of technology-mediated Trust is something both crucial and mainly dependent on the people behind the technology.

3.4 Trust and Social Networks

Social media are IT artefacts [71]. As IT artefacts, they are affected by the previously mentioned theoretical mechanism on technology-mediated Trust. For example, the number of Twitter's followers can be considered as an important indicator of the trustworthiness level toward the followed [72], therefore people more influential are also expected to detain a higher number of followers. Pentina [73] discovered that the message intention does not influence the trustworthiness of the sender: this remark is valid for all kinds of Social Networks; in other words, whether an individual or an institution is trustworthiness or not, depends on external causes rather than their posts or tweets. Consequently, there is no need to adjust or reformulate the trustworthiness evaluation statement in response of tweeting/posting activity. These considerations reinforce what discussed in the previous paragraph, remarking the issue that also when the Social Network dimension is taken into account, the individuals behind the IT artefact remain the main element to be analyzed for trust-related studies.

4   The Effect of Trust on the Four UTAUT Model's Relationships

Based on our previously defined construct of technology-mediated trust, in this chapter we show why it should act as a moderator in the original UTAUT model, and why it deserves a self-standing role in this task.

4.1   Performance Expectancy

Venkatesh et al. [8] define performance expectancy as how a human being expects that his/her job performances could increase after having adopted a given technology. High level of technology-mediated trust, that in this specific case should be the result of trustworthy issuers, developers or recommenders of the technology, are expected to generate positive effects on behavioral intention of the individual. In other words, if a person trusts who is behind the new technology that he wants to adopt, it is more likely that the same person will attribute more value in terms of performance expectancy to the technology into examination.

4.2   Effort Expectancy

The literature recognizes the effort expectancy to be directed correlated to the expected ease of use of the new technology; in fact, if a given user perceives that using a specific technology will be difficult, he or she has to put much more effort to activate the required learning mechanism: as consequence, having an expectancy of ease of use has positive effects on behavioral intention. In a similar vein, if the same user tends to trust more the issuer, developer, or recommender of the technology, he/she will be more likely to recognize as true the information about ease of use, de facto reinforcing the relationship between effort expectancy and behavioral intention.

4.3   Social Influence

In the UTAUT model social influence is characterized as how much a human being believes that important peers will judge him/her positively depending whether a specific technology is adopted or not. Trust and social influence are not isolated concepts: in fact, the definition of social influence itself contemplates the relevance of "important peers"; the level of importance is partially determined by the trustworthiness degree. As consequence, superior level of technology-mediated trust also in this case are expected to reinforce the relationship between social influence and behavioral intention, by strengthening the relevance of the social influence itself.

4.4 Facilitating Conditions

Those conditions are represented by the perception of a user about the existence of external actors or organizations that are going to be supportive after the adoption decision of a given technology. We argue that a stronger presence of technology-mediated trust is able, also in this case, to increase the credibility level that after the technology adoption, the promised supportive environment forecasted a priori, will actually realize and stands on. Clearly, this enhancement in terms of credibility should have reinforcing effects on the theoretical relationship between facilitating conditions and use behavior.

The proposed UTAUT enriched model is represented in the below Fig. 2.

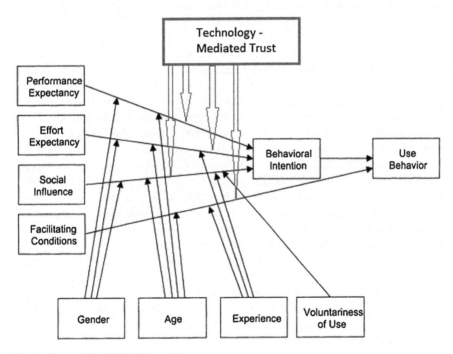

Fig. 2 The modified UTAUT model

4.5 Measuring the Level of Trust

Measuring the level of Technology-Mediated Trust is definitely not an easy task and most of the attempts have been done in the intra-individual context [74]. A possibility to measure the Trust level in the Social Networks environment is represented by using as a proxy the number of followers or fans. Following [72] we claim that the number of Twitter's followers can be considered as an important indicator of the trustworthiness level toward the followed. Anyway, at this stage we have to remark the fact that this is a work-in-progress paper and we postpone the proposal of a consistent scale to measure Trust to a more advanced stage of research.

5 Implications for Future Research

The original UTAUT model, according to its authors, claims at explaining as much as 70 % of the variance in intention [8]; in fact, as stated in the conclusions: "it is possible that we may be approaching the practical limits of our ability to explain individual acceptance and usage decisions in organizations". This statement gives us room for proposing the "fifth moderator", i.e. the technology mediated trust, in order to increase the overall explanative power of the model. This opens to wide avenues for further empirical investigations, aimed at verifying how social actors adopt and accept IT. As from our statements, every social actor will leverage on his/her level of technology-mediated trust toward a specific IT to be adopted. Thus, future research should take into account the measurement issue of different trust levels and assess its moderating impact on the UTAUT theoretical construct. In case of positive empirical validation, our contribution could trigger the exploration on how to accelerate the adoption and acceptance of IT, by promoting higher average level of trust. Given the origin of our construct, another interesting issue could be empirically investigated: the relationship between institutional trust (for example related to a public listed owner of the IT and/or an already widely diffused IT application) and the adoption and acceptance of the IT. Another interesting issue is represented by the possibility of having the level of trust as a key variable (like Performance Expectancy, Effort Expectancy, Social Influence, and Facilitating Conditions) in the UTAUT model rather than being a moderator for the existing relationship. From a theoretical point of view, it is reasonable as well: more technology-mediated trust could impact directly on both behavioral intention and use behavior. This issue confirms the necessity of performing further research aimed at empirically analyzing the role of trust in the model.

References

1. Gefen, D., Karahanna, E., Straub, D.W.: Trust and TAM in online shopping: an integrated model. MIS Q. **27**(1), 51–90 (2003)
2. Bélanger, F., Carter, L.: Trust and risk in e-government adoption. J. Strateg. Inf. Syst. **17**(2), 165–176 (2008)
3. Benbasat, I., Wang, W.: Trust in and adoption of online recommendation agents. J. Assoc. Inf. Syst. **6**(3), 72–101 (2005)
4. Venkatesh, V., Morris, M.G., Davis, G.B., Davis, F.D.: User acceptance of information technology: toward a unified view. MIS Q. **27**(3), 425–478 (2003)
5. Zaheer, A., McEvily, B., Perrone, V.: Does trust matter? Exploring the effects of interorganizational and interpersonal trust on performance. Organ. Sci. **9**(2), 141–159 (1998)
6. Venkatesh, V., Davis, F.D.: A theoretical extension of the technology acceptance model—4 longitudinal field studies. Manage. Sci. **46**(2), 186–204 (2000)
7. Venkatesh, V.: Determinants of perceived ease of use, integrating control, intrinsic motivation and emotion into the TAM. Inf. Syst. Res. **11**(4), 342–365 (2000)
8. Venkatesh, V., Morris, M.G., Davis, G.B., Davis, F.D.: User acceptance of information technology—toward a unified view. MIS Q. **27**(3), 425–478 (2003)
9. Venkatesh, V., Bala, H.: Technology acceptance model 3 and a research agenda on interventions. Decis. Sci. **39**(2), 273–315 (2008)
10. Venkatesh, V., Thong, J.Y.L., Xu, X.: Consumer acceptance and use of information technology—extending the unified theory of acceptance and use of technology. MIS Q. **36**(1), 157–178 (2012)
11. Davis, F.D.: Perceived usefulness, perceived ease of use, and user acceptance of information technology. MIS Q. **13**(3), 319–340 (1989)
12. Adams, D.A., Nelson, R.R., Todd, P.A.: Perceived usefulness, ease of use, and usage of information technology: a replication. MIS Q. **16**(2), 227–247 (1992)
13. Hendrickson, A.R., Massey, P.D., Cronan, T.P.: On the test-retest reliability of perceived usefulness and perceived ease of use scales. MIS Q. **17**(2), 227–230 (1993)
14. Segars, A.H., Grover, V.: Re-examining perceived ease of use and usefulness: a confirmatory factor analysis. MIS Q. **17**(4), 517–525 (1993)
15. Subramanian, G.H.: A replication of perceived usefulness and perceived ease of use measurement. Decis. Sci. **25**(5/6), 863–873 (1994)
16. Szajna, B.: Software evaluation and choice: predictive evaluation of the Technology Acceptance Instrument. MIS Q. **18**(3), 319–324 (1994)
17. Brown, S.A., Venkatesh, V.: Model of adoption of technology in households: a baseline model test and extension incorporating household life cycle. MIS Q. **29**(3), 399–426 (2005)
18. Karahanna, E., Straub, D.W., Chervany, N.L.: Information technology adoption across time: a cross-sectional comparison of pre-adoption and post- adoption beliefs. MIS Q. **23**(2), 183–213 (1999)
19. Bharracherjee, A., Premkumar, G.: Understanding changes in belief and attitude toward information technology usage: a theoretical model and longitudinal test. MIS Q. **28**(2), 229–254 (2004)
20. Bhattacherjee, A.: Understanding information systems continuance: An expectation-confirmation model. MIS Q. **25**(3), 351–370 (2001)
21. Rai, A., Lang, S., Welker, R.: Assessing the validity of IS success models: An empirical test and theoretical analysis. Inf. Syst. Res. **13**(1), 50–69 (2002)
22. Delone, W.H., McLean, E.R.: The DeLone and McLean model of information systems success: a ten year update. J. Manage. Inf. Syst. **19**(4), 60–95 (2003)
23. Roca, J.C., Chiu, C.M., Martínez, F.J.: Understanding e-learning continuance intention: an extension of the Technology Acceptance Model. Int. J. Hum. Comput. Stud. **64**(8), 683–696 (2006)

24. Venkatesh, V., Goyal, S.: Expectation disconfirmation and technology adoption—polynomial modeling and response surface analysis. MIS Q. **34**(2), 281–303 (2010)
25. Bretz, R.D., Judge, T.A.: Realistic job previews: a test of the adverse self-selection hypothesis. J. Appl. Psychol. **83**(2), 330–337 (1998)
26. Taylor, S., Todd, P.A.: Understanding information technology usage: a test of competing models. Inf. Syst. Res. **6**(2), 144–176 (1995)
27. Bergeron, F., Rivard, S., Serre, L.: Investigating the support role of the information center. MIS Q. **14**(3), 247–260 (1990)
28. Cragg, P., King, M.: Small-firm computing: motivators and inhibitors. MIS Q. **17**(1), 47–60 (1993)
29. Harrison, D.A., Mykytyn, P.P., Riemenschneider, C.K.: Executive decisions about adoption of information technology in small business: theory and empirical tests. Inf. Syst. Res. **8**(2), 171–195 (1997)
30. Venkatesh, V., Davis, F.D.: A model of the antecedents of perceived ease of use: development and test. Decis. Sci. **27**(3), 451–481 (1996)
31. Gefen, D., Karahanna, E., Straub, D.W.: Trust and TAM in online shopping: an integrated model. MIS Q. **27**(1), 51–90 (2003)
32. Srivastava, S.C., Chandra, S., Theng, Y.L.: Evaluating the role of trust in consumer adoption of mobile payment systems: an empirical analysis. Commun. Assoc. Inf. Syst. **27**, 561–588 (2010)
33. Bahmanziari, T., Pearson, J.M., Crosby, L.: Is trust important in technology adoption? A policy capturing approach. J. Comput. Inf. Syst. **43**(4), 46–54 (2003)
34. Lippert, S.K., Davis, M.: A conceptual model integrating trust into planned change activities to enhance technology adoption behavior. J. Inf. Sci. **32**(5), 434–448 (2006)
35. Berg, J., Dickhaut, J., McCabe, K.: Trust, reciprocity, and social history. Games Econ. Behav. **10**(1), 122–142 (1995)
36. Rapoport, A., Chammah, A.M.: Prisoner's dilemma. University of Michigan Press, Ann Arbor (1965)
37. Kreps, D.M., Milgrom, P., Roberts, J., Wilson, R.: Rational cooperation in the finitely repeated prisoners' dilemma. J. Econ. Theory **27**(2), 245–252 (1982)
38. Larzelere, R.E., Huston, T.L.: The dyadic trust scale: toward understanding inter-personal trust in close relationships. J. Marriage Fam. **42**(3), 595–604 (1980)
39. Eichengreen, B.J.: Globalizing Capital: A History of the International Monetary System. Princeton University Press, Princeton (1998)
40. Kiyotaki, N., Wright, R.: On money as a medium of exchange. J. Polit. Econ. **97**(4), 927–954 (1989)
41. Ford, D.: Trust and Knowledge Management: The Seeds Of Success. Working Paper WP 01–08. Queen's University, New York (2001)
42. Tullberg, J.: Trust—the importance of trustfulness versus trustworthiness. J. Socio Econ. **37**(5), 2059–2071 (2008)
43. Earley, P.C., Mosakowski, E.: Cultural intelligence. Harv. Bus. Rev. **82**(10), 139–146 (2004)
44. Guiso, L., Sapienza, P., Zingales, L.: Cultural biases in economic exchange. Quart. J. Econ. **124**(3), 1095–1131 (2009)
45. Kurtzberg, T. R.: Creative styles and teamwork: effects of coordination and conflict on group outcomes. Ph.D. thesis. University of Chicago, Chicago (2000)
46. De Dreu, C.K., Weingart, L.R.: Task versus relationship conflict, team performance, and team member satisfaction: a meta-analysis. J. Appl. Psychol. **88**(4), 741–749 (2003)
47. Jehn, K.A.: A multimethod examination of the benefits and detriments of intragroup conflict. Adm. Sci. Q. **40**(2), 256–282 (1995)
48. Madhok, A.: Revisiting multinational firms' tolerance for joint ventures: a trust-based approach. J. Int. Bus. Stud. **37**(1), 30–43 (2006)
49. Luo, Y.: Building trust in cross-cultural collaborations: toward a contingency perspective. J. Manage. **28**(5), 669–694 (2002)
50. Stewart, K.J.: Trust transfer on the world wide web. Organ. Sci. **14**(1), 5–17 (2003)

51. Doney, P.M., Cannon, J.P., Mullen, M.R.: Understanding the influence of national culture on the development of trust. Acad. Manag. Rev. **23**(3), 601–620 (1998)
52. Li, L.: The effects of trust and shared vision on inward knowledge transfer in subsidiaries' intra-and inter-organizational relationships. Int. Bus. Rev. **14**(1), 77–95 (2005)
53. Senge, P.M.: The fifth discipline. Meas. Bus. Excell. **1**(3), 46–51 (1997)
54. Barrett, F.J.: Creating appreciative learning cultures. Organ. Dyn. **24**(2), 36–49 (1995)
55. Cao, J., Galinsky, A.D., Maddux, W.W.: Does travel broaden the mind? Breadth of foreign experiences increases generalized trust. Soc. Psychol. Pers. Sci. **5**(5), 517–525 (2014)
56. Tonoyan, V.: Trust and Entrepreneurship: A West–East Perspective. Edward Elgar Publishing, Cheltenham (2005)
57. Lambsdorff, J.G.: How confidence facilitates illegal transactions, an empirical approach. Am. J. Econ. Sociol. **61**(4), 829–854 (2002)
58. Bjørnskov, C., Paldam, M.: The New Institutional Economics of Corruption. Routledge, London (2004)
59. Coleman, J.S.: Foundations of Social Theory. Belknap Press of Harvard University Press, Cambridge (1990)
60. Abbott, S., Freeth, D.: Social capital and health starting to make sense of the role of generalized trust and reciprocity. J. Health Psychol. **13**(7), 874–883 (2008)
61. Rose-Ackerman, S.: Trust, honesty and corruption: reflection on the state-building process. Eur. J. Sociol. **42**(03), 526–570 (2001)
62. Gillespie, N., Dietz, G.: Trust repair after organization-level failure. Acad. Manag. Rev. **34**(1), 127–145 (2009)
63. Maguire, S., Phillips, N.: 'Citibankers' at Citigroup: a study of the loss of institutional trust after a merger. J. Manage. Stud. **45**(2), 372–401 (2008)
64. Patnasingam, P., Gefen, D., Pavlou, P.A.: The role of facilitating conditions and institutional trust in electronic marketplaces. J. Electron. Commer. Organ. **3**(3), 69–82 (2005)
65. Hagen, J.M., Choe, S.: Trust in Japanese interfirm relations: institutional sanctions matter. Acad. Manag. Rev. **23**(3), 589–600 (1998)
66. Gefen, D., Pavlou, P., Benbasat, I., McKnight, H., Stewart, K., Straub, D.: ICIS panel summary: should institutional trust matter in information systems research? In: ICIS 2005 Proceedings. AIS Electronic Library (2005)
67. Lacohée, H., Cofta, P., Phippen, A., Furnell, S.: Understanding Public Perceptions: Trust and Engagement in ICT Mediated Services. Paul Co Pub Consortium, London (2008)
68. Bohmann, K.: About the sense of social compatibility. AI Soc. **3**(4), 323–331 (1989)
69. Pennington, R., Wilcox, H.D., Grover, V.: The role of system trust in business-to-consumer transactions. J. Manage. Inf. Syst. **20**(3), 197–226 (2003)
70. Gefen, D., Benbasat, I., Pavlou, P.: A research agenda for trust in online environments. J. Manage. Inf. Syst. **24**(4), 275–286 (2008)
71. Yates, D., Paquette, S.: Emergency knowledge management and social media technologies: a case study of the 2010 Haitian earthquake. Int. J. Inf. Manage. **31**(1), 6–13 (2011)
72. Anantharam, P., Henson, C.A., Thirunarayan, K. Sheth, A.P.: Trust model for semantic sensor and social networks: a preliminary report. In: Proceedings of the IEEE 2010 National Aerospace and Electronics Conference (NAECON), IEEE (2010)
73. Pentina, I., Zhang, L., Basmanova, O.: Antecedents and consequences of trust in a social media brand: a cross-cultural study of Twitter. Comput. Hum. Behav. **29**(4), 1546–1555 (2013)
74. Glaeser, E.L., Laibson, D.I., Scheinkman, J.A., Soutter, C.L.: Measuring trust. Quart. J. Econ. **115**(3), 811–846 (2000)

Digital Natives and Digital Immigrants Behaviour in Trust Choices: An Experimental Study on Social Trust Attitudes and Cognition

Alessio Maria Braccini and Francesca Marzo

1 Introduction

Some studies suggest that the intense use of information and communication technologies (ICTs) in the early years of a person's life could contribute to the development of peculiar behavioral habits and cognitive structures [1–4]. This concept finds support by several literature sources [5]. Tapscott first [4] talks about a net generation as the cohort of individuals who grew up in a digitalized world. To Prensky belongs the fatherhood of the terms *digital natives* and *digital immigrants* [3, 6], which he uses to identify the differences between those who grew up in a digitized world (the natives), and those who encountered the technology later, in a second stage of their lives (the immigrants). McMahon and Pospisil [2] finally report as a diffused habit that of interacting with technologies among millennials [7]. Though with different names, these sources refer to people who have a usual intense interaction with technology. As reported by Valkenbur and Peter [8], these persons have on average spent about 20,000 h online using different kinds of transactional systems and decision support systems to collect information, to establish social relationships, to have fun, or to cooperate with others in their lives.

This topic attracted much interest in the scientific literature, but not always with coherent and consistent results [9]. If a common trait has to be found among the literature sources discussing these individuals (that from this point on we will simply call digital natives), this is the prevailing focus on teaching and learning aspects of the natives [10], and on the inadequateness of didactic methods to teach a generation

A.M. Braccini (✉)
Dipartimento di Economia e Impresa, Università degli Studi della Tuscia,
Viterbo, VT, Italy
e-mail: abraccini@unitus.it

F. Marzo (✉)
LUISS Guido Carli, Rome, Italy
e-mail: fmarzo@luiss.it; f.marzo@gmail.com

© Springer International Publishing Switzerland 2016
F. D'Ascenzo et al. (eds.), *Blurring the Boundaries Through Digital Innovation*,
Lecture Notes in Information Systems and Organisation 19,
DOI 10.1007/978-3-319-38974-5_9

more used to digital media than books. A second aspect concerns instead the fact that some of the studies on digital natives were criticized for being anecdotal and for showing inconsistent results [5]. Following several conceptual works, empirical evidences contributed to identify a great internal variance in the characteristics of this generation [9], and further empirical investigations are necessary [11].

A keystone in the debate on digital natives is the influence that the abundant presence of ICT, and the consequent habit of interactions with it that natives developed, have produced on their skills, behaviors, habits, and principles, in relation to the way they use the technology, and the way they interact and cooperate with peers [5, 12]. Given that technology influences organizational norms, values, and behaviors [13], investigating the influence of technology intensity is important both from the perspective of information systems [12] and from the perspective of organizational behavior [10]. Therefore, we propose a study from a cognitive approach to shed light on particularly important socio-cognitive phenomena that underpin digital natives cooperation behavior in teams: trust and control dynamics. The work we propose uses an experimental methodology in order to investigate these dynamics. Section 2 presents in details the cognitive perspective on these dynamics. Section 3 will present the design of the experiment that we used for running the pilot, while Sect. 4 discuss briefly the results of the pilot we run with the aim of refining the tool for collecting data in further experimental sections.

2   Digital Natives Behavioral Traits and Socio-cognitive Model of Trust

2.1   Digital Natives Versus Digital Immigrants

The frequent use of technology could impact digital natives' motivation and capability to act proactively in organizational settings, differentiating their behaviour from digital immigrants' one. As reported by some sources [14, 15], digital natives are accustomed to the habit of receiving immediate feedback for their actions and their behaviour. We hypothesize that this is a direct consequence of the way ICTs work, where usually the interaction with such tools is a set of reiterated sequences of actions by the user and immediate reactions or feedback by the ICT tool. This might have produced a desire or a necessity of immediateness of feedback also for the other activities they perform, a kind of desire that is not frequent to be observed in digital immigrants. Such desire of immediate feedback could be a problem in situations where delayed motivation is instead necessary [10, 16] (i.e. like in the case of strategic decision making or leadership behaviour), and could end up in modifying not only the interaction between digital natives and digital immigrants (i.e. in a team work), but also the modality to manage digital natives and digital immigrants collaboration.

Adding to this, the habit of interacting with ICT tools could also have produced in digital natives the need to be able to control the environment [14]. When interacting with the ICT the user is usually in the control of the software system being used. This is ever more so for those who are so skilled (and the literature sometimes assumes digital natives all are, while this is not true for digital immigrants) that they can program the software and the hardware. We suppose thence that such habit and capability of controlling ICT systems purportedly has left digital natives with the need to be able to control the outer environment. At the same time being able to control such complex software systems also induced in digital natives a sense of self confidence [17] that might also go beyond the technological aspects. Conversely, digital immigrants, unable to accomplish this control, could feel less confident. In some cases this self confidence becomes a sense of trust [5] that influences both digital natives and digital immigrants relationship with technology and with people. Such mixed and sometimes conflicting set of behavioral traits calls for an empirical investigation of how digital natives actually behave in teams and organizations. In particular the contraposition between the sense of control and the sense of trust seems an important conflicting dichotomy that is worth of empirical investigation. Indeed, both in controlling and in feeling confident, the concept of trust is crucial.

2.2 Model of Trust

In order to understand these behavioural aspects, then, we claim that it is important to understand subjects predisposition to trust. In other terms, research questions on how different are trust attitudes and trust behaviours in digital natives and digital immigrants must be formulated. In order to allow for this formulation we would like first to introduce the concept of trust and its relationship with the concept of control.

In order to get a comprehensive model of trust, it is important both to disentangle the set of beliefs and evaluation supporting expectations about other's behavior, in order to address dispositional aspects of trust, and to take into account behavioral consequences of trust. Moreover both trust as a mental attitude and trust as a decision are intrinsically situated and must be inevitably tied to the context in which the interaction occurs [18].

The decision to delegate a task, at the basis of trust attitudes and decisions, depends on a crucial epistemic component: the expectation, considered as quantified belief that the trustee will act in an appropriate and successful manner. A cognitive model of trust has been developed in order to analyze these features. Such a model has been proposed to express the mental state of trust in cognitive terms (beliefs, goals) [19] and represents the most explicit and conscious form of trust in which the cognitive factors affecting trust are also used to make trust decisions.

Of particular importance for our study is the possibility to address the problem of trust in its dispositional aspects. Indeed, since any act of trusting and relying implies some bet and some risk [20], we need to take into account the belief about the vulnerable position the trustee put herself on [21].

When the environment and the specific circumstances are safe and reliable, less trust is necessary for delegation. Conversely, the stronger is the trust relationship, the smaller is the need of a safe and reliable environment and, then, of external monitoring and authority [22]. However, when trust is not there, there is something that can replace it (i.e. surveillance, contracts etc.). It is just matter of different kinds or better facets of trust. From this perspective an important role is played by control. The control can be considered as a meta-action aimed both at ascertaining whether a given state of the world has been realized or maintained (feedback, checking) and at dealing with the possible deviations and unforeseen events in order to positively cope with them (intervention) [21].

3 Research Design

In our study we adopt an experimental research strategy motivated on the basis of the following considerations. First of all, the inconsistency of the results in the literature of digital natives let us suppose that the birthdate is inadequate to identify the natives as a cohort. This aspect actually makes the identification of a population difficult and poses threats to the adoption of any research methodology that involves the definition of a sample (excluding the incidental one). A second aspect to be mentioned concerns also the potential bias that can be caught by self-reported measures, especially when they are used to assess behavioral traits. Finally to investigate trust and control dynamics of digital natives it would have been necessary to identify an empirical setting where these behavioral traits could be observed detached from other contextual factors. This would be necessary to exclude potential confounds (i.e. previous acquaintance and/or closeness of the ties between the trustor and the trustee, previous experiences of them in the same workgroup and similar) that might influence trust and control related decisions.

3.1 Research Questions and Experiment Design

In order to study the willingness to trust we decided to investigate how people act when the possibility of controlling others' actions is represented by the possibility of punishing them [23], on the one hand, and by the possibility of introducing some form of insurance so that the loss deriving from betrayal is significantly reduced [24], on the other. We aim at testing both mechanisms in order both to find out potential patterns in digital natives needs of control and to discover possible differences in which form of control they prefer to use.

In other terms, we aim at answering the following research questions:

Q1. What will digital natives and immigrants choose when faced with the dilemma of achieving an immediate result versus a delayed one, which relies on trusting on a second person?

Q2. What will digital natives and digital immigrants decide when faced with the possibility of controlling others' actions?

Q3. Which form of control, if any, digital natives prefer to use? Is it different from digital immigrants preferences?

In order to answer these questions, we approach the investigation of digital natives and digital immigrants "trust and control" behavior through an experimental strategy and by formulating related research hypotheses.

The experiment we run in the pilot section consists in a repeated modified trust game [25]. The subjects "trustor" TR and "trustee" TE involved in the experiments were of different kinds $k \in K = (nat, \overline{nat})$, where k_{nat} indicates a digital native, and $k_{\overline{nat}}$ indicates a non digital native. The experiment consisted of 62 rounds of the game involving a mix of different subjects to cover all the four possible combinations described below.

$$
\begin{array}{lll}
A. & TR_{nat} & TE_{nat} \\
B. & TR_{nat} & TE_{\overline{nat}} \\
C. & TR_{\overline{nat}} & TE_{nat} \\
D. & TR_{\overline{nat}} & TE_{\overline{nat}}
\end{array}
$$

We profiled natives and non natives prior the participation to the experiment through the usage of a measurement scale [1] and a basic computer skill test. We run several experiments with different groups of participants to ensure an equal number of observations for each of the previously described four combinations.

In the 62 experiments round subjects taking part to these played the roles of trustor and trustee a different amount of time in relation to their profiles (native and immigrant, cfr. Table 1). The pairings of all the four possible combinations are show in Table 2. It was not possible to ensure the same size in terms of observations for all the four pairings. Finally out of the 62 rounds, participants played 48 times the simple trust game (32 by our decision, and 16 by their decision), and 14 times the modified trust game. Out of these 14 times, in 10 cases participants opted for the punishment, and 4 times for the insurance (cfr. Table 3).

The execution of the experiments with four different groups allowed us both to investigate differences between teams formed by natives and teams formed by non natives, and between homogeneous and heterogeneous teams (i.e. teams composed both by natives and immigrants). We gave particular attention to the need of

Table 1 Player profiles

Player profile	Trustor	Trustee
Native	27	26
Immigrant	35	36

Table 2 Player profiles pairings

Pair	Frequency
Native–Native	11
Native–Immigrant	16
Immigrant–Native	15
Immigrant–Immigrant	20
Total	**62**

Table 3 Games types and frequencies

Game type	Frequency	Of which
Simple	48 (32 + 16)	–
Modified	14	10 with punishment
		4 with insurance

building experiments where dependent variables change due to those subjects' characteristics we want to consider as independent variables, namely being "natives" or "immigrants", excluding other features influence. In order to avoid that different behaviour could be due to different interpretation of context (problem that is very important when dealing with generational difference in perception), for this first study, the game will be proposed and implemented in experiment in a general form, without being directly related to typical organizational situations.

3.2 Experimental Procedures

The pilot was run in the computer laboratory of DEIM, Tuscia University, using a computer-based protocol. The experiment was compiled and conducted with SoPHIE—Software Platform for Human Interaction Experiments [26].

Upon arrival at the laboratory, participants were seated in front of individual computer-screens. Any form of communication between participants was strictly prohibited. Once all participants were seated, they began to read instructions silently at their own pace. Then, an experimenter read the instructions aloud to induce their common knowledge. The experimenter answered questions individually.

There were two phases: the first one consisted in a normal trust game, the second one consisted in a trust game with the possibility of choosing among three options: normal trust game (again), game with insurance, or game with third party punishment. At the beginning of each round, participants were assigned a token to log into the platform. Each participant for each round was randomly assigned to one of the two different roles: trustor and trustee, by calling them "Player 1" and "Player 2". Therefore each pair playing in each round consisted of one trustor and one trustee anonymously and randomly paired up.

A typical round proceeded as follows. At the beginning of a round, the computer randomly assigned an endowment of 4 points (corresponding to 4 euros) to Player 1 and 4 points to Player 2. Once a round began, Player 1 was asked to choose how many point(s) out of her endowment shall be passed to the paired Player 2. This amount was triplicated by the platform before being passed to Player 2. Player 2 was then asked to decide how many of the amount in her hands (endowment plus the sum received from the trustor) she wanted to return to her correspondent Player 1.

At the beginning of each round of the second phase, Player 1 was previously asked if either she wanted to play as in the first session or she opted for playing by using insurance or punishment. Namely, if the choice is to change the game, she can decide to pay an insurance fee or to opt for a punishment scenario. In the first case, she paid 1 point before playing; if she decided to give part of the money to Player 2 and only if Player 2 decided not to give her back anything, the researchers will give Player 1 the sum of money she offered Player 2 minus the 1 Euro paid as insurance fee. In the punishment scenario, instead, she paid 1 Euro to a "third party" which will punish Player 2 reducing his payoff if he will decide not to give back anything to Player 1. Then, the structure of the game was equal to the first session. The insurance or the punishment choices affected directly the payoffs for each single round. Participants were informed when the experiment moved from the second to the first round.

At the end of the experiment for each participant a round has been randomly selected and the payoffs of that round has been paid to subjects involved.

4 Analysis and Discussion of Data

As already mentioned in total the simple trust game was executed 48 times out of which: 32 by design, 16 by choice of participants. The modified trust game was instead executed 14 times. Out of these in 10 cases participants opted for the third party punishment, and 4 times for the insurance.

In total there were 31 homogeneous pairs (11 of which where native—native pairs, and 20 of which immigrants—immigrants pairs), and 31 heterogeneous pairs (16 of which were native—immigrant pairs, and 15 of which where immigrant—native pairs).

Figure 1 graphically shows the distribution of frequency (y axis) of the amount that has been offered by the trustor (z axis), and given back by the trustee (x axis), in all the games (regardless of being normal trust games or modified trust games). To study the different behavior of heterogeneous versus homogeneous teams these amounts are broken down to the four possible combinations of pairs in the various games.

The four area graphs in the figure show that, in terms of repetitions, homogeneous pairs tend to concentrate in few combinations. Especially in the case of pairs composed by both an immigrant trustor and trustee, the highest concentration is for

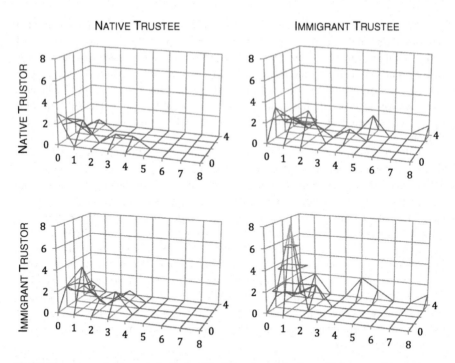

Fig. 1 Frequency of offer and giveback with different combinations of trustors and trustees

the game 1–1. Heterogeneous groups on the other side seem to combine different offers and different givebacks, as the distribution of the frequencies is sparser in this case.

Native trustors tend to offer smaller amounts to the trustee, and this behavior seem to be consistent trough the different games. Immigrant trustors in the end explore a wider breadth of the potential offers and there is less concentration among the different values passed to the trustee. A similar behavior can be observed for native trustees.

These considerations are more evident when looking at quantitative statistics of the games performed. To this regard Table 4 shows descriptive statistics (mean and variance) of the offers and givebacks in all the games, and of the payoffs of the related trustors and trustees.

Data shows that, in homogeneous groups, native trustors' offers are lower than immigrants' trustors offer. In heterogeneous groups instead there is not so much difference between native and immigrant trustors' offers.

At the same time native trustees' average givebacks are always very low (the average equals to 0.91 and 1.27 in the two cases where natives are trustees), and remarkably lower than immigrants average givebacks (0.91 and 1.27 against 1.80 and 2.06).

Table 4 Summary statistics of the games

			Offer		Giveback		Payoff TR		Payoff TE	
TR	TE	Game	Avg	Var	Avg	Var	Avg	Var	Avg	Var
ALL	ALL	Simple	1.33	0.56	1.10	2.16	3.77	1.51	6.90	3.56
		Mod	2.19	1.71	2.03	4.03	3.84	3.82	8.53	13.69
		All	1.77	1.34	1.58	3.34	3.81	2.70	7.74	9.45
			Avg	Var	Avg	Var	Avg	Var	Avg	Var
Native	Native	Simple	1.00	0.40	1.00	1.20	4.00	1.60	6.00	4.80
		Mod	1.00	1.00	0.83	2.14	3.83	2.47	6.17	9.14
		All	1.00	0.73	0.91	1.72	3.91	2.08	6.09	7.17
			Avg	Var	Avg	Var	Avg	Var	Avg	Var
Immigrant	Immigrant	Simple	1.20	0.16	0.80	0.16	3.60	0.44	6.80	1.96
		Mod	3.30	1.21	2.80	5.36	3.50	4.85	11.10	11.09
		All	2.25	1.79	1.80	3.76	3.55	2.65	8.95	11.15
			Avg	Var	Avg	Var	Avg	Var	Avg	Var
Native	Immigrant	Simple	1.88	1.11	1.75	6.19	3.88	3.61	7.88	5.11
		Mod	1.75	0.69	2.38	3.73	4.63	1.98	6.88	2.61
		All	1.81	0.90	2.06	5.06	4.25	2.94	7.38	4.11
			Avg	Var	Avg	Var	Avg	Var	Avg	Var
Immigrant	Native	Simple	1.14	0.12	0.86	0.41	3.71	0.49	6.57	1.39
		Mod	2.13	1.11	1.63	1.98	3.50	4.50	8.75	16.19
		All	1.67	0.89	1.27	1.40	3.60	2.64	7.73	10.46

Concerning payoffs, trustors' payoffs are always remarkably lower than trustee's payoffs (roughly by one half on average). Moreover native trustors' payoff is always higher than immigrant trustors' payoff.

Figure 2 shows the theoretical distribution of payoffs of the trustors and trustees in the non-modified trust game. In theory trustors' payoff increases when their offer increases (x axis) and when the amount received back from the trustees increases (y axis). For the trustee instead the payoff increases when the amount received from the trustor increases, and when the amount given back to the trustor decreases.

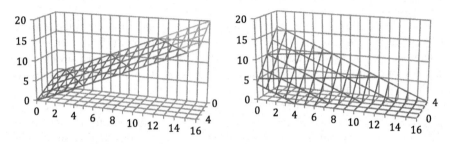

Fig. 2 Theoretical payoffs (trustor left, trustee right)

Answering the first research question (Q1), the results of these experiments seem to suggest that natives prefer an immediate result rather than trusting on a different subject to look for a delayed (even potentially higher) outcome. This support also the hypotheses formulated by the literature and discussed before that the natives seek immediate results, and do not delay their motivation to a second order objective.

The data shows that natives prefer to reduce the offer and retain as much as possible of their allowance not trusting the other to give him back a part of the investment, but looking for the immediate concretization of their payoffs. Consequently on the other side when natives are trustees, the amount of money they give back is always lower than that of immigrant trustees', again showing that they prefer to retain a higher amount for them.

Further information concerning the behaviour of digital natives can be found dis-cussing the kind of choices they adopted in the second round of the experiment, to reply to the remaining research questions. In this round participants have the choice to opt for a normal game (like that of the first round), or a modified game with two options: pay an insurance fee to receive part of the offer back if the trustee would not have given back anything, or pay a third party to punish the trustee reducing his/her payoff in case he/she would not have given back anything. The type of the game was thence the result of a trustor's choice.

Immigrants' offers are not always higher than natives' offers, while givebacks are. So, while it is not possible to state that the amount passed between players is always higher when immigrants are in the game, it is possible to affirm that immigrants tried to use the full gamut of potential offers and giveback, as showed by the frequency charts in Fig. 1. Considering that in this game higher payoffs are awarded when trustors increase the amount to be passed to the trustee to values higher than 0, in the comparison among the four different groups, the one composed by a native trustor and a native trustee shows the lowest average total payoffs (1.91 on average per each game), while the group composed by an immigrant trustor and an immigrant trustee shows the highest average total payoffs (4.05 on average per each game). In the two mixed settings (when the native is either the trustor or the trustee and the immigrant is respectively the trustee or trustor), the situation where the immigrant is the trustee shows average payoffs higher than that where the immigrant is the trustor (3.87 against 2.94). Native behavior influences than the performance of the whole team with particular detrimental effects when two natives compose the team.

Out of the 30 experiments executed in the second round, in 16 cases the trustors decided to play the normal game: 12 out of these 16 payers (75 %) were immi-grants. In reply to Q2 this datum shows that immigrants do not have strong pref-erences for control measures, while natives instead resort on this possibility in most of the cases they are offered it.

In the other 14 cases, in 10 cases players opted for the insurance, and in 4 cases players opted for the punishment. Out of the players who opted for the insurance 70 % were natives, while in the case of punishment the distribution shows not difference (50 % natives), but this scenario was chosen really few time. In reply to

Q3 these data tells us that digital natives seem to prefer insurance rather than punishment. This consideration together with the previous one seem to support the hypotheses that natives desire a more sense of control as natives more than immigrants are opting for the modified game which offered two ways of controlling the trustees: 64.28 % of the games which included control where played by a native trustor. At the same time, linked to Q1, these data tell us that digital natives prefer the immediate outcome rather than the delayed one. The preference is indeed on the insurance, which (for the way the game was structured) would have allowed them to get back part of the offer if the trustee would not have passed anything, rather than on punishment, which (for the way the game was structured) would have seen trustee's payoff reduced by a discretional amount decided by a third party (in this case the researcher). It is disputable whether not knowing the exact amount of the reduction of the payoff, rather than making a choice not affecting their immediate outcome are the drivers of this choice.

As a final comment to the results of this work it has to be pointed out that the differences emerge only when the distinction between natives and immigrants is based on behavioral traits rather than age. As explained in the research design section we classified as native those individuals who showed the behavioral traits purportedly associated with intense ICT interaction, using a specific measurement scale [1]. In this way we were able to identify two groups of different individuals with the discussed consequences. If we had to resort with the birthdate criterion usually adopted by the literature to distinguish between natives and immigrants, all our subjects would have fallen in the native cohort, loosing the possibility to identify and describe differences in their performances throughout the experiment.

5 Conclusion

We have presented a pilot for an empirical investigation of digital natives behavioral traits using a cognitive theoretical background. The aim is to begin an insight into some crucial psychological aspects whose dynamics might influence individuals' behavior in teams. This paper frames in a wider research project that will involve a cross-methodological approach mixing qualitative and quantitative analysis, on one side, and experimental and on-field data collection on the other. We posed the bases of this ambitious path in this paper, in which we presented the design of the experiment to study trust and control of digital natives and we discusses some preliminary results form data collected through the pilot section. This experiment, based on a modified version of the trust game, is aimed at working as a first step in the research program.

With the current step of the research we were able to design and test our experimental research protocol, and to fine-tune the experiments that we will run. We were also able to collect some observations to investigate three research questions, but these results shall be considered as exploratory, as larger samples shall be analyzed to draw conclusions on the trust and control dynamics of digital natives and immigrants that we have been investigating.

Further steps will consist on collecting data and analysing results of experimental sections to be run. Furthermore, after data collection and analysis future investigations will allow for deeper studies on what kind of differences exist and how their dynamics work (i.e. how to possibly manipulate these dynamics to enhance team cooperation when digital natives are involved).

References

1. Braccini, A.M., Federici, T.: A Measurement model for investigating digital natives and their organisational behaviour. In: Proceedings of the 2013 International Conference on Information Systems (ICIS 2013), Milano (2013)
2. McMahon, M., Pospisil, R.: Laptops for a digital lifestyle: millennial students and wireless mobile technologies. In: Proceedings of Ascilite Conference, pp. 421–431, Brisbane, Australia (2005)
3. Prensky, M.: Digital natives, digital immigrants. Horizon **9**, 1–6 (2001)
4. Tapscott, D.: Growing up digital: the rise of the net generation. McGraw-Hill, New York (1998)
5. Zimerman, M.: Digital natives, searching behavior and the library. New Libr. World **113**, 174–201 (2012)
6. Prensky, M.: Digital natives, digital immigrants, part II: do they really think differently? Horizon **9**, 1–9 (2001)
7. Howe, N., Strauss, W.: Millennials Rising: The Next Great Generation. Vintage, New York (2000)
8. Valkenburg, P.M., Peter, J.: Adolescents' identity experiments on the internet: consequences for social competence and self-concept unity. Commun. Res. **35**, 208–231 (2008)
9. Bennett, S., Maton, K., Kervin, L.: The "digital natives" debate: a critical review of the evidence. Br. J. Educ. Technol. **39**, 775–786 (2008)
10. Braccini, A.M.: Does ICT influence organizational behaviour? an investigation of digital natives leadership potential. In: Spagnoletti, P. (ed.) Organization Change and Information Systems—Working and Living Together in New Ways, pp. 11–19. Springer, Berlin, Heidelberg (2013)
11. Helsper, E.J., Enyon, R.: Digital natives: where is the evidence? Br. Educ. Res. J. **36**, 503–520 (2010)
12. Vodanovich, S., Sundaram, D., Myers, M.: Digital natives and ubiquitous information systems. Inf. Syst. Res. **21**, 711–723 (2010)
13. Orlikowski, W.J., Robey, D.: Information technology and the structuring of organizations. Inf. Syst. Res. **2**, 143–169 (1992)
14. Smith, K.T.: Work-life balance perspectives of marketing professionals in generation Y. Serv. Mark. Q. **31**, 434–447 (2010)
15. Cahill, T.F., Sedrak, M.: Leading a multigenerational workforce: strategies for attracting and retaining millennials. Front. Health Serv. Manage. **29**, 3–16 (2011)
16. Goleman, D.: What makes a leader? Harv. Bus. Rev. **82**, 82–91 (2004)
17. Schewe, C.D.C.D., Debevec, K.K., Madden, T.J.T.J., Diamond, W.D.W.D., Parment, A.A., Murphy, A.: "If you've seen one, you've seen them all!" are young millennials the same worldwide? J. Int. Consum. Mark. **25**, 3–15 (2013)

18. Marzo, F., Castelfranchi, C.: Trust as individual asset in a network: a cognitive analysis. In: Spagnoletti, P. (ed.) Organization Change and Information Systems, LNISO, vol. 2. pp. 167–175. Springer, Heidelberg (2013)
19. Castelfranchi, C., Falcone, R.: Trust Theory: A Socio-Cognitive and Computational Model. Wiley, Chichester, UK, UK (2010)
20. Luhmann, N.: Familiarity, confidence, trust: problems and alternatives. In: Gambetta, D. (ed.) Trust: Making and Breaking Cooperative Relations, electronic edn, pp. 94–107. Blackwell Publishers Ltd, Oxford, UK (2000)
21. Marzo, F., Braccini, A.M.: Information, technology, and trust: a cognitive approach to digital natives and digital immigrants studies. In: Rossignoli, C., Gatti, M., Agrifoglio, R. (eds.) Managing Information and Technology for Organizational Innovation and Change. Springer (2015)
22. Castelfranchi, C.: The theory of social functions: challenges for computational social science and multi-agent learning. Cogn. Syst. Res. **2**, 5–38 (2001)
23. Brandts, J., Fernanda Rivas, M.: On punishment and well-being. J. Econ. Behav. Organ. **72**, 823–834 (2009)
24. Bohnet, I., Benedikt, H., Al-Ississ, M., Robbett, A., Al-Yahya, K., Zeckhauser, R.: The elasticity of trust: how to promote trust in the arab middle east and the united states. In: Kramer, R.M., Pittinsky, T.L. (eds.) Restoring Trust in Organizations and Leaders: Enduring Challenges and Emerging Answers. Oxford University Press, Oxford (2012)
25. Berg, J., Dickhaut, J., McCabe, K.: Trust, reciprocity, and social history. Games Econ. Behav. **10**, 122–142 (1995)
26. Hendriks, A.: SoPHIE—Software Platform for Human Interaction Experiments (2012)

Part II
Crossing the Organizational Boundaries

The Exploitation of Web Navigation Data: Ethical Issues and Alternative Scenarios

Luca Vassio, Hassan Metwalley and Danilo Giordano

1 Introduction

Nowadays, almost everybody use the World Wide Web for different reasons, such as looking for news and products, accessing social networks and organizing their lives. Also in a business environment, most of the companies can not run their business without exploiting the web. For these reasons, the content that a user is consulting on the web can be classified as sensitive personal information, either if the user is a company or a private person. Thanks to the design of the web, many entities can access, partially or totally, these sensitive information. Internet Service Providers (ISPs), online services, social networks and trackers usually store as much information as possible about the users.

The data that are collected can be used in many ways: ISPs could use these information to improve their network and the quality of their services; scientists and researchers could use these data to design new services or for understanding web social implications; advertisement companies could profile users to give them specific ads; criminals could steal identities or bank information; police and public agencies could find proofs and incriminate people; companies could know what their employees are doing and decide whether to hire someone or to fire someone else.

It is clear from this partial list that the exploitation of users' web navigation data is a very complex and delicate topic, where laws are still not comprehensive and many entities are not even aware of the current scenario.

L. Vassio (✉) · H. Metwalley (✉) · D. Giordano (✉)
Dipartimento di Elettronica e Telecomunicazioni, Politecnico di Torino, Turin, Italy
e-mail: luca.vassio@polito.it

H. Metwalley
e-mail: hassan.metwalley@polito.it

D. Giordano
e-mail: danilo.giordano@polito.it

© Springer International Publishing Switzerland 2016   119
F. D'Ascenzo et al. (eds.), *Blurring the Boundaries Through Digital Innovation*,
Lecture Notes in Information Systems and Organisation 19,
DOI 10.1007/978-3-319-38974-5_10

The reminder of this paper is structured as follow: in Sect. 2 we identify and deeply explain the role of all the stakeholders in the current scenario, highlighting the connections among them. In Sect. 3 we present the ethical issues that arise for the different groups of entities. In Sect. 4 we suggest some alternative scenarios, suggesting to the different entities how they could behave and some possible counter-measures to avoid improper use of users' sensitive data. Finally, some concluding remarks are presented in Sect. 5.

2   The Stakeholders Network in the Current Scenario

The *stakeholders network* has been proposed [1] as a powerful tool for analyzing and reasoning about the difficult choices within an ICT scenario. The simple construction of this network is already a good help to identify conflicts between stakeholders and missing relationships usually not considered into the specific studied landscape. The *stakeholders network* for the web navigation data scenario is presented in Fig. 1. We will explain all the key actors of the network, as well as the connections between them.

The actors in the scenario are called *entities* and can be grouped in different families, based on the role they play.

The first group of entity is the *users* family, depicted with green background in Fig. 1. The users are the part of the network that generates data by browsing on the web; therefore they are the entities that are potentially more exposed to risks. This dangerous position is often followed by an unawareness of such risks. Indeed, as we

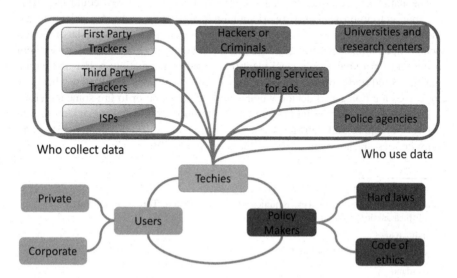

Fig. 1 The stakeholders network involved in producing, collecting, using and controlling the web navigation data

will explain later, only a small percentage of users use some techniques to protect their data. Users family can be further divided into two entities: *private* and *corporate*. Private users generate traffic for personal reasons, e.g., web surfing, entertainment or gaming. These users do not wish to disclose their data both for privacy and for security reasons; for example, they would not to share personal interests or banking information. Corporate users, instead, generate traffic for business reasons: security of these data should be fundamental for companies to avoid industrial espionage like market analysis and information about new projects.

The second group of entities is the one that could access the data, represented in yellow in Fig. 1. Within this family, each entity has a different view of the data and owns them for different reasons.

The first entity is composed by the *Internet Service Providers* (*ISPs*). They give to the users the physical access to the network, therefore an ISP receive all traffic from its users. As a consequence, ISPs are the entities that can see everything about users behaviour, except for the encrypted traffic, i.e., HTTPS.

Secondly, there are the so called *First Party Trackers*. This entity is composed by service providers, such as: *Google*, and *Facebook*. They receive some users' data directly from the users in order to receive a particular service. For example, an internaut that contacts *YouTube* to retrieve a video has to send the information about the video that wish to stream in order to watch it.

The most active, and controversial entry of this group of entities is composed by the *Third Party Trackers*. These services are embedded into the websites and are not directly linked to the original source being asked. They monetize visits and, in practice, collect users' personal information. Trackers use many solutions to identify users, ranging from storing cookies on the user's browser to tracking techniques that fingerprint users across several web sites [2–4]. Googles DoubleClick, and Yahoo YieldManager are notable examples. However, the list of companies that build their business around information collection is of the order of several hundreds of entries. A recent work based on passive measures [5], counted more than 400 active online tracking services. With 100 of them being regularly contacted by more than 50 % of users, and the most pervasive ones that are impossible to avoid. In addition, in this work the authors demonstrates that 77 % of users faced the first tracker just 1 s after starting their online web activity. This demonstrates that this phenomenon is enormously popular and it involves all Internet users.

The third group in the stakeholders network is composed by entities that wish to use users' data, depicted in blue in Fig. 1. Inside of this family there are either entities that could be legitimate to use some users' data, either others that wish to exploit them for malicious activities. As we can see from Fig. 1, this family includes all the three entities that can directly collect users' data (ISPs, First, and Third Party Trackers).

Nowadays, as explained before, ISPs have the best position to collect users' data. However, even if they have such a privileged position, they exploit them only for few operations. Currently, due to the birth of Software Defined Network (SDN), ISPs start offering new services which can heavily exploit private data. Before this scenario, ISPs already exploited users' data to extract some information to improve the users' Quality of Experience (QoE). An example is given by the so called *transparent caching* or *transparent proxy* [6]. ISPs try to understand what are the most popular content requested in their network in order to cache such contents inside some of their servers. By applying this technique, ISPs can provide smaller latency for such contents, therefore improving users' QoE. Clearly, this solution allows ISPs to save money as well. Indeed, storing contents inside of their servers is cheaper with respect to send the requests via other networks. In fact, ISPs have a non-marginal cost for sending data through networks not directly owned by them.

First Party Trackers use private information to provide some services. In addition to the needed informations, they also collect other data like cookies to allow users' login, or to remember the basket in case of e-commerce websites. However, they could also exploit such information to improve their services, targeting them to a specific subset of users. For instance, many websites target specific e-mails for advertisement of their products or services on the basis of the users' interest shown in their website.

The third party trackers are the most ambiguous since they base their business directly on the collection of personal information. Information that can be extracted either implicitly, either explicitly from the users' web browsing activity. These companies directly use the data and could also sell them. This phenomenon is ubiquitous, with all major players and hundreds of mostly unknown companies taking part in it. The research community has focused on disclosing and quantifying the vastness of this problem [2, 3, 5, 7], but proposing just few solutions [8, 9].

As a matter of facts, profiling services are fundamental for marketing purposes, e.g., knowing products browsed on a shopping website, online newspapers usually read or movies liked. These information are used to deliver customized ads for the specific user. First and third party tracker themselves, other than companies that specifically buy these information, usually exploit the data for this purpose.

Another important usage of such data are police agencies and authorities: as a matter of fact in many cases they access these data for mass surveillance. Despite this practice can be positive, as it could improve the safety of people, in many cases the authorities have overstated, taking too much information for the original purposes.[1,2] An important public example of such trend is reported by Google with the Google *Transparency Report*.[3] Indeed, by visiting this report page, it is possible to discover how many information have been requested by government agencies and how many of them have been actually disclosed by Google.

---

[1]The NSA Leaks Are About Democracy, Not Just Privacy, http://www.theatlantic.com/politics/archive/2014/01/the-nsa-leaks-are-about-democracy-not-just-privacy/282902/.

[2]Man behind NSA leaks says he did it to safeguard privacy, liberty, http://edition.cnn.com/2013/06/10/politics/edward-snowden-profile.

[3]https://www.google.com/transparencyreport/.

Also researchers in companies and universities are interested in using such data for improving the knowledge in different topics by applying data-mining and statistical techniques [10]. For example, researchers studies can be useful to find the social implications of the Web or for designing better technologies to surf the web.

Last but not least, since these data are stored somewhere in data clusters, criminals could break these systems and steal huge amount of personal data. These information can illegally be used to steal identities, bank information,[4] or passwords.[5] A historical important case of malicious activity is related to a doctor who sold a list of almost 4,000 HIV patients due to a grudge against his company.[6]

The last group of entities in the stakeholders networks consists in the policy makers, depicted in red in Fig. 1. Hard laws are mandatory policies with legal values. In this family fall UE and US government laws, as well as regional ones. Soft laws are instead the ones that are not enforced and are related to ethical issues: computer engineers, as well as general users and companies, have their own code of ethics and privacy policies.

3   Ethical and Social Implications: Open Questions

As described by Walter Maner about twenty years ago [11], the use of computing technology creates, and will create, novel ethical issues that require specific studies. In this section will be presented some ethical issues and social implications that arise for the different groups of entities introduced in Sect. 2. We will arise some open questions, that do not have strict and definitive answers. Later on, in Sect. 4 we will give some advices to address these questions.

The ethical issues implicated in the users' web data usage belong the following two domains:

1. **Privacy:** data related to navigation history are certainly confidential and sensitive. Therefore, is it possible to use and store users' navigation data without violating their privacy? How the different entities should behave in order to respect this fundamental right?
2. **Computer crimes:** hackers can use their skills to access the stored data for malicious activities. Thus, how can entities protect these data and be sure not to put in danger users? For how long entities should store users' data?

---

[4]Bank Hackers Steal Millions via Malware, http://www.nytimes.com/2015/02/15/world/bank-hackers-steal-millions-via-malware.html?_r=0.

[5]LinkedIn investigating reports that 6.46 million hashed passwords have leaked online, http://www.theverge.com/2012/6/6/3067523/linkedin-password-leak-online.

[6]Man convicted of breaking patient confidentiality, http://www.ahcmedia.com/articles/38091-man-convicted-of-breaking-patient-confidentiality.

As we saw before, each entity has different reasons to save and use users' data. Despite of the reasons, the first questions are related on the way they obtained the data: did they receive an explicit or an implicit user's consent, to store and save data? Was the user aware of being tracked? Many times the answer to both question is simple: the user was not conscious of the situation, therefore he did not give any consent at all. This is often true even in presence of an explicitly form that aware the user of the data collection. For instance, many websites present policy terms to the users that have to be explicitly accepted. However, often users do not even read these forms, since they look standards, they are long, and not easily understandable. Moreover, most of the time the user has the perception to be constrained in order to receive the service he is interested in. As a result, how can an entity be ethically legitimate to record users' data?

Starting from these points several other questions arise for the different entities.

- Should entities collecting users' data share them with other entities? In the case that the second entity is a state police agency that wish to use such data to prove a crime, is the answer the same? Even in the case where such police agency is not of the same country of the entity? In an extreme case, if in the police agency country there is the death penalty for the crime committed, what will be ethical? What should the involved entities do?
- Many companies use users' data to profile users for advertisement goals. How deep can they go into the profiling? Is there a limit due to privacy? In this case, where is this limit and who choose it? For example, is it legitimate to send advertisements related to the health-care of a person?
- Universities and research centres desire to use as much data as they can, to be able to perform better studies. However, is it fair that they could see personal data? Who can access the database where the data are stored? For what exact purpose? For example, is it an acceptable goal to study specific users' interests?
- A global network such as the internet makes usual physical boundaries obsolete. How can regional hard laws face trackers that are outside their jurisdiction? How can the freedom and anarchy of the web be balanced with a centralized regional control?

These are only a limited part of the possible questions that arise by analyzing the current internet scenario, for which fair definitive answers do not exist. However, we hope that by just proposing these questions, we can stimulate a debate between the parties that are involved in today internet network.

4 Present and Future Possible Alternative Scenarios

In Sect. 3 we identified the ethical issues related to users' web navigation data. We will now see what kind of advices and suggestions we can give to the entities of the stakeholders network presented in Fig. 1.

4.1 Users

An internet user cannot avoid to use an ISP to access the internet. However, not all the ISPs are equal. A user has the possibility, at least, to take a look at the specific ISP policy before starting a new contract. Moreover new ISPs that want to make customer privacy their top priority are emerging.[7]

Similarly, a user cannot simply block first-party trackers. However, if a user wants to still have a specific kind of service, he has the choice of moving to alternative service providers. For search engines, a possibility would be to use search engines that do not track and log any personally identifiable information. For example, DuckDuckGo[8] does not use cookies to identify users, and it discards user agents and IP addresses from its logs. Moreover it does not even generate anonymized identifier to tie searches together. Therefore, the search engine has no way of knowing whether two searches even came from the same computer and you will get the same results as everyone else in the world. If a user still prefer Googles search results, it can be possible to use services such as Startpage.[9] This service submits your search to Google and returns the results to you. In this case, Google sees a large amount of searches coming from Startpage servers, without knowing who originally requests each content. Whether these approaches ensure your privacy, you will never have personalized search based on your interests.

The are many possible counter-measures to avoid third party trackers to collect your data. The privacy-conscious users have easily available many privacy-enhancer browser plugins. These plugins are actually the most used protection from the tracking services. They automatically block the transmission of user's identifying information, depending on the user's willingness. This type of software is directly installable into web browsers and permits user to easily modify traffic, i.e. disabling cookie sending or part of javascript page, or drastically block communications to certain web services. However, these solutions is ineffective for traffic generated out of browsers (e.g., mobile application) and, additionally, the diffusion of these solutions are surprisingly very limited, as shown by Metwalley et al. [5]. Despite end-users' concerns about privacy largely increased, motivated also by exposed government surveillance programs, Internet user does not fully grasp the extent and seriousness of the problem. To this end, a common misconception is that encryption of the web would help protecting users' privacy. Accordingly, HTTPS usage increased by 100 % each year, reaching about 50 % of web flows in October 2014 [12]. In reality, encryption increases the value of data for third party trackers. Web services that deploy encryption establish a monopoly on information by precluding any other parties from exploiting it. Moreover, HTTPS prevents third parties and malicious users to check and possibly control what kind of data is

---

[7]New ISP To Make Customer Privacy Its Top Priority, http://www.themarysue.com/privacy-first-isp.

[8]https://duckduckgo.com/.

[9]https://startpage.com/.

exchanged. Another possible solution for the user would be the so-called *Do Not Track HTTP header.*[10] It is an encouraging initiative that allows users to opt out of tracking by advertising networks and analytics services. With this solution the user can choose to turn on the field in his browser, that automatically sends a special signal to the web sites telling that the user would not like to be tracked. The main problem of this solution is that, currently, there is no consensus on how the companies you encounter should interpret the *Do Not Track header.* As a result, most sites do not currently change their behaviour, with few sites supporting this solution.[11]

4.2 Hard Laws

The governments started recently to address the privacy and crime implications of the web navigation data. In 2011 the European Union [13] stated that the web navigation data shall be obtained and processed fairly. This principle generally requires that a person whose data are processed to be aware of at least the following information:

- the identity of the person who is processing the data;
- the purpose or purposes for which the data are processed;
- any third party to whom the data may be disclosed;
- the existence of a right of access and a right of rectification.

Another interesting initiative of European Union is the *Cookie Law.*[12] Thanks to this legislation, the websites must request consent from visitors to store or retrieve any information on a computer, smartphone or tablet. From June 2015 any website available to European visitors that uses cookies or any other technologies for non-essential tracking must:

1. inform users that tracking technologies are used;
2. explain the reasons for using those technologies;
3. obtain the users consent prior to using that technology and allow them to withdraw permission at any time.

While cookies are an obvious target, the law applies to all client-side technologies used to identify an individual. Additionally, user's consent must involve communication where the individual consciously indicates their acceptance, e.g., by clicking an icon or check box. The only exceptions are sites where tracking is strictly necessary for the provision of a service or communication requested by the user. Shopping baskets, some online applications and client-side caching to

---

[10]http://donottrack.us/.

[11]http://allaboutdnt.com/.

[12]The Cookie Law Explained, http://www.cookielaw.org/the-cookie-law/.

improve page speed would not require authorization. Instead, sites using analytics, advertising or customized greetings must comply.

In this context, an important problem is the difference, in terms of laws, between the European Union and the United States.[13] As a matter of fact, while the EU is trying to realize a set of laws dedicated to privacy, in the US the privacy regulation is based on a self-regulatory approach, where companies provide privacy notices that make certain promises about privacy. If these promises are violated, the *Federal Trade Commission* (FTC) might penalize the company. But this power generally extends only to the promises made, so a company can determine how stringently it wants to protect privacy by modulating the promises it makes. In many instances, people are given only a right to opt out of certain uses of their data, and often no right at all to limit the collection of data about themselves by certain companies. In the EU, the rules regarding individual consent for data collection, use, and disclosures are much stricter, and much more affirmative consent is required. Fortunately, United States government has started to collaborate with EU with the goal to improve users' privacy, and the first result of this cooperation are the *International Safe Harbor Privacy Principles.*[14] These principles forbid to transfer personal data to non-European Union countries that do not meet the European Union Directive on the protection of personal data. The aims of these principles are the protection of personal data from accidental information disclosure or loss. This task represents the first step of a process that could lead to a common lawmaking with the aim of stopping, from the point of view of hard laws, the private information leakage.

4.3 Researchers and Computer Scientists

Computer professionals should follow an ethical code while dealing with personal information. The most famous ones are the IEEE and ACM code of ethics.[15,16] In addition to these general-purpose code of ethics, recently the Oxford University propose a set of guidelines for measurement projects regarding privacy [14]. However, the problem in this scenario is not simple since researchers and engineers must face two challenges: anonymize the data used during the research and study the services that steal private information.

Regarding the first problem, some researchers [15, 16] suggested different solutions to anonymize data, while maintaining only the information that could be useful for research purpose. However, it can be very difficult to predict if in the future

---

[13]Differences between the privacy laws in the EU and the US, http://resources.infosecinstitute.com/differences-privacy-laws-in-eu-and-us/.

[14]Safe Harbor Frameworks, http://www.export.gov/safeharbor/.

[15]IEEE code of ethics, http://www.ieee.org/about/corporate/governance/p7-8.html.

[16]ACM code of ethics, http://www.acm.org/about/code-of-ethics and www.acm.org/about/se-code.

records in supposedly anonymized datasets will be re-identified. In general, a scientist should modify and present data that are not privacy invasive. It may be possible to find a compromise in which some level of aggregation and pre-processing to de-identify the data takes place before a dataset is collected and stored.

On the other side, research community is currently searching a way to solve privacy problems together with companies and institutions, maintaining the economic ecosystem created around usage of users' information. Recently Telefonica, one of the most important private telecommunications companies in the world, have started an initiative called *Data Transparency Lab*.[17] This is a collaborative effort between universities, businesses and institutions to support research in tools, data, and methodologies for shedding light on the use of personal data by online services, and to empower users to be in control of their personal data. This initiative represents a first example of how the research community can really solve privacy problems in this field.

5   Conclusions

In this paper we have discussed, from a high-level point of view, ethical issues and social implications related to the users' web navigation data. We showed that in the current scenario many entities collect, store, and use these information, affecting the users' privacy. We presented that some entities might be legitimate to access these data, e.g., researchers or police agency, while other should not have any access at all, e.g., malicious hackers. However, since people will give even more importance to the web in the near future and the web will be more pervasive in everyday life, the ethical implications could even enlarge their effects. We have shown some alternative scenarios and some countermeasures to mitigate the problems that arise. Firstly, users should be really aware of how their data are used and how they could improve their privacy. Secondly, policy makers are slowly trying to regulate these phenomena, but they should be capable of fast interventions. Finally, even scientists and engineers should put their force to make these data harmless for the users, carefully evaluating the implications of the data usage for their projects.

References

1. Gotterbarn, D., Rogerson, S.: Responsible risk analysis for software development: creating the software development impact statement. Commun. Assoc. Inform. Syst. (2005)
2. Acar, G., Eubank, C., Englehardt, S., Juarez, M., Narayanan, A., Diaz, C.: The web never forgets: persistent tracking mechanisms in the wild. In: ACM SIGSAC (2014)

---

[17]Data Transparency Lab, http://datatransparencylab.org/.

3. Krishnamurthy, B., Naryshkin, K., Wills, C.E.: Privacy leakage vs. protection measures: the growing disconnect. In: W2SP (2011)
4. Rezgui, A., Bouguettaya, A., Eltoweissy, M.: Privacy on the web: facts, challenges, and solutions. IEEE Secur. Privacy (2003)
5. Metwalley, H., Traverso, S., Mellia, M., Miskovic, S., Baldi, M.: The online tracking horde: a view from passive measurements. In: TMA (2015)
6. Blum, S., Lueker, J.: Transparent proxy server (2001) US Patent 6,182,141
7. Yen, T.F., Xie, Y., Yu, F., Yu, R.P., Abadi, M.: Host fingerprinting and tracking on the web: privacy and security implications. In: NDSS (2012)
8. Agarwal, Y., Hall, M.: ProtectMyPrivacy: Detecting and mitigating privacy leaks on iOS devices using crowdsourcing. In: ACM MobiSys (2013)
9. Enck, W., Gilbert, P., Chun, B.G., Cox, L.P., Jung, J., McDaniel, P., Sheth, A.N.: TaintDroid: An information-flow tracking system for realtime privacy monitoring on smartphones. In: USENIX OSDI (2010)
10. Kosala, R., Blockeel, H.: Web mining research: a survey. ACM Sigkdd Explorations Newsletter (2000)
11. Maner, W.: Unique ethical problems in information technology. In: ETHICOMP95, Leicester, UK (1995)
12. Naylor, D., Finamore, A., Leontiadis, I., Grunenberger, Y., Mellia, M., Papagiannaki, K., Steenkiste, P.: The cost of the "S" in HTTPS. In: ACM CoNEXT (2014)
13. European Communities Regulations 2011, Electronic Communications Network and Services, Privacy and Electronic Communications. Statutory Instruments. S.I. No. 336 of 2011. https://www.dataprotection.ie/documents/legal/SI336of2011.pdf
14. Zevenbergen, B.: Ethical privacy guidelines for mobile connectivity measurements. Oxford Internet Institute, University of Oxford, http://www.themarysue.com/privacy-first-isp
15. Chaudhuri, K., Mishra, N.: When random sampling preserves privacy. In Dwork, C., (ed.) Advances in Cryptology—CRYPTO 2006, Volume 4117 of Lecture Notes in Computer Science. Springer Berlin Heidelberg (2006)
16. Fan, J., Xu, J., Ammar, M.H., Moon, S.B.: Prefix-Preserving IP Address Anonymization: Measurement-Based Security Evaluation and a New Cryptography-Based Scheme. Computer Networks (2004)

Citizens' Health Information Privacy Concerns: Developing a Framework

Grace Kenny and Regina Connolly

1 Introduction

Patient privacy has been a vital component of healthcare delivery for centuries. Indeed, the importance of privacy is explicitly expressed in the Hippocratic Oath. Doctors around the world pledging this oath have promised to "respect the privacy of my patients, for their problems are not disclosed to me that the world may know" [27]. For centuries, this promise meant that doctors would not share the information disclosed to them with any other party. However, the meaning of privacy is changing due to the increasing prevalence of health IT solutions. On one hand, there has been huge growth in health professionals' use of systems such as electronic health records (EHRs). These technologies enable health professionals to create, store, and maintain electronic patient health records [3]. EHRs facilitate the seamless updating and transfer of patient data. On the other hand, the recent emergence of mobile health (m-health) technologies empowers individuals to monitor anything from fitness, to chronic illness [13]. The increasingly popular practice of using m-health solutions to monitor one's personal health requires the individual to disclose health information ranging from demographics, to health history and health conditions, while also automatically tracking health indicators such as steps taken. In many cases, the technology vendor offering the application shares this user data with a host of third parties. For example, a recent Federal Trade Commission report found that the 12 m-health applications reviewed had shared user data with 76 third parties [17].

G. Kenny (✉) · R. Connolly
Business School, Dublin City University, Dublin, Ireland
e-mail: grace.kenny2@mail.dcu.ie

R. Connolly
e-mail: regina.connolly@dcu.ie

© Springer International Publishing Switzerland 2016
F. D'Ascenzo et al. (eds.), *Blurring the Boundaries Through Digital Innovation*,
Lecture Notes in Information Systems and Organisation 19,
DOI 10.1007/978-3-319-38974-5_11

131

The premise of health technologies is to improve the information available to physicians and citizens, which results in the flow of sensitive health data among numerous third parties [33]. With the role of these technologies in healthcare forecast to grow, what does this mean for privacy? This paper seeks to develop a framework for understanding citizens' health information privacy concerns and the drivers of these concerns. The paper proceeds by outlining the growth of health technologies and their influence on privacy, followed by a review of the existing literature. Based on the gaps identified in the literature and the integration of varying views of privacy, we present a framework for examining citizens' health information privacy.

1.1 Changing Privacy Landscape: The Rise of Health Technologies

Health technologies used by both health professionals and citizens are becoming increasingly popular. By 2012, 78 % of physicians in the U.S. had implemented EHRs [48]. Countries such as Estonia and England have implemented EHRs on a national scale and countries such as Ireland have announced plans to implement EHRs [12]. In terms of m-health technologies, 19 % of adults in the U.S. utilized at least one m-health application in 2012 [16]. By 2013, there were approximately 97,000 m-health applications available worldwide on leading app stores [43]. While there are no statistics indicative of the use of these applications in European countries, an estimated 500 million people worldwide used m-health applications in 2015 [39]. In addition to these applications, wearable health tracking devices provided by companies such as FitBit and Jawbone, are gaining huge traction. Individuals wear these devices to track health indicators such as steps taken, sleep quality, and heart rate. Individuals can then monitor these indicators over time using a dashboard based mobile application. By 2013, 17 million wearable devices had been sold, a Tractica report estimates that this will reach 187 million by 2020 [34].

As noted, the continual growth of both EHRs and m-health solutions stimulates copious flows of health information between different health professionals, between individual citizens and technology vendors, and from technology vendors to a variety of third parties. With the increased quantity and expanded reach of health information, the meaning of privacy in this context changes. However, while the increasing prevalence of technology in many ways reduces the level of privacy automatically afforded to individuals, it does not mean privacy is no longer important in this context. In contrast, it is argued that privacy remains a pertinent issue in the health context, which must be understood and addressed. There is a great deal of support for this assertion. Firstly, health information is widely viewed as sensitive or personal. In a recent study, 93 % of Irish citizens described their health information as personal or the information they desire to protect most [14]. Secondly, many studies have found that individuals express high concerns regarding the privacy of their health information in technologies such as EHRs [9, 25]. Thirdly, privacy is viewed as a fundamental driver of health IT success or failure [12].

So how does privacy relate to EHRs and m-health technologies? To date, a number of studies have investigated the influence of factors such as privacy, on health professionals' acceptance of EHRs [20, 30, 49]. However, citizen acceptance has received little exploration. Despite this, it is widely agreed that citizen acceptance of EHRs is paramount to their success. Furthermore, citizens' privacy concerns have been described as the biggest barrier to this acceptance [8]. One study found that privacy concerns reduced individuals' intentions to accept EHRs [3]. This study supports the relevance of citizens' privacy concerns. There is a need for further research to explore citizens' concerns and the factors driving concern. Due to their recent emergence, there is an unsurprising paucity of studies exploring citizens' privacy concerns regarding m-health solutions. However, many authors have stated that privacy represents a barrier to the success of m-health technologies [11, 33, 53]. Evidently, privacy is an important factor, which warrants further exploration to understand citizens' health information privacy concerns in greater depth, and to elucidate the factors influencing these concerns.

2 Information Privacy

2.1 Defining Information Privacy

Privacy has been an issue of enduring concern across a wide variety of disciplines and throughout history. In this paper, the emphasis is on information privacy, a subset of the overall privacy concept [5]. Conversations among members of the public, increased presence in government policy and research around information privacy can be traced back to the 1960s [44]. In recent decades, privacy has garnered a great deal of attention across various academic disciplines. Despite the abundance of discussion and the myriad of attempts to define information privacy, an accepted, unambiguous definition remains lacking. Indeed, contrasting views within the same discipline are often found and critique can be presented for the majority of leading views. For instance, in the legal discipline the prevailing definition dates back to 1890 with Warren and Brandeis describing privacy as maintaining the balance between an 'individual's right to be let alone' and the information needs of society [50]. The minority view in the legal discipline refutes this view by countering that existing tort laws encompass what is described as the right to privacy [40]. In arguing against this view, Moore states that these torts share a commonality in that they are each concerned with the control of personal information [32]. While questions remain regarding the ideal amount of privacy to be legally afforded to citizens, the consensus agrees that there is a need to balance the privacy needs of the individual with the greater need of society and the information needs of organizations and governments [21].

Two leading authors in the realms of Psychology and Sociology, Altman and Westin describe privacy in terms of limiting disclosure of information about oneself, and limiting access to oneself [1, 51]. The primary criticism of the views presented by Altman and Westin is the assumption that one can control access to information about themselves and the flow of this information. Given the prevalence of technology in all aspects of life today including health, this assumption no longer holds. In recent decades, another view of privacy has emerged. Privacy economics argues that information privacy is a commodity which individuals are willing to sell or trade in return for benefits [7]. This view assumes that individuals can fully comprehend the benefits and risks of forfeiting their privacy and again that individuals have this ability to control disclosure. Within the Management Information Systems (MIS) discipline a number of definitions also exist. One of the leading conceptualizations is provided by Bélanger and Crossler [5] who build on the assertions of Clarke [10] and define privacy as an individual's desire to control how their personal information is collected and disseminated. The majority of studies in the Medical Informatics domain examining privacy do not offer a new definition of privacy nor do they adapt an existing definition. Furthermore many of these studies fail to adequately differentiate privacy from similar but distinct concepts such as security and confidentiality [45].

It is often argued that a universally accepted, unambiguous conceptualization of information privacy cannot be attained, due to the varying perspectives from which the concept is examined [35]. This paper does not seek to present an all-encompassing definition of privacy but draws from the views of various disciplines to present a comprehensive definition for the context of health information. Privacy is described here as individuals' desire to be afforded greater control over the collection, use, and dissemination of their personal health information [23]. This conceptualization draws predominately on the definition provided by Bélanger and Crossler [5] as this definition is comprehensive and does not assume individuals can exercise control. The primary differences in the definition presented here include the focus on personal health information, and the phrase 'desire to be afforded control', this follows views in the legal discipline regarding balancing individual views with the greater needs of the society or the organization in question. It is argued that individuals want to feel like they have more control than they currently are afforded, as opposed to complete control, as the majority of individuals understand complete control is not obtainable. This definition integrates privacy descriptions from the literature in the disciplines of Law, Psychology, and MIS to define privacy in the context of health information.

2.2 Examining Information Privacy

Across the plethora of information privacy studies spanning various disciplines, the majority of studies tend to examine information privacy from the single perspective of the discipline of the researchers. Thus, the calls for studies to follow a comprehensive approach using a multidisciplinary lens remain largely unanswered [37, 46]. This problem prevails across all academic disciplines concerned with understanding privacy. Upon conducting a review of the information privacy literature across several disciplines, Smith et al. [46] developed and presented the APCO framework. They positioned this framework as a guideline for future studies to ensure privacy was comprehensively investigated across any context. APCO requires the exploration of the antecedents to privacy concerns in a given context, the examining of the privacy concerns themselves, and lastly investigating how these concerns influence the outcome of interest [46]. It is argued here that the APCO framework presents a flexible guideline for future privacy studies in several contexts including health. While it is accepted that it may not be possible to develop a comprehensive framework which can be repeated across various contexts to examine privacy, it is proposed that literature in other disciplines can provide insights into which antecedents, dimensions of concern, or outcomes may or may not be relevant in the given context of the study. For example, it is widely agreed that the health status of the individual will influence their concern for the privacy of their health [3]. This is unlikely to be relevant in studies exploring privacy in non-health contexts. Other antecedents may be relevant across multiple contexts, such as trust perceptions which have been shown to influence privacy concern in the context of individual's online information [19], but are also likely to be relevant in the health context [42]. By building upon APCO using a multidisciplinary lens, different antecedents and outcomes can be tested in various contexts, thus building a strong foundation which can be retested and expanded to test the role of privacy in different contexts and situations. The paper continues with a discussion on each element of the APCO framework, prior to presenting the framework developed in this paper.

3 Antecedents: What Drives Concern?

Understanding the antecedents of information privacy concerns can provide the insights necessary to address these concerns [36]. A multitude of antecedents have been explored across a variety of contexts in the existing information privacy literature. Following an extensive review of the literature, Li [29] categorized all antecedents. Based on Li's work and the medical informatics literature, a number of potential antecedents to citizens' health information privacy concerns are presented. It is acknowledged that this list may not be comprehensive, but it provides an initial attempt to encompass both information privacy and medical informatics literature regarding antecedents.

3.1 Individual Characteristics

The role of individual characteristics on information privacy concern has been explored in a number of studies across various contexts. However, individual characteristics have received limited examination in the context of health information privacy. To date, one study has explored the influence of gender on health information privacy concern. This study found that females expressed higher health information privacy concerns [26]. This finding echoes the results in other contexts. While these findings suggest that females are likely to be more concerned regarding the privacy of their health data than males, there is a need for further examination in other countries and using more comprehensive measures of concern. Secondly, older individuals have been found to express higher health information privacy concerns [24, 26]. Again these findings complement findings in other contexts. It can thus be argued that age will have a positive influence on citizens' health information privacy concerns. The influence of education level on information privacy concern has yielded mixed results in other contexts. For example, higher education was associated with lower information privacy concerns in one study [37], but was insignificant in other studies [54]. The influence of education on health information privacy concern has not been explored to date. It would be interesting to explore this relationship to determine whether education level influences citizens' concerns regarding the privacy of their health information. Lastly, it can be argued that the health condition of an individual is likely to influence their health information privacy concern. However, the way in which health conditions influence concern and the direction of this influence remain uncertain. On one hand, it has been argued that individuals with health conditions will be less concerned about privacy, due to the benefits they can gain from physician and personal use of health IT [3]. In support of this view, a recent study found that respondents with chronic illnesses were more willing to share health data [25]. On the other hand, some argue that individuals with health conditions will be more protective of their health information, and will thus express higher privacy concerns. Some findings strengthen this view, showing that individuals with illnesses such as HIV and mental health conditions express higher health information privacy concerns [15]. It is thus argued that different health conditions are likely to influence concern in conflicting ways. Individuals who view their health condition as sensitive or likely to result in stigmatization are likely to express higher concerns than individuals who view their health conditions as chronic but not sensitive.

3.2   Individual Experiences

This section focuses on the influence experience can have on citizens' health information privacy concerns. Firstly, prior experience of privacy invasion has been found to increase information privacy concerns in a number of contexts, including the heath context. For example, a recent study found that past privacy invasion experience had a significant positive influence on health information privacy concern [4]. While further examination is required to confirm this relationship, a positive influence between privacy invasion experience and concern is expected. In other words, individuals who believe their health information has been previously misused are likely to express higher concerns regarding the privacy of this information. Secondly, awareness of privacy related media coverage has been found to impact individuals' information privacy concerns [47]. This relationship has not been examined in the health context to date. However, health technologies attract a large volume of media coverage, which may influence individuals' privacy concerns. It is thus argued that individuals who are aware of privacy media coverage regarding health technologies will be more concerned for the privacy of their personal health data.

3.3 *Individual Perceptions*

Individuals' perceptions are also likely to influence their health information privacy concerns. Firstly, an individual's perception regarding the sensitivity of information has been shown to influence their concerns for the privacy of this information. In the health context, perceived sensitivity of health data has been found to positively influence privacy concerns [4]. There is a need to further explore this relationship but it is posited that individuals who perceive health data to be highly sensitive will express high concerns regarding its privacy. Secondly, perceptions of trust have been found to negatively influence information privacy concerns in various contexts. For example, trust in technology vendors was found to reduce individuals' concerns regarding the privacy of their online data [19]. There is a need to examine the role of trust perceptions in the health context. With regards to health technology vendors such as m-health developers, it is argued that high trust will reduce individuals' health information privacy concerns. Furthermore, trust plays a large role in the relationship between patients and health professionals. It has been argued that trust in health professionals will negatively impact citizens' health information privacy concerns [42]. Thirdly, perceptions of risk, described as individuals' perceptions of the risks associated with providing a certain party with their information, have been found to increase individuals' concerns. Studies have shown that high perceptions of risk are associated with high concerns for one's personal information online [19, 31]. The role of risk perception in the health context has not been investigated to date. However, it is argued that higher perceptions of risks associated with disclosing health data to both health technology vendors and health professionals will be associated with higher health information privacy concerns.

4 Dimensions of Concern

Privacy concern is the central component of the APCO framework. This section addresses the following question: *How can we measure citizens' health information privacy concerns?* Across the various academic disciplines, there are a number of measures of privacy concern. Among these existing measures, there is no agreed upon set of dimensions or factor structure for empirically measuring privacy concerns [19]. While each measure focuses on a different context, is comprised of a different number of dimensions, factor structure, and differs in the naming of dimensions, there are evident similarities across these measures. According to the literature review conducted by Bélanger and Crossler [5], the dominant measures of privacy concern are; Concern for Information Privacy or CFIP, developed to measure individuals' concerns of how an organization uses their personal information [47] and Internet Users' Information Privacy Concerns or IUIPC which aims to measure individuals' information privacy concerns in the online environment [31]. Both measures have been applied to examine privacy concern in a number of contexts. CFIP is comprised of four dimensions; collection of personal data, unauthorized secondary use of data, improper access to data, and errors in data. CFIP has been applied in a larger number of studies than IUIPC [5], with two studies adapting the measure to examine individuals' concerns regarding their health information [3, 28]. IUIPC is formed from three dimensions; collection, control, and awareness. The six dimensions which together form CFIP and IUIPC (collection is included in both) are the most popular dimensions across all measures in the existing literature [19].

The Medical Informatics literature review failed to identify any measures of health information privacy concern. Many studies in this domain measure privacy with one item such as '*Are you concerned for the confidentiality and privacy of your health records?* To which respondents chose from three options: *yes, no, or not sure* [8]. The inclusion of confidentiality within this question obfuscates our understanding of the study's findings, as we cannot separate individuals' concern for confidentiality from their privacy concern. In 2013, Hong and Thong amalgamated the CFIP and IUIPC measures to develop the Internet Privacy Concerns (IPC) measure. It is argued that IPC represents an appropriate measure for examining citizens' HIPC for three reasons. Firstly, it is comprised of the six most popular dimensions in the information privacy literature. Secondly, the measure was empirically tested using four studies. Thirdly, IPC is suitable for inclusion in a nomological network to examine privacy in a comprehensive manner in a given context [19]. The six dimensions of IPC are reviewed at this point to justify their relevance to the health context.

The **Collection** dimension captures an individual's concerns that an organization is collecting and storing a great deal of their personal data [47]. Due to the nature of healthcare, individuals are accustomed to disclosing their personal data to health professionals. However, the storage of this information on connected systems such as EHRs is a recent development, which may cause concern, as health information is viewed as extremely personal to individuals. Furthermore, the practice of using m-health technologies requires the disclosure of personal health information to technology vendors, which individuals are not accustomed to. It is posited that the increasing volume of health data collected and stored electronically will cause concern and thus collection is a dimension relevant to examining citizens' health information privacy concerns.

The **Unauthorized Secondary Use** dimension relates to an individual's fear that their personal data is collected for one purpose and used for additional purposes without obtaining their permission [47]. In the health context, individuals are often less concerned when initially disclosing information due to the trusted relationship between patients and doctors, however when this information is shared with other healthcare providers, concern sets in [2]. Technologies such as EHRs facilitate the sharing of patient data. There are also a myriad of potential uses for health data, many of which pertain to healthcare delivery such as diagnosis and treatment, but many additional uses that individuals may not be comfortable with such as research, insurance premium calculations, marketing and media usage [22]. Data collected in both EHRs and m-health technologies could be used for these purposes. Based on this discussion, it is argued that unauthorized secondary use is pertinent to studying citizens' concern for the privacy of their health data.

The **Improper Access** dimension covers an individual's concerns that organizations do not have adequate measures in place to prevent unauthorized individuals from accessing their personal data [47]. Numerous studies have found that individuals are worried about improper access to their health information by hackers [8], malicious employees [38], or non-health professionals such as legal professionals or insurance companies [41]. Individuals also express concerns regarding the repercussions of such access [15]. Based on this empirical support, it is argued that improper access represents an important aspect of examining citizens' health information privacy concerns.

The **Errors** dimension relates to the individual's concerns that the organization does not have the adequate measures in place to prevent or correct errors in their personal data [47]. Errors in health data can have various repercussions for the individual ranging the prescription of incorrect medication, or incorrect dosage, to societal impacts such as stigmatization based on false information. Past work has shown that the possibility of errors in health information is a concern for individuals, with approximately 65 % of respondents expressing concern that digitization of health information leads to more errors [52]. These fears may not be unfounded. In a study which gave patients access to their EHR, 32 % of respondents found errors in their health data [38]. It is therefore argued that the errors dimension warrants inclusion when investigating citizens' health information privacy concern.

The **Control** dimension covers an individual's concerns that they do not have adequate control over their personal data [31]. Research has shown that individuals express a desire to exercise control over their health data on a granular level by deciding what healthcare providers can access what data [6]. Furthermore, Li and Slee [28] found when patients do not have the ability to exercise some control over their health data, they express higher privacy concerns. It is thus argued that control is a dimension of utmost relevance to studying citizens' health information privacy concerns.

The **Awareness** dimension refers to the individual's concern regarding their lack of awareness of how an organization uses and protects the privacy of their personal information [31]. It has been repeatedly highlighted that individuals are not aware of how their health information is used by health organizations [2, 18]. It has also been found that this lack of awareness can increase privacy concerns [8]. It can be argued that individuals will express high privacy concerns if they feel unaware of how their health information is used by health entities or technology vendors. Therefore awareness is an important dimension when examining citizens' health information privacy concerns.

5 Framework and Conclusion

Based on the previous discussion, a framework for examining the antecedents to citizens' health information privacy concerns and the dimensions of concern is presented below. It is posited that citizens' health information privacy concerns will reduce individuals' acceptance and adoption of health ITs such as EHRs and m-health solutions (Fig. 1).

Health technology solutions present many benefits to both health professionals and citizens. However, these technologies also change the nature of privacy in this context. It is widely accepted that citizens' health information privacy concerns represent a barrier which could hinder the growth of health technologies. In order to address and reduce citizens' health information privacy concerns, these concerns and the factors driving them must be identified and understood. This paper integrates literature from various disciplines to offer a definition of what privacy means in the health context. A number of individual characteristics, experiences, and perceptions are presented as possible antecedents to citizens' health information privacy concerns. A comprehensive six dimensional measure is adapted to measure information privacy concern in this context. Lastly, a framework based on the APCO model for examining information privacy is presented. This framework is empirically tested in an upcoming study. Testing this framework will provide initial insights into the factors driving and reducing citizens' health information privacy

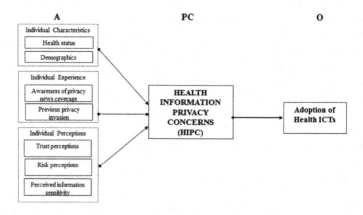

Fig. 1 Framework

concerns, and the relationship between concern and citizen adoption of health technologies. These insights will further our understanding of the role information privacy plays in this context and will strengthen the literature by extending many constructs to the health context. The insights developed can also be leveraged by policymakers, health organizations, and technology vendors for two purposes. Firstly, health technologies can be designed in ways which ensure privacy is maintained and respected. Secondly, they can develop approaches to educate citizens on health technologies in ways which address their information privacy concerns and ensure their acceptance and adoption of these valuable technologies.

References

1. Altman, I.: The Environment and Social Behavior: Privacy, Personal Space, Territory, Crowding. Brooks/Cole, Monterey, CA (1975)
2. Angst, C.: Protect my privacy or support the common-good? Ethical questions about electronic health information exchanges. J. Bus. Ethics 90(2), 169–178 (2006)
3. Angst, C., Agarwal, R.: Adoption of electronic records in the presence of privacy concerns: the elaboration likelihood model and individual persuasion. MIS Q. 33(2), 339–370 (2009)
4. Bansal, G., Zahedi, F.M., Gefen, D.: The impact of personal dispositions on information sensitivity, privacy concern and trust in disclosing health information online. Decis. Support Syst. 49(2), 138–150 (2010)
5. Bélanger, F., Crossler, R.E.: Privacy in the digital age: a review of information privacy research in information systems. MIS Q. 45(4), 1017–1041 (2011)
6. Caine, K., Hanania, R.: Patients want granular privacy control over health information in electronic medical records. J. Am. Med. Inf. Assoc. JAMIA 20(1), 7–15 (2013)
7. Chellappa, R.K., Sin, R.G.: Personalization versus privacy: an empirical examination of the online consumer's dilemma. Inf. Technol. Manage. 6(2–3), 181–202 (2005)
8. Chhanabhai, P., Holt, A.: Consumers are ready to accept the transition to online and electronic records if they can be assured of the security measures. Medscape General Med. 9(1), 8 (2007)
9. Clarke, I., Flaherty, T.B., Hollis, S.M., Tomallo, M.: Consumer privacy issues associated with the use of electronic health records. AHCMJ 5(2), 63–77 (2009)
10. Clarke, R.: Internet privacy concerns confirm the case for intervention. Commun. ACM 42(2), 60–67 (1999)
11. Connelly, K.H., Faber, A.M., Rogers, Y., Siek, K.A., Toscos, T.: Mobile applications that empower people to monitor their personal health. e and i Elektrotechnik und Informationstechnik 123(4), 124–128 (2006)
12. Department of Health.: eHealth strategy for Ireland. http://health.gov.ie/wpcontent/uploads/2014/03/Ireland_eHealth_Strategy.pdf (visited on 02/12/2015) (2013)
13. Eng, D.S., Lee, J.M.: The promise and peril of mobile health applications for diabetes and endocrinology. Pediatr. Diabetes 14(4), 231–238 (2013)
14. Eurobarometer.: Attitudes on Data Protection and Electronic Identity in the European Union. http://ec.europa.eu/public_opinion/archives/ebs/ebs_359_en.pdf (2011). Accessed 22 Mar 2014
15. Flynn, H., Marcus, S., Kerber, K., Alessi, N.: Patients' concerns about and perceptions of electronic psychiatric records. Psychiatr. Serv. 54(11), 1539–1541 (2003)
16. Fox, S., Duggan, M.: Mobile Health 2012. http://www.pewinternet.org/files/old-media//Files/Reports/2012/PIP_MobileHealth2012_FINAL.pdf (2012). Accessed 9th Jun 2014

17. FTC.: Consumer Generated and Controlled Health Data. https://www.ftc.gov/system/files/documents/public_events/195411/privacyseries-healthdata-agenda.pdf (2013). Accessed 10th Jun 2015
18. Goodwin, L. Courtney, K. Kirby, D., Iannacchione, M.A.: A pilot study: Patients' perceptions about the privacy of their medical records. Online J. Nursing Inf. **6**(3) (2002)
19. Hong, W., Thong, J.: Internet privacy concerns: an integrated conceptualisation and four empirical studies. MIS Q. **37**(1), 275–298 (2013)
20. Hsieh, P.-J: Physicians' acceptance of electronic medical records exchange: an extension of the decomposed TPB model with institutional trust and perceived risk. Int. J. Med. Inf. 1–14 (2014)
21. Hughes, K.: A behavioural understanding of privacy and its implications for privacy law. Modern Law Rev. **75**(5), 806–836 (2012)
22. Järvinen, O.P.: Privacy management of patient-centered e-health. In: Wilson, E.V. (ed.) Patient-Centered E-Health, pp. 81–97. PA IGI Global, Hershey (2009)
23. Kenny, G., Connolly, R.: Citizens' health information privacy concerns: a multifaceted approach ECIS 2015 Research-in-Progress Papers. In: Paper 22. ISBN 978-3-00-050284-2. http://aisel.aisnet.org/ecis2015_rip/22 (2015)
24. King, T., Brankovic, L., Gillard, P.: Perspectives of Australian adults about protecting the privacy of their health Information in statistical databases. Int. J. Med. Inf. **81**(4), 279–289 (2012)
25. Lafky, D.B., Horan, T.A.: Personal health records: consumer attitudes toward privacy and security of their personal health information. Health Inf. J. **17**(1), 63–71 (2011)
26. Laric, M.V., Pitta, D.A., Katsanis, L.P.: Consumer concerns for healthcare information privacy: a comparison of US and canadian perspectives. Res. Healthc. Finan. Manage. **12**(1), 93–111 (2009)
27. Lasagna, L.: Hippocratic Oath, Modern version. John Hopkins Sheridan Libraries. http://guides.library.jhu.edu/content.php?pid=23699&sid=190964. Accessed 10 Aug 2014 (1964)
28. Li, T., Slee, T.: The effects of information privacy concerns on digitizing personal health records. J. Assoc. Inform. Sci. Technol. **65**(8), 1541–1554 (2014)
29. Li, Y.: Empirical studies on online information privacy concerns: literature review and an integrative framework. Commun. Assoc. Inform. Syst. **28**(28), 453–496 (2011)
30. Maillet, E., Mathieu, L., Sicotte, C.: Modeling factors explaining the acceptance, actual use and satisfaction of nurses using an electronic patient record in acute care settings: an extension of the UTAUT. Int. J. Med. Inf. 1–12 (2014)
31. Malhotra, N.K., Kim, S.S., Agarwal, J.: Internet Users' Information Privacy Concerns (IUIPC): the construct, the scale and a causal model. Inform. Syst. Res. **15**(4), 336–355 (2004)
32. Moore, A.D.: Privacy: its meaning. Am. Philos. Q. **40**(3), 215–227 (2003)
33. Mosa, S.M., Yoo, I., Sheets, L.: A systematic review of healthcare applications for smartphones. BMC Med. Inform. Decis. Mak. **12**(67), 1–31 (2012)
34. Mottl, J.: Wearables primed for big growth, with Apple Watch driving adoption. FierceMobile Healthcare. http://www.fiercemobilehealthcare.com/story/reports-wearables-primed-big-growth-apple-watch-driving-adoption/2015-02-22. Accessed 19 Jun 2015 (2015)
35. Pavlou, P.: State of the information privacy literature: where are we now and where should we go? MIS Q. **35**(4), 977–989 (2011)
36. Phelps, J.E., D'Souza, G., Nowak, G.J.: Antecedents and consequences of consumer privacy concerns: an empirical investigation. J. Interact. Market. **15**(4), 2–17 (2001)
37. Phelps, J., Nowak, G., Ferrell, E.: Privacy concerns and consumer willingness to provide personal information. Am. Market. Assoc. **19**(1), 27–41 (2000)
38. Powell, J., Fitton, R., Fitton, C.: Sharing electronic health records: the patient view. Inf. Primary Care **14**(1), 55–57 (2003)
39. Privacy Rights Clearinghouse.: Mobile Health and Fitness Apps: What Are the Privacy Risks? https://www.privacyrights.org/mobile-medical-apps-privacy-alert (visited on 30/11/2014) (2013)

40. Prosser, W.: Privacy. Calif. Law Rev. **48**(3), 83–423 (1960)
41. Pyper, C., Amery, J., Watson, M., Crook, C.: Patients' experiences when accessing their on-line electronic patient records in primary care. Br. J. Gen. Pract. **54**(498), 38–43 (2008)
42. Rahim, F.A., Ismail, Z., Samy, G.N.: Information privacy concerns in electronic healthcare records : a systematic literature review. In: 3rd International Conference on Research and Innovation in Information Systems—2013 (ICRIIS'13), pp. 504–509, (2013)
43. Ralf-Gordon, H.: The market for mHealth app services will reach $26 billion by 2017. http://research2guidance.com/the-market-for-mhealth-app-services-will-reach-26-billion-by-2017/ (visited on 02/01/2015) (2013)
44. Regan, P.M., FitzGerald, G., Balint, P.: Generational views of information privacy? Innovation Eur. J. Soc. Sci. Res. **26**(1–2), 81–99 (2013)
45. Shaw, N.T., Kulkarni, A., Mador, R.L.: Patients and health care providers' concerns about the privacy of electronic health records: a review of the literature. Electron. J. Health Inf. **6**(1), 1–5 (2011)
46. Smith, H.J., Dinev, T., Xu, H.: Information privacy research: an Interdisciplinary review. MIS Q. **35**(4), 989–1015 (2011)
47. Smith, H.J., Milberg, S.J., Burke, S.J.: Information privacy: Measuring individuals concerns about organizational practices. MIS Q. **20**, 167–196 (1996)
48. U.S. Department of Health and Human Services.: More physicians and hospitals are using EHRs than before. http://www.hhs.gov/news/press/2014pres/08/20140807a.html (visited on 18/08/2014) (2014)
49. Venkatesh, V., Sykes, T., Zhang, X.: Just what the doctor ordered: a revised UTAUT for EMR system adoption and use by doctors. In: Proceedings of the 44th Hawaii International Conference on System Sciences, Hawaii, 1–10, (2011)
50. Warren, S., Brandeis, L.: The right to privacy. Harvard Law Rev. 193–220 (1890)
51. Westin, A.: Privacy and Freedom. Athenbaum, New York (1967)
52. Westin, A.: Public attitudes toward electronic health records. Privacy Am. Bus. **12**(2), 2–6 (2005)
53. Whittaker, R.: Key issues in mobile health and implications for New Zealand. Healthc. Inf. Rev. Online **16**(2), 2–7 (2012)
54. Zhang, Y., Chen, J., Wen, K.W.: Characteristics of internet users and their privacy concerns— a comparative study between China and the United States. J. Internet Commer. **1**(2), 1–16 (2002)

Designing a Scenario-Based Questionnaire to Assess Behavioral Intention in Social Networking Sites' Ethical Dilemmas

Hosein Jafarkarimi, Alex Tze Hiang Sim, Robab Saadatdoost and Jee Mei Hee

1 Introduction

In the context of Information and Communication Technology (ICT), behavioral studies are very important. The influential factors that have an impact on people to engage with certain activities are well studied and different sets of theories and models are proposed in this field. In these kinds of researches, the focus is to find influential variables that cause a certain behavior, or use of a system. With these studies, people are asked to report their behavior in the topic of interest. However, in some cases, the behavior is not possible to be observed or asked since the topic of interest is not that usual to happen for everyone, every day. For instance, when the focus is to find ethical decision making of people in different contexts, it is hard to ask whether or not they behave ethically. In these cases, a common practice is to design a scenario and ask respondents to answer a set of questions regarding that particular scenario. Although this is an accepted approach in these researches, a comprehensive guideline for designing these kinds of questionnaires is not easy to find. For instance, Lind [1] has an instruction to design ethical dilemma scenarios

H. Jafarkarimi (✉)
Department of Computer, Damavand Branch, Islamic Azad University, Damavand, Iran
e-mail: karimi@damavandiau.ac.ir

A.T.H. Sim
Faculty of Computing, Universiti Teknologi Malaysia, Johor Bahru, Malaysia
e-mail: alex@utm.my

R. Saadatdoost
Department of Computer and Information Technology, Parand Branch,
Islamic Azad University, Parand, Iran
e-mail: saadatdoost@piau.ac.ir

J.M. Hee
Faculty of Education, Universiti Teknologi Malaysia, Johor Bahru, Malaysia
e-mail: jmhee@utm.my

© Springer International Publishing Switzerland 2016   145
F. D'Ascenzo et al. (eds.), *Blurring the Boundaries Through Digital Innovation*,
Lecture Notes in Information Systems and Organisation 19,
DOI 10.1007/978-3-319-38974-5_12

for his famous Moral Judgment Test (MJT); but, it is not clear how to insure the proposed criteria are fulfilled. Here, the aim is to propose a guideline to set an example for designing a scenario-based questionnaire to investigate influential factors that affect individual's intention. The focus in this paper guideline is set to the field of Social Networking Sites' (SNSs) ethical dilemmas. In this regard, this research aims to find answers for the following questions:

1. What are the potential important factors that make individuals intend to carry out unethical behavior in SNS context?
2. How to design and select proper ethical dilemma scenarios for a survey instrument?
3. How to check the reliability and validity of the designed instrument to make it ready for main survey?

The remainder of this paper is organized as follows. Section 2 discusses influential factors that hypothetically have impact on the ethical decision making process. In Sect. 3, the method through which a set of scenarios are designed is discussed. In Sect. 4, the method of data collection is elaborated and in Sect. 5, the method through which appropriate scenarios are selected is discussed. Section 6 provides detailed steps for formulating measurement model to check validity and reliability of the instrument. Finally, conclusion and future work is presented in Sect. 7.

2 Influential Factors

In order to investigate the process of an individual's moral decision making, the first step is to find the influential factors that have an impact on this process. Different theories and models have been proposed to examine the relationship between different factors and behaviors [2]. Among them, Wicker [3] looked at the relationship of attitude and behavior and concluded that these two probably have no relation. "Out of frustration with traditional attitude-behavior researches, much of them found weak correlation between attitude and performance of a volitional behavior" [4, p. 259], Fishbein and Ajzen [5] proposed the theory of reasoned action (TRA) which aimed to explain volitional behaviors. Later, they extended TRA and the outcome was the TPB [6]. TRA and TPB became the most widely researched models of behavior since [7].

TRA aimed to provide a prediction model of attitude and behavior. TRA is based on previous theories of attitude and is rooted in social psychology settings [8]. According to TRA, people's behavior can be influenced by two general factors, namely, attitude and SN. TRA recommends that an individual's intention is a precursor of their actual behavior. Attitude refers to the individual's evaluation of whether the performance of an act is favorable or unfavorable. SN are the individual's perception about an idea of those who are important to him or her regarding the act under question.

To increase the predictive power of TRA, Ajzen [6] proposed TPB by adding percieved behavioral control (PBC) as another independent variable that predicts intention. TPB suggests that attitude, SN and PBC are good predictors of intention and consequently of behavior. The first two antecedents are the same as the TRA constructs, and the third one, PBC, can be defined as how easy or hard it is to perform a certain behavior. The TPB claims that the performance of deliberate intentional behaviors could be predicted with high accuracy from intentions and perceptions of behavioral control [9].

In line with these variables, and based on a literature review, we include another two constructs namely personal normative belief (PNB) and perceived threat of legal punishment (PTLP) to be embedded in the TPB to investigate behavioral intention in SNS dilemma cases. PNB refers to an individual's feeling about his or her moral obligation to do or not to do an act. Finally, PTLP is defined as the probability of legal punishment in the case of doing an act and the perception of the severity and impact on the individual's life if they should do a certain act and be punished for it [10].

2.1 Attitude

Despites some researchers' claim that attitude is an insignificant factor in TPB [11], many other studies reflected the opposite [12–19]. An individual's evaluation of favorability of a particular act is called attitude towards that act [9]. Attitude depends on individual's evaluation of their beliefs regarding engaging with a certain act [20] which is rooted in their character and their moral development [21]. It is expected that people will engage more in activities that they believe they are more in favor of.

2.2 Subjective Norms

Although SN is one of the main factors of TPB, its impact on intention has been under question. There are scholars who believe that SN explains a small proportion of variance in intention [22–25]. For this reason, several researchers removed SN from their behavioral models [e.g. 11, 26–28]. However, Trafimow [22] reviewed 30 behavioral studies and stated that SN might not be as influential as attitude, but it still has a considerable impact on people's behavioral intention depending on the context. According to Sheppard [24], SN is the weakest variable in TPB and Ajzen [9] stated that SN might be negated by the influence of personal considerations. In line with this view, some researchers have omitted SN from their studies and include PNB instead [e.g. 11, 24, 26, 28]. Conversely, other scholars believe that

SN is still significant for behavioral intention prediction [16, 29–32] and its poor performance might lie in the weakness of its measurement especially due to the use of single item measures [7]. Armitage and Conner [7] reviewed 185 TPB studies and reported that in studies in which SN is measured using multi-item measures, it has a reasonably strong impact on behavioral intention. Hence, in this research, SNS is included with other factors to be examined for any possible impact on behavioral intention. It is expected that people will engage in activities that are more acceptable by people who are important to them.

2.3 Perceived Behavioral Control

Madden [33] states that in a certain scenario, if people could deliberately control a behavior, PBC would not be a relevant construct anymore. In other words, PBC is only important in actions in which individuals are not in full volitional control [7]. For example, if someone does not want to listen to music, it is not important how hard it is for him to download pirated music. In contrast, if he intends to download pirated music, PBC will be the simplicity of access to websites with such content. It is expected that people engage more in those behaviors that seem to be easier to achieve [34].

2.4 Personal Normative Beliefs

Individuals' feeling about their moral obligation to engage with a particular act is referred to as PNB. Same as SN, there are some doubts about the relevance of this factor in predicting behavioral intention [35, 36]. To scrutinize the claims regarding the influence of PNB, it is included in present study in addition to SN to investigate its potential role on behavioral intention in case of SNS ethical dilemmas. It is expected that people engage less in unethical activities to which they feel morally obligated.

2.5 Perceived Threat of Legal Punishment

PTLP is defined as the possibility of legal punishment should an individual perform an act and the perceived threat of the severity of that punishment on his or her life [10]. Most people try to avoid actions that might cause punishment by law and as the law becomes more strict its impact on individuals' behavior becomes stronger [37]. Consistent with this idea, different researchers include this variable as an influential factor on predicting individuals' behavioral intention [e.g. 10, 38, 39]. In this regard, PTLP included influential factors of this research and it is expected that people engage less in activities that they perceive to have more threat of legal punishment.

Regarding these definitions and since the behavior is not possible to be investigated in ethical dilemmas, the focus here is to design a survey instrument to capture behavioral intention and its influential factors including attitude, SN PBC, PNB and PTLP. To this end, five constructs are aimed to be measured using ethical dilemma scenarios. For each of the constructs, three questions were asked. These measures are presented in Table 1.

Table 1 Measurement of each construct

Construct	Items	Refined Items	Adapted from
Intention	INT01	If I were X[a], I would do as s/he did.	[40]
	INT02	Depending on the situation, I could do as X did.	[32]
	INT03	I may do as X did in future.	[40]
Attitude	ATT01	X's decision is good.	[41]
	ATT02	X's decision is wise.	[41]
	ATT03	X's decision is beneficial.	[41]
SN	SN01	If I do what X did in this scenario, most of the people who are important to me would not care.	[14]
	SN02	If I do as X did, most of the people who are important to me would approve.	[40]
	SN03	Most people who are important to me think that I should do as X did in this scenario.	[13]
PBC	PBC01	If I wanted to, I would easily do as X did.	[40]
	PBC02	Technically it is easy for me to act as X did in this scenario.	[7]
	PBC03	I would be able to do what X did even if there was no one to show me how.	[32]
PNB	PNB01	In my opinion, it is morally wrong to do as X did.	[40]
	PNB02	I would not feel guilty if I do what X did. (R)	[14]
	PNB03	In my opinion, X's act is wrong.	[40]
PTLP	PTLP01	If I do what X did, I might be arrested.	[10]
	PTLP02	If I do what X did and I get arrested, I will be in a big problem.	[10]
	PTLP03	If I do as X did and I get arrested, the punishment that I will face will create a big problem for my life.	[10]

[a]In the questionnaire, depending on the scenario that was used, different names were replaced by "X"

3   Scenario Development

The actual behavior of people in ethical dilemma cases, especially in the SNS context, is almost impossible to observe. As there is a need to see their actions when facing these dilemmas, and due to the fact that it is not possible to observe individuals' decisions in ethical dilemma cases, this research employed designed scenarios to check individual intentions in the presented scenarios. Scenario-based questionnaires are widely used in behavioral studies [e.g. 11, 20, 27, 28, 32, 42–46]. In this approach, instead of observing people in different situations, a scenario (case) is presented to them and some questions regarding that particular scenario are asked. To this end, several scenarios were designed as potential dilemma cases to be included in the survey questionnaire in the present study. For this aim, Lind's [1] instructions for the "construction of new dilemmas for moral judgment test" were followed. Lind [44] proposed the MJT to assess moral reasoning of individuals based on Kohlberg's theory of moral development. The test employs ethical dilemmas. Lind [1] proposed the following criteria for the design of new ethical dilemmas:

1. "There should be two new dilemmas to make sure that we will have one fully certifiable at the end.
2. It should deal with the story of a fictitious person who is very likely to exist in real; s/he should have a name.
3. It should be clear from the beginning that there is a difficulty ahead (title of the story; first sentence).
4. It should contain a clear decision under time pressure; an evasion of the decision or postponing it should not be an option.
5. It should be short and easily understandable (not too technical language).
6. It should appeal to people with high moral ideals, but also to people with lower ideals.
7. It should appeal equally to people who agree with the decision of the protagonist as to people who disagree."

Based on the above instruction and its seven criteria, 23 possible dilemmas were constructed. The scenarios included previously studied ethical issues such as privacy, piracy, copyright infringement, cyberbullying, false accusations, impersonation, and fraud. These constructed dilemma cases were presented to a panel of experts including three professors. The panel was presented with a questionnaire which asked them to evaluate the scenarios in terms of ethicality and importance to this research. Those scenarios with a low rate of agreement about their un-ethicality were removed from the poll. To fulfill Lind's [1] first criterion for scenario construction, since this research needed four final scenarios, eight of those with higher relevance ranks were selected to be included in the study (Appendix).

In the first scenario, a job applicant is being rejected by Jack. He finds about her pregnancy on Facebook. This act is unethical since the applicant is being rejected based on her gender. The second scenario is about Mark, who develops a code to make reports of his girlfriend's activity on Facebook to see if their relationship is stable or if there is someone else in whom she is romantically interested. This is a case of stalking and breaching someone's privacy and is unethical. The third scenario is based on a real story. In the scenario, Dom's laptop has been stolen and pictures of the new owner were sent to Dom's email address [47]. Dom then posts the pictures all over the Internet and claims the new owner as the thief. The scenario finishes here but later on he discovers that the new owner is not a thief and she is an innocent girl who happened to buy his laptop as a new one [48]. Later on, Dom apologizes to her and regrets what he has done. It is not ethical since he was accusing someone without her being convicted in the court of law. The fourth scenario is about a student society and is based on a personal experience. In this case, Michael, a representative of the student society is facing some students who use the freedom of expression in a wrong way and use harsh words and false accusations. The representative thinks that it is wrong to put the society's reputation at stake and fights them back in their own game. Finally, he decides to make a fake ID and use the same method to reply to them and defend the society. It is unethical since he is using harsh words, false accusations and a fake identity to achieve his aim. The fifth scenario is about Jeremy who is a journalist. His Facebook friend becomes murdered and a focus of media. He decides to use the information available to him in Facebook to make a story about the murder and get use of situation in order to sell it to newspapers. This is wrong since the information is only available to him and can be considered as breaching someone's privacy. Sixth scenario is about Aida who sees a picture of monk throwing a child into a grave. In the caption it is stated that monks are burying children from a certain religion alive in a country. She decides to share the news without investigating if it is right or wrong. It is also unethical since it might be a forged picture or another story might be behind the picture so her act can be considered as spreading lie or false news. In the seventh scenario, Maria shares an advertisement for a medicine and states that its results were great on her. However, she does not know anything about the medicine and did it to have a chance to win a lucky draw which is conducted by that particular medicine factory. It is unethical since she is lying and her act can harm others. In the last scenario, Kevin develops a website with fake picture of children who have cancer to get money from people as charity. It goes without saying that this is against the law and ethics and is considered as fraud.

All the characters in the eight scenarios were given names and their stories were completely probable in the real world (Criterion 2). For the third criterion, each story had a difficulty which was stated at its very beginning. At the end of each scenario, a clear decision about the character in the case was stated (Criterion 4). The scenarios were as short as possible with a maximum word length of 120 and average word length of 86 which is appropriate for Criterion 5. Fulfilling criterion 6 and 7 was done through data collection.

4   Data Collection

Due to the unique design of this research and in order to reduce the time and cost of the data collection process, two types of questionnaire were used in the data collection phase. Each of these questionnaires had four different scenarios, meaning eight scenarios were included in the pilot study and each respondent was asked to answer a set of questions regarding four different scenarios. This step was done using the Google Form survey instrument which was distributed to 400 individual Facebook users. Of these 48 individuals answered the two questionnaires (response rate of 12 %) which meant 192 sets of results for all eight scenarios together (24 answers for each scenario). These results were used to fulfill Lind's criteria 6 and 7 and also for the validity and reliability check. A summary of the criteria and the procedure of fulfillment are presented in Table 2.

5   Scenario Selection

Since the data collection was done using all eight scenarios, the result was used to ensure that the scenarios were appealing to different people (Criterion 6) and also appealing for both those who agree with the given decision and those who did not (Criterion 7). To check Criterion 6, the mean and standard deviation of the attitude construct were used. The top four scenarios with a mean nearer to 3 (the middle of a 5-point Likert scale which was used in this research) and larger in variance (which reflects the spread of a set of observations) showed that this was not the result of neutral responses. The same was done for the mean and standard deviation of the intention construct to make sure that the respondents were spread in terms of deciding to do or not to do the presented task. The results are presented in Table 2.

The four main scenarios were then selected based on a higher disagreement about respondents' intention in the presented case. To this end, the skewness and kurtosis test values were examined. Skewness assesses how symmetrically distributed the variables are, and kurtosis shows the extent to which the values of the variables are peaked. The four scenarios were selected with skewness and kurtosis values nearer to zero, which are the first four scenarios presented in Table 2. This was done to ensure that the cases were dilemmas, and that people with different points of view would decide differently. If the ethicality of an act becomes so clear and people feel that something is clearly wrong, most of them will decide not to get involved with it or at least state it in the questionnaire. This case cannot be a good representative of an ethical dilemma. Hence, this process would ensure the feeling of uncertainty among the individuals regarding whether or not to get involved with the action proposed in the scenario.

Table 2 Designed scenarios and their scores to be used for current research

Criterion 1	Criterion 2	Criterion 3	Criterion 4	Criterion 5	Criterion 6		Criterion 7		Selection scale	
Scenarios	Name	Issue	Decision	Word count	Attitude mean	Attitude standard deviation	Intention mean	Intention standard deviation	Skewness	Kurtosis
1	Jack	SNS and workplace	To reject an applicant due to her pregnancy	82	2.62	0.95	2.63	1.195	0.586	−0.509
2	Mark	Privacy and stalking	To monitor his girlfriend's online behavior	71	3.24	1.37	3.51	1.19	−0.480	−0.66
3	Dom	False accusation, breaching privacy	To send new owner's picture as a thief	82	3.48	1.19	3.48	1.05	0.516	−0.394
4	Michael	Impersonation and harsh words	To build a fake ID and use harsh words	80	3.77	1.25	3.32	1.23	−0.163	−1.091
5	Jeremy	Privacy	To share private information of a dead person	120	3.28	0.97	3.69	1.012	−1.417	0.821
6	Aida	False news	To share news which is not authenticated	76	4.03	1.18	3.66	0.88	−0.110	−1.867
7	Maria	False claim in advertising	To tell others a lie about using a certain medicine	72	3.96	1.14	4.18	1.14	−0.852	−1.514
8	Kevin	Fraud	To advertise for a fake charity program	109	3.56	1.00	3.67	1.2	−1.353	1.447

6 Formulating Measurement Model

The outcome of the scenario development phase was used in line with a set of questions to measure the proposed variables as the conceptual model's constructs. The relationships among constructs and their corresponding indicators are specified by a measurement model or outer model [49]. Different constructs can be measured using either single-item or multiple-item measures. Single items ensure higher rates of responses since the questions can be easily and quickly answered [50]. However, using single items causes fewer degrees of freedom, less information is available to handle missing values and, unlike multiple items, it is not possible to adjust measurement errors and consequently the reliability is decreased [49]. It is suggested to have at least three observed indicators for a construct to make it identified [51]. Due to the challenging and time-consuming nature of this study's questionnaire, only three questions were asked for the measurement of each construct. In current study, all five constructs were measured using reflective measures as mentioned in Sect. 2. The respondents were asked to answer each question by choosing one of five alternatives ranging from "strongly agree" to "strongly disagree" as proposed by Likert [52] (5-point Likert scale). The final step in designing a proper survey instrument is checking its validity and reliability. To assess reflective constructs, internal consistency, convergent and discriminant validity are used. Cronbach's alpha and composite reliability were checked for internal consistency; for convergent validity, factor outer loading and Average Variance Extracted (AVE). Table 3 summarizes the results of these tests.

Table 3 Reliability and convergent validity check results for reflective measures

Constructs	Internal consistency reliability		Convergent validity		
Name	Cronbach's alpha (>0.6)	Composite reliability (>0.7)	AVE (>0.5)	Outer loading (>0.7)	
Attitude	0.808	0.884	0.720	ATT01	0.888
				ATT02	0.889
				ATT03	0.761
Intention	0.926	0.895	0.872	INT01	0.931
				INT02	0.927
				INT03	0.943
Perceived behavioral control	0.871	0.863	0.792	PBC01	0.889
				PBC02	0.898
				PBC03	0.882
Subjective norms	0.851	0.908	0.768	SN01	0.767
				SN02	0.933
				SN03	0.921
Personal normative beliefs	0.760	0.724	0.605	PNB01	0.750
				PNB02	0.731
				PNB03	0.720
Perceived threat of legal punishment	0.869	0.901	0.796	PTLP01	0.804
				PTLP02	0.938
				PTLP03	0.927

Table 4 Fornell–Larcker criterion results

	ATT	INT	PBC	PNB	PTLP	SN
ATT	**0.849**					
INT	0.753	**0.934**				
PBC	0.418	0.567	**0.890**			
PNB	−.417	−0.557	−0.451	**0.778**		
PTLP	−.246	−0.339	−0.275	0.339	**0.892**	
SN	0.478	0.546	0.441	−0.516	−0.320	**0.876**

As inferred from Table 3, all the measures perfectly passed the required thresholds. To ensure the discriminant validity, Fornell–Larcker criterion was assessed. The results are presented in Table 4. According to Table 4, all the amounts of the square roots of each construct's AVE were larger than its correlation with other constructs and, hence, this instrument was found to have discriminant validity.

Following these validity and reliability tests, the questionnaire was finalized and ready to be used as the survey instrument. In order to finish the process of questionnaire design, demographic questions can be included in the beginning of this questionnaire to make it ready for the main survey.

7 Conclusion

This paper presented the method in which a scenario-based questionnaire was designed to be used in a real survey to test a number of hypotheses regarding individuals' ethical decision making in the context of SNS ethical dilemmas. To this end, different steps that were taken were presented. First an instruction to design ethical dilemma cases was adopted from Lind's (2007) MJT. Based on this instruction, a number of scenarios were designed and went through a process for selecting the most appropriate ones. To insure each of Lind's (2007) criterions, a clear procedure is proposed to be used. In addition, the measurement model was tested which resulted to a finalized scenario-based questionnaire for the actual survey. Although different steps of designing a questionnaire were discussed in current paper, all the constructs were measured reflectively. This might be considered as a limitation for this study; however, formative measures could also be included in this method since their presence does not impact the process through which the scenarios were selected. The only consideration in such a case is that formative measurement model assessment has its own criteria to be fulfilled which are not the same with the reflective measurement model. The proposed approach can be adopted in future researches in different contexts in which the focus is on ethical dilemmas and individual behavioral intentions in these cases. In future researches, other constructs can be included as predictors of behavioral intention following the same steps that were stated in this paper.

Acknowledgments Authors would like to thank Islamic Azad University, Damavand branch (Iran) for supporting this research. This work is also supported by the Fundamental Research Grant Scheme (FRGS) of Ministry of Higher Education (MOHE) and Universiti Teknologi Malaysia (UTM), with reference to FRGS/1/2014/ICT01/UTM/02/2 (Vot: 4F441).

Appendix

Scenarios

1. Jack is a manager of a newborn company which is employing new staff for an important position. Reviewing applicants' resumes, He finds two potential engineers for the job. He doubts which one to employ. He decides to check their Facebook where he discovers that one of the applicants is pregnant and speculate that she might not be able to work properly. He decides to reject her application and employ the other applicant.

2. Recently, Mark feels something has changed in his relationship with his girlfriend. He felt that there is another man in her life. Being a skillful web programmer, he decides to program a code to trace all her Facebook activities including comments, likes and shares. This application makes a report each day and sends it to Mark's email. He hopes to find important information to keep track of her daily activities.

3. Dom's laptop was stolen recently. Luckily, he installed a program taking pictures in a schedule and sending it to his email. After a while, he receives some pictures of the new laptop owner in different conditions of her personal life. He is not sure whether the new owner is the thief or an innocent person. Yet he considered that the only option to get his laptop back is to start a Facebook page and spreading the picture of the new owner as the thief.

4. Michael is the admin of a page on Facebook which represents a student society in his university. Recently, some users have started to criticize this society with harsh words. They use a very impolite language to tell their ideas and Michael is not able to use their language to reply them because he considers the reputation of the student society. Considering the only option he makes a fake ID in Facebook and starts to fight them back in their own way.

5. Jeremy is a normal journalist. Recently, one of his Facebook friends was murdered and became an important topic for newspapers. He was only a Facebook friend and he did not know him in the real world. Jeremy has access to many private issues of the murder and he can write a complete story about this case. This can make him a famous journalist and affects the rest of his professional career. However, his friend, set many issues only visible for his friends list and he might not want others to know about them. Thinking as the only opportunity in his life, Jeremy decides to use his Facebook information to write the story and sell it to a good newspaper.

6. Checking Facebook, Aida sees a picture of a monk, throwing a child into a grave. In the caption, it is stated that this is about a country in which, monks,

bury people alive who are of a certain religion because of their belief. Without checking the fact and becoming certain of reliability of the source, she shares the picture because she believes that it is genocide and people all around the world should know it.

7. Checking her Facebook, Maria encountered a page announcing that sharing an advertisement about a certain medicine, will have a chance to win a good amount of money in a lucky draw. Whoever wants to share the advertisement have to state that he or she used the stuff and it was great. Without knowing anything about the medicine and its side effects, Maria decides to share the picture and write the requested statement.

8. Kevin's father has lost a lot of money in a gambling spree and threatened to be killed by his gambling opponents. They asked his father to produce $20,000 in two weeks' time, or else his life will be in danger. Since they have no money, Kevin, who is a web programmer considered the last option. He then developed a website in which he uploaded fake pictures of children who have cancer and need people's help. He also gives an account number for people to send money for the charity. He used his popular page in Facebook which has more than 300,000 members to spread the fake charity webpage.

References

1. Lind, G.: Constructing New Dilemmas for the Moral Judgment Test (MJT). 2/7/2014]; http://www.uni-konstanz.de/ag-moral/mut/mjt_new_dilemma_construction.htm (2007)
2. Olson, J.M., Zanna, M.P.: Attitudes and attitude change. Annu. Rev. Psychol. **44**(1), 117–154 (1993)
3. Wicker, A.W.: Attitudes versus actions: the relationship of verbal and overt behavioral responses to attitude objects. J. Soc. Issues **25**(4), 41–78 (1969)
4. Hale, J.L., Householder, B.J., Greene, K.L.: The theory of reasoned action. In: Dillard, J.P., Shen, L. (eds.) The Sage Handbook of Persuasion: Developments in Theory and Practice. Sage Thousand Oaks, CA, USA. pp. 259–286 (2002)
5. Fishbein, M., Ajzen, I.: Belief, attitude, intention and behavior: an introduction to theory and research, 1st edn. Addison-Wesley Series in Social Psychology, Addison-Wesley Pub (Sd) (1975)
6. Ajzen, I.: From intentions to actions: a theory of planned behavior. In: Kuhl, J. (ed.) Action control: from cognition to behavior. Springer, Berlin and New York. pp. 11–39 (1985)
7. Armitage, C.J., Conner, M.: Efficacy of the theory of planned behaviour: a meta-analytic review. Br. J. Soc. Psychol. **40**(4), 471–499 (2001)
8. Ajzen, I., Fishbein, M.: The prediction of behavioral intentions in a choice situation. J. Exp. Soc. Psychol. **5**(4), 400–416 (1969)
9. Ajzen, I.: The theory of planned behavior. Organ. Behav. Hum. Decis. Process. **50**(2), 179–211 (1991)
10. Grasmick, H.G., Green, D.E.: Legal punishment, social disapproval and internalization as inhibitors of illegal behavior. J. Crim. Law Criminol. (1973) **71**(3), 325–335 (1980)
11. Banerjee, D., Cronan, T.P., Jones, T.W.: Modeling IT ethics: a study in situational ethics. MIS Q. **22**(1), 31–60 (1998)

12. Ajzen, I., Madden, T.J.: Prediction of goal-directed behavior: attitudes, intentions, and perceived behavioral control. J. Exp. Soc. Psychol. **22**(5), 453–474 (1986)
13. Arvola, A., Vassallo, M., Dean, M., Lampila, P., Saba, A., Lähteenmäki, L., Shepherd, R.: Predicting intentions to purchase organic food: the role of affective and moral attitudes in the theory of planned behaviour. Appetite **50**(2–3), 443–454 (2008)
14. Beck, L., Ajzen, I.: Predicting dishonest actions using the theory of planned behavior. J. Res. Pers. **25**(3), 285–301 (1991)
15. Chiang, F.K., Sun, C.S., Wuttke, H.D., Rainer, K.: Design and development of students' attitudes questionnaire towards innovative information technology for learning. In: Gibson, I. et al. (eds.) Society for Information Technology & Teacher Education International Conference 2009, AACE, Charleston, SC, USA. 1786–1791 (2009)
16. Cox, J.: Information systems user security: a structured model of the knowing-doing gap. Comput. Hum. Behav. **28**(5), 1849–1858 (2012)
17. Debatin, B., Lovejoy, J.P., Horn, A.-K., Hughes, B.N.: Facebook and online privacy: attitudes, behaviors, and unintended consequences. J. Comput-Mediat. Commun. **15**(1), 83–108 (2009)
18. Durndell, A., Haag, Z.: Computer self efficacy, computer anxiety, attitudes towards the internet and reported experience with the internet, by gender, in an East European sample. Comput. Hum. Behav. **18**(5), 521–535 (2002)
19. Paradice, D.B.: Ethical attitudes of entry-level mis personnel. Inf. Manag. **18**(3), 143–151 (1990)
20. Ellis, T.S., Griffith, D.: The evaluation of IT ethical scenarios using a multidimensional scale. SIGMIS Database **32**(1), 75–85 (2000)
21. Kohlberg, L.: The cognitive-developmental approach to moral education. The Phi Delta Kappan **56**(10), 670–677 (1975)
22. Trafimow, D., Finlay, K.A.: The importance of subjective norms for a minority of people: between subjects and within-subjects analyses. Pers. Soc. Psychol. Bull. **22**(8), 820–828 (1996)
23. Tarkiainen, A., Sundqvist, S.: Subjective norms, attitudes and intentions of finnish consumers in buying organic food. Brit. Food J. **107**(11), 808–822 (2005)
24. Sheppard, B.H., Jon, H., Warshaw, P.R.: The theory of reasoned action: a meta-analysis of past research with recommendations for modifications and future research. J. Consum. Res. **15**(3), 325–343 (1988)
25. Godin, G., Kok, G.: The theory of planned behavior: a review of its applications to health-related behaviors. Am. J. Health Promot. **11**(2), 87–98 (1996)
26. Sparks, P., Shepherd, R., Wieringa, N., Zimmermanns, N.: Perceived behavioural control, unrealistic optimism and dietary change: an exploratory study. Appetite **24**(3), 243–255 (1995)
27. Leonard, L.N.K., Cronan, T.P.: Illegal, inappropriate, and unethical behavior in an information technology context: a study to explain influences. J. Assoc. Inform. Syst. **1**(1), 1–31 (2001)
28. Leonard, L.N.K., Cronan, T.P., Kreie, J.: What influences IT ethical behavior intentions—planned behavior, reasoned action, perceived importance, or individual characteristics? Inf. Manag. **42**(1), 143–158 (2004)
29. Johnston, A.C., Warkentin, M.: Fear appeals and information security behaviors: an empirical study. MIS Q. **34**(3), 549–566 (2010)
30. Knapp, K.J., Marshall, T.E., Rainer, R.K., Ford, F.N.: Information security: management's effect on culture and policy. Inform. Manage. Comput. Secur. **14**(1), 24–36 (2006)
31. Chan, M., Woon, I., Kankanhalli, A.: Perceptions of information security in the workplace: linking information security climate to compliant behavior. J. Inform. Privacy Secur. **1**(3), 18–41 (2005)
32. Chatterjee, S.: Unethical Behavior Using Information Technology. College of Business, Washington State University, Washington. 107 (2008)
33. Madden, T.J., Ellen, P.S., Ajzen, I.: A comparison of the theory of planned behavior and the theory of reasoned action. Pers. Soc. Psychol. Bull. **18**(1), 3–9 (1992)

34. Bandura, A.: Guide for Constructing self-efficacy scales. In: Pajares, F., Urdan, T.C. (eds.) Self-Efficacy Beliefs of Adolescents. Information Age Publishing, USA. pp. 307–337 (2006)
35. Schwartz, S.H., Tessler, R.C.: A test of a model for reducing measured attitude-behavior discrepancies. J. Pers. Soc. Psychol. **24**(2), 225–236 (1972)
36. Godin, G.: The theories of reasoned action and planned behavior: overview of findings, emerging research problems and usefulness for exercise promotion. J. Appl. Sport Psychol. **5** (2), 141–157 (1993)
37. Bommer, M., Gratto, C., Gravander, J., Tuttle, M.: A behavioral model of ethical and unethical decision making. In: Poff, D.C., Michalos, A.C. (eds.) Citation Classics from the Journal of Business Ethics. Springer Netherlands, pp. 97–117 (2013)
38. Paternoster, R., Saltzman, L.E., Waldo, G.P., Chiricos, T.G.: Estimating perceptual stability and deterrent effects: the role of perceived legal punishment in the inhibition of criminal involvement. J. Crim. Law Criminol. **74**, 270 (1983)
39. Morton, N.A., Koufteros, X.: Intention to commit online music piracy and its antecedents: an empirical investigation. Struct. Equ. Model. **15**(3), 491–512 (2008)
40. Chen, M.F., Pan, C.T., Pan, M.C.: The joint moderating impact of moral intensity and moral judgment on consumer's use intention of pirated software. J. Bus. Ethics **90**(3), 361–373 (2009)
41. Ajzen, I.: Attitudes, personality, and behavior. In: Manstead, T. (ed.) Mapping Social Psychology, 2nd ed. McGraw-Hill International, England (2005)
42. Haines, R., Leonard, L.N.: Individual characteristics and ethical decision-making in an IT context. Indus. Manage. Data Syst. **107**(1), 5–20 (2007)
43. Jung, I.: Ethical judgments and behaviors: applying a multidimensional ethics scale to measuring ict ethics of college students. Comput. Educ. **53**(3), 940–949 (2009)
44. Lind, G.: An Introduction to the Moral Judgment Test (MJT). In: Unpublished manuscript. University of Konstanz, Konstanz (1998)
45. Rest, J.R.: Development in Judging Moral Issues. University of Minnesota Press (1989)
46. Yoon, C.: Ethical decision-making in the internet context: development and test of an initial model based on moral philosophy. Comput. Hum. Behav. **27**(6), 2401–2409 (2011)
47. Deltorto, D.: Dom's Laptop Is in Iran. [Online Article] 2/7/2014]. http://laptopiniran.tumblr.com/ (2013)
48. Beaumont, P.: Owner of Stolen Laptop That Sends Spy Photos from Iran Regrets Exposing Users. The Guardian [Online Article] 12/4/2013]. http://www.theguardian.com/technology/2013/apr/12/owner-stolen-laptop-spy-iran (2013)
49. Hair, J.F.J., Hult, G.T.M., Ringle, C., Sarstedt, M.: A Primer on Partial Least Squares Structural Equation Modeling (PLS-SEM), 1st edn. SAGE Publications, Incorporated (2013)
50. Fuchs, C., Diamantopoulos, A.: Using single-item measures for construct measurement in management research. Die Betriebswirtschaft **69**(2), 195–210 (2009)
51. Gefen, D., Rigdon, E.E., Straub, D.: An update and extension to sem guidelines for administrative and social science research. MIS Q. **35**(2), iii-xiv (2011)
52. Likert, R.: A technique for the measurement of attitudes. Arch. Psychol. **140**, 5–55 (1932)

A Firm's Activity in Social Media and Its Relationship with Corporate Reputation and Firm Performance

Heikki Karjaluoto, Hanna Mäkinen and Joel Järvinen

1 Introduction

Currently, no company can say it is not affected by social media. Even if a company is not active in social media, communication about its brands still occurs in those channels [1]. Social media has caused consumers to be more demanding; therefore, one-way communication from companies to consumers is no longer sufficient [2]. Instead, the importance of communication and conversation with consumers is emphasized [3] as consumers want companies to listen to them as well as engage with and respond to them [1]. Consumers want to participate, interact, and create value by themselves. As a matter of fact, it can be said that power has shifted from companies to consumers [4].

For this reason, many companies have increased their social media activity. Furthermore, the financial crisis led companies to seek more cost-effective marketing methods, and social media has become a good channel for this [5]. Despite that, there are still many companies who do not sufficiently understand social media and so just ignore it [1]. Therefore, it is important to determine if it is beneficial for a company to be active in social media and what the advantages are of being active.

Literature about the subject is growing, but there is still little scholarly evidence that addresses how the utilization of social media influences company performance. Prior evidence has suggested that social media is important from a public relations (PR) and reputation point of view [6, 7] whereas others have linked it to overall

H. Karjaluoto (✉) · H. Mäkinen · J. Järvinen
School of Business and Economics, University of Jyväskylä, Jyväskylä, Finland
e-mail: heikki.karjaluoto@jyu.fi

H. Mäkinen
e-mail: hanna.u.makinen@gmail.com

J. Järvinen
e-mail: joel.jarvinen@jyu.fi

© Springer International Publishing Switzerland 2016
F. D'Ascenzo et al. (eds.), *Blurring the Boundaries Through Digital Innovation*,
Lecture Notes in Information Systems and Organisation 19,
DOI 10.1007/978-3-319-38974-5_13

equity value [8]. Nevertheless, little research has been conducted on how a company's appearance and activity in social media affect reputation and firm performance. Hence, this study aims to fill this gap in the literature by examining the relationship between social media activity and three variables, namely, corporate reputation, firm performance, and firm size (control variable). This study analyzes the relationships between the constructs but does not propose or discuss the direction of these effects or, in other words, the causal linkages between the variables.

2 Literature Review

Social media is defined in various ways, but all the definitions share the idea that it is a way to connect and interact with other people using various communication techniques through online media [1, 5, 9, p. 152]. While traditional media is focused on delivering a message (outbound marketing), social media is user-driven (inbound marketing) and includes, for example, building relationships and conversing with an audience [10]. Social media consists of various channels and platforms that allow communication, networking, and sharing of content and information [1, 11].

Social media has been classified into six categories based on two key elements: media research (social presence, media richness) and social processes (self-presentation, self-disclosure) [12]. The greater the social presence/media richness, the greater the social influence of users on the behavior of other users. The greater the self-presentation/self-disclosure, the more willing people are to talk about and reveal aspects of themselves to others. The six categories based on these elements are blogs, social networking sites, virtual social worlds, collaborative projects, content communities, and virtual game worlds [12]. In this study, we focus on social networking sites (Facebook, LinkedIn), content communities (YouTube), and one form of blogging, namely, microblogging (Twitter) as these are the most widely adopted social media tools among companies. On social networking sites, users can create profiles, share information, including photos, videos, audio files, and blogs, and ask friends to join or connect to their profiles [12].

Facebook is to date the largest and most popular social media channel [13, 14, p. 127] where users find and add friends and contacts to share content through personal profiles [15]. LinkedIn is a business-networking tool that is more focused on networking [1] with other professionals or companies. On the consumer side, LinkedIn is not used for finding customers [13, p. 63], but on the business-to-business side, it is used for acquiring customers, gathering market information, and recruiting, for instance [14, p. 97].

Content communities allow people to share content with other users who can comment on it. Content communities include, for example, YouTube for sharing videos and Flickr for sharing photos. Considering the 100 million videos that YouTube serves up each day, it is easy to understand the wide accessibility of content communities [12]. More recently, YouTube has also been used as a channel for publishing video blogs [16].

The most popular microblogging service is Twitter, which allows people to send and read short messages of 140 characters or less from their profile to users who follow them [15]. It is also possible to add links to other pages or send direct messages to other users by including a username in a post (in the form of @username) [13, p. 57].

Social media has become a tool for companies to communicate and engage with customers at lower cost and more effectively than traditional channels [12]. At the present, social media is increasingly being seen as a tool for creating and maintaining customer relationships and, for this reason, has also become an important tool for CRM [2]. Customers can no longer be seen simply as objects for a sale but instead must be considered as decision makers with their own needs and the option to choose what and where they are buying. Just as the entire web has turned into a social web, the customer has also turned into a social customer, standing at the center of the business ecosystem [17]. These social customers also have social needs and by filling them companies can build long lasting and meaningful relationships with their customers. The idea of social customers significantly affects companies and drives the need for social CRM [17], which can be considered a CRM strategy that emphasizes customer relationship communication via new communication technologies.

2.1 Social Media and Corporate Reputation

Corporate reputation refers to how stakeholders perceive a company and how the company responds to those perceptions [18]. A strong corporate reputation provides a competitive advantage to a company and is very difficult for others to imitate [19]. The more a company differentiates itself from its competitors, the stronger its reputation and the greater its reputational capital [20, p. 392]. Hence, reputation can be seen as an intangible and strategic asset of a company [21]. Earlier studies have shown that company reputation is positively linked with customer loyalty [22], attractiveness of company offerings [20, p. 8], employee commitment and job satisfaction [23, 24], reduction of transaction [25] and operating costs [26, p. 75], and firm performance [21, 26].

In traditional media, corporate reputation is seen as the interaction between a company's communicative actions and stakeholders' reactions. Accordingly, when a company communicates through their marketing channels, for example, their reputation depends on how stakeholders perceive the message and react to it [4]. In the social media era, it is not enough merely to communicate a message to consumers; instead, companies must engage consumers in conversation through social media [3].

In the social media era, companies have lost the power to control discussion about them, which makes it more difficult to influence reputation [6]. Social media has enhanced customers' need to be active and, at the same time, is what enables companies to address these needs. Customers want to participate, interact, and create value on their own, and social media provides an opportunity for companies to enable that through participation and interaction with customers. This participation leads to greater involvement with and commitment to a company, which has been suggested to increase customer satisfaction [2], which, again, has been proven in earlier research to lead to better corporate reputation [27]. Therefore, a positive relationship between a firm's social media activity and its corporate reputation can be proposed:

Proposition 1 *A firm's social media activity and corporate reputation have a positive relationship.*

2.2 Social Media and Firm Performance

Many companies are interested in learning how to benefit financially from social media. To justify investment, it is essential to determine the financial value of social media [8, 28]. The use of social media has expanded exponentially among both consumers and corporations, but still only a small amount of money earmarked for marketing is dedicated to social media. One reason for this is the difficulty of measuring the value of investments in social media marketing [28]. Despite the difficulty of measuring the value of social media, many researchers have attempted to measure its return on investment (ROI). However, the value of a customer to a firm is not only the amount of money they spend, but also the influence they have on other people's opinions by spreading their thoughts through social media; the actual value of a customer is based on far more than their spending [29].

Measuring and calculating social media ROI begins with measuring costs and then attempting to determine the return on sales. When dealing with social media, however, this is insufficient. Companies should also consider which marketing objectives are met by social media utilization. These can be, for example, brand engagement, providing knowledge about new products, or delivering information to customers. Hence, returns are not always financial [30] or recognized in the short-term.

Nevertheless, several studies have examined the relationship between social media and financial figures [2, 31, 32]. Luo et al. [8] suggested that social media has strong predictive power of a firm's future equity value. Their research revealed that through positive blog posts, consumers' trust and advocacy can be improved, leading to higher firm value. Naturally, negative blog posts can instead harm reputations, leading to weaker firm performance [8]. Schniederjans [31] studied the relationship between firm performance and social media from the perspective of impression management and found a partial positive connection between the use of social media and financial performance, depending on the impression management strategy used. Yu et al. [32] argued that social media has a stronger impact on firm stock performance than conventional media does. Additionally, compared to other media, effects from social media occur much faster. Furthermore, the harmful effects from negative opinions and ideas occur more quickly than the beneficial effects from positive opinions and ideas. Therefore, negative publicity in social media in particular can rapidly affect firm performance [8].

Social media has fostered customers who are more willing to participate in company activity, which may also increase commitment to the company. It has been suggested that customers' higher involvement and commitment to a company increase satisfaction and loyalty [2], which, in earlier studies, was revealed to have a positive impact on firm equity value [8, 33].

Proposition 2 *Social media activity and firm performance have a positive relationship.*

3   Methodology

Three data collection procedures were used in this study. First, self-gathered data on companies' social media activity were collected from selected companies' social media channels between March 2014 and April 2014. Social media channels selected for this research were Facebook, Twitter, LinkedIn, and YouTube. Data consisted of number of likes, talks, and activity (Facebook); number of followers, tweets, and activity (Twitter); number of followers and activity (LinkedIn); and number of subscribers, views, and videos (YouTube). The channels were chosen because they are the most popular social media channels currently used by firms.

The amount of activity depends on the duration a given social media channel was utilized by a company. Activity was evaluated by the amount of activity such as Facebook posts a company made on their page during 2013 so it could be compared among companies. Detailed classification and measurement of activity is shown in Table 1.

Some companies did not have a profile on Facebook for the whole of 2013. For these companies, the number of posts used for analysis was calculated by dividing the number of posts by the number of months the company had a Facebook presence and multiplying the result by 12 for a whole year average.

Second, corporate reputation data were obtained from a market research firm. The data are from a 2013 survey that measured the reputation and responsibility of Finnish companies (see Appendix Fig. 1). The survey had 9,802 respondents from different age, gender, and regional groups in Finland and examined 59 companies that operate in the country. These same 59 companies were chosen as the sample for this research in order to have comparable data about reputation. The companies operate in seven different industries: food, retail, service, finance, energy, industry, and ICT. The reputation index covers different dimensions. The survey questions evaluated perceptions of five different fields: overall evaluation of reputation, impression about the company, trust, financial success, and the quality of products

Table 1 Classification of social media activity

Activity	Scale
Activity on Facebook	
No Facebook page	1
Facebook page but no activity	2
Less than 50 posts a year	3
50–100 posts a year	4
100–500 posts a year	5
More than 500 posts a year	6
Amount of likes on posts	
No Facebook page	1
Less than 10 likes/post	2
10–50 likes/post	3
50–100 likes/post	4
100–1000 likes/post	5
More than 1000 likes/post	6
Activity on Twitter	
No Twitter account	1
An account but no tweets	2
Less than every other day	3
Max once a day	4
1–2 tweets a day	5
Many tweets a day	6
Activity on LinkedIn	
No LinkedIn profile	1
Profile but no activity	2
Profile but no regular activity	3
1–5 posts a month	4
5–15 posts a month	5
More than 15 posts a month	6

and services. The questions were divided into three dimensions so that questions dealing with overall evaluation of reputation explained overall reputation; questions dealing with impression of the company and trust explained relationship and emotional attraction; and questions dealing with financial success and quality of the products and services explained competence and rational attraction.

Third, data on firm performance and size (used as a control variable) were gathered from secondary sources, i.e., companies' annual reports. The data included revenue, profits, and the number of personnel in the companies for financial year 2013. If financial data from 2013 were not available, data from 2012 were used. Net profit was used to indicate firm performance and revenue, and number of personnel was used to indicate company size.

The relationships between the study constructs were analyzed with two-tailed Pearson's correlation.

4 Results

The largest share was in the food and industry groups with 13 companies (22 %) in each. The second largest group was energy with nine companies (15.3 %). The next largest group was finance with eight companies (13.6 %) followed by service and retail with six companies (10.2 %) each. The smallest group was ICT with four companies (6.8 %). Most companies were B2C (75 %).

Of the 59 companies, almost all had a LinkedIn page (97 %) and YouTube channel (83 %). Approximately three out of four had a Facebook presence (76 %) and Twitter account (73 %). The ICT and service sectors were the most active on social media. All companies in the ICT sector participated in all four types of social media (Facebook, Twitter, LinkedIn, and YouTube). In addition, all companies in the service sector participated in all four types of social media, with the exception of two companies that did not have Twitter accounts. Energy and retail were the most inactive sectors, with 33 % of companies having no Facebook, Twitter, or YouTube accounts. In the retail sector, 83 % of companies had no Twitter account.

A majority of the numeric data were not classified but used directly as ratio variables. On Facebook, a majority of the companies (49 %) made 50 to 100 posts during 2013 (Table 2).

Table 2 Firms' social media activity	N	%
Activity on Facebook		
No Facebook page	14	23.7
Facebook page but no activity	0	0.0
Less than 50 posts a year	2	3.4
50–100 posts a year	29	49.2
100–500 posts a year	11	18.6
More than 500 posts a year	3	5.1
Activity on Twitter		
No Twitter account	18	30.5
An account but no tweets	2	3.4
Less than every other day	6	10.2
Max once a day	13	22.0
1–2 tweets a day	5	8.5
Many tweets a day	15	25.4
Activity on LinkedIn		
No LinkedIn profile	5	8.5
Profile but no activity	11	18.6
Profile but no regular activity	9	15.3
1–5 posts a month	19	32.2
5–15 posts a month	11	18.6
More than 15 posts a month	4	6.8

Every company with a Facebook profile had at least some activity, and only two companies (3.4 %) made fewer than 50 posts during the year. One-fourth (25 %) of the companies tweeted multiple times per day. On LinkedIn, the largest group, 19 companies (32.2 %), made one to five posts per month. Social media activity was also related to whether the company was serving consumers (B2C) or other organizations (B2B). In general, B2C companies were found to be more active on Facebook, Twitter, and YouTube whereas B2B companies were more active on LinkedIn.

4.1   The Relationship Between a Firm's Social Media Activity and Corporate Reputation

Within the overall sample, social media activity and company reputation (based on reputation index values) are not related (at the $p < 0.05$ level). However, when examining this relationship between industries and in B2B versus B2C companies, significant correlations were found. In the service industry, there is a positive relationship among Facebook activity ($r = 0.843$, $p < 0.01$), number of Twitter followers ($r = 0.976, p < 0.01$), tweets ($r = 0.976, p < 0.01$), and reputation. In the food industry, reputation correlates with number of LinkedIn followers ($r = 0.976$, $p < 0.01$) and LinkedIn activity ($r = 0.577$, $p < 0.05$). In this industry, there were also correlations between YouTube channel subscribers and reputation ($r = 0.690$, $p < 0.05$) and between YouTube views and reputation ($r = 0.663$, $p < 0.05$).

When examining B2B and B2C companies separately, the only correlation found was among B2B companies between reputation and people talking about a company on Facebook ($r = 0.784$, $p < 0.05$).

4.2   The Relationship Between Firm's Social Media Activity and Firm Performance

Within the overall sample, when examining the relationship between variables of Facebook activity (likes, talking about, activity) and financial numbers (net revenue, net profit), the only significant correlations were between the amount of people talking about a company on Facebook and net revenue ($r = 0.313, p < 0.05$) and between the amount of people talking about a company on Facebook and a control variable, namely, number of personnel ($r = 0.500, p < 0.01$). This indicates that people are talking more about companies that are larger and more profitable on Facebook. No significant relationships were observed between net profit and other values.

With respect to Twitter, significant correlations were found between the number of tweets and net profit ($r = 0.384$, $p < 0.05$), between the number of tweets and number of personnel ($r = 0.591$, $p < 0.01$), and between overall activity and net revenue ($r = 0.280$, $p < 0.05$). This indicates that more profitable companies and companies with more personnel made more tweets, and companies with higher net revenue had more yearly activity.

On LinkedIn, significant correlations were found between activity and net revenue ($r = 0.311$, $p < 0.05$), between activity and net profit ($r = 0.319$, $p < 0,05$), and between activity and number of personnel ($r = 0.391$, $p < 0.01$). This indicates that more profitable companies and companies with more personnel are more active on LinkedIn. Amount of followers did not correlate with revenue, profit, or number of personnel.

On YouTube, there were no significant correlations between any variables (subscribers, amount of videos, views, financial figures).

5 Discussion

The aim of the study was to examine the relationship between a company's activity on social media and corporate reputation and firm performance. The two propositions developed were not supported by the data. The first proposition claimed that activity on social media would have a positive relationship with corporate reputation. This proposition is based on the idea that customers want to participate, interact, and create value by themselves, and social media provides the possibility for companies to participate and interact with customers, leading to higher involvement and commitment and greater bigger customer satisfaction [2], which again has been proven to lead to better corporate reputation [27]. This leads to the conclusion that social media has an indirect effect on corporate reputation.

The second proposition argued that firm's activity on social media would have a positive relationship with firm performance. This proposition is based on the idea that social media usage can increase customers' involvement and commitment to a company, leading to increased satisfaction and loyalty [2], which again have been found to have a positive impact on firm equity value [8, 33]. Hence, an indirect effect of social media participation is better firm performance. However, this study provides some evidence of the partial relationship between social media and firm performance. The relationship was identified in use of Twitter and LinkedIn. Larger companies with more personnel had more tweets overall and were also more active on LinkedIn than smaller companies with fewer personnel.

Additionally, companies with larger net revenue were more active on both Twitter and LinkedIn than were companies with smaller net revenue. More profitable companies (with larger net profit) registered more activity on LinkedIn and more tweets than less profitable companies did. On Facebook, people talked more about profitable and larger companies, but a companies' own activity on Facebook had no relationship to firm performance or size. On YouTube, there was no relationship between companies' activity and firm performance and size.

The main theoretical contribution of the study is that it demonstrates that the more active companies have better reputations than that are not active in social media. However, a partial link can be found between social media activity and firm performance. In terms of managerial implications, this research presents a good argument that managers should not believe that simply being active in different social media channels is sufficient to enhance corporate reputation or increase financial performance. Even if a company itself is active on social media, reputation and financial performance are not inherently positive as a result.

These rather counterintuitive findings are limited by the sampling frame, analysis methods, and firm perspective. Despite companies' activity on social media, most of the things that happen in social media occur regardless of how active companies are in this arena. Social media has caused power to shift from companies to consumers and, as a result, companies' ability to control their reputation and what is said about them on the Internet has diminished [4]. Nevertheless, companies have not lost all their power as they still control the rules and framework of how the company and its brands participate in social media. Companies can decide, for example, what is posted, who is posting, and where it is posted [30]. Thus, we encourage researchers to further examine the relationship between firms' social media activity and corporate reputation/firm performance.

Appendix

See Fig. 1.

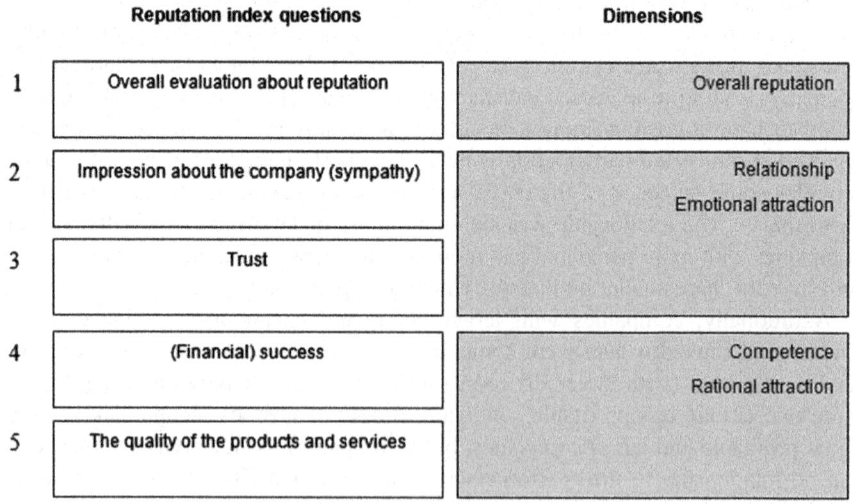

Fig. 1 The dimensions of reputation index

References

1. Kietzman, J.H., Hermkens, K., McCarthy, I.P., Silvestre, B.S.: Social media? get serious! understanding the functional building blocks of social media. Bus. Horizons. **54**, 241–251 (2011)
2. Trainor, K.J.: Relating social media technologies to performance: a capabilities-based perspective. J. Pers. Selling Sales Manage. **32**, 317–331 (2012)
3. Jones, B., Temperley, J., Lima, A.: Corporate reputation in the era of web 2.0: the case of Primark. J. Market. Manage. **25**, 927–939 (2009)
4. Bunting, M., Lipski, R.: Drowned out? rethinking corporate reputation management for the internet. J. Commun. Manage. **5**, 170–178 (2000)
5. Kirtiş, A.K., Karahan, F.: To be or not to be in social media arena as the most cost-efficient marketing strategy after the global recession. Procedia-Social Behav. Sci. **24**, 260–268 (2011)
6. Aula, P.: Social media, reputation risk and ambient publicity management. Strat. Leadersh. **38**, 43–49 (2010)
7. Firestein, P.J.: Building and protecting corporate reputation. Strat. Leadersh. **34**, 25–31 (2006)
8. Luo, X., Homburg, C., Wieseke, J.: Customer satisfaction, analyst stock recommendations, and firm value. J. Market. Res. **47**, 1041–1058 (2010)
9. Ryan, D., Jones, C.: Understanding Digital marketing: Marketing Strategies for Engaging the Digital Generation. Kogan Page Ltd, London (2009)
10. Drury, G.: Opinion piece: social media: should marketers engage and how can it be done effectively? J. Direct Data Digital Market. Pract. **9**, 274–277 (2008)
11. Bowman, N.D., Westerman, D.K., Claus, C.J.: How demanding is social media: understanding social media diets as a function of perceived costs and Benefits—a rational actor perspective. Comput. Hum. Behav. **28**, 2298–2305 (2012)
12. Kaplan, A., Haenlein, M.: Users of the world, unite! the challenges and opportunities of social media. Bus. Horiz. **53**, 59–68 (2010)
13. Funk, T.: Social media playbook for business: reaching your online community with Twitter, Facebook, Linkedin and More. ABC-CLIO, Santa Barbara, CA (2011)
14. Bodnar, K., Cohen, J.L.: B2B social media book: become a marketing superstar by generating leads with blogging, LinkedIn, Twitter, Facebook, Email, and more. Wiley, Hoboken, NJ (2011)
15. Berthon, P.R.: Marketing meets Web 2.0, social media, and creative consumers: implications for international marketing strategy. Bus. Horiz. **55**, 261–271 (2012)
16. Biel, J., Gatica-Perez, D.: The YouTube lens: crowdsourced personality impressions and audiovisual analysis of vlogs. IEEE Trans. Multimedia **15**, 41–55 (2013)
17. Greenberg, P.: The impact of CRM 2.0 on customer insight. J. Bus. Indus. Market. **25**, 410–419 (2010)
18. Williams, R.J.: The impact of corporate strategy on a firm's reputation. Corp. Reputation Rev. **8**, 187–197 (2005)
19. Hall, R.: A framework linking intangible resources and capabilities to sustainable competitive advantage. Strat. Manage. J. **14**, 607–618 (1993)
20. Fombrun, C.J., Van Riel, C.B.M.: Fame and Fortune: How Successful Companies Build Winning Reputations. Pearson, Upper Saddle River, NJ (2003)
21. Eberl, M., Schwaiger, M.: Corporate reputation: disentangling the effects on financial performance. Eur. J. Market. **39**, 838–854 (2005)
22. Keh, H.T.: Corporate reputation and customer behavioral intentions: the roles of trust, identification and commitment. Indus. Market. Manage. **38**, 732–742 (2009)
23. Alniacik, U.: Independent and joint effects of perceived corporate reputation, affective commitment and job satisfaction on turnover intentions. Procedia—Soc. Behav. Sci. **24**, 1177–1189 (2011)
24. Helm, S.: Employees' awareness of their impact on corporate reputation. J. Bus. Res. **64**, 657–663 (2011)

25. Walsh, G.E.: Customer-based corporate reputation of a service firm: scale development and validation. J. Acad. Market. Sci. **35**, 127–143 (2007)
26. Fombrun, C.J.: Reputation: Realizing Value from the Corporate Image. Harvard Business School Press, Cambridge, MA (1996)
27. Carmeli, A.A.C., Tishler, A.: Perceived organizational reputation and organizational performance: an empirical investigation of industrial enterprises. Corp. Reputation Rev. **8**, 13–30 (2005)
28. Gilfoil, D.M., Jobs, C.: return on investment for social media: a proposed framework for understanding, implementing, and measuring the return. J. Bus. Econ. Res. **10**, 637–650 (2012)
29. Fisher, T.: ROI in social media: a look at the arguments. J. Database Market. Customer Strat. Manage. **16**, 189–195 (2009)
30. Hoffman, D.L., Fodor, M.: Can you measure the roi of your social media marketing? MIT Sloan Manage. Rev. **52**, 41–49 (2010)
31. Schniederjans, D.: Enhancing financial performance with social media: an impression management perspective. Decis. Support Syst. **55**, 911–918 (2013)
32. Yu, Y., Duan, W., Cao, Q.: The impact of social and conventional media on firm equity value: a sentiment analysis approach. Decis. Support Syst. **55**, 919–926 (2013)
33. Anderson, E.W., Fornell, C., Mazvancheryl, S.K.: Customer satisfaction and shareholder value. J. Market. **68**, 172–185 (2004)

The Relationships Between Customer Brand Engagement in Social Media and Share of Wallet

Heikki Karjaluoto, Juha Munnukka and Severi Tiensuu

1 Introduction

Many companies have fully integrated social media into their marketing and brand building activities. For example, in recent years, several companies have created brand communities on social media such as Facebook, which currently has around 890 million active daily users on average [1]. This increase in the use of social media and other technologies has led to the development of new tools, and consequently, it has also led to new practices of contacting and engaging with customers. Customer engagement has become increasingly important for companies' customer relationship management [2–4] and often results in repeated interactions that strengthens customers' emotional, psychological, or physical investment in a brand [5]. Furthermore, academic research has been quick to respond to this development, resulting in new theories and empirical evidence regarding customer brand engagement [2, 6]. It has been suggested that the consumers' share of spending on companies' offerings (i.e., share-of-wallet) becomes a focal measure of business value and behavioral loyalty in the context of consumer marketing [7, 8]. This is particularly true for retailers who continuously search for more effective methods of extracting a higher share of total grocery expenditures from their customers' share-of-wallet (SOW) [9]. In recent years, social media has been recognized as a highly effective channel for contacting and engaging with consumers. For example, Zheng et al. [10] have recently shown that companies can effectively

H. Karjaluoto (✉) · J. Munnukka (✉) · S. Tiensuu
School of Business and Economics, University of Jyväskylä, Jyväskylä, Finland
e-mail: heikki.karjaluoto@jyu.fi

J. Munnukka
e-mail: juha.t.munnukka@jyu.fi

S. Tiensuu
e-mail: severi_tiensuu@hotmail.com

© Springer International Publishing Switzerland 2016
F. D'Ascenzo et al. (eds.), *Blurring the Boundaries Through Digital Innovation*,
Lecture Notes in Information Systems and Organisation 19,
DOI 10.1007/978-3-319-38974-5_14

strengthen brand loyalty by engaging customers in online brand communities. However, brand engagement and its consequences on consumer buying behavior are relatively new concepts in the academic information systems and business literature. More empirical research is needed especially in the context of online communities [11–13]. Therefore, our study aims to provide new information regarding the drivers of customer engagement in online brand communities and how this impacts customer spending on company products.

Literature proposes that engagement results from motivation [14–17]. McQuail [18] classified motivation into four main components: social interaction, need for information, entertainment, and developing personal identity. In the subsequent literature, economic benefit has been presented as a driver of engagement [10, 19]. Studies show numerous benefits of customer engagement, such as higher brand satisfaction, trust, commitment, emotional connection/attachment, empowerment, consumer value, and loyalty [6, 14, 16]. However, current research lacks empirical evidence regarding the impact of engagement on consumer spending and choice between different brands.

One well-documented example of engagement on social media is Coca-Cola, which has successfully capitalized on social media in brand management. Coca-Cola actively participates in the social media brand community to inspire optimism and happiness and to build the Coca-Cola brand [20]. Coca-Cola has nearly 80 million fans and more than 640,000 people talking about the company and its products on Facebook. Coca-Cola strives to build personal relationships with millions of people, thus accruing brand loyalty which enhances business value.

In addition to an increase in the use of social media and online brand communities, the impact of social media on customer buying behavior has become a valid concern. A common goal of most virtual brand communities has been to attract members to community sites and encourage them to engage in online activities as often as possible. This frequency of visit has been considered as one of the key indicators of customer brand engagement [21–23]. In addition, previous literature suggests that customers' brand behavior is strengthened by frequent exposure to brand communication [24]. De Valck et al. [25] have found similar positive effects that exist in online brand communities, and they suggest that the frequency of exposure to brand-related messages on community site, directly impacts members' behavior. However, current research continues to be limited regarding the relationship between customers' frequency of visiting an online brand community site and brand engagement-buying behavior.

This study seeks to contribute to the identified limitations of existing knowledge by constructing and testing a conceptual model of customer brand engagement in the context of social media. This study examines behavioral and experiential motives that affect customer brand engagement in a social media context in addition to the effect of engagement on SOW. We combine engagement and SOW theories to develop a framework for the associations between the aforementioned concepts. This research concurs with the suggestions of [12, 14, 21] that note the need for more empirical studies on customer engagement to identify different types of brand communities and similarities in engagement behaviors. In addition, the Marketing

Science Institute (MSI) identified customer engagement as a key research priority [26]. This research contributes to current literature by first showing the key drivers of customer engagement in online brand communities; it also discusses how brand community engagement impacts the brand's share of the consumers' wallet (SOW). Third, we examine the effect of consumers' frequency of visiting the online community site in the proposed model.

The remainder of the paper is structured as follows: (1) we briefly describe the research framework and develop hypotheses on how motivational factors, brand engagement, share of wallet and frequency of visit are connected; (2) we describe the methods and measures applied to test the research model; and (3) we present the results and discuss the findings from both theoretical and managerial aspects.

2 Sources of Brand Engagement and Influence on Share-of-Wallet

2.1 Research Model and Hypotheses

The conceptual model of this study and six hypotheses that are derived from the existing literature are presented in Fig. 1. This study examines the impact of five types of motives on customer engagement in the social media context in addition to analyzing the impact of brand engagement and frequency of visits to the social media forums (Facebook and Twitter) of the brand on SOW. The model is controlled for gender and age.

In the online context, virtual brand communities constitute an important platform for customer engagement behavior [14, 27–29]. According to Hanna et al. [30], the main objective of social media presence is to capture consumers' attention and engage them with the brand. Existing research suggests that customer engagement is a strategic imperative for establishing and sustaining a competitive advantage and is a valuable predictor of future business performance [14]. Other research claims that customer engagement improves profitability [31] and promotes customers' WOM behavior, such as increasing customers' tendency to make referrals and recommendations on specific products, services, and/or brands to others [14]. Furthermore, consumers' active participation in positively valenced brand-related activities in online brand communities has been found to positively affect their self-brand connection and brand use intentions [32] as well as increase the effectiveness of brand-related messages on building the customer-brand relationship [33]. In this study, customer brand engagement in social media is defined as "an interactive and integrative participation in the fan-page community" [12, p. 349].

Engagement stems from multiple motivations [10, 14–16]. This study analyses five relevant motivations in the social media context: community motivations (c.f. social interaction motivations), information motivations, entertainment motivations, personal identity motivations and economic motivations [18, 34, 35]. Research [12, 13] revealed that community value is among the strongest drivers of

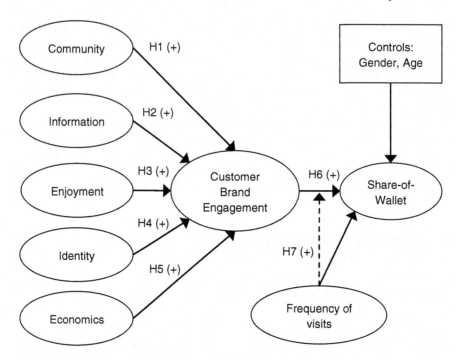

Fig. 1 Research model and hypotheses (*dashed lines* represent moderating effects)

brand fan page use. Need for information is another key motive for participating in online brand communities [36, 37]. In addition, entertainment is an important motivation for viewing user-generated content [37]. Experiential value is created for customers that use online services such as social media [21, 38]. Similarly, impression management and identity expression have been identified as motivators of social network sites access [39] where users can express their individuality by adjusting their profiles, linking to particular friends, displaying their "likes" and "dislikes," and joining groups [40]. Finally, economic benefits provide an impetus for joining brand communities [10]. For example, economic incentives such as discounts, time savings, or opportunities to participate in raffles and competitions are important motivational drivers for consumers to engage in online brand communities [19].

The following hypotheses have been constructed regarding these five motivations that drive consumers' brand engagement in social media:

H1: Community experience is positively associated with customer brand engagement

H2: Information experience is positively associated with customer brand engagement

H3: Enjoyment experience is positively associated with customer brand engagement

H4: Identity-related experience is positively associated with customer brand engagement

H5: Economic-related experience is positively associated with customer brand engagement

SOW is defined as the percentage of the volume of total business transactions between a firm and a customer within a year [41]. For example, in retail banking, it is "the stated percentage of total assets held at the bank being rated by the customer" [42, p. 365]. According to Perkins-Munn et al. [43], a firm's efforts to manage customers' spending patterns tend to represent greater opportunities than simply trying to maximize customer retention rates. In fact, rather than concentrating on customer retention rates, a more effective method to increase profitability is to concentrate on serving existing customers [44] and increasing the company's SOW [see 8]. For example, Vivek et al. [23] show that engaged consumers lead to positive organizational outcomes, such as increased SOW.

Consumers' share of spending is an important measure of behavioral loyalty [7, 45] and provides essential information to retailers regarding how and why customers allocate their purchases across different brands and stores [9]. This information enables retailers to formulate strategies that motivate their customers to allot a higher share of their expenditures to the retailer's products. Therefore, it has been suggested that SOW is a more reliable measure of loyalty than other loyalty measures [8, 46]. Although engagement has been linked with satisfaction, commitment and loyalty [6, 14, 15], only Vivek et al. [23] has specifically investigated the associations between consumer brand engagement and SOW. This preliminary study indicated a positive association between these constructs and strong support exists for the positive relationship between customer engagement and loyalty [16, 47, 48]. We theorize that a consumer's increased engagement in an online brand community leads to a higher share of the consumer's wallet for that brand. Therefore, the next hypothesis postulates the following:

H6: Customer brand engagement has a positive effect on SOW.

The frequency of customer participation in brand community activities is an important indicator of customer brand engagement [21] as well as the strength of the customer-brand relationship [24]. In addition, the frequency of customer participation in brand community activities includes the frequency of communication and community member interaction [49]. The frequency of communication or interaction between community members is a crucial aspect of engagement behavior [23], communication quality and collaborative communication behavior [50]. Existing research indicates that customers' frequency of visits to a brand site is positively associated with loyalty behavior [51]. In addition, frequency of visits is likely to strengthen the effectiveness of community content on the customer-brand relationship [25]. Literature shows that exposure frequency strengthens the effectiveness of information on consumer behavior [52]. Therefore, the frequency that consumers engage in brand community activities is expected to strengthen the brand engagement-SOW relationship.

H7: Frequency of visits moderates the positive relationship between engagement
     and SOW such that when frequency of visits is high, the relationship will be
     stronger.

3 Methodology

The hypotheses were tested using data obtained from Facebook fans and Twitter
followers of a global consumer electronics company. Within a two-week response
time, 818 people submitted completed questionnaires. The effective response rate
was 57 %. Established scales ranging from 1 "strongly disagree" to 5 "strongly
agree" were utilized to measure the study constructs. Community (four items) and
enjoyment (three items) scales were adapted from [35, 53]. Identity and information
motives were measured with three items each adapted from [35]. Two items from
[22] were applied to measure economic benefits. The customer brand engagement
(seven items) scale was adapted from [12, 21, 37]. SOW was measured using two
items from [45].

The data were first subjected to an exploratory factor analysis, and the
hypotheses subsequently were tested with partial least squares structural equation
modelling software SmartPLS 3.0 [54]. All the study constructs are reflective.

Common method bias had been minimized in the data collection stage by
rearranging the items in the questionnaire and ensuring that the respondents'
identities remained confidential. In the analysis phase, we ran a PLS model with a
method factor. The results suggested that the average variance explained by the
indicators (0.704) was considerably higher than the average method-based variance
(0.016). Given the magnitude of the method variance, common method bias is
unlikely to be of serious concern in this study.

Nonresponse bias was examined by comparing the early respondents (N = 100)
to the late respondents (N = 100). No statistically significant differences ($p < 0.05$)
between the groups were found in their responses to the study constructs. Thus,
nonresponse bias is not likely to occur in the survey.

4 Results

The majority of the respondents were male 547 (67 %). Most respondents reported
ages between 26 and 35 years (25 %). The next largest groups were those aged 36–
45 (19.9 %) and 18–25 (18.9 %). Most of the respondents visited the fan page
either 1–3 times per week (30 %) or 2–3 times per month (24 %). This composition
aligns with the profile of the visitors to the case company's Facebook fan page,
where the female population accounts for approximately 40 % of the community's
population.

4.1 Measurement Model

The confirmatory factor analysis was acceptable because the factor loadings were high (>0.75) and significant, the composite reliabilities for the scales were larger than 0.840, the AVE values exceeded the cut-off criteria 0.50, and discriminant validity was achieved when the square root of AVE exceeded the value of correlation between the factors (see Table 1).

The model's predictive relevance was medium-high, as the model explains more than 50 % of the R^2 of customer brand engagement ($R^2 = 0.695$). The R^2 for SOW was 0.182. The Q^2 values were larger than 0.15 for SOW and larger than 0.35 for customer brand engagement, indicating that the path model's predictive accuracy for SOW and engagement are medium and large, respectively [55].

4.2 Structural Model

Figure 2 shows the results of the hypotheses testing.

The proposed five motivational factors were studied, and four of the drivers exhibited positive relationships with brand engagement, thus confirming H1, H3, H4 and H5. The effects of community is the strongest ($\beta = 0.469$, $p < 0.01$), followed by the effect of economic motives ($\beta = 0.222$, $p < 0.01$), identity motives ($\beta = 0.193$, $p < 0.01$) and enjoyment motives ($\beta = 0.106$, $p < 0.01$). No relationship between information motives and engagement was found, thus H2 was rejected. Moreover, customer brand engagement (H6) was positively associated with SOW ($\beta = 0.249$, $p < 0.01$), confirming H6. The test of the moderating effect (H7) of frequency of visits showed that it strengthens ($\beta = 0.062$, $p < 0.05$) the effect of engagement on SOW, thus supporting H7. A review of the control variables indicated that the effects of gender and age on SOW were not significant.

The results suggest that (1) community benefits are the strongest motivator of customer brand engagement in the social media context, (2) customer brand engagement is positively associated with SOW, and (3) the effect of brand engagement on SOW is strengthened when frequency of visiting is high.

5 Discussion

Customer brand engagement has become more important in companies' customer relationship and brand management activities in conjunction with the growth of social media. However, theories and conceptual models still need more empirical testing. Research is especially needed that analyses the drivers of customer brand engagement in social media, how customer brand engagement affects consumers' buying behavior, and how consumers' frequency of visiting a brand community site

Table 1 Discriminant validity

	AVE	(1)	(2)	(3)	(4)	(5)	(6)	(7)	(8)	(9)	(10)
COM[b] (1)	0.645	**0.803**									
INF[c] (2)	0.719	0.618	**0.848**								
ENJ[d] (3)	0.711	0.578	0.685	**0.843**							
IDE[e] (4)	0.683	0.654	0.580	0.630	**0.826**						
ECO[f] (5)	0.727	0.388	0.326	0.352	0.444	**0.852**					
CBE[g] (6)	0.687	0.765	0.583	0.602	0.686	0.539	**0.829**				
SOW[h] (7)	0.867	0.248	0.246	0.287	0.283	0.190	0.358	**0.931**			
FV[i] (8)	n/a	0.352	0.327	0.420	0.341	0.241	0.452	0.360	**n/a**		
Gender (9)	n/a	0.114	0.143	0.010	0.038	0.080	0.039	-0.055	-0.102	**n/a**	
Age (10)	n/a	-0.017	0.011	-0.059	-0.095	-0.042	-0.016	-0.073	0.065	0.142	**n/a**
Mean	–	2.99	3.44	3.33	2.67	3.29	2.75	4.17[j]	3.28		
s.d.	–	1.10	1.00	0.96	1.05	1.17	1.14	2.55	1.24		
CR[a]	–	0.879	0.884	0.881	0.866	0.840	0.939	0.929	n/a	n/a	n/a

Notes [a]*CR* Composite reliability; [b]*COM* Community; [c]*INF* Information; [d]*ENJ* Enjoyment; [e]*IDE* Identity; [f]*ECO* Economics; [g]*CBE* Customer brand engagement; [h]*SOW* Share of wallet; [i]*FV* Frequency of visits; [j]SOW item scale recoded from 0–100 to 0–10
n/a Not applicable. Construct measured through a single indicator; composite reliability and AVE cannot be computed

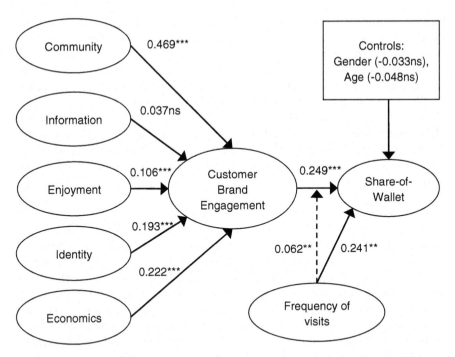

Fig. 2 Hypotheses testing (path coefficients). *Notes* ***p < 0.01, **p < 0.05, ns = Not significant

affects these relationships. One of the key measures of behavioral loyalty is share of wallet (SOW). However, existing research is limited in examining the effect of customer brand engagement in social media on SOW [14, 23].

This study contributes to existing customer brand engagement literature with three important findings. First, we refined the model of social media engagement suggested by [10] by identifying four specific motivations that positively influence consumers' brand engagement in social media. The results indicated that consumers who follow a brand in social media and receive benefits related to community, enjoyment, identity and economics are more intensively engaged with the brand than those receiving fewer benefits. Interestingly, information motives were not found to be related to engagement [cf. 13]. Our findings confirmed the existence of four motivational drivers of brand engagement in social media [12, 17, 37], and we add to the literature by identifying community experience as the key driver of customer brand engagement in social media and demonstrating that information motives had no impact on engagement. The latter conflicts with [13], who stated that information plays an important role in engaging consumers in companies' microblog sites. A possible explanation for the contradicting result may be that Facebook brand communities focus on the other four motives that we identified. Second, we make an important contribution to literature by investigating the relationship between brand engagement in social media and SOW. The relationship between customers' engagement with a company's Facebook site and the brand's share of the customers' spending has not been previously studied. Our results show that customer engagement is positively associated with SOW [c.f. 23]. Specifically, the percentage of expenditures that engaged customers allocate to a brand is larger than that allocated by customers who are unengaged with the brand in social media. Finally, we add to current knowledge by showing that the customers' frequency of visiting a brand's online community positively affects the brand engagement and SOW relationship. Thus, the higher the visiting frequency, the stronger is the positive relationship between brand engagement and SOW [c.f. 25] [c.f. 52]. Therefore, brand engagement in social media is a stronger driver of SOW among consumers with higher visiting frequency than among consumers with lower visiting frequency.

Three managerial implications can be concluded from our findings. First, our results verified that four (out of five) motivational factors drive brand engagement in social media. Of these four motives, community motives were found to be the most important. Thus, we recommend that managers should develop social media sites that foster we-intentions and belongingness [c.f. 25]. In addition, we encourage managers to offer economic benefits on Facebook communities. Second, the results confirmed a positive link between brand engagement in social media and SOW, and we encourage brands to invest in fostering engagement in social media brand sites. Third, the results indicated that managers should implement social media strategies that maximize the users' frequency of visits and consequently increase the effectiveness social media. Companies should invest in generating current information and innovative activities for those customers that are identified as high-frequent visitors of the brand's social media site. Acting on these implications should result in an increase of the brand's share of the customers' wallet.

Finally, the study has limitations that may offer opportunities for future studies. The sample may be biased towards more motivated social media users because participation was voluntary. Thus, in generalizing the results, caution must be made. Future studies should strive to utilize data that includes respondents that are less motived users of the brand. Although we minimized common method bias in the survey design, its effect can only be ruled out with a longitudinal study design. Last, this study analyzed brands sold only in household appliance stores in Finland, which limits the generalization of these results to other types of brands or to geographic areas outside of Finland. It is recommended that future research be conducted to study multiple geographic locations and include multiple brands.

Appendix

See Table 2.

Table 2 List of survey items

Items	Factor loadings
Community	
I am as interested in input from other users as I am in the content generated by company	0.789
I like the company's FB site because of what I get from other users	0.871
The company's FB site gets its visitors to converse or comment	0.734
I have become interested in things, which I otherwise would not have, because of other users on the site	0.813
Information	
I get good tips from the content	0.786
The content shows me how people live	0.870
The content helps me learn what to do or how to do it	0.884
Enjoyment	
I find following content enjoyable	0.861
Following content helps me improve my mood	0.810
The content entertains me	0.858
Identity	
Following content makes me a more interesting person	0.849
Contributing to this content makes me feel like I belong to a group	0.776
I want other people to know that I am reading this content	0.853
Economic	
I write comments and/or like posts on a virtual platform because of the incentives I can receive	0.937
I write comments and/or like posts on a virtual platform because I can receive a reward for the writing and liking	0.758
Brand engagement	
I am an engaged member of this fan-page community	0.821
I am an active member of this fan-page community	0.754
I am a participating member of this fan-page community	0.858
I engage in conversations and comment in company's FB-site	0.823
I often like (like-function in FB) contents from company's FB-site	0.823
I use to contribute in conversations in company's FB-site	0.873
I often share company's contents in FB	0.845
Share of wallet	
What percentage of your total expenditures for domestic appliance technologies do you spend for company's products?	0.933
Of the 10 times you select to buy domestic appliance technologies, how many times do you select company?	0.929
Frequency of visits	
How often you visit the community?	n/a

References

1. Facebook: Annual Report 2014. Facebook Inc, http://investor.fb.com/annuals.cfm (2015)
2. Libai, B.: Comment: the perils of focusing on highly engaged customers. J. Serv. Res. **14**, 275–276 (2011)
3. Sashi, C.M.: Customer engagement, buyer-seller relationships, and social media. Manag. Decis. **50**, 253–272 (2012)
4. Kumar, V., Aksoy, L., Donkers, B., Venkatesan, R., Wiesel, T., Tillmans, S.: Undervalued or overvalued customers: capturing total customer engagement value. J. Serv. Res. **13**, 297–310 (2010)
5. Sedley, R.: 4th Annual Online Customer Engagement Report 2010, http://issuu.com/richardsedley/docs/customer-engagement-report2010 (2010)
6. Bowden, J.L.H.: The process of customer engagement: a conceptual framework. J. Market. Theory Pract. **17**, 63–74 (2009)
7. Keiningham, T.L., Aksoy, L., Perkins-Munn, T., Vavra, T.G.: The brand-customer connections. Market. Manage. **14**, 33–37 (2005)
8. Zeithaml, V.A.: Service quality, profitability, and the economic worth of customers: what we know and what we need to learn. J. Acad. Market. Sci. **28**, 67–85 (2000)
9. Meyer-Waarden, L.: The effects of loyalty programs on customer lifetime duration and share of wallet. J. of Retail. **83**, 223–236 (2007)
10. Zheng, X., Cheung, C.M., Lee, M.K., Liang, L.: Building brand loyalty through user engagement in online brand communities in social networking sites. Inform. Technol. People **28**, 90–106 (2015)
11. Cheung, C. M. K., Lee, M. K. O., Jin, X-L.: Customer engagement in an online social platform: a conceptual model and scale development. In: Proceedings of the 32nd International Conference on Information Systems (ICIS), Shanghai, China, December 4–7 (2011)
12. Jahn, B., Kunz, W.: How to transform consumers into fans of your brand. J. Serv. Manage. **23**, 322–361 (2012)
13. Zhang, H., Zhang, K.Z., Lee, M.K., Feng, F.: Brand loyalty in enterprise microblogs: influence of community commitment, IT habit, and participation. Inform. Technol. People **28**, 304–326 (2015)
14. Brodie, R.J., Hollebeek, L.D., Juric, B., Ilic, A.: Conceptual domain, fundamental propositions and implications for research. J. Serv. Res. **14**, 252–271 (2011)
15. van Doorn, J., Lemon, K.N., Mittal, V., Nass, S., Pick, D., Pirner, P., Verhoef, P.C.: Customer engagement behavior: theoretical foundations and research directions. J. Serv. Res. **13**, 253–266 (2010)
16. Hollebeek, L.: Exploring customer brand engagement: definition and themes. J. Strateg. Market. **19**, 555–573 (2011)
17. Ouwersloot, H., Odekerken-Schröder, G.: Who's who in brand communities—and why? Eur. J. Market. **42**, 571–585 (2008)
18. McQuail, D.: Mass Communication Theory: An Introduction. Sage, London (1983)
19. Gwinner, K.P., Gremler, D.D., Bitner, M.J.: Relational benefits in service industries: the customer's perspective. J. Acad. Market. Sci. **26**, 101–114 (1998)
20. Coca Cola: Social Media Principles, http://www.coca-colacompany.com/stories/online-social-media-principles (2014)
21. Gummerus, J., Lijander, V., Weman, E., Pihlström, M.: Customer engagement in a facebook brand community. Manage. Res. Rev. **35**, 857–877 (2012)
22. Hennig-Thurau, T., Gwinner, K.P., Walsh, G., Gremler, D.D.: Electronic word-of-mouth via consumer-opinion platforms: what motivates consumers to articulate themselves on the internet? J. Interact. Market. **18**, 38–52 (2004)
23. Vivek, S.D., Beatty, S.E., Morgan, R.M.: Customer engagement: exploring customer relationships beyond purchase. J. Market. Theory Pract. **20**, 127–145 (2012)

24. Keller, K.L.: Building Customer-Based Brand Equity: A Blueprint for Creating Strong Brands. Marketing Science Institute, Working Paper. 01–107, pp. 3–38 (2001)
25. De Valck, K., van Bruggen, G.H., Wierenga, B.: Virtual communities: marketing perspective. Decis. Support Syst. **47**, 185–203 (2009)
26. Marketing Science Institute (MSI): Research Priorities 2014–2016, http://www.msi.org/research/2014-2016-research-priorities (2014)
27. Dholakia, U.M., Bagozzi, R.P., Pearo, L.K.: A social influence model of consumer participation in network- and small-group-based virtual communities. Int. J. Res. Market. **21**, 241–263 (2004)
28. Kane, G.C., Fichman, R.G., Gallaugher, J., Glaser, J.: Community relations 2.0. Harvard Bus. Rev. **87**, 45–50 (2009)
29. McAlexander, J., Schouten, J., Koenig, H.: Building brand community. J. Market. **66**, 38–54 (2002)
30. Hanna, R., Rohm, A., Crittenden, V.: We're all connected: the power of the social media ecosystem. Bus. Horiz. **54**, 265–273 (2011)
31. Voyles B.: Beyond Loyalty: Meeting the Challenge of Customer Engagement. Economist Intelligence Unit, http://www.adobe.com/engagement/pdfs/partI.pdf (2007)
32. Hollebeek, L.D., Glynn, M.S., Brodie, R.J.: Consumer brand engagement in social media: conceptualization, scale development and validation. J. Interact. Market. **28**, 149–165 (2014)
33. Habibi, M.R., Laroche, M., Richard, M.O.: The roles of brand community and community engagement in building brand trust on social media. Comput. Hum. Behav. **37**, 152–161 (2014)
34. Heinonen, K.: Consumer activity in social media: managerial approaches to consumers' social media behaviour. J. Consum. Behav. **10**, 356–364 (2011)
35. Mersey, R.D., Malthouse, E.C., Calder, B.J.: Focusing on the reader: engagement trumps satisfaction. J. Mass Commun. Q. **89**, 695–709 (2012)
36. Brodie, R.J., Ilic, A., Juric, B., Hollebeek, L.D.: Consumer engagement in a virtual brand community: an exploratory analysis. J. Bus. Res. **66**, 105–114 (2013)
37. Muntinga, D.G., Moorman, M., Smit, E.G.: Introducing COBRAs: exploring motivations for brand-related social media use. Int. J. Advertising **30**, 13–46 (2011)
38. Men, L.R., Tsai, W.-H.S.: Beyond liking or following: understanding public engagement on social networking sites in China. Public Relat. Rev. **39**, 13–22 (2013)
39. Boyd, D.: Why youth (Heart) social network sites: the role of networked publics in teenage social life. In: Buckingham, D. (ed.) MacArthur Foundation Series on Digital Learning—Youth, Identity, and Digital Media Volume, pp. 119–142. MIT Press, Cambridge, MA (2008)
40. Tufekci, Z.: Grooming, Gossip, Facebook and Myspace. Inform. Commun. Soc. **11**, 544–564 (2008)
41. Keiningham, T.L., Perkins-Munn, T., Evans, H.: The impact of customer satisfaction on share of wallet in a business-to-business environment. J. Serv. Res. **6**, 37–50 (2003)
42. Keiningham, T.L., Cooil, B., Aksoy, L., Andersson, T.W., Weiner, J.: The value of different customer satisfaction and loyalty metrics in predicting customer retention, recommendation, and share-of-wallet. Manag. Serv. Qual. **17**, 361–384 (2007)
43. Perkins-Munn, T., Aksoy, L., Keiningham, T.L., Estrin, D.: Actual purchase as a proxy for share of wallet. J. Serv. Res. **7**, 245–256 (2005)
44. Reinartz, W.J., Kumar, V.: On the profitability of long-life customers in a noncontractual setting: an empirical investigation and implications for marketing. J. Market. **64**, 17–35 (2000)
45. De Wulf, K., Odekerken-Schröder, G., Iacobucci, D.: Investments in consumer relationships: a cross-country and cross-industry exploration. J. Market. **50**, 33–50 (2001)
46. Jones, T.O., Sasser Jr, E.W.: Why satisfied customers defect. Harvard Bus. Rev. **73**, 88–99 (1995)
47. Algesheimer, R., Dholakia, U.M., Hermann, A.: The social influence of brand community: evidence from european car clubs. J. Market. **69**, 19–34 (2005)
48. Matzler, K., Krauter, S.G., Bidmon, S.: Risk aversion and brand loyalty: the mediating role of brand trust and brand affect. J. Prod. Brand Manage. **17**, 154–162 (2008)

49. Farace, R.V., Monge, P.R., Russell, H.: Communicating and Organizing. Addison-Wesley, Reading, MA (1977)
50. Mohr, J., Fisher, R., Nevin, J.R.: Collaborative communication in inter firm relationships: moderating effects of integration and control. J. Market. **60**, 103–115 (1996)
51. Thorbjørnsen, H., Supphellen, M.: The impact of brand loyalty on website usage. J. Brand Manage. **11**, 199–208 (2004)
52. Broussard, G.: How advertising frequency can work to build online advertising effectiveness. Int. J. Market Res. **42**, 439–457 (2000)
53. Calder, B.J., Malthouse, E.C., Schaedel, U.: An experimental study of the relationship between online engagement and advertising effectiveness. J. Interact. Market. **23**, 321–331 (2009)
54. Ringle, C.M., Wende, S., Becker, J-M.: SmartPLS 3. SmartPLS, Hamburg. http://www.smartpls.com
55. Sarstedt, M., Ringle, C.M., Smith, D., Reams, R., Hair Jr, J.F.: Partial least squares structural equation modeling (PLS-SEM): a useful tool for family business researchers. J. Family Bus. Strateg. **5**, 105–115 (2014)

Religiosity, Hedonism, Social Image and E-banking Acceptance in Lebanon

Antoine Harfouche, Soraya Ezzeddine and Michèle Kosremelli Asmar

1 Introduction

With the rapid diffusion of Internet, e-banking has become a real alternative to the physical channel [1]. In Lebanon, even though banks are investing more in financial e-services, e-banking has still not replaced traditional banking. Despite the fact that Internet usage in Lebanon is increasing (more than 60 % of Lebanese people are using the Web in their everyday life), e-banking is not used by the majority of banks customers in Lebanon.

This leads us to the following questions: What are the reasons of this delay in banking e-services acceptance in Lebanon? Does the Lebanese culture have an impact on the acceptance/rejection of these e-services? Does religion have a role in the acceptance/rejection of e-services?

The individuals' behaviour toward ICT acceptance/rejection has been the subject of research from academics around the world. Over time, a dozen of models were developed (TAM1, TAM2, TRA, DTRA, TPB, DTPB, MATH, MPCU, TIB, MM, UTAUT) mobilizing hundreds of variables. In this paper, our aim is not to create such a model; instead, it is to contextualize the acceptance/rejection of e-banking services. We therefore seek the local and situational variables related to the Lebanese context and, as Orlikowski and Suzanne Iacono [2] and Ben Boubaker and Barki [3], we consider the acceptance/rejection of banking e-services as a phenomenon embedded in a socio-economic, historical, psychological, political and

A. Harfouche (✉)
Université Paris Ouest Nanterre La Défense, Nanterre, France
e-mail: antoineharfouche@icto.info

S. Ezzeddine (✉) · M. Kosremelli Asmar (✉)
Saint Joseph University, Beirut, Lebanon
e-mail: soraya.ezzeddine@gmail.com

M. Kosremelli Asmar
e-mail: michele.asmar@usj.edu.lb

© Springer International Publishing Switzerland 2016   187
F. D'Ascenzo et al. (eds.), *Blurring the Boundaries Through Digital Innovation*,
Lecture Notes in Information Systems and Organisation 19,
DOI 10.1007/978-3-319-38974-5_15

legal context. In other words, the adoption of banking e-services is a cultural dependant phenomenon. Thus, based on the Model of Adoption of Technology in Households (MATH) [4], we propose a model that is rooted in the Lebanese culture and which emphasizes the Lebanese context. Our model connects three characteristics of the Lebanese cultural context to the acceptance/rejection of e-banking services: religiosity, affect, and social image. Lebanon is characterized by a heterogeneous population comprised of 18 religious communities [5]. This heterogeneity creates a difficult, hostile, and risky environment [6]. Religiosity plays an important role in the everyday life of Lebanese citizens. They see their life as directed by the will of God [6]. Another feature of the Lebanese culture is the salient role of emotions in the people's choice. Weir [7] and Harfouche [8] showed that the actions of Lebanese are guided by their emotional state rather than by a utilitarian rationale. Finally, Lebanese, like other Arabs, seek membership in social groups offering them the potential of lifting their social standing [9, 10]. Since Lebanese social self-image is considered very important. Some researchers proved that the Lebanese individual is ready to adopt certain behaviour just in order to impress his social group [11]. Therefore, the adoption/rejection of e-services in Lebanon can be influenced by religion, the hedonic and social potential outcomes that result from using the banking e-services.

Research linking religion, emotion, and social image to the acceptance of e-services are rare. Thus, our research provides new theoretical and empirical contributions. This paper presents the results of an empirical research that was conducted in 2011. The survey was conducted among 147 potential users of e-banking randomly chosen. The data was analysed and tested using structural equation modelling approach (SEM) using Partial Least Squares Path Modeling (PLS). This approach estimates structural models according to variance [12, 13]. Data were processed using the software SmartPLS [13].

2 Internet Banking and Banking E-services Acceptance

Banking has always been a highly information intensive activity [14]. The web gives the possibility to offer quick and updated information to online customers but it also offers the possibility to make distance transactions. Therefore, the multichannel strategy has become popular worldwide.

2.1 E-banking

E-banking allows customers to perform a wide range of banking transactions electronically via the bank's Web site. E-banking started as an information tool used to market banks products and services. Today, banks are introducing more and more transactional services whereas users can perform common banking transactions through the web such as managing their finances and investments, open new accounts and apply for new services, have access to e-statements and do international transfers,. Consequently, internet banking has evolved into a "one stop service" offering quick, easy and secured services with instant access to accounts from anywhere in the world. All these services are possible at low cost and constitute an alternative to brick and mortar branch banking.

2.2 The Banking E-services Acceptance Bounded in the Lebanese Context

Unfortunately, there has been no scientific research linking Lebanese culture with ICT acceptance. There is also very little research that compares Lebanon to other Arab countries. Rose and Straub [15], Straub et al. [16], for example, compared ICT acceptance in four Arab countries: Jordan, Saudi Arabia, Lebanon, and Sudan. They however considered these four Arab countries as one unique culture. Lebanese culture cannot be considered as a pure Arab culture since it has specificities of its own. In fact, Lebanon is known as a heterogeneous society characterized by the existence of 18 religious communities. Many civil wars in the 19th and 20th centuries have plagued the Lebanese citizens. The difficult history of cohabitation between these different communities has created a very specific environment. Lebanese for example developed local management tools such as the "Wasta" (or connections) as methods that can ensure trust in their daily transactions [17]. Affiliation to a bank is usually chosen on a communitarian basis. Religious affiliation of the owner is clear and used as a marketing positioning. This is a deeply rooted practice among all Lebanese communities. Lebanese are religious people who consider their life, to be defined by the Lord wills [6]. The Religious social norms are deeply embedded in everyday life and have an impact on the citizen's beliefs. Therefore, we consider that it is important to take into account, in our research, the potential impact of the Lebanese culture on the attitudinal, normative, and control beliefs.

Among the abundant literature that has been developed to explain the voluntary behaviour of acceptance of ICT by potential users, two theories, the Rogers [18]' innovation diffusion theory (IDT) and the Brown and Venkatesh [4] Model of of Adoption of Technology in Households (MATH)' raise a particular interest. The IDT shows that the process of ICT acceptance begins when the information goes through the social system of potential adopters meaning that adoption is a social phenomenon that depends largely on the adopters' context. The latter influences the perceptions of ICT attributes that potential adopters develop toward an ICT. Subsequently, these perceptions serve as drivers for the decision to accept/reject the ICT by influencing attitude, intention, and ultimately the behaviour of adopters (TRA) [19]. Our research fits in these perspectives. Our objective is to describe the contextual reasons that may explain the acceptance/rejection of e-banking services within the Lebanese population through the development of a contextualized acceptance/rejection model of banking e-services based on inhibitors and facilitators in the Lebanese culture. To meet this challenge, we have adapted the MATH theory, which is an extension of the well-known theory of planned behaviour [20]. According to MATH, the acceptance/rejection of e-services is a weighted function of attitudinal (AB), normative (SN) and control beliefs (PBC), each of which can be decomposed into a multidimensional structure. A review of the literature has enabled us to decompose the attitudinal, normative, and control beliefs related to the adoption of banking e-services to which we added religiosity that is specific of the Lebanese cultural context.

Attitudinal Beliefs include [21]: Utilitarian (OU), Hedonic (HO), Social (SO), and Control (CO) consequences that results from accepting and using banking e-services. Attitudinal beliefs result from the adaptation of the theory of reasoned action (TRA) which states that e-services attributes have little predictive power of the acceptance/rejection. E-services attributes are generally insufficient to predict the behaviour but they influence the beliefs about the consequences associated with the acceptance and usage of these e-services, which in turn influence the intention to accept/reject banking e-services. *Utilitarian consequences* will measure the extent to which the use of banking e-services will increase the effectiveness of the user. *Hedonic consequences* can be defined as the pleasure derived from the usage of banking e-services. *Social consequences* refer to the social image provided to users by the utilization of banking e-services. *Control consequences* refer to the perceived characteristics of banking e-services directly related to the control such as the relative cost of access to the banking e-services, the possibility to try the e-services, the ease of use …

Research in the Lebanese context, has shown that utilitarian consequences had an impact on the adoption/rejection of e-services but it seems that hedonic consequences had a stronger influence [21]. This reflects the importance of emotions and feelings in this country.

In addition, in Lebanon, as in most of the Arab world, the social image determines the status of the person [11, 22]. Therefore, people behave in a way that raises their social status [9, 10]. Therefore, social consequences (gain in terms of image and prestige) of banking e-services may have an important role in the acceptance/rejection of banking e-services in Lebanon. As for the control consequences, the ease/difficulty of use of banking e-services, constituted an important factor in the acceptance process.

The Subjective Norms (SN) influence the intention to use banking e-services (IB) in two ways: directly through the social influences or through the banks commercial influences, and indirectly through attitude by influencing the social outcomes.

In Lebanon, social relations are very important. Thus, parents, friends, and formal and informal groups have a decisive influence on individual's behaviour [6]. Past research found that social norms strongly explained ICT adoption in this region [23]. Bank influences can also be determinant in the acceptance of banking e-services. They can launch marketing campaigns to convince and encourage individuals to accept e-services.

The Perceived Behavioural Control (PBC) reflects the perception of an individual concerning the presence or absence of resources and opportunities necessary to use the banking e-services. It reflects perceptions of internal and external constraints on the acceptance of banking e-services (adapted from Ajzen [20, 24], and Mathieson [25]). Control constructs were separated into internal and external factors depending on whether the construct is linked to psychological stress or internal capacity of the individual such as computer self-efficacy, confidence in the safety, confidence in the Privacy [21] or external environmental constraints such as situational factors [4] as bank support. In the Lebanese context, computer self-efficacy can be determinant in the use of the banking e-services. E-skills are an essential resource for web usage [8] and some people do not have the minimum skills required to use banking e-services [26]. Confidence in the security and confidence in the privacy may also play an important role in the acceptance of e-services [21]. Technical support offered by Lebanese bank is also a determining factor of the acceptance of banking e-services.

In our model, the Lebanese cultural context is taken into account by adding the **Religiosity** to the MATH variables. According to Mokhlis [27], the effect of religion on people's behaviour depends mainly on their level of religiosity and on the importance of religion in their lives. According to Kids [28], religiosity plays an important role in defining individual and societal attitudes and represents part of the history and heritage of Lebanon. In the Web domain, Armfield and Lance Holbert [29] found that "the more religious a person is, the less likely it will use Internet".

The Intention to Accept/Reject Banking E-Services represents the probability that a person agrees to use the web in order to perform banking transactions. The usage may happen at any time and from any place but must be Web based.

3   Method and Results

3.1   The Research Method

The investigation method used is quantitative. The research model is constituted of five meta-constructs: Four exogenous (attitudinal beliefs, normative beliefs, control beliefs, religiosity) and one endogenous (intention to accept/reject banking e-services). To understand the role and importance of each factor, we decomposed these meta-constructs into several reflexive constructs. *Attitudinal beliefs* were measured through four reflexive constructs: Utilitarian outcomes (CAU), Hedonic outcomes (CAH), Social outcomes (CAS) and Control outcomes (CAC). *Normative beliefs* were decomposed into two constructs: social influences and companies commercial influences. Social influences (CNS) have been considered as a single-item constructs. Perceived companies commercial influences (CNC) were considered as a reflexive construct measured using three items. *Control beliefs* were decomposed into four constructs: self-efficacy, confidence in the e-services safety, confidence in the e-services privacy and perceived banks support. Self-efficacy (CCA) was defined as reflective and measured with three items. Confidence in the security (CCS), confidence in the respect of privacy (CCV) and perceived banks support (CRB) have been considered as mono-items. Acceptance/rejection intention (IAeservices) was measured with three items. Data was collected on a 7 point Likert scale ranging from 'strongly disagree' to 'strongly agree'. To take into account the religious individuals in our model, we adopted the Allport and Ross scale [8] which measures the religious orientation of a person (Religious Orientation Scale). This scale measures the degree of religiosity of a person based on two criteria: intrinsic religiosity and extrinsic religiosity. According to Allport and Michael Ross [30], people who are intrinsically religious are those for whom religion is a central part of their lives. These people give great importance to standards, ethics, and discipline. People who are extrinsically religious consider religion as an opportunity [31]. Intrinsic religiosity is related to extrinsic religiosity [30].

In Structural Equation Modelling, the validation of the measurement model is a key step before analyzing the structural model [32]. Therefore, we will start by checking the validity of the measurement used and then, we will interpret the structural model results of our research.

3.2   Validation of the Auxiliary Theory

All constructs of the model are reflexive. Their assessment is based on four elements: (1) convergent validity, (2) the reliability/consistency/uniformity/or internal consistency of each construct, (3) discriminant validity, (4) the reliability of the indicators.

As a first step of validation, we first verify that the items converge well to their respective constructs. As Table 1 (item construct correlations) shows, all constructs in the model have items that have a loading greater than 0.7 ($\lambda > 0.7$) except RIN and REX which include some items with loading below 0.7. Therefore, we perform a purification of these two scales by eliminating all items that have a loading lower than 0.7, a Student's t lower than 1.96 (t < 1.96) and an error greater than 0.05 (p > 0.05). Thus, we eliminated REX1, REX2, REX5, REX6 and RIN1, RIN3, RIN6 who had respectively the following λ 0.34, 0.66, 0.30, 0.28 and 0.67, 0.32, 0.06 and 1.62 following Student's t, 5.70, 1.49, 1.30 and 8.1, 2.07, 0.35.

Convergent validity was measured using the average variance extracted (AVE) [33]. Variables composed of a single item (CNS, CCS, and CCV CRB) pose no problem in their convergent validity. Therefore, we checked the convergent validity of other reflexive constructs. As shown in Table 2, the AVE of the nine reflexive constructs of our model (CAU, CAH, CAS, CAC, NCC, CCA, RIN, REX, and IAe-services) are 0.77, 0.70, 0.67, 0.70, 0.74, 0.71, 0.75, 0.63 and 0.70. All AVE, including RIN and REX (AVERIN = 0.63, AVEREX = 0.75), are well above the threshold value of 0.50 (AVE > 0.5) (see Table 2).

Table 1 Item to construct correlations

Items	CAU	CAH	CAS	CAC	CNS	CNC	CCA	CCS	CCV	CRB	REX	RIN	IAeser
CAU1	**0,86**	0,58	-0,01	0,33	-0,01	0,10	0,37	0,21	0,27	0,20	0,11	0,17	0,41
CAU2	**0,89**	0,60	0,02	0,33	-0,04	0,19	0,41	0,30	0,23	0,29	0,12	0,13	0,44
CAU3	**0,89**	0,68	0,04	0,33	-0,03	0,15	0,44	0,27	0,27	0,27	0,14	0,20	0,46
CAH1	0,67	**0,89**	0,08	0,42	0,05	0,24	0,50	0,38	0,36	0,27	0,14	0,18	0,54
CAH2	0,54	**0,85**	0,12	0,39	0,11	0,22	0,46	0,33	0,29	0,26	0,13	0,17	0,48
CAH3	0,55	**0,76**	0,10	0,33	0,11	0,24	0,43	0,28	0,19	0,23	0,08	0,17	0,41
CAS1	0,01	0,10	**0,83**	-0,01	0,28	0,10	0,03	0,14	0,01	0,01	-0,10	-0,05	0,18
CAS2	0,14	0,21	**0,84**	0,13	0,34	0,17	0,15	0,31	0,15	0,04	-0,06	0,03	0,18
CAS3	-0,08	-0,01	**0,79**	0,04	0,50	0,06	0,10	0,08	0,02	-0,01	-0,02	-0,01	0,21
CAC1	0,34	0,42	0,05	**0,87**	0,12	0,32	0,61	0,40	0,34	0,36	0,16	0,21	0,36
CAC2	0,36	0,43	0,12	**0,87**	0,20	0,32	0,57	0,36	0,38	0,32	0,18	0,23	0,35
CAC3	0,23	0,29	-0,01	**0,75**	0,10	0,20	0,45	0,22	0,18	0,31	0,17	0,21	0,30
CNS1	-0,03	0,10	0,46	0,16	**1,00**	0,26	0,11	0,16	0,22	0,08	0,10	0,09	0,32
CNC1	0,15	0,26	0,05	0,31	0,21	**0,86**	0,25	0,28	0,38	0,29	0,24	0,23	0,27
CNC2	0,16	0,25	0,14	0,27	0,20	**0,86**	0,24	0,23	0,22	0,28	0,14	0,18	0,21
CNC3	0,11	0,21	0,15	0,29	0,25	**0,86**	0,26	0,22	0,28	0,38	0,18	0,22	0,25
CCA1	0,39	0,50	0,14	0,52	0,12	0,27	**0,83**	0,43	0,43	0,37	0,16	0,17	0,48
CCA2	0,37	0,46	0,07	0,55	0,09	0,32	**0,87**	0,35	0,30	0,45	0,27	0,31	0,43
CCA3	0,41	0,44	0,08	0,59	0,06	0,16	**0,82**	0,26	0,25	0,35	0,17	0,25	0,44
CCS1	0,29	0,40	0,21	0,40	0,16	0,28	0,41	**1,00**	0,61	0,27	0,20	0,25	0,30
CCV1	0,29	0,34	0,07	0,37	0,22	0,35	0,39	0,61	**1,00**	0,37	0,24	0,30	0,31
CRB1	0,29	0,31	0,02	0,39	0,08	0,37	0,46	0,27	0,37	1,00	0,34	0,30	0,30
REX1	-0,03	-0,03	0,22	-0,02	0,29	0,07	-0,01	0,06	0,07	0,06	**0,34**	0,15	0,09
REX2	0,03	0,00	0,06	0,17	0,16	0,15	0,18	0,09	0,14	0,19	**0,66**	0,40	-0,02
REX3	0,18	0,19	-0,16	0,15	-0,07	0,22	0,21	0,15	0,16	0,31	**0,80**	0,65	-0,01
REX4	0,13	0,12	-0,16	0,19	0,04	0,13	0,18	0,21	0,25	0,27	**0,78**	0,56	-0,07
REX5	-0,07	0,01	0,24	-0,06	0,33	0,09	-0,01	0,14	0,09	0,00	**0,30**	0,08	0,09
REX6	-0,07	-0,02	0,24	-0,03	0,32	0,09	0,01	-0,02	0,02	0,10	**0,28**	0,09	0,13
RIN1	0,19	0,22	-0,08	0,27	0,03	0,22	0,28	0,28	0,25	0,19	0,46	**0,67**	-0,02
RIN2	0,17	0,22	-0,06	0,26	0,08	0,14	0,26	0,20	0,27	0,19	0,53	**0,78**	0,03
RIN3	0,11	0,13	0,11	0,07	0,13	0,01	0,02	0,05	-0,09	-0,06	-0,16	**-0,32**	0,20
RIN4	0,25	0,22	-0,09	0,22	0,00	0,18	0,25	0,21	0,29	0,29	0,54	**0,81**	0,07
RIN5	0,07	0,14	0,06	0,18	0,08	0,21	0,24	0,16	0,17	0,28	0,55	**0,80**	0,07
RIN6	0,14	0,17	0,13	0,18	0,09	0,21	0,16	0,09	0,05	-0,01	-0,05	**-0,06**	0,12
RIN7	0,10	0,07	0,12	0,13	0,18	0,23	0,12	0,16	0,17	0,19	0,59	**0,72**	0,08
IAE1	0,50	0,55	0,18	0,33	0,25	0,18	0,44	0,15	0,24	0,31	-0,04	0,01	**0,87**
IAE2	0,44	0,53	0,08	0,31	0,19	0,29	0,40	0,25	0,24	0,24	0,01	0,09	**0,84**
IAE3	0,30	0,37	0,32	0,37	0,35	0,26	0,50	0,35	0,29	0,20	-0,01	0,03	**0,79**

All loading items on their built are significant with p < 0.05 unless REX1, REX5, REX6, RIN3 and RIN6

Internal validity is also important because it confirms that the items selected to measure a construct converge on meaning of this construct and diverge from other constructs. It confirms that measures chosen overlap to capture the essence of the construct [1]. According to Petter et al. [34], internal consistency is important for reflexive constructs. For this reason, the Cronbach's alpha [35] is used as an indicator to measure the reliability and to ensure that the items are compatible. According to Igalens and Roussel [36], this coefficient allows verifying if all items of the construct refer to a common notion or whether each item is consistent with all other items of the construct. As shown in Table 2, all reflective constructs have good Cronbach's alpha greater than 0.7 except for REX (0.66) which is still acceptable.

Table 2 AVE, CR, and Cronbach's alpha of the reflective constructs

Construits	AVE	Composite reliability	R square	Cronbachs alpha	Communality	Redundancy
CAU	0.77	0.91	0.00	0.85	0.77	0.00
CAH	0.70	0.87	0.00	0.78	0.70	0.00
CAS	0.67	0.86	0.00	0.76	0.67	0.00
CAC	0.70	0.87	0.00	0.78	0.70	0.00
CNC	0.74	0.89	0.00	0.82	0.74	0.00
CCA	0.71	0.88	0.00	0.79	0.71	0.00
REX	0.75	0.86	0.49	0.66	0.75	0.36
RIN	0.63	0.87	0.00	0.80	0.63	0.00
IAservices	0.70	0.87	0.52	0.78	0.70	−0.01

The Dillon and Goldstein composite reliability index (Dillon and Goldstein's Rho) is also used to validate the reliability of constructs by checking the internal consistency of each block of indicators. An acceptable level is 0.70. We note that the CR of our constructs (or the Rho Dillon and Goldstein) are as follow: 0.91, 0.87, 0.86, 0.87, 0.89, 0.88, 0.86, 0.87, 0.87 and this is well above the Nunnally minimum (minimum of 0.60)

To check the external validity, we examine the discriminant validity of each reflexive construct. Indeed, according to Fornell and Larcker [37], a latent construct should explain better the variance of its indicators than the variance of other latent constructs. There is discriminant validity when the square root of the average variance shared between each construct and its indicators are greater than the correlations with the other constructs of the model [37]. Thus, we can see that this rule is respected in our model. Table 3 summarizes these results.

After examining convergent and discriminant validities of each construct, we can conclude that each indicator converges on its construction more than it does with the other constructs and that the entire model's constructs meet the reliability requirements. The fact that there are no reliabilities with less than 0.85 can be considered as a second proof of convergent validity [38]. Therefore, our results suggest that the validity and the reliability of the reflective constructs are adequate to test the structural model.

Table 3 The discriminant validity of the reflexive constructs of the model

Construct	CAH	CAU	CCA	IAeservices	REX	RIN
CAH	0.8343*		–	–	–	–
CAU	0.7067	0.8792*	–	–	–	–
CCA	0.5564	0.4636	0.8417*	–	–	–
IAeservices	0.5807	0.5010	0.5326	0.8345*	–	–
REX	0.1863	0.1797	0.2277	−0.0426	0.8645*	–
RIN	0.2087	0.1938	0.2761	0.0814	0.6997	0.7916*

*Variances between the latent constructs

3.3   The Test of the Structural Model

The model of this research tests the relationship between the CAU, CAH, CAS, CAC, NAC, NCC, CCA, CCS, CCV, CRB, REX, RIN and the IAe-services. As shown in Table 4, CAU, CAH, CNS, CSF and REX have a relationship with the intention to accept/reject e-services. RIN and are also connected to REX. Therefore, assumptions H1a, H1b, H2a, H3a, and H4b H4C are validated while all other hypotheses are rejected. These results are summarized in Table 4 and Fig. 1a, b.

To assess the predictive power of the structural model, we applied the method proposed by Ahuja and Thatcher [39] that uses the R^2 coefficient to estimate the variance proportion of (the) endogenous(s) variable(s) that comes directly from the variance of the exogenous variables. The results show an acceptable R^2 of 0.51 for the intention to accept e-services. In order to estimate the Students t, we opted for a bootstrap of 200 resampling. The bootstrap enabled us to check the stability of the relationship between items and constructs and between constructs themselves. All structural relationships were considered significant (error < 0.05).

Results Interpretation

The results of our research show that among the four-attitudinal beliefs, only the utilitarian and hedonic consequences are positively related to the intention of acceptance of e-banking services. The social consequences have no impact on the intention to accept/reject e-services. This can be explained by the fact that our research studied only the early stages of acceptance/rejection process. This corroborates the results of Karahana et al. [40] that show that improving the perceived image related to the ICT usage is not a good predictor of the adoption of ICT in the early stages of the adoption process but it can predict the continuous usage of ICT in the following stages.

The consequences of control have no impact on the intention to accept/reject banking e-services. The same logic can be applied to this construct. Indeed, the ease/difficulty of use is related the continuous usage of e-services. In our research, the intention level is still upstream of nd therefore this factor is not yet salient for potential adopters.

Social norms influence the intention of acceptance of e-banking only on the social level and not at the commercial level. Social relations are crucial in the Lebanese context. Moreover, communicational campaigns and ads are increasingly perceived as suspicious by consumers due to the fact that there are few regulations on this subject. Companies often exaggerate in their advertising campaigns and Lebanese consumers often react by increasing their perceptual filter.

Among control beliefs, only those related to self-efficacy seemed to have an impact on the intention of potential adopters. Indeed, in order to use the banking e-services, potential users must have a minimum of e-skills. The lack of technical skills reduces the intention of potential adopters.

Table 4 The research results

Hypotheses	Path coefficient	T value (t > 1.96)	Results
H1a. CAU → IAe-services (Utilitarian outcomes affect positively the intention to accept/reject e-services in Lebanon)	0.200	2.168*	Validated
H1b. CAH → IAe-services (Hedonic outcomes affect positively the intention to accept/reject e-services in Lebanon)	0.266	2.525*	Validated
H1c. CAS → IAe-services (Social outcomes (in term of image) affect positively the intention to accept/reject e-services in Lebanon)	0.007	0.068	Rejected
H1d. CAC → IAe-services (Control outcomes (ease of use) affect positively the intention to accept/reject e-services in Lebanon)	−0.023	0.210	Rejected
H2a. CNS → IAe-services (Social influences (the influence of the people who are important to the potential adopter) affect positively the intention to accept/reject e-services in Lebanon)	0.237	2.311*	Validated
H2b. CNC → IAe-services (Perceived companies commercial influences have a positive impact on the intention to accept/reject e-services in Lebanon)	0.058	0.592	Rejected
H3a. CCA → IAe-services (Self-efficacy affects positively the intention to accept/reject e-services in Lebanon)	0.284	2.375*	Validated
H3b. CCS → IAe-services (Confidence in the security affects positively the intention to accept/reject e-services in Lebanon).	−0.021	0.210	Rejected
H3c. CCV → IAe-services (Confidence in the respect of privacy affects positively the intention to accept/reject e-services in Lebanon)	0.021	0.266	Rejected
H3d. CRB → IAe-services (Perceived banks support affects positively the intention to accept/reject e-services in Lebanon)	0.072	0.893	Rejected
H4a. RIN → IAe-services (Intrinsic religiosity is negatively related to the intention to accept/reject e-services in Lebanon)	0.014	0.135	Rejected
H4b. REX → IAe-services (Extrinsic religiosity is negatively related to the intention to accept/reject e-services in Lebanon)	−0.231	2.249*	Validated
H4c. RIN → REX (Intrinsic religiosity is positively related to extrinsic religiosity)	0.700	14.542**	Validated

*Variances between the latent constructs, **AVE square root

(a)

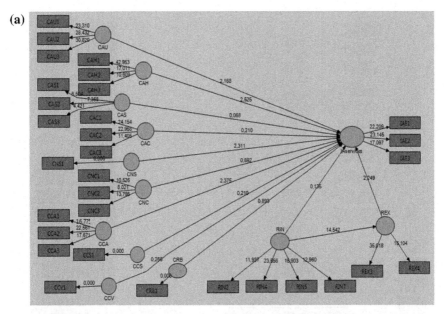

(b)

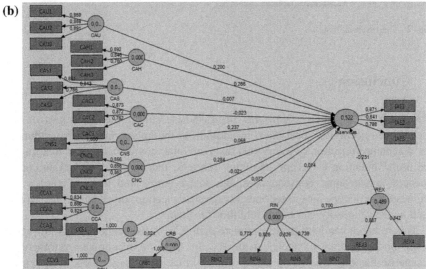

Fig. 1 **a** and **b** The PLS results

The results of our research show that religiosity has a negative impact on the intention of acceptance of e-services. These results are in line with those of Armfield and Holbert [29]; however in our case, it is mainly the extrinsic religiosity that has a negative impact. It also plays a mediating role on intrinsic religiosity (Fig. 2).

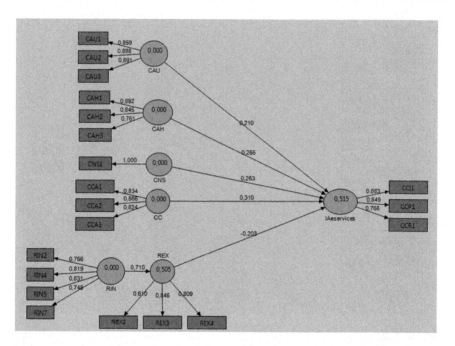

Fig. 2 The research results

4   Conclusion

The results of this study show that the Lebanese culture has an impact on the acceptance/rejection of e-services. In addition to the known factors that influence the acceptance/rejection of e-services, there are other contextual factors that impact the users' intention to accept e-banking services. Indeed, if the utilitarian consequences, the hedonic consequences, the social norms and the self-efficacy are universal facilitators for t e-services acceptance/rejection, other contextual factors such as the religiosity can be an inhibitor for them.

This research can help banks optimize their ICT investments and this through a better understanding of their customers. In fact, to encourage customers to accept/use banking e-services, we recommend that banks target those who believe they can enjoy from the benefits of e-services. In other words, banks must target those who find these e-services useful. Banking ads can emphasize the perceived usefulness of these e-services especially in timesaving, travel, and at experiential levels... But ads are not efficient as actually used. Indeed, banks must rely more on social influences and opinion leaders especially in the dissemination of information. In Lebanon, the indirect communication is more powerful than the marketing ads. Banks ads must take into account all these factors to promote banking e-services.

Banks e-services must also be redesigned. The fun appearance and enjoyment should be an integral part of the website. These findings underscore the importance of underlying the potential entertainment of the Web. The self-efficacy or the perceived e-skills of potential adopters must also be underlined. An, indoor agency communication can alter the perception of those who do not believe they can do. In 1981, IBM succeeded with the character of Charlie Chaplin to show to the potential users that they do not have to be rocket scientists' engineers to use a computer. Following this communication, sales of computers have increased and IBM who planned to sell 100,000 units sold 500,000 computers in one year.

Finally, we note that our research has several limitations. First, its main limitation is that the responses of interviewees may be biased. A second limitation concerns the choice of banking e-services that have been considered in this research. Indeed, the fact that we did not include specific e-banking services focused the attention of potential adopters on certain benefits and certain inhibitors of banking e-services. Therefore, the relation between religiosity and rejection of banking e-services should be deepened in the future.

References

1. Straub, D., Boudreau, M.C., Gefen, D.: Validation guidelines for IS positivist research. Commun. Assoc. Inf. Syst. **13**(1), 380–426 (2004)
2. Orlikowski, W.J., Suzanne Iacono, C.: Research commentary: desperately seeking the "IT" in IT research—a call to theorizing the IT artifact. In: Information Systems Research, vol. 12, no. 2, pp. 121–134 (2001)
3. Ben Boubaker, K., Barki, H.: La crise identitaire du champ des systèmes d'information: une tentative de délimitation des frontières. HEC Montréal, Chaire de recherche du Canada en implantation et gestion des technologies de l'information, (2005)
4. Brown, S.A., Venkatesh, V.: Model of adoption of technology in households: a baseline model test and extension incorporating household life cycle. In: Management Information Systems Quarterly, pp. 399–426 (2005)
5. Moufarrege, J.C.: State and community in lebanon: reflections from the lebanese social movement. http://www.cetri.be/spip.phparticle1380&lang=en (2009)
6. Yahchouchi, G.: Employees' perceptions of Lebanese managers' leadership styles and organizational commitment. Int. J. Leadersh. Stud. **4**(2), 127–140 (2009)
7. Weir, D.: Management in the Arab world: a fourth paradigm? The European Academy of Management (EURAM 2002), May 9–11, Stockholm, Sweden. http://www.leadersnet.co.il/go/leadh/forums_files/4845731437.pdf (2002). Accessed 29 Aug 2010
8. Harfouche, A.: The same wine but in new bottles. Public e-services divide and low citizens' satisfaction: an example from Lebanon. In: International Journal of Electronic Government Research (IJEGR), vol. 6, no. 3, pp. 73–105 (2010)
9. Ali, A.J.: Management theory in a transitional society: the Arab's experience. In: International Studies of Management & Organization, vol. 20.3, pp. 7–35 (1990)
10. Ali, A.J.: Cultural discontinuity and Arab management thought. In: International Studies of Management & Organization, vol. 25.3, pp. 7–30 (1995)
11. Neal, M., Finlay, J., Tansey, R.: My father knows the minister a comparative study of Arab women's attitudes towards leadership authority. Women Manag. Rev. **20**(7), 478–497 (2005)

12. Wold, H.: Soft modelling: the basic design and some extensions. In: Jöreskog, K.G., Wold, H. (eds.) Systems Under Indirect Observation, Part II. North Holland Press, Amsterdam (1982)
13. Wold, H.: Partial least squares. In: Kotz, S., Johnson, N.L. (eds.) Encyclopedia of Statistical Sciences, vol. 6, pp. 581–591. Wiley, New York (1985)
14. Tan, M., Thompson, SHT.: Factors influencing the adoption of Internet banking. In: Journal of the AIS 1, no. 1es. http://jais.isworld.org/articles/1-5/ (2000)
15. Rose, G., Straub, D.: Predicting general IT use: applying TAM to the Arabic world. J. Glob. Inf. Manag. 6(3), 39–46 (1998)
16. Straub, D., Lock, K., Hill, C.: Transfer of information technology to developing countries: a test of cultural influence modeling in the Arab world. J. Glob. Inf. Manag. 9(4), 6–28 (2001)
17. Colli, A.: The history of family business, 1850–2000, vol. 47. Cambridge University Press, Cambridge, England (2003)
18. Rogers, E.M.: The diffusion of innovations, 3rd edn. Free Press, New York (1983)
19. Fishbein, M., Ajzen, I.: Belief, attitude, intention and behavior: an introduction to theory and research. Reading, Mass.; Don Mills. Addison-Wesley Pub. Co, Ontario (1975)
20. Ajzen, I.: From intentions to actions: a theory of planned behavior. In: Springer, Berlin, Heidelberg, New York (1985)
21. Harfouche, A., Robbin, A.: Inhibitors and enablers of public e-services in Lebanon. J. Organ. End User Comput. 24(3), 45–68 (2012)
22. Al Omian, M., Weir, D.: Leadership in the Arab world. University of Jordan (2005)
23. Loch, K.D., Straub, D.W., Kamel, S.: Diffusing the Internet in the Arab world: the role of social norms and technological culturation. IEEE Trans. Eng. Manag. 50(1), 43–63 (2003)
24. Ajzen, I.: The theory of planned behavior. Organ. Behav. Hum. Decis. Process. 50(2), 179–211 (1991)
25. Mathieson, K.: Predicting user intentions: comparing the technology acceptance model with the theory of planned behavior. Inf. Syst. Res. 2(3), 173–191 (1991)
26. Bélanger, F., Carter, L.: The impact of the digital divide on e-government use. Commun. Assoc. Comput. Mach. 52(4), 132–135 (2009)
27. Mokhlis, S.: Consumer religiosity and the importance of store attributes. J. Human Res. Adult Learn. 4(2), 122–133 (2008)
28. Kids, Global English.: PC Online Software (2008)
29. Armfield, G.G., Lance Holbert, R.: The relationship between religiosity and internet use. In: Journal of Media and Religion, vol. 2, no. 3, pp. 129–144 (2003)
30. Allport, G.W., Michael Ross, J.: Personal religious orientation and prejudice. In: Journal of Personality and Social Psychology, vol. 5, no. 4, pp. 432–443 (1967)
31. Wiebe, K.F., Roland Fleck, J.: Personality correlates of intrinsic, extrinsic, and nonreligious orientations. In: The Journal of Psychology, vol. 105, no. 2, pp. 181–187 (1980)
32. Bagozzi, R.P.: Measurement and meaning in information systems and organizational research: methodological and philosophical foundations. Manag. Inf. Syst. Quart. 35(2), 261–292 (2011)
33. Chin, W.W.: The partial least squares approach to structural equation modeling. In: Marcoulides, G.A. (ed.) Modern Methods for Business Research, vol. 295, no. 2, pp. 295–336. Lawrence Erlbaum Associates, Mahwah, NJ (1998)
34. Petter, S., Straub, D., Rai, A.: Specifying formative constructs in information systems research. Manag. Inf. Syst. Quart. 31(1), 623–656 (2007)
35. Cronbach, L.J.: Coefficient alpha and the internal structure of tests. Psychometrika 16(3), 297–334 (1951)
36. Igalens, J., Roussel, P.: Méthodes de recherche en gestion des ressources humaines. Economica, Paris (1998)
37. Fornell, C., Larcker, D.F.: Evaluating structural equation models with unobservable variables and measurement error. J. Mark. Res. 39–50 (1981)
38. Nunnally, J.C., Bernstein, I.H.: The assessment of reliability. In: Psychometric Theory, vol. 3, pp. 248–292. McGraw-Hill, New York (1994)

39. Ahuja, M.K., Thatcher, J.B.: Moving beyond intentions and toward the theory of trying: effects of work environment and gender on post-adoption information technology use. Manag. Inf. Syst. Quart. **29**(3), 427–459 (2005)
40. Karahana, E., Straub, D.W., Chervany, N.L.: Information technology adoption across time. Manag. Inf. Syst. Quart. **23**(2), 183–214 (1999)

Power to the (Shopping) People! Changing Traditional Customer-Vendor Interaction in Online Markets by ICT-Enabled "Group Buying"

Andreas Mladenow, Christine Bauer and Christine Strauss

1 Introduction

Information and communication technologies (ICT) are enablers that bring together consumers with similar interests around the world. Thereby, the vast availability of such technologies also stimulates cooperative and collective online shopping [1]: consumers perform shopping in groups, whereby they either act collectively or in assigned roles. This phenomenon is referred to as "group buying" and "collective buying" [2, 3]. Group buying is not restricted to the online setting; however, ICT is a strong enabler supporting and improving the entire process of buying, including group forming, discussion among group participants, bargaining with vendors, decision making (e.g., selection of vendor, selection of product or service), post-purchase services, etc. [3, 4].

Recently, online group buying has become a widespread shopping alternative worldwide and numerous online platforms have emerged that support all activities involved in group buying (e.g., LivingSocial.com, Groupon.com, Teambuy.com.cn, Dianpin.com, Meituan.com). Besides the emergence of online group buying platforms that are operated by intermediaries (top-down approach), ICT also enable users to form and self-manage a cooperative group via various communication channels (bottom-up approach) [5].

A. Mladenow (✉) · C. Strauss
Department of E-business, University of Vienna, Vienna, Austria
e-mail: andreas.mladenow@univie.ac.at

C. Strauss
e-mail: christine.strauss@univie.ac.at

C. Bauer
Department of Information Systems and Information Management,
University of Cologne, Cologne, Germany
e-mail: bauer@wim.uni-koeln.de

© Springer International Publishing Switzerland 2016
F. D'Ascenzo et al. (eds.), *Blurring the Boundaries Through Digital Innovation*,
Lecture Notes in Information Systems and Organisation 19,
DOI 10.1007/978-3-319-38974-5_16

Considering the leading online group buying platforms in various markets and/or countries, it can be observed that the success of the different approaches to online group buying varies [3, 6]. Furthermore, the online group buying phenomenon has developed into diverse directions. The main questions are: What are the success factors for online group buying business models? And what are the influencing factors that drive the differed developments and changes in the various markets?

Against these major research questions of our ongoing research, the present paper engages with a thorough analysis of the top-down and bottom-up business models of online group buying with different pricing models covering both, fixed as well as dynamic pricing mechanisms. For instance, a group buying platform may facilitate communication between the participants and provide all necessary communication functionalities for the involved stakeholders. Each individual customer or consumer has his/her own notion of the maximum amount he/she is willing to pay for the specific product or service in which every member of the collective is interested. This personal reserve price serves as a benchmark of whether the price offered is perceived as too cheap or too expensive. The higher the difference between final and reserve price, the more satisfied the consumer will be. Another key factor that may vary between consumers covers the time span that he/she is willing to wait for the purchase of the product or service. If it takes too long for the consumer to receive a product as a member of a group buying purchase, he/she might choose to join another collective for which the transaction finalizes earlier or even buy the product on his/her own directly from a vendor at retail price.

This paper analyses recent developments regarding enablers and inhibitors of ICT-based group buying approaches in different markets. After outlining the theoretical background of our work in Sect. 2, we will perform a SWOT (strengths, weaknesses, opportunities, and threats) analysis in Sect. 3 that will allow for discussing the enablers and the inhibitors of ICT in the different approaches to online group buying in Sect. 4. In this final Section, we also conclude with a brief summary of our work and point to future research opportunities.

2 Theoretical Background

In this section, we first provide details on group buying; then we continue with outlining different online group buying approaches as currently observed on the market.

2.1 Group Buying

"Group buying" or "collective buying" is a shopping strategy in B2C (business-to-consumer) as well as B2B (business-to-business) interactions between vendors and purchasers in which consumers form a collective. In our work, we focus on the B2C setting. With a group buying strategy consumers aim at obtaining price reductions or better conditions for purchases than they would obtain as individuals [2, 7]. Volume discounts and the opportunity to obtain additional services or customized package solutions are main motivators for consumers to engage in group buying [8, 9]. For instance, when groups buy higher quantities of items, they may bargain with the vendor to obtain volume discounts [5, 6]. Furthermore, a collective, which is willing to buy a high quantity of the same product or service, has increased bargaining power; consequently the group may negotiate on better conditions, additional services, or customized package solutions [10]. In addition, there is an incentive for uninformed individuals to cooperate with intermediaries as well as knowledgeable consumers that have a better understanding of the market and good negotiation skills [7].

Besides consumers, vendors equally benefit from group buying [11]. One advantage for vendors lies in the potentially increased sales, which they may realize due to a high(er) demand generated by collective buyers [12]. As a result, the vendor may generate profits despite lower prices compared to traditional retailing strategies due to the quantities sold [12]. Higher sales quantities lead to higher demand between vendor and wholesaler or supplier, which raises the vendors' negotiating power in his interaction with his supplier. Higher sales quantities also result in financial flexibility, as cash flow and, thus, liquidity might increase significantly. Furthermore, large batches of goods (sales and purchase) lead to a reduction of proportional fixed cost per unit. From a vendor's perspective, a deal with a group buying collective is typically cost-effective: since they do not have to deal with each of the consumers individually. Consequently, group buying transactions involve lower communication and bargaining costs [13].

While the online group buying phenomenon has flourished worldwide, it can be observed that the adopted business models have developed into diverse directions across the markets. The major two online group buying approaches are described in the next section.

2.2 Online Group Buying Approaches

The major two types of online group buying approaches are the top-down approach and the bottom-up approach. Based on these two generic model types several derivative variants have developed.

Regarding the top-down group buying approach, the shopping process is not initiated by potential consumers, but by the platform providers themselves [5]. There are two variants: in the dynamic price-level variant, the vendor provides a prepackaged offer, which consumers may either accept or decline as is within the offer's validity period. Thus, the vendor does not warrant the consumers any negotiation possibilities. The rationale behind this group buying variant that offers prepackaged "deals" is the following: the more users who are willing to buy a particular product or service, the lower the price. Example platforms are Mercata. com, LetsBuyIt.com, and Mobshop.com that were already launched in the 1990s. In early 2008, a second variant of the top-down approach was initiated by Groupon. com [14, 15]. The prepackaged "deals" (typically special discounts) have a fixed price; a minimum number of required customers that has to be exceeded for the respective offer within a certain time period (typically a day) in order to obtain the discount, which may be redeemed after payment [1, 16].

An example for the bottom-up approach is a concept that allows for so-called group buying discounts, i.e., quantity discounts [5]. In the dynamic price level variant, the crowd formation is the first process phase; the crowd searches for potential merchants offer; then, a selected group representative negotiates with the merchant. This phase may also take place in the merchant's premises. The group discusses the available deals and, finally, the merchant's offer might be accepted to the agreed conditions.

This variant of the bottom-up approach is particularly popular in Asia (e.g., TeamBuy.com.cn, liba.com) [2, 5, 17]. It brings together consumers who intend to buy a specific product or service. The crowd participants may enjoy discounted pricing through collective bargaining. They have the opportunity to meet on an online forum or on specific websites, which might speed up the process of crowd formation. Another variant is the bottom-up approach with fixed price level.

Figure 1 provides an overview of approaches and variants of online group buying and lists some example applications (cf. Fig. 1).

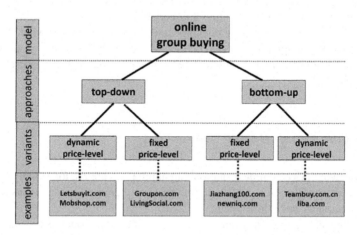

Fig. 1 Overview of approaches, variants, and application examples of the group buying concept

3   Enablers and Inhibitors of Online Group Buying

Web-based interaction between consumers provides new opportunities for innovative forms of cooperation between customers and suppliers [18, 19], which go in
line with the social shopping experience that is recently emphasized in practice.
Having extensive market knowledge is a key to success for companies offering
demand-oriented services [20]. Thereby, web-companies may not only gain an
advantage over competitors in the long term but they might also achieve a quality
advantage [21].

The SWOT matrix of the dominant top-down approach is depicted in Table 1.
The major platform providers using this approach typically provide a broad portfolio of offerings with additional services. A specific strength of Groupon.com and
TeamBuy.com.cn lies in the good navigability of the platform thanks to a good user
interface. From the provider's perspective, the high number of non-redeemers is
advantageous, as it allows for higher profits [22]. As the platforms are typically
large, economies of scale can easily be accomplished. A remarkable strength of the
platforms lies also in the fact that they localize their products and services and
provide a recognizable share of localized offers in their portfolio. As the top-down
approach does not require user interaction, the platforms do not have to support and
facilitate interaction among users. The low interaction of consumers also means that
the consumers rarely influence each other, which is beneficial for the provider in
terms of achieved profits.

Table 1 SWOT analysis of the top-down group buying approach

Strengths	Weaknesses
• Broad portfolio of offerings • Good additional services • Good navigation/user interface • High number of non-redeemers • Economies of scale • Localized offers • Low interaction and influence among consumers	• Low price margins • Transactions not profitable for suppliers • Dependent on the offers by the suppliers • Offer has to be adapted to every market (high evaluation and transaction costs) • Broad mass of suppliers are on the platform • No differentiation from competing platforms • Low switching costs for consumers • Low social shopping experience for consumers
Opportunities	Threats
• Improvement of apps for mobile devices • Investing in broader portfolio • Branding for companies/suppliers • Entry in new markets (e.g., Eastern Europe) • Targeted offers for customer loyalty • Auction system • Relationship guidelines for partners for return business	• Tight competition • Low entry barriers into market for new companies • Potential bad reviews/evaluations • High number of redeemers • Bad calculations by suppliers may lead to bad reputation of platform

A weakness of the concept lies in the low price margins that may be achieved. For the suppliers the transactions are on a wide scale not profitable. Accordingly, the approach may rather be considered as a marketing tool. A challenge for platform providers is to keep participating supplying companies, since their participation may not be profitable for them. When acting on different markets, the offer has to be adapted to every market, which includes high evaluation and transaction costs. The localization of offers therefore puts further burden on the platform providers. A further weakness can be ascribed to the broad mass of suppliers on the platforms. First, there may be quality issues or at least large quality differences. Second, there is hardly any differentiation in the supply from competing platforms. In addition, there are low switching costs for consumers, as they may switch to another provider by the click of a button. Furthermore, although the group buying concept would allow for a social shopping experience, the top-down approach does not exploit this capability as low interaction among the consumers is involved.

The opportunities for platform providers taking a top-down approach to group buying are versatile. Investing in additional channels such as in applications for mobile devices would be an asset. Offering a(n) (even) broader portfolio of products and (additional) services could be a further opportunity. Allowing participating supplier companies to have their own branding could be another driver for potential market growth. Addressing the weakness of low switching-costs for customers, targeted offers could strengthen customer loyalty by rewarding repeated purchases. Furthermore, the way that suppliers act, strongly influences a platform's reputation; relationship guidelines for such partner companies may positively impact the consumers' perception of the platform. Particularly with respect for the return business, such guidelines appear advantageous.

A present threat for platform providers is the tight competition in the field. The low entry barriers into the market for new companies intensify this threat. Potential bad user reviews and evaluations may cause consumers to switch to other, similar platforms [23, 24]. The strong dependency on its suppliers is also affected by the calculations performed by the latter; if calculations concerning quantities are not well elaborated, this may negatively impact the platforms reputation in two ways; first, suppliers that overestimate the (marginal) profits may not feel as equally treated partners; second, if a supplier cannot provide the quantities sold due to capacity problems consumers might be disappointed.

The SWOT matrix of the bottom-up approach is depicted in Table 2. Strength lies in the potential revenue, as the approach may be considered as an advertising channel, because consumers "spread the word". In contrast to the top-down approach, a high degree of social shopping experience is involved as consumers vividly interact in this approach. The other strength of the bottom-up approach may be considered as rather similar to the top-down approach.

The waiting time until the ultimate purchase transaction represents a central challenge. Waiting time refers to the period in which the group is waiting for further growth in terms of group members, in order to generate higher demand and hence to achieve a higher order volume. The higher the number of orders within the crowd, the higher are the benefits from economies of scale (up to a certain limit) [25–29]

Table 2 SWOT analysis of the bottom-up group buying approach

Strengths	Weaknesses
• Revenue (advertising channel) • Economies of scale • High social shopping experience for consumers • Good navigation/user interface • Broad portfolio of offerings by vendors • Localized offers • Good additional service	• Difficult to determine the suitable waiting time • Insecurities concerning participating consumers' purchase intention and perceived obligation to purchase • No income for transactions • Low switching costs for consumers • Highly dependent on the offers by the suppliers • Offer has to be adapted to every market (high evaluation and transaction costs) • Not applicable in many countries • No differentiation from competing platform
Opportunities	Threats
• Improvement of apps for mobile devices • Investing in additional services • Branding for companies/suppliers • Targeted offers for customer loyalty • Relationship guidelines for partners for return business	• Tight competition • Low entry barriers into market for new companies • Negative word-of-mouth

and the higher is thus also the quantity discount offered by the service provider to group members. However, this causes a dilemma that, for instance, the intermediary is confronted with when it comes to waiting time: on the one hand, a longer waiting period leads to a higher order volume and thus higher discounts; on the other hand, by waiting too long, the patience of the participants is challenged. As a consequence, if the waiting time is too long, some potential customers might drop out, as they are not willing to wait any longer. Therefore waiting causes a degree of uncertainty affecting the result of the entire crowd shopping project. The task of the crowd manager is, in this case, to analyse the market and to estimate a suitable waiting time for the specific situation (including product or service, market situation, already received offers, etc.) in order to find a good balance between a sufficiently large quantity of orders and a timely date of purchase or auction. Another challenge arising from implementing the crowd shopping concept as bottom-up instrument is that of ensuring that all participating consumers ultimately feel a certain obligation to actually purchase the respective product or service. If this is not the case, consumers who are not willing to go through the entire crowd shopping process or who are not willing to buy a product or service will be carried through halfway of the process. Accordingly, in order to achieve a certain seriousness and commitment and to reduce the dropout rate of participants, one viable solution could, for instance, be to ask participants to state their credit card details. Furthermore, there is no revenue directly associated with the transactions involved when using the bottom-up approach of group buying. Similar to the top-down approach the offer has to be adapted to every market, which includes high evaluation and transaction costs. In addition, the bottom-up approach to group buying is currently not applicable in many countries. The low differentiation of platforms from competing ones is a weakness that the bottom-up approach shares with the top-down approach to group buying.

The opportunities for platforms using the bottom-up approach are similar to the ones for platforms applying a top-down approach. Investing in additional services, branding for suppliers, and investing in customer loyalty are among the opportunities with potentially the highest impact.

The threats for bottom-up approach platform providers are the tight competition and the low entry barriers into the market for new companies. The negative word-of-mouth is particularly threatening for this type of group shopping as consumers highly interact and bad reputation may spread as easily as positive experience and the invitation to participate.

4 Discussion and Outlook

'Group buying' as a term is not used consistently. One can find it in connection with grouponing as a marketing tool (top-down approach) as well as a bottom-up approach, where consumers that share the intent to purchase a specific product or service engage in forming buying groups. In the latter case a price reduction is achieved primarily by means of attaining a higher market share and—as a consequence—bargaining power. The common intent to purchase a product or service leads to a common interest within a community, which strives through the coordination and organization among the members to achieve their target of acquiring a product or service and thus to benefit from the cooperation. In addition to the described differences, both approaches serve the principle of benefiting from high accessibility thanks to the Internet. Thus, there is also the need for a sufficiently high number of interested people necessary for the implementation of both approaches. Furthermore, the two approaches are similar in terms of offering very time-limited deals. Different, however, are the initiators who act at the beginning of the group-buying approach.

Interestingly, the top-down platform concept with dynamic price level such as LetsBuyIt.com, Mobshop.com, and Mercata.com vanished; so did recent successor Jasmere.com. In this regard, this concept turned out as being too complicated for customers as the selected pricing strategy is based on the number of participating customers throughout the entire offer period. The more customers accept the current price, the faster the next lower price level is reached. In this respect, customers have often not been aware of the currently valid price.

When it comes to group buying, the basic question is whether the new business model variant will be accepted or not; just as Mobshop.com was confronted with around the turn of the millennium. This question of acceptance includes the risk of not reaching a critical mass of customers at an early stage, which is required in order to implement the model successfully. In addition, a trustworthy and professional online appearance is essential for the company. The aim is to build quickly a community of consumers who are willing to participate actively. Be it by participating in crowd shopping as buyers, or by contributing suggestions and ideas that will be later implemented by the company, or by participating in some other form. The exact business concept may vary depending on the offered products and services (or the companies in the B2B area). In this regard it is important to provide an appropriate combination or the most promising overall package of options and features, coupled with an efficient marketing campaign to catch attention.

Interestingly, while there has been a trend towards predefined vendor-initiated "daily deals" in countries such as the USA, in other countries, platforms such as China's market leader TeamBuy.com.cn, where forum members initiate crowd shopping activities, have flourished.

Overall, group buying allows companies to serve larger quantities of solvent customers, resulting in additional profit margins.

A disadvantage for participating companies arises from the increased influence of customers on pricing negotiations in a group buying setting [15, 30]. The bargaining power of customers is particularly strong in the bottom-up approach implementation of the group buying instrument. As a result, unit contribution margins may be lowered compared to traditional customer-vendor settings. To counteract lower margins, suppliers may set prerequisites in the price negotiations; for instance, a frequently used instrument is it to require a particular number of overall sales for granting a certain price. From the perspective of the supplier, determining the ideal group size is a major challenge, because quoting unrealistic sales volumes in negotiations will deter potential customers while asking for small group sizes may allow for lower profits only. If the required number of potential buyers has not yet been reached, consumers are typically motivated to distribute product information to other people. The success for group buying, thus, depends largely on the efficiency of consumers as sales promoters.

The fact that consumers may not know in advance which price they finally have to pay, the group buying approach with dynamic pricing mechanisms might turn out as too complex for consumers, which may result in a lack of consumer acceptance on a broader basis. Granting discounts for recommending other users to join a purchase on the platform may represent an incentive to (still) participate.

While small and medium-size enterprises (SMEs) show an increased interest in cooperating with the consumers [31–33], larger companies are frequently less willing to respond to consumer groups regarding pricing, sometimes due to image reasons. For smaller companies, though, group buying offers the possibility to attract the attention of a large number of consumers and build a positive reputation [34]. The strategy to engage in group projects buying also suits companies that are geographically isolated. Despite their remoteness they may build up a base of customers who value beneficial business relations more than vicinity. Providing localized offers, though, is one of the strengths of current platforms, which should not be underestimated in the implementation of group buying concepts.

The thorough analysis in our work provides a basis for explaining changes and developments of online group shopping variants and may contribute to the development and improvement of future business models.

As the types of group shopping vary tremendously with regard to communication, coordination, and collaboration among participants, a potentially interesting line of research would be the analysis of the various interaction requirements in the different group buying approaches The support of ICT in the different phases of the customer buying process would be a further interesting field of investigation, as ICT could help to improve the involved shopping process and the underlying notion of the different business models.

References

1. Shin, D.H.: User experience in social commerce: in friends we trust. Behav. Inf. Technol. **32** (1), 52–67 (2013)
2. Wang, J.J., Zhao, X., Li, J.J.: Group buying: a strategic form of consumer collective. J. Retail. **89**(3), 338–351 (2013)
3. Liu, Y., Sutanto, J.: Online group-buying: literature review and directions for future research. ACM SIGMIS Database **46**(1), 39–59 (2015)
4. Luo, X., Andrews, M., Song, Y., Aspara, J.: Group-buying deal popularity. J. Mark. **78**(2), 20–33 (2014)
5. Mladenow A, Bauer C, Strauss C (2015), Collaborative shopping with the crowd. In: The 12th International Conference on Cooperative Design, Visualization & Engineering. CDVE 2015, Mallorca, Spain, September 20–23. LNCS 9320. Springer, pp. 162–169. doi:10.1007/978-3-319-24132-6_19
6. Jing, X., Xie, J.: Group buying: a new mechanism for selling through social interactions. Manage. Sci. **57**(8), 1354–1372 (2011)
7. Lee, E.: 2013 China's Group-buying Turnover Rockets 67.7 % YOY to 35.88 Billion Yuan. http://technode.com/2014/01/15/2013-group-buying-turnover-rockets-68-percent-yoy-in-china/. Accessed 22 Nov 2015
8. Chen, W.Y., Wu, P.H.: Factors affecting consumers' motivation in online group buyers. In: 2010 Sixth International Conference on IEEE, Intelligent Information Hiding and Multimedia Signal Processing (IIH-MSP), pp. 708–711 (2010)
9. Kauffman, R.J., Lai, H., Ho, C.T.: Incentive mechanisms, fairness and participation in online group-buying auctions. Electron. Commer. Res. Appl. **9**(3), 249–262 (2010)
10. Chung, W., Chen, L.: Group-buying e-commerce in China. IT Professional **14**(4), 24–30 (2012)
11. Yu, M., Lang, K., Pelaez, A.: Evaluating electronix market designs: the effects of competitive arousal and social facilitation on electronic group buying. In: 47th Hawaii International Conference on System Science, pp. 4148–4157 (2014)
12. Leitner, P., Grechenig, T.: Collaborative shopping networks: sharing the wisdom of crowds in E-commerce environments. In: BLED 2008 Proceedings, vol. 21 (2008)
13. Zhang, J.J., Tsai, W.H.S.: United we shop! chinese consumers' online group buying. J. Int. Consum. Mark. **27**(1), 54–68 (2015)
14. Edelman, B., Jaffe, S., Kominers, S.D.: To groupon or not to groupon: the profitability of deep discounts. Market. Lett. 1–15, (2011)
15. Dickinger, A., Kleijnen, M.: Coupons going wireless: determinants of consumer intentions to redeem mobile coupons. J. Interact. Mark. **22**(3), 23–39 (2008)
16. Sharif-Paghaleh, H.: Analysis of the waiting time effects on the financial return and the order fulfillment in web-based group buying mechanisms. In: Proceedings of the 2009 IEEE/WIC/ACM International Joint Conference on Web Intelligence and Intelligent Agent Technology-Volume 01. IEEE Computer Society, pp. 663–666 (2009)

17. Tan, W.K., Tan, Y.J.: Online or offline group buying?. In: 2010 Seventh International Conference on Fuzzy Systems and Knowledge Discovery, vol. 6, pp. 2853–2857 (2010)
18. Bauer, C., Mladenow, A., Strauss, C.: Fostering collaboration by location-based crowdsourcing. In: Cooperative Design, Visualization, and Engineering: 11th International Conference, CDVE 2014, Seattle, WA, USA, 14–17 Sept 2014. Proceedings Vol. 8683, pp. 88–95. Springer (2014)
19. Cho, N., Park, S.: Development of electronic commerce user-consumer satisfaction index (ECUSI) for internet shopping. Ind. Manag. Data Syst. **101**(8), 400–406 (2001)
20. Liao, S.H., Chu, P.H., Chen, Y.J., Chang, C.C.: Mining customer knowledge for exploring online group buying behavior. Expert Syst. Appl. **39**(3), 3708–3716 (2012)
21. Hsu, M.H., Chang, C.M., Chu, K.K., Lee, Y.J.: Determinants of repurchase intention in online group-buying: the perspectives of DeLone & McLean IS success model and trust. Comput. Hum. Behav. **36**, 234–245 (2014)
22. Zhang, Z., Zhang, Z., Wang, F., Law, R., Li, D.: Factors influencing the effectiveness of online group buying in the restaurant industry. Int. J. Hospitality Manag. **35**, 237–245 (2013)
23. Novak, N. M., Mladenow, A., Strauss, C.: Avatar-based innovation processes-are virtual worlds a breeding ground for innovations? In Proceedings of International Conference on Information Integration and Web-based Applications & Services. ACM. ISBN: 978-1-4503-2113-6, p. 174 (2013)
24. Forbes: http://www.forbes.com/sites/tomiogeron/2011/08/26/facebook-shutting-down-deals-service/. Accessed 22 Nov (2015)
25. Mladenow, A., Bauer, C., Strauss, C.: Crowdsourcing in logistics: concepts and applications using the social crowd. doi:10.1145/2837185.2837242. Edition: ICPS—International Conference Proceedings Series, Publisher: ACM, Editors: Indrawan-Santiago, Steinbauer, Khalil, Gabriele Anderst-Kotsis, pp. 244–251 (2015)
26. Hyben, B., Mladenow, A., Novak, N.M., Strauss, C.: Consumer acceptance on mobile shopping of textile goods in Austria: modelling an empirical study. In: The 13th International Conference on Advances in Mobile Computing and Multimedia (MoMM 2015), ACM, ISBN: 978-1-4503-3493-8, pp. 402–406 (2015)
27. Mladenow, A., Novak, N. M., Strauss, C.: Mobility for 'Immovables'–clouds supporting the business with real estates. In: The 6th International Conference on Emerging Ubiquitous Systems and Pervasive Networks (EUSPN 2015). Procedia Computer Science, 63, pp. 120–127 (2015)
28. Kopetzky, R., Günther, M., Kryvinska, N., Mladenow, A., Strauss, C., Stummer, C.: Strategic management of disruptive technologies: a practical framework in the context of voice services and of computing towards the cloud. Int. J. Grid Utility Comput. **4**(1), 47–59 (2013)
29. Mladenow, A., Bauer, C., Strauss, C., Gregus, M.: Collaboration and locality in crowdsourcing. doi:10.1109/INCoS.2015.74. In: 2015 International Conference on, Intelligent Networking and Collaborative Systems (INCOS), pp. 1–6 (2015)
30. Xie, G., Zhu, J., Lu, Q., Xu, S.: Influencing factors of consumer intention towards web group buying. In: 2011 IEEE International Conference on IEEE, Industrial Engineering and Engineering Management (IEEM), pp. 1397–1401 (2011)
31. Mladenow, A., Novak, N.M., Strauss, C.: Online Ad-Fraud in search engine advertising campaigns, prevention, detection and damage limitation. In: Information & Communication Technology-Eurasia Conference ICT-EurAsia 2015, LNCS 9357. Springer, pp. 109–118. doi:10.1007/978-3-319-24315-3_11 (2015)
32. Mladenow, A., Novak, N.M., Strauss, C.: Micropayments in virtuellen Welten—Prozessmodell und Nutzung bei 7- bis 12-jährigen Besuchern. In GI-Edition: Informatik 2015, editors: Douglas Cunningham, Petra Hofstedt, Klaus Meer, Ingo Schmitt. 28.9–2.10. 2015, Cottbus. Lect. Notes Inf. 1267–1278 (2015)
33. Mladenow, A., Fröschl, K.: Kooperative Forschung. Peter Lang, Frankfurt am Main (2011)
34. Tan, C.H., Goh, K.Y., Teo, H.H.: An investigation of online group-buying institution and buyer behavior. In: Human-Computer Interaction. HCI Applications and Services. Springer, pp. 124–131 (2007)

Part III
Societal Challenges and ICT Adoption Outside the Organizational Boundaries

Socio-technical Process Design—The Case of Coordinated Service Delivery for Elderly People

Thomas Herrmann, Michael Prilla and Alexander Nolte

1 Introduction: Integration of Pen&Paper Technology and Service Delivery as a Socio-technical Process

The project Service4home [1] investigated the usefulness of Pen&Paper technology for elderly people to order services. In order to coordinate and conduct these services in a cost-efficient way, we established a service agency. Creating such a solution requires a holistic approach, which not only considers human-computer interaction aspects but also the design of the interplay between technical infrastructure and organisational processes. We thus ran Service4home as a project which takes into account various influences on work and combined different methods into an approach of socio-technical design [2].

Literature on "Socio-technical Systems Design" such as ETHICS [3] or literature on basic principles of socio-technical design [4, 5] and socio-technical systems engineering [6] is closely oriented towards companies as organisational units, in which tasks are supposed to be conducted more efficiently through the integration of organisational and technical systems and processes. In this context, the term 'system' in socio-technical system design refers either to a software-system [6] or—more holistically—to an organizational unit (such as a company or a department) that will include the technical components. The term system implies on the one hand a unit—consisting of related elements—which is clearly separated from its

T. Herrmann (✉) · A. Nolte (✉)
Information and Technology Management, Ruhr-University of Bochum,
Bochum, Germany
e-mail: thomas.herrmann@rub.de

A. Nolte
e-mail: nolte@iaw.rub.de

M. Prilla (✉)
Department of Informatics, TU Clausthal, Clausthal-Zellerfeld, Germany
e-mail: michael.prilla@tu-clausthal.de

© Springer International Publishing Switzerland 2016   217
F. D'Ascenzo et al. (eds.), *Blurring the Boundaries Through Digital Innovation*,
Lecture Notes in Information Systems and Organisation 19,
DOI 10.1007/978-3-319-38974-5_17

environment [7]. On the other hand, a holistic approach attempts to see the relations within the system in the context of the environment's influences to understand or design its behaviour in accordance with system thinking [8]. In the project Service4home however, it was not reasonable to identify an organizational unit to be designed. We rather had to include various organisations such as a housing society, the households of the renters, the neighbourhood of households, and a local subsidiary of a social welfare organisation, which took the role of a service agency throughout the course of the project. To integrate them into a single socio-technical system would have enlarged the focus in a way that would have made it impractical to carry out the project. Therefore we took the whole (service) process as a design focus, and holistically included the relevant influences which shape the activities within this process. This implies a shift form socio-technical **systems** design to socio-technical **process** design. This is methodologically reflected by e.g. using a visualization of the socio-technical process throughout the project and by applying several walkthroughs on this visualization [9]. These walkthroughs were facilitated and pursued participation and collaboration of several stakeholders to communicatively integrate a variety of perspectives. We identify structured discourses as a crucial contribution to the evolution of social systems in accordance with Luhman [10] and Habermas [11]. We used a variety of methods to inform and support the development and deployment of the socio-technical process being designed by the Service4home project.

The aim of this paper is to reflect on how different methods can be combined and arranged to support the focussing of socio-technical design on a process, and how this focus provides an orientation to select the relevant aspects which have to be taken into account. In what follows, we start by describing the socio-technical solution that we developed during the course of the project (Sect. 2). It should be noted that the focus of design was not on the technical quality of the solution (i.e. whether the most suitable technology was chosen) but on the methodological approach. This is based upon the fact that the Pen&Paper technology we used was predefined from the beginning of this project. Then, we describe the methods used in the project (Sect. 3) and discuss them (Sect. 4) before we summarize our insights (Sect. 5).

2 Pen&Paper Technology and Service Coordination as a Socio-technical Solution in a Neighborhood

Service4home was run to investigate whether Pen&Paper technology and a corresponding infrastructure are useful for people to send orders to a service agency (run by a welfare organization). We put a special emphasis on offering services for elderly people that help them to live on their own and in their homes for as long as possible. A service order is placed by filling in a (simple) paper form and using a digital pen equipped with a camera (e.g., pens by Anoto™). The pen recognizes the writing on the paper form and transmits the data to the agency. This allows for people to order services digitally without requiring the use of a computer device. The data is then included into an excel sheet which is used by the service agency to coordinate service delivery. After an order is processed successfully by the service agency, the clients are notified via telephone about when and where the service will be conducted.

The services are offered to the renters of the housing society. They include services such as home care, shopping support, cleaning and many others. By establishing a service agency as a part of a citizen center, services can be offered flexibly and on demand. This flexibility can be considered a huge competitive advantage compared to common offers, where services are available only at given times and certain rhythms during the week. Given that orders were available digitally and beforehand, the agency could also efficiently use staff capacities by bundling services (e.g. by offering a shopping companion to two or three people which wanted to visit the same shop thus reducing the cost per person).

Figure 1 shows an example for such a service where elderly people are accompanied during their weekly shopping. The process described there includes technical components and spatial constraints. It also shows how activities are integrated into the social interactions within the neighborhood. This actual process was developed and implemented during the course of the project [12]. It includes different roles (actors) and places, which are connected by the technical infrastructure:

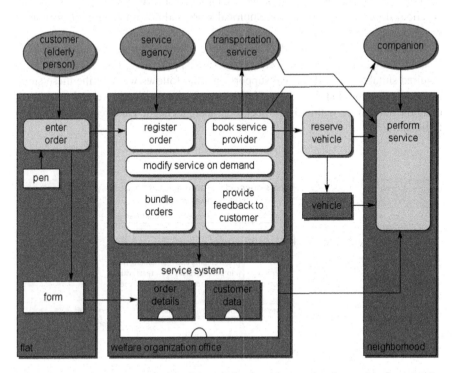

Fig. 1 Roles, activities, components of the solution by the example of a combined service for transportation and shopping support ("Shopping companion", modelled using SeeMe [13])

- A customer (elderly person), who starts the process by filling in a form at home,
- the service agency, to which the order is sent to be processed and bundled with other orders; contacts to service providers (e.g. a transportation service) and customer feedback was organized there as well,
- the neighborhood, where services such as "shopping companion" were conducted.

3   Methodology and Course of the Project

The usability and acceptance of a new process like the one described before depends on various aspects, such as the quality of the paper forms and the perceived quality of the cooperating partners (e.g., services providers) and other helpers (e.g., voluntary shopping companions).

Methods that aim at designing and implementing such solutions need to enable designers to get an understanding of these aspects and to tailor solutions to them. Literature however, mostly focusses on the description of frameworks for such designs rather than providing guidance on the application of concrete methods. Support can be found in approaches such as Contextual Design [14], which describes different approaches for empirical work and documentation of insights in the design process.

According to the needs described above, Service4home included multiple methodological steps, which were partly overlapping (c.f. Fig. 2). These steps required suitable methodological support. In what follows we describe these steps. It should be noted that they do not follow a certain process but were chosen based upon the necessities within the project (e.g., insights needed and requirements to be fulfilled).

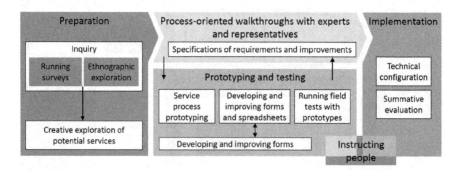

Fig. 2 Procedure of the design project

3.1 Explorative Data Gathering

In the beginning of the project empirical investigations covering the application context and constraints were run. These investigations included a survey as well as ethnographic methods (c.f. Fig. 2 left).

To analyze the potential demand for services, we ran a survey covering 10 % of the renters in the neighborhood where the services were to be offered in (n = 120 households). The survey consisted of questions on the demographic background, willingness and potential to pay for services, assessment of value perceived by certain services and questions on the acceptance of the Pen&Paper technology. The results of the survey were used as a basis for choosing appropriate services and for designing concrete service processes. For example, according to the results, the acceptance of Pen&Paper technology was above 50 % across all age groups.

A complementary exploration was conducted as an ethnographic study to collect qualitative data and to identify specific constraints within the neighborhood. This was conducted by talking with elderly people about their habits, exploring the area, working with the people in the citizen center etc. Results were included into the design of the services, contrasting them with the ideas and visions of project staff. The ethnographic study included observations as well as conversations with renters of the area. For example, from a conversation with an elderly lady it became obvious that despite some physical problems she regularly went to the office of the welfare organization to help others—providing help also manifested as a major prerequisite of taking help in the study. Based upon the results of the ethnographic study we developed stories that guided the further course of the project. We deliberately chose a pragmatic approach to ethnography, which brought forward many insights and ideas but also allowed for (partial) incompleteness. Results form both the survey and the ethnography served as a basis for preparing the creativity techniques described in the following section.

3.2 Exploration of Potential Solutions with Creativity Techniques

After the inquiry phase a workshop was conducted (c.f. Fig. 2 bottom left), in which new ideas for services were developed [4]. From a collection of ideas provided in the workshop, the participants chose services they perceived to be well suited for the renters of the neighborhood and that could be supported by Pen&Paper technology.

The duration of the workshop was three and a half hours. In the beginning, the moderator asked the participants (organizers of the services, software developers, welfare organization staff and researchers) to answer the question "*Why is it helpful for elderly people to be integrated into a network of people (professionally, voluntary, personally related)?*" individually. The answers were written on paper cards. Then, groups of three people used these cards as a basis to answer the question *"Which offerings for and by elderly people can be derived from the collection of ideas?"*. The resulting ideas were collected digitally before they were compacted and associated with new ideas that came in during this process. After that, the groups of three were merged to groups of six before all groups came together in order to exchange ideas. During this transition phase ideas were sharpened and concretized.

The workshop featured different means to facilitate ideation and creative thinking:

- Questions such as *"Which kind of support would be helpful for elderly people"* and the questions mentioned above,
- Randomly chosen pictures of elderly people in different life situations,
- A loop of presentation slides with results from the inquiry phase, including insights on interest and demands for services as well as leisure activities of elderly people,
- Stories created by one of the researchers that was part of the ethnographic study,
- A provocation: people were asked to envision the wishes of an elderly person, who could afford anything due to her being famous.

From a large number of resulting ideas, we prioritized those ideas that were perceived by the participants as valuable for the later services processes.

We also used brainstorming techniques afterwards to concretize the process on which the socio-technical process was to be based. We identified six fields of action, which needed to be designed in more detail afterwards: Preparing a service, transferring order data, communicating about a service, processing and coordinating orders, conducting the service, and following up on the service conducted. Based upon these fields a basic process representation was created and discussed. For the discussion we used guiding questions such as *"Which steps need to be regarded?"*, *"Which data is needed?"*, and *"For which areas of work can the digital pen be supportive?"*. A detailed description of this procedure can be found in [15, 16].

3.3 Participatory Design with the Socio-technical Walkthrough

One of the main challenges we faced during the course of the project was to choose a reasonable set of participants for the workshops and to organize their participation [4, 17]. Participation was a key aspect to identify potentials and barriers of technology usage and to adapt the socio-technical solution accordingly. As target groups and potential participants we identified elderly people, welfare staff and management, potential staff of the service agency, representatives of the housing society, external service providers and technology developers. For these groups we used different ways of integrating them into the project [1]: service providers, welfare and housing society staff and management as well as developers were directly integrated into modelling walkthrough workshops (c.f. Fig. 2 top middle) and the prototyping of service processes (c.f. Fig. 2 bottom middle). Elderly people were indirectly involved in order to get their feedback on the quality of service processes and their fit to daily needs. Elderly people were also integrated by discussing marketing material with them, in which the services offered and the procedure for their delivery was described alongside paper forms that were designed to order the services [18].

The indirect involvement of elderly people into the design of the processes proved to be helpful, as it enabled them to assess the results of process design after each phase of design and deployment: This enabled them to look at the processes from the angle of potential clients and to add a perspective that was decisive for the development of the processes—this perspective was not provided by any of the other participants (developers, experts, researchers). Foci of the feedback given by the elderlies involved can be found in transparency of prices and value proposition (*"What do I get for my money?"*) and reliability regarding the services ordered (e.g. expressing the need of approval after orders via telephone). The implementation of this feedback into the processes was supported by researchers, who acted as representatives of the elderly people during workshops. The researchers intervened when they thought it was necessary from the perspective of the elderly people.

3.4 Usability Test and Field Tests of the Prototypes

The design of the paper forms was evaluated in intensive usability tests with elderly people (c.f. Fig. 2 bottom middle). These tests showed a lot of minor problems handling the forms (e.g. for filling in the date, we had provided boxes for each digit that were not recognized by some participants in the test), which resulted from the fact that using a paper form provides less restrictions than filling in a web form. During evaluation, the participants were asked to perform sample tasks (service orders) with the forms and to fill in all data needed to order the service. This was done in two iterations.

The improved forms were used to run a field pretest of the prototyped service processes (c.f. Fig. 2 bottom middle). In order to do this we created Excel sheets containing data that represent service offerings. Furthermore, we trained the staff of the service agency with respect to the process of coordinating services. This was done by a test that was run for 3 months with four households. For this time period, data was not sent electronically but the forms were collected from the households manually. These visits also offered researchers the opportunity to talk to and interview participants of the pretest and to identify difficulties and barriers when ordering services. The forms were then transferred manually to the corresponding sheets by the staff of the service agency, which in turn offered possibilities to observe and discuss problems in data processing and service coordination.

3.5 Deriving Improvements in a Walkthrough

To connect insights and other results from the pretest closely to the design of the service process, we analyzed the process again using the approach of the socio-technical walkthrough (STWT) [9, 16]. A Walkthrough [19] is done in a step-by-step process following a documentation—in our case the documentation came in the form of a process model. The socio-technical walkthrough promotes the discussion with respect to the details of a process model (i.e. process steps) by using guiding questions. We used questions such as *"Where did we encounter problems?"* or *"Which tasks need to be adapted?"* as the basis for discussion. The walkthrough was conducted in a workshop in which all participants of the pretest served as workshop participants (c.f. Fig. 2 top middle). Researchers brought in the results from the discussions and feedback given by agency staff and elderly people—thus representing them as discussed above (c.f. Sect. 3.3). While discussing the process model step by step comments were added to the process model. These comments served as a basis for re-design after the workshop. Whenever it appeared feasible and reasonable the process model was altered right away. Figure 3 shows a part of the process model, illustrating the amount of comments created. After the workshop the comments were processed and included into a new process design. One of the results from this procedure was to set priorities in service delivery and to reduce the amount of options in service orders. This included the number of different services to be offered as well as service details such as the number of supermarkets for which the shopping companion service was offered.

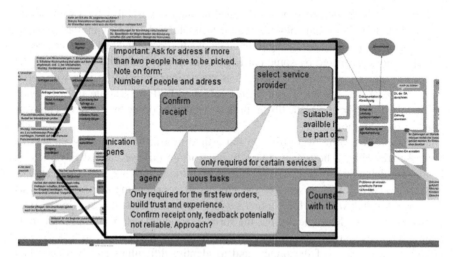

Fig. 3 Comments containing improvement needs in the process model of the service (including zoomed part)

3.6 Establishing Organizational Processes and Evaluation

In parallel to the analysis of the pretest, the technical components were designed and implemented (servers, data transmission, processing via Excel sheets, c.f. Fig. 2 right). We found that the technical challenges were far less complex in comparison to the establishment of the organizational procedures in the socio-technical process. Such establishment is referred to by Baxter and Sommerville [6] as "Change Process", which accompanies the technical development. In Service4home this included choosing and training agency staff as well as integrating suitable service providers and voluntary helpers (e.g. shopping companions). Recruiting elderly people who are willing to pay for the services offered by the agency proved to be a challenge. For this the abovementioned marketing material can be considered crucial. In addition building trust also was an important factor. As an example, all members of agency staff were provided with a special ID to show when they arrived at the different households. Elderly people were mostly recruited via personal conversations during information events run by the welfare organization. Testimonials provided by clients of the agency (e.g. those who were part of the pretest) also were helpful. In addition we also made sure to only record a minimal amount of personal. As an example data on special needs of clients was asked for each time when filling in forms again in order not to store them as standing data of clients.

The services proved to be quite successful: The five most active clients ordered 77 service in the first 9 months of the service agency. The Pen&Paper technology was also used cooperatively. For example we were told that two clients, who wanted to use the shopping companion service together, talked on the telephone when filling in the forms to ensure that they would be able to go shopping together.

4 Reflection: Relevance of the Methods for Socio-technical Redesign

The literature describes a variety of methods, e.g. with respect to usability design, ethnography, interviewing techniques, participator design (cf. [6]) which can be employed to develop complex socio-technical solutions. However, the challenge is to go beyond analytical and technical considerations, to extend design to the realm of organizing work processes and their continuous evolution, and to find an appropriate focus and extend of details to be taken into account.

With respect to the **qualitative exploration** of the social aspects it became obvious, that the magnitude of potentially relevant details cannot be taken into account in accordance with ethnographical standards. A manageable focus of ethnographical gathering of data can be to challenge pre-assumptions being made about the context of a solution. For example we erroneously supposed that groups of people can meet somewhere to be picked up by a taxi although there was no shelter available where people could wait e.g. during bad weather. In this context it is most important to identify potential for social conflicts which can potentially compromise a socio-technical solution. To inform redesign activities it is important to repeatedly collect stories about how a technical system is used as well as rumors about the success or failures. We gained valuable date by working with people at the citizen center at the beginning of the evaluation. This should have taken place earlier to inform in the first phases of design.

Creativity techniques support the emergence of a variety of helpful and innovative ideas. Via brainstorming potentially important details of the newly designed collaboration process could be anticipated. Involving experts such as caregivers into brainstorming was not only relevant with respect to the experience and background they could bring to the table. Involving different participants from different backgrounds also stimulate creativity. It was expected that not every innovative idea was brought into reality in the first design cycle. The early phases of combining creativity and development of requirements should consequently rather be used to establish an idea pool which is continuously maintained and to which one can go back to inform continuous redesign. Since creativity techniques produce a variety of ideas, they help to overcome sticking with the first draft for a solution. However, it has to be taken into account that practitioners and analytically oriented experts may have a critical attitude towards creativity techniques.

Improving and adapting a socio-technical solution by inspecting the process model proved reasonable since the approx. 115 modeled activities had to be discussed with respect to several questions. It turned out that it is a challenge to motivate participating experts to actively take part in these repeated walkthroughs. It was necessary to prepare the workshops carefully and to avoid long phases of documenting results of the discussion. The participants should always perceive that their active involvement is solicited and helpful. It was reasonable to intertwine walkthroughs with phases of brainstorming to collect proposals of how the recognized problems can be overcome. Walking through the draft of a organizational work process helped to derive requirements for the socio-technical solutions. It also helped to realize how technical features and social measures had to be related to each other.

Offering and supporting **participation** was highly relevant to achieve acceptance for the project. It turned out to be inappropriate to directly include elderly people in the discussion since the caretakers did not want to disclose their experience if their clients are present. Therefore we included representatives of the elderly who were familiar with their needs and we also took the results of the ethnographical analyses into account. We knew that these representatives might have a biased view. But we also expected that the evaluation of the field test provides correcting information if necessary. When starting the project we thought that the biggest barrier to be overcome would be the acceptance of the technology and the services by the elderly people. In contrast, we faced the highest skepticism by the people who worked in the welfare organization and whom we asked to run the coordination agency. They were skeptical about the possibilities for informal communication if the orders were submitted electronically. This kind of skepticism did not become obvious during the walkthrough workshops since the participants felt obliged to behave supportive with respect to the group dynamics. The problems rather surfaced when members of project took over some tasks at the service agency. Similar to action research they had the opportunity to get a more direct impression of how people think and act. Concluding, it is reasonable to combine participatory approaches taking place in workshops with action research activities where members of a project directly interact with people that are part of a socio-technical process. This is useful to detect potential conflicts as early as possible.

Usability-Testing as well as practical **pretests** in the systems environment were indispensable for the success of the project. They helped to detect mistakes early on and promote focusing on realistic goals. The problem of pretest is that they influence the participants' first impression of the socio-technical concept and therefore sustain opinions about it. This opinion can be negative since pretests usually help to make deficits apparent and take place while not every question is sufficiently answered. For example, questions about the costs for the services could not be answered during the pretest. This vagueness led to an uncertainty which was communicated between potential clients and proved as an obstacle when marketing started.

When the new processes of ordering and coordinating services were eventually established a **gradual deployment** of the solution was necessary. Accordingly, the potential users had the possibility to become familiar with the Pen&Paper technology by testing it at the citizen center before they ordered it for their household. During the test they were assisted to perform real ordering of services by filling in a form. Offering the possibility of such a type of testing in the citizen center implied the need to have two types of forms: one where the name of the user had to be filled in explicitly and another where this was avoided since each form was assigned to an household. Furthermore, a gradual introduction of the new technique included that it could have been tested at home before the payment of a fee for every usage had been started.

It is necessary to combine such a gradual introduction of new socio-technical processes with the need of continuous adaptation and evolutionary redesign of the solution. The possibilities for adaptation have to be taken into account in advance for instance by applying principles of meta-design [20]. This includes under design —an approach which avoids the specification and determination of details which restrict the flexibility of the usage processes. Only those aspects which ensure the compliance with legal norms and similar restriction have to be fixed by technical features so that they cannot be bypassed. An example of meta-design in our project was to avoid programming the digital pens in a way that every special form had its own software. By contrast, the pens we used more abstract variables to program the pens. Consequently, we were able to change forms without changing the digital pens' software.

5 Conclusion and Summary

Conducting the project Service4home we faced the challenge to create a socio-technical solution where we had to set up a service agency that coordinates services for elderly people. In order to do so, the support of different service providers and volunteers had to be acquired. Our experience from using different methods during the project provides initial insights on how to support socio-technical design being focused on a process (rather than a system).

The centerpiece of our methodological approach (c.f. Fig. 2 top middle) are facilitated discourses within walkthroughs which repeatedly refer to models of the designed process. As a preparation we conducted interviews and surveys as well as ethnographic data gathering in order to cover the details and constraints that can and will potentially influence the socio-technical process. To our understanding, designing a socio-technical process requires a cyclic approach that involves multiple phases of prototyping, testing, and (re-)design or adaptation. Pretests in the real future field proved to be especially helpful as they create insights—which supplement the views of the walkthrough participants—on additional and changing requirements and before finally implementing the process. Therefore, we suggest that design and deployment consequently are organized step-by-step in cycles which include informing and orienting actors towards a future solution (c.f. Fig. 2 middle).

It is reasonable to accompany the cycles by socio-technical walkthroughs which employ the linear structure of processes to decide step-by-step how the experience with the prototypical solution is translated into improved design. This allows for systematically analyzing the current state of the solution, anticipating potential flaws and identifying details that have to be adapted. This systematic linear approach should however be accompanied by phases of creative divergence. Approaches that foster creativity such as brainstorming support divergence and allow for new ideas to be created or factors to be collected that have to be considered when designing a socio-technical process [21]. Linear walkthroughs consequently serve as a convergence phase that accompanies these divergent phases in order to shape the socio-technical process and prepare its delivery.

References

1. Prilla, M., Herrmann, T.: Gestaltung von AAL-Lösungen als sozio-technische Systeme: Selbstgesteuerte Alltagsunterstützung. i-com. Zeitschrift für interaktive und kooperative Medien. (2012)
2. Mumford, E.: The story of socio-technical design: reflections on its successes, failures and potential. Inf. Syst. J. **16**, 317–342 (2006)
3. Mumford, E.: Effective Systems Design and Requirements and Analysis—the ETHICS aproach. Macmillan Press LTD, Houndsmill, Basingstoke, Hampshire and London (1995)
4. Carell, A., Herrmann, T.: Interaction and collaboration modes for integration inspiring information into technology-enhanced creativity workshops. In: Proceedings of the 43rd Hawaii International Conference on System Science (HICCS 43) (2010)

5. Cherns, A.: Principles of sociotechnical design revisted. Hum. Relat. **40**, 153–162 (1987)
6. Baxter, G., Sommerville, I.: Socio-technical systems: from design methods to systems engineering. Interact. Comput. **23**, 4–17 (2011)
7. von Bertalanffy, L.: General System Theory: Foundations, Development, Applications. Braziller, New York (1968)
8. Alter, S.: Desperately seeking systems thinking in the information systems discipline. ICIS 2004 Proceedings. 61 (2004)
9. Herrmann, T.: Systems design with the socio-technical walkthrough. In: Whitworth, B., de Moor, A. (eds.) Handbook of Research on Socio-technical Design and Social Networking Systems. Information Science Reference (2009)
10. Luhmann, N.: Soziale Systeme. Grundriß einer allgemeinen Theorie. Suhrkamp Verlag, Frankfurt (1993)
11. Habermas, J.: Theorie des kommunikativen Handelns, vol. 1. Handlungsrationalität und gesellschaftliche Rationalisierung. Suhrkamp, Frankfurt (1981)
12. Prilla, M., Rascher, I., Skrotzki, R.: Digitale Stift-Technologie zur Vermittlung von Dienstleistungen: Auswahl und Anpassung geeigneter Dienstleistungsprozesse. In: Proceedings AAL-Kongress 2011 (2011)
13. Herrmann, T.: SeeMe in a nutshell—the semi-structured, socio-technical modeling method (2006)
14. Beyer, H., Holtzblatt, K.: Contextual Design: Defining Customer-Centered Systems. Morgan Kaufmann (1998)
15. Herrmann, T., Nolte, A., Prilla, M.: Awareness support for combining individual and collaborative process design in co-located meetings. Comput. Support. Coop. Work **22**, 241–270 (2013)
16. Herrmann, T.: Kreatives Prozessdesign - Konzepte und Methoden zur Integration von Prozessorganisation. Technik und Arbeitsgestaltung. Springer, Berlin Heidelberg (2012)
17. Prilla, M., Nolte, A.: Fostering self-direction in participatory process design. In: Bodker, K., Bratteteig, T., Loi, D., Robertson, T. (eds.) Proceedings of the Eleventh Conference on Participatory Design 2010, pp. 227–230. ACM, New York (2010)
18. Turnwald, M., Frerichs, A., Prilla, M.: Usability Testing für und mit Senioren. In: Brau, H., Lehmann, A., Petrovic, K., Schroeder, M.C. (eds.) Tagungsband Usability Professionals 2011, pp. 216–220. German UPA e. V, Stuttgart (2011)
19. Yourdon, E.: Structured Walkthroughs. Yourdon Press Upper Saddle River, NJ, USA (1989)
20. Fischer, G., Herrmann, T.: Socio-technical systems: a meta-design perspective. Int. J. Sociotechnol. Knowl. Dev. **3**, 1–33 (2011)
21. Herrmann, T.: Design heuristics for computer supported collaborative creativity. In: HICSS'09. 42nd Hawaii International Conference on, System Sciences, 2009, pp. 1–10 (2009)

Organizing e-Services Co-production in Multiple Contexts: Implications for Designers and Policymakers

Paolo Depaoli

1 Introduction

The concept of co-production in public services has been explored and debated for a long time [1] and the potential usefulness of service-dominant approaches to the delivery of public services highlighted [2]. Some caveats limit but do not cancel its applicability; for example, choices of how to approach co-production become more complex when vital professional expertise is required or when coerced users are involved (ibid. p. 150). In this paper such complexity is explored by examining a case in point, i.e. the characteristics and outcomes of a European Commission program concerning the development of age-aware information technologies (e-services) for the elderly. Vital expertise is needed in this field both because impairment and chronic diseases affect this growing part of the population and because trade-offs between 'presence' and 'distance' have to be carefully weighted. Indeed, leaving aside for a moment the adoption of information and communication technologies (ICTs), the role of the elderly as co-producers (and not as mere users) for the delivery of effective domiciliary care has been underscored by the literature for a long time [3, 4]. More recently, the relevance of co-production for addressing the needs of an ageing population has been mentioned in several contributions of a collective book edited by Pestoff et al. [5]. In general, there is a growing diversity in the actors involved in the delivery of these services: there are public, not for profit and for profit organizations that need to be managed and governed. Thus, to the original co-production concepts—whereby individual citizens participate at least in part to the production of public services—two other concepts have been developed to better understand the phenomenon: 'co-governance' and 'co-management'. The former refers to the involvement of non-public organizations to the planning phase

P. Depaoli (✉)
CeRSI-LUISS "Guido Carli" University, Rome, Italy
e-mail: pdepaoli@luiss.it

© Springer International Publishing Switzerland 2016
F. D'Ascenzo et al. (eds.), *Blurring the Boundaries Through Digital Innovation*,
Lecture Notes in Information Systems and Organisation 19,
DOI 10.1007/978-3-319-38974-5_18

of public services and the latter to the production of services in collaboration with the state [6, p. 29].

The adoption of ICTs based services adds to the complexity of designing and developing services for the elderly [7]. Actually, these technologies are being explored to evaluate their potential in finding solutions to concerns relating both to the shrinking of national welfare budgets and to the social standing of the elderly and their right to be both as independent as possible and integrated in their living and working communities [8]. For example, distance monitoring of conditions of patients in appropriate 'smart houses' can reduce hospitalization time, thus decreasing costs, especially when chronic diseases are encountered [9]. The access to the Internet can facilitate the acquisition of information on leisure services or on-line purchase of goods and services for the elderly with weakened mobility, thus increasing the instances of independent action [10]. Appropriate information systems (IS) applications can facilitate the use and circulation of the experience of older knowledge workers [11] if interfaces are properly designed to balance the diminished visual and hearing capabilities that start affecting people in their fifties [12]. Nevertheless, a number of caveats have been pointed out concerning both the risks of techno-centric approaches in designing the systems (even though they can be mitigated by co-productive relationships) [13] and the ethical implications and dilemmas in conducting research on ageing [14].

The aim of this paper is therefore to understand to what extent co-production concepts and principles are being considered in the development of e-services for the elderly and what approaches can enhance it.

2 Research Strategy

The appearing of new concepts in the co-production literature, namely the above mentioned 'co-governance' and 'co-management', shows that policy building issues are indeed relevant in social welfare provision especially in emerging social care markets. This is certainly the case of ICT enhanced services for the elderly for at least three reasons. First, it is a market which is still in its infancy because both demand and supply have to overcome barriers that hinder their development [15]. Second, economists have acknowledged the fact that an ageing population is one major societal change that challenges governments to adopt a decisive, 'transformational' and innovative, role [16]. Third, governments and international institutions have decided to finance research programs in this field [17, 18]. Notably, in 2007 within an e-inclusion strategy, the European Union (EU) launched the Action Plan on ICTs and Ageing supported by a 2008–2013 specific joint research program on Ambient Assisted Living (AAL). The aim of the program was to provide "equipment and services for the independent living of elderly people" [15, p. 64]. At the end of the program, an evaluation report was commissioned by the European Commission [19].

A through literature review and Delphi study concerning age-aware services, even though limited to e-government, shows that research in this area is scant and rather descriptive concluding that both better theoretical explanations and a detailed differentiation of 'the elderly' are needed. This would help overcome the current basic, anachronistic, understanding and "develop services that are better suited to the individual needs of members of this group" [17, p. 314]. The term 'co-production' does not appear in the cited review and the role of information technologies in the delivery of social services (in general and not specifically on services for the elderly) has been explored in only two papers according to a literature review on co-production [1]. Both works make positive comments on the benefits of ICTs for co-production in general: Cahn and Gray [20] stress the reduction in coordination costs enabled by these technologies while Meijer [21], after considering two cases, concludes that "new media hold the promise of strengthening co–production in an information age" (p. 200). Since 2012 the combination of co-production and ICT in elderly care started to be considered in papers based on research funded by either national or supranational initiatives [22–24]. These investigations (centred on telecare) consider co-production as an appropriate, inclusive approach to the development of age-aware services and reach the following converging conclusions: (i) rather than 'advanced' technologies, the key success factors for in place programs "depend on effortful alignments in the technical, organisational and social configuration of support" and the way "to facilitating the co-production of ageing in place is to provide better support for the routine collaboration between members of formal and informal care networks" [25, pp 245, 263]; (ii) specific project experiences suggest "a renewed focus on design in use rather than the engagement of users in prior design" which means to concentrate research and development efforts on "how infrastructures can be nurtured to support the co-production of service environments within which such systems and artefacts might be better appropriated by their users" [19, p. 21]; (iii) consequently, co-production has to take place "in the context of 'user' engagement in the visioning and re-thinking of the context into which such systems and devices are to be procured and deployed." [20, p. 1138].

Building on these results, since this paper considers the European AAL joint research program which has a scope wider than the development of telecare, the following research question is posed: what is the role of co-production among the relevant contextual factors that have been considered in designing and evaluating the AAL program and which other ones could be considered to further policy support to the development of e-services for the elderly?

A recent work edited by Christopher Pollitt, Context in Public Policy and Management [26], is used to define the guiding principles to interpret the relevant AAL Program documents issued by the European Commission (EC) in order to gain an understanding of what contexts have been considered by the European policymakers, by the EC staff and consultants that prepared the calls and the guidelines, and by the group of experts that prepared the evaluation report. Since the objective of the program is the development of e-services, the paper draws on the basic tenets of 'service science' [27, 28] and on the central propositions of 'service-dominant logic' [29, 30] as the theoretical underpinnings to frame co-production in the European service innovation (ICT based) undertaking. Indeed, Osborn and co-authors also draw on these concepts to argue for a 'public service dominant' approach in re-considering public services: "[b]y taking a public service-dominant approach, coproduction becomes an inalienable component of public services delivery that places the experiences and knowledge of the service user at the heart of effective public service design and delivery." [2, p. 146]

The paper is structured as follows. The next section outlines the key traits of 'service science' and of 'service dominant logic' as prerequisite for an effective co-production. In section four the AAL case is described using Pollitt's principles of contextual analysis. The case is discussed in section five in the light of the AAL evaluation report prepared by an expert panel appointed by the European Commission (EC). In this section suggestions are made to deal with some of the challenges and recommendations put forth by the report and relevant for the extension of the AAL program. Summary of the work done and implications resulting from it conclude this contribution.

3 The Key Tenets of 'Service Science' as a Prerequisite for Co-production When Approaching e-Services

In his brief note on the Harvard Business Review, when describing the reasons why the discipline of 'services science' seemed to be a promising area of research, Chesbrough [27] stressed the role of intangibility as the specific trait of services. In his work also the question of the transfer of tacit knowledge is particularly relevant since services promote encounters among people that have to learn from each other for an effective service to occur. The accent on tacit knowledge was kept at center stage in the article that Chesbrough co-authored with Spohrer the following year [28].

Other literature on service science defines service as "the application of competences (knowledge and skills) by one entity for the benefit of another" [31, p. 145] so that knowledge is once again at center stage in the discussion concerning the development of a theoretical framework for service science. This definition of service is particularly useful in avoiding a technology driven approach to AAL projects. Since a large number of important factors (i.e. contexts) are to be considered when designing a service, they must not be obscured by letting technologies play a dominant role. In the work of Vargo and Lusch [29, 30], the ten 'Foundational Premises (FP) of Service-Dominant Logic' are helpful to avoid such technological determinism. In this work, five of them seem relevant [26, p. 7]: FP 3, Goods (both durable and non-durable) are a 'distribution mechanism', i.e. they "derive their value through use—the service they provide"; FP 6, "The customer is always a co-creator of value" which implies that "value creation is interactional";

FP 8, "A service centered view is inherently customer oriented and relational"; FP 9, "All social and economic actors are resource integrators". It implies that "the context of value creation is networks of networks (resource integrators)". Finally, the tenth FP: "Value is always uniquely and phenomenologically determined by the beneficiary" since "Value is idiosyncratic, experiential, contextual, and meaning laden". A possible interpretation of these principles for the aims of this paper is: the development of age-sensitive technologies is meaningful if such technologies are considered as distribution mechanisms that derive their value (not per se but) from the use that a network of interacting actors (users and researchers-designers) experience in a certain context.

This interpretation supports (is a prerequisite for) the mutual backing of co-production and the Internet underlined by Meijer when he criticizes current dyadic models based on public service providers on the one hand and on individual consumers on the other hand: "The perspective of co–production opens up the arena to other actors who could possibly play a role in the provision of public services. From this perspective, involvement of citizens, intermediaries and stakeholders strengthens the provision of public services. This idea fits recent shifts in thinking about Internet technology: from the Internet as an information medium to the Internet as a platform for communication and interaction" [21, p. 203].

4   Drawing on Pollitt's 'Contextual Analysis' to Describe the Case of the AAL Programme

In considering social services, Pestoff [6] confirms the multiplicity of actors engaged in the co-production process and he underlines the importance of the notion of 'interdependence'. Indeed, "[m]ost social services are long-term and involve repeated interactions between the professional staff and their clients... When an organization cannot produce the service without some customer input, they are considered interdependent." (ibid. p. 30). He refers to this type of services as 'enduring social services' where it is necessary "to have a realistic assessment of the range of diverse interests and varying motives for engaging in co-production from the perspective of various stakeholders, that is, the municipal authorities, professional staff and users/citizens. The authorities and staff will have various economic, political and professional motives, such as lower costs, higher quality service and more legitimacy. Citizens' motives are based on economic, social, political and quality considerations. It is also important to understand these differences and try to bridge the gap between them in order for co-production to be sustainable." (ibid p. 32).

It is thus apparent that new ICT based services can be developed appropriately by considering the different contexts that affect their design and implementation. As mentioned above in section two, in order to find out what contexts have been considered by the European Commission AAL program, Pollitt's framework [26] is adopted here. In the preface to the book he edited, he agrees with a large number of scholars who remark that contextual factors are crucial to explain why certain reforms have been successful (or not). Yet, he argues that context is an umbrella term with limited explanatory value since it bundles together different elements and influences. The purpose of the book he edited was therefore to develop a typology of contexts so that some basic issues can be addressed with the support of a theoretical background: for example, contexts can be either constraints or facilitators for change, they have a level or scale (micro, meso or macro), and they have different durations. The closing chapter of the book summarizes the 21 contributions highlighting the following six main concerns that have emerged. Contexts "(a) should be defined, theorized and operationalized; (b) they may be factual and/or conceptual; (c) they are multiple and intersecting; (d) they may be constitutive for action; (e) policymakers should look for the mechanisms and processes that animate contexts and enable them to have effects; (f) comparison can play a valuable role in the analysis" (ibid. p. 374). In what follows, with the exception of the last one, such principles have been applied to the relevant AAL Program documents issued by the European Commission to gain an understanding of what contexts have been considered by the European policymakers, by the European Commission staff and consultants that prepared the calls and the guidelines, and by the group of experts that prepared the evaluation report.

Context definition: the European policy on e-inclusion. The European Union policy for e-inclusion of the European Union (EU) is stated in the "Riga Ministerial Declaration on an Inclusive Information Society" dated June 11, 2006. In the declaration the term e-inclusion stands for both inclusive ICTs and ICTs to be considered as enablers with respect to inclusion objectives.

One year after the Riga Declaration, in 2007, the staff of the European Commission prepared an impact assessment [32] of the afore mentioned targets and initiatives so that appropriate action plans could be developed. The study showed that overcoming divides in the Internet use was not only socially correct but also economically rewarding. In general, "[t]he wellbeing of a vibrant European society depends also on human capital, social capital, health, and reduction of the costs of social exclusion and in general on the quality of life" [ibid., p. 7]. The costs of social exclusion for the 27 European countries were estimated to range between 440 and 764 billion euro every year so that, if the Riga targets were met, "a digitally included society could boost economic growth in Europe by an estimated 85 billion euro in the next 5 years" [ibid.].

Specific factual and conceptual contexts: definition of an action plan for the elderly. The "Action Plan on Information and Communication Technologies and Ageing—Ageing well in the information society" [33], claims to pursue not only advantages for senior citizens (independent and active living, updated competencies, increased social participation) but to be set out also to benefit both European companies (increased market size in Europe in the business area of ICT and ageing, a stronger position in the world market, a better skilled workforce) and authorities (enhancing e-Government solutions leading to reduction in costs and better quality in health and social care systems). Given these sets of needs to be satisfied (and the expected direct and indirect benefits), the Action Plan is structured around four action areas and objectives. The first one is 'raising awareness' on existing barriers and opportunities (financial and regulatory) and 'establishing consensus and common strategies' among the numerous stakeholders: older persons and their representatives, national and local authorities, industry and providers, employers, health insurers, telecommunications and construction companies, researchers, and standardization bodies. The second area relates to 'putting the enabling conditions in place' which entails (on the part of the Commission) further assessment on legal, technical, and market barriers, in addition to preparing guidance for their removal. The third area relates to 'promoting take-up' whereby the Commission intends to launch pilot projects (on independent living and chronic disease monitoring, on the potential of ICT for active ageing at work) led by industry, service providers and national and local authorities to conduct socio-economic assessment and validation for scaling up.

The 'multiple and intersecting' AAL contexts. In order to pursue the objectives of the 'action areas', the Action Plan defined a specific research activity on Ambient Assisted Living (AAL) which aims at providing:

> equipment and services for the independent living of elderly people, via the seamless integration of info-communication technologies within homes and extended homes, thus increasing their quality of life and autonomy and reducing the need for being institutionalised. These include assistance to carry out daily activities, health and activity monitoring, enhancing safety and security, getting access to social, medical and emergency systems, and facilitating social contacts, in addition to context-based infotainment and entertainment [15, p. 64].

By stating these priorities for research, the European policy maker intended to ensure that the three basic areas of needs addressed (work—community—home) would continue to guide an age-aware ICT policy in a complex network of interconnections. Each year a call was to ensure that the different contexts would be covered.

The AAL context as a basis for action. The program was expected to mobilize at least 600 million euro of private and public funding in 6 years. In fact, in 2008 the European Union (EU) decided to make a financial contribution of 150 million euro to be doubled by member states, thus making 50 % of the budget, while the other 50 % would come from the private organizations in charge of carrying out the research projects. The rationale of this funding approach was both to create a critical mass with the support of EU and to link the research programs of member states while supporting private R&D efforts [25].

Animating the AAL context, enabling it to have effects. The AAL Program has an Internet site (http://www.aal-europe.eu/) to support consortia when they prepare the project to be submitted. Besides the administrative procedures that have to be followed, three documents explain the rationale of the program across all the calls (besides a specific document prepared for each call): (i) Guideline: The Art and Joy of User Integration in AAL Projects—White paper for the integration of users in AAL projects, from idea creation to product testing and business model development; (ii) Knowledge base: AAL Stakeholders and Their Requirements—A collection of characteristics and requirements of primary, secondary, and tertiary users of AAL solutions, and a guideline for user-friendly AAL design; (iii) Toolbox: Methods of User Integration for AAL Innovations. As the titles show they focus on how users and stakeholders are to be involved in the different phases of the project from the understanding of user needs to the building of a viable idea, to the testing of the system while developing a business model. Furthermore, each year a 'Forum' was to be held in a different country where project participants and experts in the relevant fields would meet and discuss the emerging issues and solutions being developed.

5 Discussion: From the AAL Program Outcomes to Three Proposals

In the following two sub-sections, first the results achieved by the program, and highlighted by a panel of experts appointed by the European Commission [19], are summarized; then, supported by some of the recommendations present in the evaluation report, three areas of concern are suggested here to support downstream innovation and market validation activities within a co-production perspective in successive editions of the program.

5.1 The Program Evaluation: Outcomes, Challenges, and Recommendations

As the chairman of the panel of experts notes in the foreword to the report, not enough time has elapsed to measure the full effects of the investments made. However, the program is considered a success since it has mobilized some euro 630 million (an amount higher than expected) that funded 130 projects along the duration of the program from 2008 to 2013 with the participation of 20 member countries. The multiple and intersecting contexts addressed by the program where covered by the six calls on 'ICT based solutions' concerning Prevention and Management of Chronic Conditions', Social Interaction, Independence and Participation in the "Self-Serve Society", Mobility, (Self-) Management of Daily Life, and Supporting Occupation in Life of Older Adults.

Furthermore, some other key achievements have been highlighted in the report, e.g.: pan European communities have been seeded; strong catalytic effects on national initiatives have been observed; almost one-third of the organizations involved have a user role; 40 % of participants are small and medium size enterprises (SMEs), a higher presence than in other European programs; 50 % of the projects have secured intellectual property rights (of these about one-third are being funded to take their results to market).

There are however some strategic challenges that have to be addressed. The first one is the need for a broad-based view of innovation. Since it is "an innovation programme (as opposed to purely a research programme) ... a more broad-based view of innovation is required that fully embraces service innovations and social innovations alongside development of ICT-based solutions." (ibid., p. 20 emphasis in the original). The second challenge is the need for "a stronger strategic focus on creating the marketplace in which products and services can flourish rather than on the development of products and services per se." (ibid). This need to intensify the market orientation in a transnational setting requires a "much more focused attention to exploitation and commercialization" (ibid.) which is based on the solving of problems concerning interoperability, standardization and harmonization. A first step in this direction would be the use of the results of projects by other projects to create an AAL ecosystem.

To respond to these challenges the report proposes 10 recommendations to set up a second edition of the program. In this work, that uses the lens of service-science, four of them seem particularly relevant. Recommendation 1 and 2 are considered of strategic relevance and they concern: (i) the need for a "widening of demand side participation in the Programme" which entails, inter alia, "improving the quality of users' involvements and drawing new actors into the value chain" and "implementing demonstrations and pilots operating under realistic, real-world conditions, including under differing national conditions" (ibid. p. 21); (ii) "The Programme should further enrich the ecosystem surrounding the AAL community in Europe through initiatives and actions that promote networking and stimulate uptake. Emphasis should be on novel measures that have not been tried up to now, such as: sub-programmes involving lead customers and owners; new models of co-creation and living lab solutions" (ibid., emphasis added). To further operational performance, Recommendations 6 and 9 are relevant. The first one concerns, inter alia, the strengthening of implementation and monitoring of the Programme, by experimenting with new, more flexible instruments that are more responsive to market demands; for example, calls should be defined so as to take better account of economic and societal challenges, not just technological options, and the evaluation criteria adapted accordingly (ibid. p. 23). The second one stresses the need to further "enhance and extend the multidisciplinary approach, including the close involvement of end-users at all stages of programme design and execution, and engagement with new stakeholder communities".

The comments and suggestions present in the evaluation Report stress the importance of an overall approach for the successive edition of the Program to be more sensitive to the service science and service dominant principles, described in section three above. Table 1 below shows which service-dominant logic principles [30] can be usefully applied to meet the above mentioned challenges and recommendations.

Table 1 Service science principles and AAL challenges

Challenges (C) and Recommendations (R)	Applicable S-D logic principles (adapted from Vargo and Lusch [30])
C1: Stronger attention to service and social innovation	FP 3: Goods (here technologies) are distribution mechanisms; value generated through use
R1: Widening demand through realistic conditions	FP 6: Value creation is interactional
	FP 8: Customer orientation
R2: Increase networking	FP 9: Actors as resource integrators
R9: Extend multidisciplinary approaches	FP 10: Value is contextual

5.2 Strengthening Both the 'Conceptual Context' and the 'Basis for Action' Context: Co-creation, Intermediaries, and Gatekeepers

The above mentioned recommendations are meant both to mitigate the influence of technologies in the way the AAL projects are designed and to orientate the projects towards service and social innovation. They acknowledge the danger that technological aspects overweigh the social ones. Undeniably, both organizational contexts and processes of development of AAL systems were not properly considered. The following paragraphs outline three proposals to help overcome such risks and to promote co-production in age-aware e-services.

A—'Co-creation' as a basis for co-production in e-services development. The need for new evaluation criteria recommended in the Report and mentioned above convey the idea that the evaluation course becomes itself "a socially embedded process in which formal procedures entwine with the informal assessments by which actors make sense of their situation" [30, p. 94] Since situations evolve, sensemaking is a process by which actors give meaning to their experience and orientate their choices and actions so that the evaluation process is open-ended— whereby, from the AAL artifact design onwards, outcomes are interpreted and used to guide successive action toward improved performances. As Weick and his co-authors point out [34], besides being retrospective (built on experience) and onward looking (aimed at identifying successive actions), sensemaking is also social (actors are interdependent) and it entails communication so that interactive talk and exchange of interpretations allow organizing and decision making in the different circumstances at hand. In sum, the AAL artifact development cycle has to do with organizational change and is a complex matter intertwined with numerous aspects besides the (however crucial) technological ones. Specifically, as Weick et al. argue (supra), important tacit knowledge is created by the interaction of people in the sensemaking process and this fact should be considered when both evaluating and designing AAL e-services. When the size or complexity of the project is significant, the issues in organizing change (and sensemaking) to pursue a certain accomplishment become ever more crucial because of both the time required for the development of the specific system and the large number of heterogeneous actors involved.

This entails that the introduction and diffusion of AAL based services has to take into account the way "traditional" systems are deployed and in what way the change affects both the 'beneficiaries' and the practitioners involved within the network of organizations they belong to. This is why two principles of the service-dominant approach should be kept at the forefront when defining the rationale of programs, calls, and projects: "all social and economic actors are resource integrators" (FP9) and "value is always uniquely and phenomenologically determined by the beneficiary" (FP 10).

B—'Intermediaries' as facilitators in the co-production process for e-services deployment. To facilitate the adoption and spreading of the services derived from AAL projects, some useful suggestions can be found in the e-government literature and experiences. These have shown the advantage of using 'intermediaries'. What has become clear is that the engagement of 'users' and the contextualization of e-government projects require not only the bridging of the 'digital divide' but also the promotion of 'intermediate entities' to act as a go-between in connecting people with services [35]. The important role of 'intermediaries' becomes apparent because the attitude of people towards ICT-intensive services has not been encouraging [36]. Thus, any strategy concerning the delivery of public services must leverage other resources in order to integrate digital with in-presence public services. Essentially, there are positive effects when a service-dominant logic is being built and a number of intermediate service providers ('intermediaries') develop their value propositions in a sort of supply chain, where different techniques are employed (both digital and in-presence). The emergence of 'intermediaries' and their potential influence on the qualities of a service relationship has been studied specifically by the literature [37]. Adopting a 'beneficiary'-centric perspective, the intermediaries are seen as a way to help a broad range of users to access the information/resources they need through more tailored services. In that sense, the intermediaries have the potential to bridge inequalities, above all in terms of the adoption, access, and use of the ICT resources within a climate of trust. The type of individuals receiving assistance from social intermediaries, compared to those not receiving assistance, tends to be those who are otherwise beyond the digital divide, excluded from other information society benefits. The presence of intermediaries who add human skills and knowledge to the ICT environment is critical for projects that want to reach less advantaged citizens [38]. Sorrentino and Niehaves [37] slot the intermediaries into the "institutional carrier" category (a concept worked on by Scott [39]) and highlight its dual nature: relational agents (i.e., "systems made up of connections among actors, including both individual and collective actors" [35, p. 886]), and symbolic agents (i.e., "systems that can be used to convey information about rules (...), values and norms (...), or mental schema or models" [ibid, p. 882]. In the former role, the intermediaries (for example professional associations) reshape organizational boundaries and "stimulate managers to reconsider who and what are inside versus outside" [ibid, p. 887]. The second role (i.e., symbolic agents) played by the intermediaries, especially those who interact directly with individuals, is particularly crucial for the carrying of tacit knowledge, i.e., non-codified knowledge embedded in the skills and routines of performers. For instance, an elderly may see the pharmacist as a kind of access point to an abstract system, i.e., the national health service.

C—Gatekeepers as co-producers of relevant information for e-services diffusion. Another role, that of 'gatekeepers', seems important for the penetration of AAL based services: the AAL evaluation Report refers explicitly to a number of decision-makers "who will be critical gatekeepers in enabling solutions to reach the market" (p. 19). The connection among different actors and the bridging of inequalities (while including different kinds of knowledge) can be seen through the lens of the Network Gatekeeping Theory. In an extensive review [40] of the meaning of gatekeeping in the literature of different disciplines (including information systems management) the word gatekeeping "refers broadly to the process of controlling information as it moves through a gate or filter, and is associated with different types of power" (ibid. p. 1). For our discourse on intermediaries and co-creation of meaningful knowledge in age-aware e-services three are the points of interest concerning gatekeeping. First, the role of the 'gated' (e.g., the users of an e-service) and not only that of the gatekeepers needs to be taken into account because both roles interact dynamically. Second, in the management of information systems, gatekeepers are 'facilitators' who "improve or maintain internal processes and help new gated entering the network (gatekeepers … in many cases serve as educators)" (ibid., p. 12). Third, the gated are also considered capable of 'challenging' gatekeepers given: (i) the high rate of exchanges between the two parties; (ii) the useful information potentially generated by the gated; (iii) the choice of alternatives available to the gated; and (iv) the fact that the gated are not powerless.

Furthermore, the "gatekeepers and the gated are not monolithic social and political entities… dynamism is important to represent an environment where the interests and goals of the stakeholders constantly change, as do their gatekeeping and gated roles" (ibid., p. 47). Second, the phenomenon of gatekeeping is large yet sensitive to specific contexts. Third, there are multiple dimensions to gatekeeping whereby, for example, gatekeepers are both 'guardians of boundaries' and 'messengers of the community'.

In sum, the reason for the flourishing of services within services (such as 'intermediaries' and 'gatekeepers') is acknowledging the fact that value is basically idiosyncratic and contextual, as was underscored in this work.

6   Concluding Remarks

The paper has highlighted the following aspects. First, the ageing of the population raises economic issues, in relation to the affordability for national budgets to satisfy their needs, and social issues concerning the right of the elderly to be both as independent as possible and integrated in their living and working communities. Second, the potential of age-aware services based on the development of ICTs is significant; their development, however, is hampered by questions concerning their dependability, their complex integration with different organizational milieus, their intrusive character, and the ability of many older people to deal with them effectively. Third, approaching the design and development of these emerging services using the 'service science' principles appears to help coping with these issues and with the dangers of technological determinism; indeed, the 'one size fits all' approach is still looming wide over this kind of innovations. Fourth, the 'contextual analysis' conducted on the AAL program and the evaluation Report show that the initiative on the whole has been successful: the seeding of transnational communities, the substantial number of SMEs and of user role organizations, the funding already obtained by a considerable number of projects to further their development. Fifth, there are challenges to cope with and recommendations to be followed stressed in the Report: (i) most AAL solutions are technology driven and they are not adequately centered on service innovations and social innovations (as a consequence the selection criteria of the projects to be funded should better consider this problem); (ii) they should be more focused on exploitation and commercialization as well as proposing pilots operating under realistic conditions; furthermore, (iii) the quality of users' involvements should be improved (i.e. co-production should be enhanced). Sixth, consequently, the 'conceptual context' (more specifically the 'conceptual context of ideas and doctrines' [21, p. 395] should be strengthened to support these challenges; to this end, drawing on neo-institutional theory and on network gatekeeping theory, three suggestions are made as specific contributions of this paper: promoting co-creation while leveraging the roles of 'intermediaries' and 'gatekeepers'. In the light of the outcomes of the case-in-point described above, these suggestions seem to sustain the realization of a 'service-dominant logic' as a prerequisite for an effective co-production in designing and deploying e-services for an ageing population.

References

1. Verschuere, B., Brandsen, T., Pestoff, V.: Co-production: The State of the Art in Research and the Future Agenda. Voluntas. 23, 1083–1101 (2012)
2. Osborne, S.P., Radnor, Z., Nasi, G.: A new theory for public service management? toward a (public) service-dominant approach. Am. Rev. Public Adm. 43, 135–158 (2012)
3. Wilson, G.: Co-production and self-care: new approaches to managing community care services for older people. Soc. Policy Adm. 28, 236–250 (1994)
4. Bode, I.: Co-governance within networks and the non-profit—for-profit divide. Public Manag. Rev. 8, 551–566 (2006)
5. Pestoff, V., Brandsen, T., Verschuere, B. (eds.): New Public Governance, the Third Sector and Co-Production. Routledge, New York (2012)
6. Pestoff, V.: Co-production and third sector social services in europe—some crucial conceptual issues. In: Pestoff, V., Brandsen, T., Verschuere, B. (eds.) New Public Governance, the Third Sector and Co-production, pp. 25–45. Routledge, New York (2012)
7. Niehaves, B.: Iceberg ahead: on electronic government research and societal aging. Gov. Inf. Q. 28, 310–319 (2011)

8. Edwards, P.: Active Ageing: a Policy Framework Geneva, 2002. World Health Organization Press, Geneva (2002)
9. Vergados, D., Alevizos, A., Caragiozidis, M., Mariolis, A.: Intelligent services for assisting independent living of elderly people at home. In: Pervasive Technologies Related to Assistive Environments. ACM, New York (2008)
10. Czaja, S.J., Lee, C.C.: The impact of the internet on older adults. In: Charness, N., Schaie, K. W. (eds.) Impact of Technology on Succesful Ageing. Springer, New York (2003)
11. Börsch-Supan, A., Brugiavini, A., Jürges, H., Kapteyn, A., Mackenbach, J., Siegrist, J., Weber, G.: First Results from the Survey of Health, Ageing and Retirement in Europe (2004–2007): Starting the Longitudinal Dimension. MEA, Mannheim (2008)
12. Hanson, V.L.: Age and web access: the next generation. In: Proceedings of the 2009 International Cross-Disciplinary Conference on Web Accessibililty (W4A). ACM, New York (2009)
13. McLoughlin, I., Maniatopoulos, G., Wilson, R., Martin, M.: Hope to die before you get old? Techno-centric versus user-centred approaches in developing virtual services for older people. Public Manag. Rev. 11, 857–880 (2009)
14. Bowes, A., Dawson, A., Bell, D.: Ethical implications of lifestyle monitoring data in ageing research. information. Commun. Soc. 15, 5–22 (2012)
15. Stack, J., Zarate, L., Pastor, C., Mathiassen, N.E., Barbera, R., Knops, H., Kornsten, H.: Analysing and federating the European assistive technology ICT industry—Final Report., Bruxelles (2009)
16. Mazzucato, M., Penna, C. (eds.): Mission-Oriented Finance for Innovation: New Ideas for Investment-Led Growth. Rowman & Littlefield, London (2015)
17. OECD: Science and technology perspectives on an ageing society. In: OECD Science, Technology and Industry Outlook 2012. pp. 97–113. OECD Publishing, Paris (2012)
18. Obi, T., Auffret, J.P., Iwasaki, N. (eds.): Aging Society and ICT: Global Silver Innovation, vol. 5. IOS Press. IOS Press (2013)
19. Aarts, E., Dózsa, C., Mollenkopf, H., Uusikylä, P., Sharpe, M.: Final Evaluation of the Ambient Assisted Living Joint Programme (2013)
20. Cahn, E., Gray, C.: Co-production from a normative perspective. In: Pestoff, V., Brandsen, T., Verschuere, B. (eds.) New Public Governance, the Third Sector and Co-production. Routledge (2012)
21. Meijer, A.: Co-production in an information age. In: Pestoff, V., Brandsen, T., Verschuere, B. (eds.) New Public Governance, the Third Sector and Co-production, pp. 199–217. Routledge, New York (2012)
22. Procter, R., Greenhalgh, T., Wherton, J., Sugarhood, P., Rouncefield, M., Hinder, S.: The day-to-day co-production of ageing in place. Comput. Support. Coop. Work 23, 245–267 (2014)
23. McLoughlin, I., Maniatopoulos, G., Wilson, R., Martin, M.: Inside a digital experiment: Co-producing telecare services for older people. Scand. J. Inf. Syst. 24, 3–26 (2013)
24. Wilson, R., Maniatopoulos, G., Martin, M., McLoughlin, I.: Innovating relationships. information. Commun. Soc. 15, 1136–1163 (2012)
25. European Commission Staff: Working document: Ageing Well in the Information Society. Action Plan on Information and Communication Technologies and Ageing. Bruxelles (2007)
26. Pollitt, C.: Context in public policy and management: the missing link?. Edward Elgar Publishing, Cheltenham (2013)
27. Chesbrough, H.W.: Toward a new science of services. Harv. Bus. Rev. 83, 43–44 (2005)
28. Chesbrough, H., Spohrer, J.I.M.: A research manifesto for services science. Commun. ACM 49, 35–40 (2006)
29. Vargo, S.L., Lusch, R.F.: Evolving to a new dominant logic for marketing. J. Mark. 68, 1–17 (2004)
30. Vargo, S.L., Lusch, R.F.: Service-dominant logic: continuing the evolution. J. Acad. Mark. Sci. 36, 1–10 (2008)

31. Vargo, S.L., Maglio, P.P., Akaka, M.A.: On value and value co-creation: a service systems and service logic perspective. Eur. Manag. J. **26**, 145–152 (2008)
32. European Commission Staff: Accompanying Document to the Initiative On E-Inclusion: To Be Part Of The Information Society. Bruxelles (2007)
33. European Commission Staff: Working Document: Ageing well in the Information Society—Action Plan on Information and Communication Technologies and Ageing (2007)
34. Weick, K.E., Sutcliffe, K.M., Obstfeld, D.: Organizing and the process of sensemaking. Organ. Sci. **16**, 409–421 (2005)
35. OECD: The e-Government Imperative. OECD Publishing (2003)
36. Miller, E.A., West, D.M.: Where's the revolution? digital technology and health care in the internet age. J. Health Polit. Policy Law **34**, 261–284 (2009)
37. Sorrentino, M., Niehaves, B.: Intermediaries in E-inclusion: a literature review. In: Proceedings of the 43rd Hawaii International Conference on System Sciences (HICSS), pp. 1–10 (2010)
38. Rajalekshmi, K.: E-governance services through telecenters: the role of human intermediary and issues of trust. Inf. Technol. Int. Dev. **4**, 19–35 (2007)
39. Scott, W.R.: Institutional carriers: reviewing modes of transporting ideas over time and space and considering their consequences. Ind. Corp. Chang. **12**, 879–894 (2003)
40. Barzilai-Nahon, K.: Gatekeeping: a critical review. Annu. Rev. Inf. Sci. Technol. **43**, 1–63 (2009)

Organizational Engines for Smart Territorial Networks: The Case of an Initiative for Food Waste Reduction

Sabrina Bonomi, Francesca Ricciardi and Cecilia Rossignoli

1 Introduction

New technologies are opening up immense opportunities not only for businesses, but also for the common good. Many problems, in effect, have to be addressed at the level of territorial systems, because entire territorial areas are often heavily impacted by the negative consequences of economic development, such as pollution, waste, overpopulation, traffic, social exclusion, population ageing, and so forth. Intelligent, far-sighted collaboration, supported or enabled by new technologies, is often perceived as the sole possible solution to such dramatic challenges [1].

The so-called "smart revolution" movement stems precisely from this idea. A vast global community is growing, including people from governmental bodies, businesses and research institutions, focusing on the opportunities offered by high technologies in order to address the emerging societal and ecological challenges. The vigorously growing research streams on smart cities, smart regions and smart communities all converge in suggesting that high technologies should be leveraged to boost intelligent collaboration aiming at the common good, and especially the sustainability, resilience and quality of life of the systems (e.g., cities) where daily life concretely takes place [2].

This heterogeneous, multi-disciplinary movement shares the idea that we must build a "smarter world", where economic prosperity is coupled with higher social

S. Bonomi (✉)
eCampus University, Novedrate, CO, Italy
e-mail: sabrina.bonomi@uniecampus.it

F. Ricciardi · C. Rossignoli
University of Verona, Verona, Italy
e-mail: francesca.ricciardi@univr.it

C. Rossignoli
e-mail: cecilia.rossignoli@univr.it

© Springer International Publishing Switzerland 2016
F. D'Ascenzo et al. (eds.), *Blurring the Boundaries Through Digital Innovation*,
Lecture Notes in Information Systems and Organisation 19,
DOI 10.1007/978-3-319-38974-5_19

and ecological sustainability, a better quality of life for all, and a higher resilience (i.e., robustness and adaptability) of critical social systems such as local communities or economic districts [3, 4].

Most of the research on smart initiatives have mainly focused on technological aspects so far. On the other hand, it is becoming growingly clear that technological innovation is not enough. Consistent changes in practices, shared values, roles, and rules of the game are also needed to achieve a smarter world through high technologies. The research focusing on traditional, for-profit firms has already started addressing these issues, and a great deal of studies is being dedicated to investigate the new organizational forms, business models and business eco-systems that allow a better exploitation of the opportunities offered by high technologies, and ICTs in particular. Conversely, the research focusing on smart innovation for the common good lags critically behind the unprecedented management issues emerging in today's scenario.

If high technologies, and ICTs in particular, offer crucial opportunities to address many dramatic problems at the level of territorial systems, what are the (new) organizational forms and eco-systems that may enable to better exploit these emerging opportunities? What are the key (and possibly new) managerial challenges implied?

This study contributes to address these research questions, which are to date surprisingly under-investigated by the scholarly community. To do so, we explore a case of a pioneering project of a not for profit organization in Italy. R.e.b.u.s. is an acronym that means 'Recovery of goods in surplus, usable for charities' (Recupero, Eccedenze, Beni, Utilizzabili, Solidalmente). This project implemented a recovering process to reduce the impairment of food. Thanks to an ICT-enabled network created by a supervisor, the surplus of food in the area is donated, instead of wasting it; the donated food is immediately delivered to people in need of it by aid organizations. R.e.b.u.s. is an example of value co-creation because the food that would have been otherwise wasted becomes a resource with social and economic importance, thanks to the interaction of several organizations.

We gained in-depth understanding of this case, through the combined contribution of participatory action research, design oriented research and long-term participant observation. Our results confirm that the smart organization (SO) under study, thanks to a relatively simple technological solution and consistent, innovative organizational strategies, achieves four important goals, and namely:

- the SO transforms a negative externality (food waste) into a common resource;
- the SO creates and fine-tunes a set of rules that contribute to improve the use of common resources in the whole territorial system;
- the SO plays a pivotal role in day-by-day management of common resources; and
- the SO triggers beneficial institutional changes in the wider social environment, including governmental norms, community expectations, and practices in both businesses and charity organizations.

We found that the phenomena observed in this case could not be explained through the lens of a single existing theory: we suggest that a cross-fertilization is needed, between (1) the studies on smart cities, regions and communities; (2) the studies on institutional entrepreneurship; and (3) the studies on socio-technical systems (STS) and socio-ecological systems (SES).

Therefore, this study suggests that management and information systems scholars cooperate to develop a new research area. This research area should focus on the emerging knowledge-based, network-shaped organizational forms, which have a great potential to create value at the level of territorial systems and trigger positive changes in the social environment. We label these new organizational forms as "smart organizations". This study suggests that SOs could be the key engine for the socio-technical transition to sustainability and resilience of territorial systems. We suggest that this approach is likely to yield relevant contributions and could leverage the complementarities of research traditions that have remained separated so far: smart city/region/community, institutional entrepreneurship, and STS/SES studies.

2 Background

2.1 The Studies on Smart Cities, Regions and Communities

The idea of an imminent "smart revolution" emerged in the late 1990s as a bottom-up trend, stemming from local initiatives carried out by citizens, associations, not-for-profit organizations, and for-profit companies [2]. This movement takes root at the crossroads of different and multidisciplinary debates of both research and practice communities [5, 6]. Its basic assumptions are: (1) social and ecological systems (such as regions) face severe, unprecedented challenges (such as pollution, traffic, population ageing, social exclusion, global competition, climate change, and so forth), which need to be addressed innovatively, otherwise the systems will collapse; and (2) collaborative innovation and full exploitation of high technologies are the key strategies to address such challenges [1].

Studies on smart projects and initiatives usually focus on territorial systems (usually labelled as smart cities or smart regions) but also on virtual networks of geographically distant people, linked by common interests or purposes (smart communities). The literature has to date mainly concentrated on the technological aspects of the smart revolution, whilst the organizational and managerial implications of these technological opportunities remain substantially under-investigated [7]. In other words, the literature on the smart phenomenon is today similar to how the literature on e-business looked like in the 1990s: then too, whilst the technological implications arose a great deal of interest, the organizational and managerial issues remained a sort of black box. The scholarly community studying the e-business phenomenon soon realized that such a gap needed closing, and a viable stream of studies emerged to investigate the new organizational forms, business models and business eco-systems that allow a better exploitation of the opportunities offered by ICTs in the new, globalized business scenario.

We think that, similarly, also the literature on smart cities/regions/communities will soon concentrate on the key governance and management implications of the opportunities offered by new technologies. In particular, the role of organizational factors in the interplay between technological and institutional innovation seems a very promising research area.

2.2 The Studies on Institutional Entrepreneurship

Institutions are commonly defined as the formal and informal rules, norms, values and beliefs that shape action in a certain social environment. Institutions provide stable designs for activities, because deviations from institutionalized expectations are socially sanctioned in some manner [8]. Organizations exist in an environment of institutions, which exert some degree of pressure on them. Since organizations need support and legitimacy, they seek to align their behaviors with the institutionalized expectations of their environment [9].

Studies on the role of institutions in organizational life tend to polarize into two opposing view: the so-called realist institutionalism, or old institutionalism, on the one side; and social institutionalism, or new institutionalism, on the other side [10].

These two views on the relationships between organizations and institutions, corresponding to new and old institutionalism respectively, are unable to explain the phenomena observed in the case presented here. In fact, the organization we investigated has been very actively engaged in institutional design to maximize the territorial system's sustainability and quality of life, instead of its own payoff. In addition, also the triggering and enabling role of new technologies observed in the "smart" initiative under analysis could not be explained by leveraging the traditional neo- and old institutional approaches.

The former assumes the primacy of human agency, i.e. the capacity of people to act independently and to make free, rational choices. According to old institutionalism, humans (and organizations) pursue alignment between (organizational) behaviors and institutional expectations by struggling to adapt institutions to their own interests [11].

New institutionalism, conversely, assumes the primacy of social structure over human agency. Legitimacy is a necessary pre-condition to interact in a certain institutional environment, and then conformity and adherence to norms are more important than efficiency or power. As a consequence, humans (and organizations) pursue alignment between (organizational) behaviors and institutional expectations by strictly and passively conforming to existing norms, rules and expectations [12].

If taken in isolation, both new and old institutionalisms are subject to easy criticism. Tolbert and Zucker [11] suggest that real-world institutionalization processes (i.e., the rise of novel institutional structures) can be explained only through a hybridization between old and new institutionalism, by assuming that the success and persistence of an institutional structure is not independent of its concrete impact on actors' desires and needs.

Studies on institutional entrepreneurship, in particular, provide interesting attempts to bridge the views of old and new institutionalism [8]. These studies focus on the activities of actors who leverage resources to transform existing institutions or to create new ones, in order to build and stabilize a novel institutional arrangement that is favorable to their interests [13]. These studies highlight that social structures, while constraining actors to some extent, also provide the fabric allowing initiatives and change. An important stimulus for, and enabler of, institutional activism is technological innovation; some interesting studies focus on the intertwining between technological change and institutional entrepreneurship (for example, [14]).

In most studies, the institutional entrepreneur is assumed to act upon self-interest in the classical sense, in order to maximize just his or her own power and/or profit. But a wider view of the possible consequences of institutional entrepreneurship is emerging.

New institutional structures are often framed through cooperation and collective action, therefore institutional entrepreneurship often implies the ability to provide the other actors with common meaning and a new collective identity [15]. Institutional entrepreneurs are active arbitrageurs that intervene to find common solutions to collective problems; in this way, they may take advantage of convergent interests and rely on collective action to influence higher-level institutions [16]. For this reason, Pacheco et al. [8] suggest that management studies in institutional theory should distinguish the collective and individual outcomes that arise from institutional entrepreneurship efforts.

But if the institutional entrepreneur's actions can also result in influencing collective interests, this poses unprecedented questions to organizational scholars. What is exactly the nature of the most relevant common interests that (techno-) institutional design can impact? How could the institutional entrepreneur contribute to the common good? Should this contribution be considered a "rational" goal for managerial action? Organization and management scholars have completely overlooked these questions so far; but extremely interesting answers are provided by the literature on SES and STS.

2.3 The Studies on Socio-ecological and Socio-technical Systems (SES and STS)

Ostrom [17] authoritatively criticizes the idea that the momentum for change when market fails must come from the government (typically advised by economists) rather than from the reflection, creativity and collaborative efforts of those within the market-failure situation to restructure their own patterns of interaction for higher collective payoff.

Two important and complementary streams of studies have developed around the basic idea of the bottom-up co-evolution of environments, institutions and technologies: Socio-ecological Systems (SES) studies, and Socio-technical Systems (STS) studies. The former focuses on resource management, by studying the interactions between a specific natural environment and a specific social system [18], described through its institutional and technological structures. The latter pays less attention to environmental impact and concentrates on innovation processes, by studying the co-evolution between technologies and institutions in social systems [19].

SES studies include the researches on common pool resources [20]: those scarce, fragile, critical common resources, such as clean water, fisheries, or development aid, that are subject to over-exploitation and irreversible destruction (the so-called "tragedy of the commons") unless effective institutions protect them [21]. The findings on how institutions can protect strategic resources are being extended also to intangible resources, such as digitally shared knowledge, or a community's innovation attitudes [22, 23].

STS studies, on the other hand, originate from Trist's seminal paper [24], which claimed that institutions, including legitimated habits, power structures and cooperation rules, can be changed by the effects of technological triggers. This statement does not imply any techno-centric determinism: on the contrary, STS scholars study also how institutions, in turn, affect technologies, and suggest that institutions should not be used just to explain inertia and stability, but also to explain dynamism and innovation [19, 25, 26]. STS scholars criticize the disciplinary traditions of sociology for having almost entirely neglected the material nature of societies [27]. Human beings are surrounded by technologies and artifacts, ranging from vehicles, cell phones, buildings, web pages, etc. These artifacts cannot be assumed as neutral and merely material instruments: they shape our perceptions, relationships, behaviors and habits. Socio-technical systems thus form a structuring context for human action. Indeed, "the rules that drive societies are not just shared in social groups and carried inside actors' heads, but can also be embedded in artifacts and practice" ([19], p. 903). Rules and beliefs embedded in artifacts, on the other hand, may be harder to change, often because of economic aspects, such as sunk costs.

Overall, SES and STS studies encourage new, more advanced ways to understand institutional change and design [28]. They provide sound scientific bases to explain how, at any level of analysis (e.g. industrial cluster, metropolitan area, harbor system) the social community's institutions interact with the resources and technologies that the community can rely on. This interaction determines the whole system's sustainability, robustness to crises, and adaptability [29].

In the last decades, SES and STS studies have accumulated a critical mass of findings on the factors that facilitate positive processes of techno-institutional (re) design, likely resulting in enhanced system sustainability and resilience. Many of these success factors have relevant organizational implications: for example, the bottom-up polycentrism of institutional activism, or the transparence (thanks to real-time information management) of the system [30]. On the other hand, SES and STS studies are rooted in economics, and therefore have been blind to *organizational* phenomena so far. This makes the cross-fertilization with the studies on institutional entrepreneurship and those on smart cities/regions/communities extremely promising and interesting.

3   Method

Given the explorative nature of this study, a process of qualitative data collection and analysis [31] has been chosen as the most appropriate.

The case presented in this paper describes a new, networked organizational form that leverages ICTs to mobilize resources for higher territorial system resilience, sustainability and quality of life. Therefore, it can be considered a representative case of SO, selected through the maximum intensity criterion [32].

This research builds upon both non-participant observation and participatory action research [32]. One of the authors was directly involved in the project since the beginning, whilst the other authors could witness some meetings where the project was discussed, and posed questions as participating observers. This allowed diversity and complementarity in the researchers' views.

The longitudinal data collection process started in 2008, when the project was launched, and it is still in progress. Thanks to reflective practice and discussion of the experiences, the authors achieved a direct and in-depth understanding of the concrete opportunities and problems, as implied by a SO "in action".

The research activities provided the authors with a multi-faceted experience of the phenomenon under study, as well as rich and diverse text and data archives, resulting from institutional and corporate reports, website texts, social network texts, interview recordings, and researchers' field notes. The analyses of these archives were conducted through a collaborative effort to gain in-depth understanding of the actors' views. The texts were independently analyzed by the three researchers, and then thoroughly discussed. This process lead to a shared interpretation of the case, which was then compared to the explanatory power of the existing literature.

4   Case Analysis

The R.e.b.u.s. network has two intertwined purposes: (1) reducing waste throughout the food value chain, and (2) reducing malnutrition of socially disadvantaged people. The project was officially launched in 2008—but groundwork and pilots had started in 2004—by a non-profit association in Verona (in the North of Italy).

Of course, initiatives of food donation to charity organizations already existed, but had proved quite inefficient. Charity organizations traditionally collected donated food and stored it in warehouses, which resulted in paradoxically high costs. Moreover, the logistical process of food collection and distribution were typically managed in a naïve, opaque fashion, which resulted in further waste, and even opportunistic behaviors. Last but not least, the nutritional quality of the food provided to people in need was poorly cared for, due to the prevalence of pasta, rice and preserved food. Therefore, the amount of food actually saved from waste and successfully utilized by people in need was very unsatisfactory, and potential donors (such as supermarkets, canteens or farmers) were scarcely motivated to donate, also because donation did not provide donors with immediate, tangible payoff.

The R.e.b.u.s. project was launched to create a new, financially self-sustaining network organization aimed at addressing the problems listed above. The basic idea was to involve three categories of actors (for-profit organizations, charity organizations, and public administration bodies) in a network linked by smooth information management (through ICT) and a set of rules developed ad hoc, in order to advantage all the partnering organizations.

The free food provided by the R.e.b.u.s. network allows charity organizations to save money and time and also guarantee a better nutrition to disadvantaged people, thanks to the balanced foods and fruit, vegetables and fresh food supplied. In addition, the charity organizations can also recruit unemployed people to provide food distribution services, thus promoting social inclusion. On the other hand, the donor companies reduce their fiscal costs and enhance their legitimation through a Corporate Social Responsibility (CSR) initiative. Finally, local governmental institutions foster a good practice that reduces waste production and its environmental impact (the action of the R.e.b.u.s. network reduced organic waste of 5 % in the involved area in 2012. Source: Arpav, the Regional agency for environmental prevention and protection). In addition, thanks to the R.e.b.u.s. network, the governmental bodies involved co-create value and improve public health, thus gaining higher reputation among taxpayers and voters [33].

The R.e.b.u.s. network, in effect, thanks to the "just-in-time" logistics allowed by its information system, needs no warehouse and has extremely low coordination costs. The non-profit organizations directly collect the surplus of food from donors as soon as donors inform the system that the food is made available. The charity organizations, after collecting the food, immediately distribute it for consumption. Probably, the direct involvement and collaboration of all the three groups of organizations (public administration, donors, and charity organizations), coordinated by an association of second level and linked by stable and reciprocals relationships, allows to reach the goals with efficiency and efficacy.

Today, at the steady state, the R.e.b.u.s. network works thanks to its information system, a full-time person coordinating the activities, and about three part-time volunteers. Most of the work (updating the database, making food available, collecting and distributing it) is carried out directly by the partnering organizations.

The coordinating association cooperates with the public administration in the procedures check, prepares the agreements with donors for the administrative and fiscal transparency, trains the non-profit organizations to respect the regulations, verifies the controls thus ensuring the accuracy of the procedure, elaborates the results that are to be communicated to all the stakeholders, finds new donors and beneficiaries and supervises the entire process (Fig. 1).

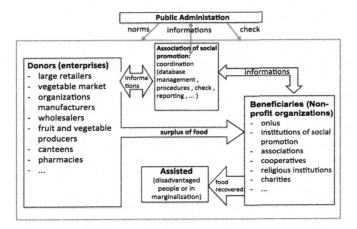

Fig. 1 The R.e.b.u.s. process

Procedures, processes and norms are standardized, which allows the replication of the model and its diffusion. Nowadays, the project is fully operational in the Verona area. Additionally, the supervisor fosters the reproduction of the model in other northern Italy cities, such as Vicenza, Padua, Rovigo, Bergamo and Mantua.

In 2014, about 1,430 tons worth of food were reused and the economic value of the recovered food is about 1,800,000 euro. There is an increase of about 32 % compared with 2013; the food recovering comes from one large retailer, 21 schools and two company canteens, a fruit and vegetable market and five agricultural producers' organizations. The recovered food is given for free to more than 70 non-profit organizations that assist over 60,000 economically disadvantaged people, becoming a resource with social and economic importance (Fig. 2).

In 2010, a new initiative was launched, called 'R.e.b.u.s. Informs', an educational program that considers several topics, such as waste reduction, correct nutrition, respect for the environment, subsidiarity. This educational initiative aims at children, students and citizens to encourage a positive change in the populations' behaviors.

The public organizations involved are the local government of Verona, the Province of Verona, the local health authority, the prefecture; an important role is

Fig. 2 The trend of recovery from the beginning of the project (testing) to today

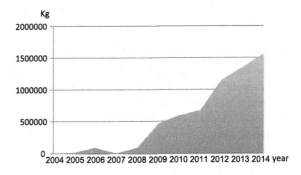

also played by the municipal organization responsible for waste logistic management. Thanks to the undertaking of the latter organization, indeed, a regulatory change was introduced, to incentive participation in the R.e.b.u.s. network. According to this new policy, developed ad hoc, the organizations that contribute to the prevention of food waste, redistributing food and meals, obtain a reduction of the waste tax (*TIA: Tassa di Igiene Ambientale*).

Information systems have a pivotal role in the R.e.b.u.s. project. On one hand, ICTs foster the efficiency of the project and consequently facilitate its sustainability. On the other hand, the R.e.b.u.s. information system supports transparency and legality; therefore the credibility of the project increases.

Without ICT, indeed, the wide network of collaborative relationships of the R.e.b.u.s. project could not have been activated, because it would have been impossible to provide the partners with just-in-time, low-cost information flows on the availability of fresh food. In addition, also the incentive provided by the waste tax discount (TIA) would have been impossible, because only an IT solution can provide a transparent, certified and sustainable monitoring and supervision of the process of food donation.

5 Conclusions

The R.e.b.u.s. network proved a very interesting case of smart organization (SO) as we defined it above: a networked, knowledge-based organization that leverages new technologies to enhance the sustainability, resilience and/or quality of life of a territorial system.

In fact, thanks to its information system, the R.e.b.u.s. network reduces environmental damage caused by waste, and makes free food available for people in need. Interestingly, we also found that the R.e.b.u.s. network acts as an institutional entrepreneur for a better governance and management of important common goods such as free food, public health, social cohesion and the environment. In fact, the R.e.b.u.s. network:

- guarantees fiscal and administrative fulfillments, transparency and legality throughout the logistic processes of food collection and distribution, and, in this way, contrasts the opportunistic behaviors that would deplete the common resources;
- contributes to nutritional education;
- contributes to community pride and identity;
- encourages the cross-fertilization of values, practices and mentality between for-profit, non-profit and governmental organizations;
- creates and enables new practices throughout the food system;
- creates the conditions for, and actively promotes, regulatory change that boosts the network.

Our analysis suggests that the successful coevolution of individual and collective interests, observed in this case, should be attributed to the SO's concerted efforts to align those interests with a strategic vision of a better configuration of the territorial system seen as a common resource.

In our opinion, the phenomena we observed in the R.e.b.u.s. case cannot be explained by any of the existing theories, if taken in isolation. Conversely, we suggest that a cross-fertilization between studies on smart city/regions/communities, institutional entrepreneurship, and SES/STS may prove very fertile to explain these new emerging organizational phenomena.

Our findings confirm that the paramount consequences of technological change go far beyond the single firm's competitiveness and open up immense opportunities to address much more complex higher-level problems.

In traditional economies, face-to-face social interactions and community discussions were sufficient to establish institutional arrangements that allowed to protect critical resources at the level of the territorial system, as Ostrom's studies demonstrated [20]. Today, instead, territorial systems are continuously challenged and subject to ever-changing, complex conditions. New forms of organizational engines are likely to be needed to allow full exploitation of new technologies for the common good. This appears to be as one of the most relevant and interesting issues for organization and management studies for the years to come.

References

1. Dameri, R.P., Ricciardi, F.: Smart City Intellectual Capital: an emerging view of territorial systems innovation management. J. Intellect. Cap. **16**, 1–15 (2015)
2. Ricciardi, F., Za, S.: Smart city research as an interdisciplinary crossroads: a challenge for management and organization studies. In: Mola, L., Pennarola, F. (eds.) From Information to Smart Society: Environment, Politics and Economics, LNISO, vol. 5, pp. 163–171. Springer (2014)
3. Fiksel, J.: Sustainability and resilience: toward a systems approach. Sustain. Sci. Pract. Policy **2**, 14–21 (2006)
4. Folke, C.: Resilience: The emergence of a perspective for social-ecological systems analyses. Glob. Environ. Change **16**, 253–267 (2006)
5. Giffinger, R., Fertner, C., Kramar, H., Kalasek, R., Pichler-Milanovic, N., Meijers, E.: Smart Cities-Ranking of European Medium-Sized Cities. Vienna University of Technology (2007)
6. Nam, T., Pardo, T.: Smart city as urban innovation: focusing on management, policy, and context. In: Proceedings of the 5th International Conference on Theory and Practice of Electronic Governance (2011)
7. Ricciardi, F., Rossignoli, C., De Marco, M.: Participatory networks for place safety and livability: organisational success factors. Int. J. Networking Virtual Organ. **13**, 42–65 (2013)
8. Pacheco, D.F., York, J.G., Dean, T.J., Sarasvathy, S.D.: The coevolution of institutional entrepreneurship: a tale of two theories. J. Manage. **36**, 974–1010 (2010)
9. Rossignoli, C., Ricciardi, F.: Inter-Organizational Relationships. Towards a Dynamic Model for Understanding Business Network Performance. Springer International Publishing, Berlin (2015)
10. Heugens, P.P.M.A.R., Lander, M.W.: Structure! agency! (and other quarrels): a meta-analysis of institutional theories of organization. Acad. Manag. J. **52**, 61–85 (2009)

11. Tolbert, P.S., Zucker, L.G.: The institutionalization of institutional theory. In: Studying Organization. Theory and Method, pp. 169–184 (1999)
12. Powell, W.W., Di Maggio, P.J.: The New Institutionalism in Organizational Analysis. University of Chicago Press, Chicago (2012)
13. Battilana, J., Leca, B., Boxenbaum, E.: How actors change institutions: towards a theory of institutional entrepreneurship. Acad. Manag. Ann. **3**, 65–107 (2009)
14. Munir, K.A.: The birth of the "Kodak Moment": institutional entrepreneurship and the adoption of new technologies. Organ. Stud. **26**, 1665–1687 (2005)
15. Fligstein, N.: Social skill and institutional theory. Am. Behav. Sci. **40**, 397–405 (1997)
16. Wijen, F., Ansari, S.: Overcoming inaction through collective institutional entrepreneurship: insights from regime theory. Organ. Stud. **28**, 1079–1100 (2007)
17. Ostrom, E.: Beyond markets and states: polycentric governance of complex economic systems. Am. Econ. Rev. **100**, 641–672 (2010)
18. Brondizio, E.S., Ostrom, E., Young, O.R.: Connectivity and the governance of multilevel social-ecological systems: the role of social capital. Ann. Rev. Environ. Resour. **34**, 253–278 (2009)
19. Geels, F.W.: From sectoral systems of innovation to socio-technical systems: Insights about dynamics and change from sociology and institutional theory. Res. Policy **33**, 897–920 (2004)
20. Ostrom, E.: Governing The Commons: The Evolution of Institutions for Collective Action. Oxford University Press, Oxford (1990)
21. Gibson, C.C., Andersson, K., Ostrom, E., Shivakumar, S.: The Samaritan's Dilemma: The political economy of development aid. Polit. Econ. Dev. Aid. **13**, 105–124 (2005)
22. Rose, C.M., Roset, C.: The comedy of the commons: commerce, custom, and inherently public property. Univ. Chicago Law Rev. **53**, 711–781 (1986)
23. Lessig, L.: The future of ideas: the fate of the commons in a connected world, Vintage (2002)
24. Trist, E.: The evolution of socio-technical systems. Occas. Pap. **2** (1981)
25. Geels, F.W.: The multi-level perspective on sustainability transitions: responses to seven criticisms. Environ. Innov. Soc. Transitions **1**, 24–40 (2011)
26. Smith, A.: Translating sustainabilities between green niches and socio-technical regimes. Technol. Anal. Strateg. Manag. **19**, 427–450 (2007)
27. Geels, F.W.: Ontologies, socio-technical transitions (to sustainability), and the multi-level perspective. Res. Policy **39**, 495–510 (2010)
28. Young, O.R.: Institutional dynamics: resilience, vulnerability and adaptation in environmental and resource regimes. Glob. Environ. Change **20**, 378–385 (2010)
29. Berkes, F., Folke, C., Colding, J. (eds.): Linking Social and Ecological Systems: Management Practices and Social Mechanisms for Building Resilience. Cambridge University Press, Cambridge (2000)
30. Ostrom, E.: Understanding Institutional Diversity. Princeton university press, Princeton (2009)
31. Yin, R.K.: Case Study Research: Design and Methods. Sage publications, Thousand Oaks (2013)
32. Bryman, A., Bell, E.: Business Research Methods. Oxford University Press, Oxford (2011)
33. Bonomi, S., Ricci, M., Tommasi, M.: The relationships between different organizational units for the development of an integrated strategy to reduce food waste and waste management. In: Proceeding for SUM Symposium of Urban Mining, CISA publisher (2014)

Exploring Smart City Vision
by University, Industry and Government

Annalisa Cocchia and Renata Paola Dameri

1 Introduction

During the latest 20 years, urbanization has been accelerating all over the world. People moves from country to cities to find better opportunities for living, working, studying, developing their entrepreneurial ideas [1, 2]. However, urbanization produces also several diseases such as pollution, traffic, congestion, waste, and social exclusion.

The smart city movement was born just from these opposite circumstances: the pivotal role of cities and the urban problems deriving from urbanization. A smart city is conceived like a urban strategy using high technology and especially ICT for supporting a participated social and economic development of the urban area, preventing pollution and reducing the environmental footprint.

Until now, smart cities have been implemented especially applying a spontaneous, bottom-up process; municipalities, companies, not-for-profit organizations and the citizens themselves pursue the smartness of their city suggesting or directly implementing smart projects, initiatives, solutions. The final aim of this trend is to improve the citizens' quality of life and the environmental preservation.

Universities all over the world have been the first actor interested in studying and experimenting smart city pilots, starting this wave now interesting a very large set of heterogeneous stakeholders. As technology is the core component of a smart city, solution vendors are also first movers in designing and suggesting smart city solutions. Municipalities are involved as both players and coordinators of smart city plans interesting the city as a whole.

A. Cocchia (✉) · R.P. Dameri (✉)
University of Genova, Department of Economics, Genoa, Italy
e-mail: annalisa.cocchia@gmail.com

R.P. Dameri
e-mail: dameri@economia.unige.it

© Springer International Publishing Switzerland 2016
F. D'Ascenzo et al. (eds.), *Blurring the Boundaries Through Digital Innovation*,
Lecture Notes in Information Systems and Organisation 19,
DOI 10.1007/978-3-319-38974-5_20

The involvement of universities, industries, and (local) governments in the smart city implementation responds to the triple helix idea [3, 4]; where citizens or their representatives are involved too, it becomes a quadruple helix. A smart city emerges therefore like an innovation ecosystem, exploiting social and economic development thanks to the hybridization of elements from university, industry and government to generate a creative renewal in the knowledge economy and society.

However, to produce benefits the smart city triple-helix should be based on the same idea of smart city shared by all the key actors aiming at the same smart goals. As a sound definition of smart city lacks so far, it is not possible to refer to a shared theoretical concept, but a common smart city idea is the necessary conceptual basis to support a long-term, synergic, successful implementation of innovative smart cities thanks to the cooperation of all the involved actors and stakeholders.

This work aims at verifying the conceptual idea of smart city belonging to these different key players: university, industry, and government. For pursuing this aim, the authors carry out a deep analysis of a large set of documents issued by all these players: the set includes scientific papers, institutional reports, industry surveys focused on the smart city topic and issued by the most representative actors in the international panorama. The content analysis permits to compare not only several smart city definitions, but also aims, components, and instruments included in the smart city vision defined by each category of actors and to understand if and how much these visions are similar or different each other. Implications are derived, regarding public policies and private strategies for a better integration between university, industry and local government in smart city implementation.

2   Literature Review

During the latest 5 years, the smart city topic has been increasing its weight in research activities of universities all over the world. Papers and reports issued about this theme have been exponentially increasing after 2010 so far.

This vibrant topic is until now immature and in progress; indeed, a shared and sound definition of smart city has not been recognised by the scientific community yet. However, some most cited definitions are able to depict the main contents and aspects characterising this new urban trend (Table 1).

Hall [5] defines a smart city like a place where infrastructures—both traditional and ICT—are the core of a urban system. This pioneer and still immature definition already outlines the role of technology and the citizens as final addressees of the smart city policies.

Also Caragliu et al. [6] define smart city depending on infrastructures and technologies, but they add also two more crucial components: environmental preservation and participation to city governance. The smart city emerges as an integrate subject of both technological and political solutions with a high degree of innovation not only in the physical layer of the city, but also in the human and knowledge component of it.

Table 1 Most cited definitions of smart city

> "A city that monitors and integrates conditions of all of its critical infrastructures, including roads, bridges, tunnels, rails, subways, airports, seaports, *communications*, water, power, even major buildings, can better optimize its resources, plan its preventive maintenance activities, and monitor security aspects while maximizing services to its citizens".

• **Hall, 2000**

> "A city to be smart when investments in human and social capital and traditional (transport) and modern (*ICT*) communication infrastructure fuel sustainable economic growth and a high quality of life, with a wise management of natural resources, through participatory governance".

• **Caragliu et al., 2009**

> "Smart City is a city in which it can combine technologies as diverse as water recycling, advanced energy grids and mobile communications in order to reduce environmental impact and to offer its citizens better lives".

• **SETIS-EU 2012**

> "A smart city is a well-defined geographical area, in which high technologies such as *ICT*, logistic, energy production, and so on, cooperate to create benefits for citizens in terms of well-being, inclusion and participation, environmental quality, intelligent development; it is governed by a well-defined pool of subjects, able to state the rules and policy for the city government and development".

• **Dameri, 2013**

The European Commission [7] in its program SETIS defines a smart city especially in order to harmonize technological innovation and economic development with environmental preservation. The environmental component has in the EU vision a central role and EU smart policies are explicitly addressed to use innovative technologies for reducing the environmental footprint of smart cities.

Dameri [8] summarizes these and many other definitions and introduces some other aspects, such as: the role of good city governance, the territorial component and the social and inclusive aims of a smart city.

All these definitions outline the innovative role of a smart city; as a city is necessarily a territorial system, a smart city emerges like an innovation ecosystem, that is, "the network of institutions in the public and private sectors whose activities and interactions initiate, import, modify and diffuse new technologies" [9]. However, the condition to realize such an ecosystem is that all players would act in synergy each other.

Several papers analyze the smart city like an ecosystem, based on the triple helix model joining all the players and stakeholders involved in the smart city implementation, i.e. local governments, universities and private corporations. Deakin and Leydesdorff [10] in their paper try to demonstrate how the triple-helix model enables the study of a smart city like an innovation system. Lombardi et al. [11] suggest a modified model of a triple helix focusing on the production of knowledge by universities and government and the production of innovations that are patented by industry and universities as an index of intellectual capital in smart cities.

In all these cases, the smart city emerges like a complex system, where both heterogeneous actors play a pivotal role and several components are strictly interrelated each other. To give a framework to this complexity, some authors design a smart city model suggesting a framework to explore all the smart city components and their relations.

Giffinger [12] design six smart dimensions that are nowadays the most used to define the smart city components. They are: Smart economy, Smart mobility, Smart environment, Smart governance, Smart people, and Smart living. Chourabi et al. [13] define a smart city model built on two levels: in the internal level, Technology, Organization and Policy directly influence the Smart city initiative; in the external level, People Infrastructure, Environment, Technology and Governance put their direct influence on the internal components. Nam and Pardo [14] suggest a smart city model like a complex system deriving from the interactions of three dimensions: Technology, People, and Institutions.

All these models are useful to understand what a smart city is and how much different subjects involved in the smart city implementation converge or diverge in their own smart city vision. A shared smart city vision is indeed the premises for successful and synergic smart city programs involving all the triple helix subjects and to transform a smart city in a veritable innovation ecosystem.

3 Research Method

This paper aims at understanding and comparing the smart city vision of the three key actors—university, industry and government—composing the triple helix, whose activities support the Smart city implementation. The research method is based on a deep content analysis conducted on a selected subset of both scientific and not-scientific documents published during the latest 20 years. This choice derives from the observation that the smart city concept evolves along with two different paths, not ever coordinated each other: scientific research and empirical implementation [14]. Therefore, scientific papers furnish the proof of theoretical evolution of the smart city concept and non-scientific papers collect the case studies of implemented smart projects all over the world.

The paper collection has been made differently for scientific and not-scientific documents:

- scientific documents have been searched on Scopus database between April and May 2015 requesting to the system to search the keywords "*Smart City*" in the title and in the abstract of contribution. Thereby, the scientific documents found were 264 and they included only English academic papers published within 1995–2015 range. Afterwards, the authors analysed the paper containing the most cited smart city definitions;
- non-scientific documents have been searched on Google in November 2014 requesting to the system to search on the web the keywords "*Report*" AND "*Smart City*". The results of this research showed many reports concerning Smart City, the authors selected the most important industrial and institutional reports

Fig. 1 The Nam and Pardo
smart city model [14]

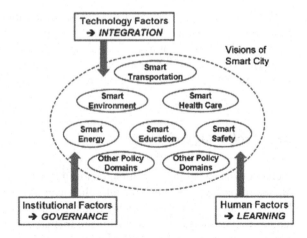

issued by the following institutions: ABB (2014), Between (2014), Ericsson (2013), Forrester (2011), IBM (2014), IDC (2013), Siemens (2013), Gartner (2012), Mc Kinsey (2014), Boston Consulting Group (2012), Northstream (2010), Cassa Depositi e Prestiti (2014), European Commission (2014), EU-Setis (2012), California Institute (2001), UK Government (2013), Anci Cittalia-Forum PA (2014).

Collected documents have been classified depending on the nature of their issuer: public body, university, or private company. The content is further analysed applying the Nam and Pardo Smart city model (see Fig. 1), chosen because it designs the smart city model on three dimensions, Technology, Institutions, and People, well representing the multi-layer architecture of a Smart city and the interests of the three key actors—public bodies, universities and research centres, and private companies [14].

The analysis is then executed using manual coding and applying the keywords representing the Nam and Pardo dimensions. Finally, contents are compared respect to these three dimensions to understand if and how much the key actors share or not the same smart city vision.

In the following paragraphs, the results of this survey are shown analysing and comparing the contents of the selected documents.

4 The Comparison of Smart City Vision Among University, Industry and Government

At a glance, it seems that all the aforementioned actors share the same vision of the smart city: a new way to understand the city of the future [5, 12, 15, 16] to realize economic sustainability and social inclusion, preserving the environment [17–20] with the aim to improve the quality of life of citizens [6, 7, 21, 22].

However, each category of actors has different aims and these aims influence their smart city vision. The content analysis permits to compare not only several smart city definitions, but also aims, components and instruments included in the smart city vision defined by each category of actors and to understand if and how much these visions are similar or different each other.

4.1 Technology Factors

Technology is one of the most important enabling factors to implement a smart city. Authors especially consider ICT like the main enabler of a smart city [13, 14]. Thanks to high technologies such as Smart Computing [23, 24], it is possible to support traditional hardware and software interaction [25], to collect data from the urban sensors and to deliver real time information to support better decisions [26]. These technologies need an adequate ICT infrastructure, including broadband, optic fibre, Wi-Fi networks, wireless hotspots [27, 28]. Technology and infrastructures are therefore the premises to create a smart city [14, 29].

Respect to technology, the examined three key actors have different ideas.

Universities and Research centres develop and experiment the use of innovative technologies in urban areas and their cost and benefits, to transfer their technological knowledge to solution vendors [3]. Research activities regard both positive and negative impacts of such technologies on citizens' quality of life. On the one hand, technology is examined as a positive factor able to support and improve the quality of life [5]. On the other hand, doubts arise as regard as the real capability of technology to positively change the daily life of all citizens, especially thinking at digital divide [30, 31]. Sometimes implementing ICT in smart cities could generate several problems, such as a reduction in ICT security and data privacy, high cost of implementation and low returns [32, 33]. Universities generally study the most innovative technological solutions, but not ever these solutions are suitable to the smart city and especially to a large number of heterogeneous users; instead they are niche solutions useful for few recipients.

Private companies play the role of technology enablers [26, 34]. They project and implement the smart city technological infrastructure; obviously each of them is especially focused on its own technological products and solutions, i.e., smart transport, smart energy systems, ICT systems, healthcare solutions, efficient building, and so on [8, 14]. Overall, they try to implement the most profitable solutions, conditioning the prioritization expressed by local governments and better suitable with the citizens' needs.

Advisors and consultancy officers are involved in studying the better technological solutions for the smart city implementation; they are the link between the innovative solutions suggested by universities and the vendors able to produce technical facilities [26, 35, 36]. They offer their knowledge and competencies to support local governments in smart city strategic planning, economic evaluation and estimate, technological prioritization about the best smart solutions to be implemented for the first [21].

Local governments are involved in planning and implementing the smart city; they generally play the director role, coordinating all the other players in their own territory [37]. A local government establishes relationships with private companies charged to implement technical infrastructure and smart technologies; the most applied instruments for supporting these relationships are public-private partnerships (PPP) [7]. Municipalities and also the central governments are required to rule all the new topics emerging from the smart technologies implementation, such as the security and privacy requirements for cloud computing, the open data rules, and so on [32, 38].

This survey shows that the three smart city key actors are playing an interconnected role in implementing smart cities, sharing some basic concepts but pursuing their own goals. The analysis of a large set of smart projects in some champions smart city [39] and the direct involving in a Municipality government reveal that the key actors are sometimes in synergy, sometimes in conflict each other. Respect to the Technology factor, their ideas regarding the smart city—emerging from both the examined documents and the empirical observation—are quite different and confrontational for the following reasons:

- universities and research centres consider smart city like an innovative place where to implement their pilots and experimental solutions, neglecting the digital divide, the difficulties in funding innovative facilities and the lack of competences in Municipalities to manage the highest innovation;
- private companies try to force Municipalities to prioritize their own technical solutions, neglecting the real needs of citizens and sometimes offering standard systems, instead of projecting ad hoc solutions for a specific urban area;
- Municipalities are trying to transform cities in smart cities, but both political bodies and public managers and officers often are not capable nor to define strategic planning for the smart city implementation, nor to manage the change program; the topic is too much immature and new and public bodies need official education and support from the central state to face such a complex topic.

From this survey it emerges also that all the actors are not enough considering the role of knowledge and human capabilities in using smart technologies. For this reason, two situations occur:

1. solution vendors mainly suggest the implementation of technologies not requiring the citizens participation (such as smart public lighting, reducing energy consumption but impacting remotely on the citizens' quality of life) [37];
2. innovative technological solutions are implemented, but scarcely used; also in this case, the impact on the citizens' daily life is minimum, because very low is the rate of use [25].

4.2 Human Factors

Human factors regard the role of people in smart city. Smart citizens and communities play a pivotal role, both because they are the main addressees of smart initiatives, and because often their involvement and participation is required for the complete success of a smart project [12, 14, 40]. The Human factor is considered not only regard to the citizen participation, but also regarding the human and social capital existing in a city and knowledge, culture, and values characterising a community [6].

Respect to this factor, the key actors have some shared basic ideas and different points of view.

Universities and research centres recognise the role of a smart city program in supporting the human factor development, by attracting talented people [40], developing work and entrepreneurship [12, 41], settling excellent schools and universities [41]. Universities coined the phrase "Smart people" just to outline the role of citizens in the smart city implementation success [12].

Private companies consider people like the addressees of their technological solutions. Therefore, companies and advisory officers often have been settled where the local community is more interested in smart projects, offering their technological solutions or consulting. For example, in China large companies such as IBM are finding fertile ground for their business, in cities strongly oriented towards smartness. To have success, companies need to invest in smart employees, educating their work force to the smart city vision [26]. Private companies represent therefore an enabler factor for smarter people, attracting talented workers, educating employees and inducing the settling of better schools and universities [11, 18, 34, 42].

Public bodies should create the better conditions for implementing a smart city for all, reducing digital divide and promoting smart social inclusiveness. A key role for these aims has been played in Europe by the European Commission with acts such as the European Digital Agenda [22, 37, 38].

However, the smart city has been developing especially like a bottom-up phenomenon [39], where the citizens themselves have been the main characters in the smart city implementation [43]. People are moving independently from the governments, cooperating and implementing their own smart solutions; governments should enforce their role, promoting the citizens' involvement and participation in smart city planning, coordinating all the initiatives to gain higher synergies.

4.3 Institutional Factors

With the phrase "Institutional factors" Nam and Pardo [14] mean the set of actions forming the smart city governance; they individuate the following smart actions: collaboration, cooperation, partnership, citizen engagement, participation. Institutional factors therefore enable the multi-stakeholders smart city, supporting interactions and communication amongst all the players. Also in this case, the three key actors have different visions about this component.

Universities and research centres coined the phrase "smart governance" to outline the pivotal role played by governance in realizing a successful smart city [12, 14, 26]. During the latest years, academic papers suggest the importance of a comprehensive governance by both local and central governments, aiming at designing a urban smart strategy [44, 45]. This vision suggests a top-down path for implementing the smart city, where the government plays a central, directive role.

Private companies suggest a mix solution between top-down and bottom-up approach. Indeed, the bottom-up approach does not consider enough the citizens' needs and preferences, the bottom-up approach lacks of coordination and often is nor efficient nor effective [26, 35]. A mix solution could balance strengths and weaknesses of both the approaches.

Public bodies are often driven by financial constraints instead of by smart city vision; local governments are influenced by funding policies by national or supranational bodies and sometimes lack of their own smart city vision. In Europe, for example, the European Commission defines the guidelines to pursue and implement a smart city, sustaining its own priorities with large financial amounts and influencing the local choices. However, the EU does not define common goals for the smart city and for this reason results are heterogeneous and lack of synergies [2, 37]. Also private companies adhere to this trend, as EU funds can support the purchase of smart solutions from technology vendors [7, 22, 36]. This situation reduces the importance of governance aspects, such as citizen engagement and participation [14]. A crucial role in supporting the citizen's role in smart city is played by the so-called civil society, for example association, foundations, observatories, and so on. They are playing a central role in sharing and communicating the smart city idea suggesting more participated and people-centred smart city models [46].

5 Conclusions

Our survey permits to discover the different orientation that three key players have towards the smart city concept. Both scientific papers and practitioner reports reveal the presence of a triple helix, as theoretical defined by Lombardi et al. [11] or Deakin and Leydesdorff [10], even if each key player has different aims: research and knowledge spreading for universities, business and profit for private companies, local well-being and political consensus for public bodies.

Different aims synergetic linked together should drive the smart city towards its veritable final aim, that is, the quality of life for citizens. However, our survey shows that the people not ever are at the core of the smart city efforts and key actors are more interested in pursuing their own objectives than to reach the common good.

Several institutional reports or empirical survey outlines that people are few aware about the smart city projects occurring in their city [46, 47]; it generally depends on the lack of local initiatives by the key actors to inform and support the use of smart devices and services [26, 47].

The comparison amongst all the papers and reports included in our survey reveals that the first stage of smart city implementation is not more suitable for the future. If in the pioneer phase a spontaneous, bottom-up wave has been useful to stimulate innovative and original initiatives, now the smart city needs comprehensive, integrated strategies to support long-term, profitable and effective smart projects. The analysis of reports collecting smart projects in Italy or Europe [12, 37, 46, 48] outlines that until now smart initiatives are heterogeneous, unfocused, less effective, regarding few people, poorly funded. Without a central direction, coordinating the interests of all the key actors with the stakeholders expectations and needs, the smart city will remain an interesting innovative laboratory, but failing in creating public and private value for all in the long term. An effective strategic planning, based on a shared smart city definition collected by the participation of both key actors and stakeholders would be the right basis for a long lasting well-being in smarter cities.

References

1. OECD.: OECD Regions at a Glance. OECD Publishing (2013)
2. European Commission: Quality of life in cities. Perception survey in 79 European Cities (2013)
3. Etzkowitz, H.: The Triple Helix: University-Industry-Government Innovation in Action. London Routledge (2008)
4. Etzkowitz, H., Leydesdorff, L.: The dynamics of innovation: from national systems and "mode 2" to a triple helix of university–industry–government relations. Res. Policy **29**(2), 109–123 (2000)
5. Hall, P.: Creative cities and economic development. Urban Stud. **37**(4), 633–649 (2000)
6. Caragliu, A., De Bo, C., Nijcamp, P.: Smart city in Europe. In: 3rd Central European Conference in Regional Science (2009)
7. Setis-Eu: setis.ec.europa.eu/implementation/technology-roadmap/ (2012)
8. Dameri, R.P.: Defining an evaluation framework for digital cities implementation. In: IEEE International Conference on Information Society (i-Society) (2012)
9. Freeman, C.: Technical innovation, diffusion, and long cycles of economic development. In: The Long-Wave Debate, pp. 295–309. Springer, Berlin, Heidelberg (1987)
10. Deakin, M., Leydesdorff, L.: The triple-helix model for smart cities: a neo-evolutionary perspective. J. Urban Technol. **18**(2), 53–63 (2011)
11. Lombardi, P., Giordano, S., Farouh, H., Yousef, W.: Modelling the smart city performance. Innovation Eur. J. Soc. Sci. Res. **25**(2), 137–149 (2012)
12. Giffinger, R.: Smart Cities: Ranking of European Medium-Sized Cities. Centre of Regional Science, Vienna (2007)
13. Chourabi, H., Nam, T., Walker, S., Gil-Garcia, J.R., Mellouli, S., Nahon, K., Scholl, H.J.: Understanding smart cities: an integrative framework. In: 2012 45th Hawaii International Conference on, System Science (HICSS), pp. 2289–2297. IEEE (2012, January)

14. Nam, T., Pardo, T.A.: Conceptualizing smart city with dimensions of technology, people, and institutions. In: Proceedings of the 12th Annual International Digital Government Research Conference: Digital Government Innovation in Challenging Times, pp. 282–291. ACM (2011, June)

15. IDC (2013): IDC MarketScape: US business consulting services for Smart Cities 2013 vendor analysis. https://www.idc.com/getdoc.jsp?containerId=242453

16. California Institute for Smart Communities (2001): Smart communities guide book. http://www.smartcommunities.org/guidebook.html

17. Hollands, R.: Will the Real Smart City Please Stand up? Intelligent, Progressive or Entrepreneurial?. City: analysis of urban trends, culture, theory, policy, action (2008)

18. Ericsson: Networked society—city index 2013. http://www.ericsson.com/res/docs/2013/ns-city-index-report-2013.pdf (2013)

19. Boston Consulting Group: Smart Cities—How to Master the World's Biggest Growth Challenge. Boston Consulting Group (2014)

20. Dameri, R.P., Sabroux, C.: Smart city and value creation. In: Dameri, R.P., Sabroux, C. (eds.) How to Create Public and Economic Value with High Technology in Urban Space, pp. 1–12. Springer International Publishing (2014)

21. Gartner.: Market Insight: 'Smart Cities' in Emerging Markets. Gartner Report (2010)

22. CDP.: Smart City. Progetti di sviluppo e strumenti di finanziamento. Cassa Depositi e Prestiti (2013)

23. Washburn, D., Sindhu, U., Balaouras, S., Dines, R.A., Hayes, N.M., Nelson, L.E.: Helping CIOs Understand "Smart City" Initiatives: Defining the Smart City, Its Drivers, and the Role of the CIO. Cambridge (2010)

24. Su, K., Li, J., Fu, H.: Smart City and the applications. In: IEEE International Conference on Electronics, Communications and Control (ICECC), pp. 1028–1031 (2011)

25. Bolici, R., Mora, L.: Dalla smart city alla smart region—Governare la transizione Intelligente delle polarità urbane. Forum PA (2012)

26. Forrester: Helping CIOs understand Smart City initiatives. Forrester (2010)

27. Anthopoulos, L., Tougountzoglou, T.: A viability model for digital cities: economic and acceptability factors. Web 2.0 Technologies and Democratic Governance, vol. 1, pp. 79–96 (2012)

28. Al-Hader M., Rodzi A.: The smart city infrastructure development & monitoring. Theor. Empirical Res. Urban Manag. 2 (2009)

29. Lindskog, H.: Smart communities initiatives. In: Proceedings of the 3rd ISOneWorld Conference, Las Vegas, 14–16 April 2004

30. Odendaal, N.: Information and communication technology and local governance: Understanding the difference between cities in developed and emerging economies. Comput. Environ. Urban Syst. 27(6), 585–607 (2003)

31. Foster, S.P.: The digital divide: some reflections. Int. Inf. Libr. Rev. 23, 437–451 (2000)

32. Ebrahim, Z., Irani, Z.: E-government adoption: architecture and barriers. Bus. Process Manag. J. 5(11), 589–611 (2005)

33. Dameri, R.P.: Using the balanced scorecard to evaluate ICT investments in non profit organisations. Electron. J. Inf. Syst. Eval. 8(2), 107–114 (2005)

34. IBM: Smarter Thinking for a Smarter Planet (2010)

35. McKinsey: How to make a city great—a review of the steps city leaders around the world take to transform their cities into great places to live and work. http://www.mckinsey.com/insights/urbanization/how_to_make_a_city_great (2013)

36. UK Government: The Smart City Market: Opportunities for the UK. Department for Business Education and Skills, Oct 2013

37. European Parliament: Mapping Smart Cities in the EU, Directorate General for Internal Policies Policy Department A: Economic and Scientific Policy, Jan 2014

38. EU Digital Agenda: www.agenda-digitale.it/agenda_digitale/index.php/agenda-digitale-europea (2012)

39. Dameri, R.P.: Comparing smart and digital city: initiatives and strategies in amsterdam and genoa. are they digital and/or smart? In: Dameri, R.P., Sabroux, C. (eds.) Smart City. How to Create Public and Economic Value with High Technology in Urban Space, pp. 45–88. Springer International Publishing (2014)
40. Winters, J.V.: Why are smart cities growing? Who moves and who stays. J. Reg. Sci. **10**(20), 1–18 (2010)
41. Glaeser, E.L., Berry, C.R.: Why are smart places getting smarter?. In: Taubman Center Policy Briefs, PB-2006, vol. 2 (2006)
42. Florida, R.: The Rise of the Creative Class: and How It's Transforming Work, Leisure, Community and Everyday Life. Basic Books, New York (2002). http://www.washingtonmonthly.com/features/2001/0205.flor ida.html
43. Coe, A., Paquet, G., Roy, J.: E-governance and smart communities: a social learning challenge. Soc. Sci. Comput. Rev. **19**(19), 80–93 (2001)
44. Batty, M.: "Cities and Complexity: Understanding Cities with Cellular Automata", Agent-Based Models, and Fractals. The MIT Press, ACM (2007)
45. Conroy, M.M., Evans-Cowley, J.: E-participation in planning: an analysis of cities adopting on-line citizen participation tools. Environ. Plan. C Gov. Policy **24**(3), 371–384 (2006)
46. Anci Cittalia: Vademecum per la città intelligente. Edizioni Forum PA (2013)
47. Cisco: Smart city framework—a systematic process for enabling smart + connected communities. https://www.cisco.com/web/about/ac79/docs/ps/motm/Smart-City-Framework.pdf (2012)
48. Between: Smart City Index—Confrontarsi per diventare Smart. http://www.between.it/SmartCityIndex/Between_SmartCityIndex2014.pdf (2014)
49. Dameri, R.P., D'Auria, B.: Modelli di governo e di governance delle smart cities, il caso italiano. Electron. J. Manag. Impresa Progetto (4) (2014)

Exploring Collective Action Dynamics in Online Communities from a Critical Realist Perspective

Alessio Maria Braccini, Tommaso Federici and Øystein Sæbø

1 Introduction and Motivation

Online Communities (OCs) are persistent collections of people that share common or complementary interests, mainly communicating through the Internet [1] citing [2]. Scholars have investigated several aspects within the setting of OCs, such as their potential to sustain shared knowledge production processes [3–8], the individual motivation to participate (and factors influencing on motivation) [1, 9–11] and governance mechanisms supporting the coordination of the people and resources composing the OC [12–15].

The three main components of OCs (people, technologies, and organizational structures) influence each other, but are frequently discussed separately in the literature. We posit that they should be studied together, to generate new knowledge and to challenge current, sometimes unfit, understanding of the organization side of OCs [15]. In this paper we therefore aim at answering the following research question: *which mechanisms sustain the collective action dynamics of OCs?*

We conducted a study of the OC management and use by an Italian political movement, the Five Star Movement (Movimento 5 Stelle, M5S). M5S represents a pertinent research unit for online communities from two perspectives: (i) its size, influence and technological configuration for the political context, and (ii) its diversity from the software development and knowledge sharing communities that are the prevailing target in literature on OCs.

A.M. Braccini (✉) · T. Federici (✉)
Università degli Studi della Tuscia, Dipartimento di Economia e Impresa, Viterbo, Italy
e-mail: abraccini@unitus.it

T. Federici
e-mail: tfederici@unitus.it

Ø. Sæbø (✉)
University of Agder, Department of Information Systems, Kristiansand, Norway
e-mail: oystein.sabo@uia.no

© Springer International Publishing Switzerland 2016
F. D'Ascenzo et al. (eds.), *Blurring the Boundaries Through Digital Innovation*,
Lecture Notes in Information Systems and Organisation 19,
DOI 10.1007/978-3-319-38974-5_21

By assuming the ontological inseparability of the three components of OCs, we conducted qualitative research from a critical realist perspective, to identify the mechanisms that support the working dynamics of OCs. We introduced the concept of affordance, as the possibility for goal-directed actions provided by an object in a relation to a goal-oriented actor, to identify generative mechanisms [16]. We identified four affordances for collective action in OCs; Circulating Information, Connecting People, Triggering Actions and Crossing Boundaries. The results and lessons to be learned from this paper should help practitioners to better manage OCs, as well as researchers to progress the study and the understanding of OCs working dynamics, to better understand the relationship between technology and social actors [17].

2 Theoretical Background

2.1 Online Communities

A community consists of a group of people in a closed area who share values, historical experiences and beliefs, being identifiable by specific geographical boundaries and membership status [18]. An OC is a community where the usage of technology allows to overcome the limitations imposed by the geographical boundaries [13], and is a persistent collection of people sharing common interests, who primarily communicate through the Internet [2].

OCs offer many different opportunities to organize social discussion and establish connections with people. Shirky [19] provides a simplified, yet illustrative classification of various forms of OCs, by proposing a three-step ladder of group compilation. *Sharing* is the most basic form of OC, and corresponds to a setting where every participant is called to share online. *Cooperation* is a more complex form of OC, where every participant shall behave in a way to synchronize with the others and sustain a collaborative production [20]. Community members have to establish cooperation to negotiate and make collective decisions. *Collective action* is the most advanced form of OC. In such an OC, members share responsibilities, hence the identity of the individual blurs in favor of that of the group. Community members are called to make community decisions, which will bind both the behavior of individuals and that of the community as a whole. A strong and shared vision is a necessary guiding force to keep the community together, in spite of episodic decisions that will inevitably displease some of the members [19].

Managing an OC for collective action is more difficult than managing one for information sharing or collaboration. Collective action implies that members with common interests and objectives, and a shared understanding of everyone being better off with that objective being achieved, logically will work together to achieve that purpose [21].

The organization of collective actions is usually an uncertain and complex undertaking, in which boundaries and internal characteristics must be established. The ways in which collective action is organized, coordinated, and produces collective outcomes, are frequently discussed in the literature [15]. The management of collective actions within online communities may be influenced by complexity related to size, diversity, and the type of work being created.

2.2 Critical Realism

The inseparability of technology and human agency is seen as a promising direction for fruitful investigation of technology, people, and organizational related phenomena within the field of information systems [22, 23]. *Critical realism* recently emerged in the information systems literature [24, 25] where researchers leveraged on its capabilities of understanding complex technological and organizational structures as inseparable entities [17], recognizing that the deep interconnectedness of technology and organization materializes through patterns of interactions [16, 17, 26].

Critical realism is based on the foundational work of the philosopher Bhaskar [27, 28], and raises as an alternative to both the positivist and the interpretive paradigms, leveraging on both of them to provide a new approach to generating knowledge [29]. Critical realism is based on a realist ontology, a fallible, *critical* in a Kantian sense, epistemology [30], and supports the need of a pluralism of methods and methodologies to investigate reality [24]. Since correlational analysis fails to identify the mechanisms that produce observed associations [31], there is a need to study complex patterns to explicate mechanisms that generate and explain associations between events [31]. Ontologically critical realism posits for a three layers stratification of the reality encompassing the *real*, the *actual*, and the *empirical* layer. Consequently phenomena are reflected differently at the three levels [16]. The *real* contains all the objects that exist in the reality and produce effects regardless of individual perceptions. The *actual* layer contains all the mechanisms that allow objects of the *real* layer to produce effects, events or outcomes, both observable and non-observable. The *empirical* layer contains a subset of the mechanisms of the actual, which can be empirically observed.

To understand a phenomenon in a critical realist perspective it is necessary to uncover the generative mechanisms that are associated with it, and that retroduce empirically observable things, to the structures and the properties of objects in the reality [17], to provide a causal explanation of how and why things happen [16]. Mechanisms are 'frequently occurring and easily recognizable causal patterns that are triggered under generally unknown conditions' [32, p. 45]. A *retroduction* is hence a path that extends from the observable events to the underlying mechanisms that could logically have produced them [17]. Retroducing means moving from experience to the potential existing structures or mechanisms in the real domain investigating the interactions which may potentially have generated the event [24]. This is done through what may be called an 'analytic induction' process, where researchers postulate mechanisms based on intensive examination of particular cases, working backwards from the observed outcome to the theoretical mechanisms [33].

Generative mechanisms possess capacities to induce an effect, either by enabling or constraining actions arising from the structure, relationship between structures, or relationship between structures and actions [16]. Generative mechanisms are causal in nature [34].

2.3 Affordances as Generative Mechanisms

The concept of affordance originates from the work of Gibson [35, 36]. An affordance is the interaction between an actor and the environment surrounding it, and the properties of both the actor and the environment [36]. The affordance concept suggests that individuals perceive objects in the environment not just for what they are (i.e. for their properties), but for what they allow them to do (i.e. afford) [37]. Affordances are neither properties of the environment, nor characteristics of the individual. Affordances emerge in the interaction between an actor and an artifact [38], and are related to the action capabilities of the actor reflecting the action potential of the artifact [39]. Affordances need to be perceived and actualized by goal-oriented actors to achieve outcomes [37, 40].

The concept of affordance has become popular in the area of IS to explore how the materiality of objects favors, shapes, invites, and constrains specific uses [41]. Also, it was used to describe action possibilities allowed by material properties within IS [37]. Within studies of the symbioses of IT and organizations, Zammuto et al. [41] propose the concept of affordances for organizing as a bridging concept to explain the intersection between IT systems and organizational systems. Affordances allow the examination of how goal-oriented individuals interpret (and actualize) material properties within IS to create changes in organizational practices [42]. Hence affordances not only relate to the individual level, but also to the action potential level for what an organization can do with information systems with the intent to support organizational goals [39].

Organizational affordances relate to "the potential actions enabled are associated with achieving organizational-level immediate concrete outcomes in support of organizational level goals" [43], produced by the collective actions of the individuals. Aligned with this view, Leonardi [44] introduces the concept of shared affordances, in which individual actors manifest a similar use of technology features, and argues that affordances at the organizational level are only actualized when (individuals) actors agree on the usage of a similar sequence of technology features.

Our motivation for introducing the concept of affordances within critical realism originates from the contributions in the literature that find the entanglement of technology/people/and organization, on which we are focusing in this paper, embedded in the concept of affordance [16, 44]. Moreover, Volkoff and Strong make a parallelism between the concept of affordance and that of generative mechanism [16]. They find that affordances help clarify the stratification process (within the critical realist domain) in several ways.

First, affordances exist in the real domain, representing the potential for action rather than action itself. Second, affordances exist whether or not we are aware of them, where the actual affordance being observed allows the retroduction to underlying real affordances. Third, while actualized phenomena are specific, the underlying real affordances are more generic, allowing for theories of IT-associated organization change to be developed [16], opening up the black box of IT systems to better explain interactions over time in virtual collaborations [41].

In this paper we adopt the concept of affordance to retroduce from the empirical layer to the real layer to identify the mechanisms that support OCs working dynamics with a qualitative research strategy focusing on the investigation of M5S' OC, relying on the prescriptions of Wynn and Williams [29] for critical realist studies.

3 Research Design

Data were collected from different sources including interviews, observations of software platforms, technical reports and documents. The data were organized and recorded in a research database for qualitative analysis. The semi-structured interviews served as the primary basis for our analytical efforts, while the other data sources complemented it to provide the contextual background and to achieve a good understanding from which researchers could reflect on the research subject [45].

We interviewed various key actors of the M5S' OC. Since the community is active on the whole Italian territory, we interviewed actors with different roles—representatives in national and regional assemblies, subscribers, followers non members—coming from two cities (sites), and from the national parliament, to give us a good perspective on the internal working dynamics at the different levels. 19 semi-structured interviews were conducted, tape-recorded, and transcribed. Archival data included the M5S' website (its headquarter), several units' web pages at national, regional and local levels, the statute and other internal documents from the movement.

The data collection and analysis were conducted in tandem to benefit from the emerging recursive understanding between theoretical concepts and empirical material. Hence, theory generation is not the result of a linear process, but rather of an iterative process in which data and insights from the first round influenced data-gathering activities in the second round. The analysis began with the evidence emerging from the data, proceeding with the description of structures and contexts aligned with the second prescription of Wynn and Williams [29].

First, we used open coding individually to identify concepts. This process yielded an initial set of concepts that were discussed by us in order to identify the main concepts and structures. Second, we identified affordances to retroduce observations to the structures existing at the real level. At the same time, we confronted our hypotheses on the existence of mechanisms and structures and their causal power.

A main criterion for the identification of mechanisms and structures and the formulation of causal explanations was the empirical corroboration of findings [29]. The affordances produce immediate outcomes and events that are empirically observable: we looked for them in our empirical material by investigating our data sources to identify actual events, allowing us to identify the existence of an affordance in use and therefore to retroduce it at the real level. While identifying affordances, we were aware of the potential existence of different kinds: empirically observed, actualized but not empirically observed, exercised but not actualized, not exercised and desired, and the interrelation among different affordances.

4   Case Description and Findings

Due to space limitations this section briefly introduces and discusses the Italian M5S. A more detailed description is provided by Federici et al. [46]. M5S is an Italian political movement that sharply distinguishes itself from traditional Italian parties, as it claims to be more open, transparent, and participative. Since the origin the M5S has developed to a large nation-wide OC, managed through a different and evolving set of ICT tools, with approximately 100,000 people already enrolled, and 700,000 in line to be. The M5S uses the OC to perform activities related to the dissemination of political information, consultation, and decision-making processes involving citizens, who must subscribe to the movement in order to perform actions online. It is also used by citizens to discuss and debate topics of common interests and is divided into groups of local, regional, and national interest. The OC developed out of the blog of Beppe Grillo, who is one of the founders of the movement and still its most prominent member. The M5S' OC used at its birth the Meetup social networking platform (www.meetup.com) to better coordinate the activities of groups, which since then are called *meetups*. Later on, they started to use several ICT tools to manage the OC. A set of core tools allows the interaction between representatives elected in the parliament subscribers, and local groups. Currently, there are 1,487 active groups in 1,216 different cities and across 21 countries. Tools adopted by M5S' OC consist of a mixture of general-purpose social networking platforms (like Facebook and Twitter), and specifically developed tools (like the M5S Operating System and the Parelon).

The OC works under the coordination of the M5S's legal entity, which was officially established in 2009. Actors in the M5S' OC are differentiated into 'certified' (whose application has been approved by the movement's staff), and 'not yet certified' (whose application approval is still pending). Only certified actors have full access to the M5S' OC. Non-certified users are limited in their ability to act in the community.

One of the main reasons for people to take part in an OC is to do things together. This involves both creating and circulating information, and making decisions on aspects of interest both for the individual and for the community: *"Usually I get a general overview, and then I go into details when I find news that it is interesting to me."* [Follower non member].

Another need is that of facilitating the establishment of direct relationships for information circulation, providing continuous feedback and feeding a debate. *"My aunt sympathizes for the movement, she is not an activist, but she is in the activists' group. So she can post in the activists' group, ... she can communicate her own ideas."* [Subscriber in charge of communication in a local group]. Such connections are supported by technologies for cross-individual communication, including social networking platforms, micro blogging, instant messaging tools, and e-mail. All members, whatever their role in the community, and also non-members are allowed and encouraged to participate to discussion, both collective and one-to-one.

Nevertheless the community has also mechanisms to call members to their duties in specific moments of the community life: *"I just use [the system] when Grillo calls to the participation on the blog."* [Subscriber of a local group]). The aims of such calls to action are of two levels: first allowing members to be continuously in touch with current processes, getting informed in a timely manner of actions to be taken. At a different level this makes collective actions easier for members, possibly increasing the number of active members in each process. Members in charge to call to action use for this aim technologies with which they can even target communication directly to specific community members, like social networking platforms, micro blogging platforms, and instant messaging tools. Recipients are free to ignore the call to action.

The mechanisms, through which the community members are explicitly asked to perform actions online, are usually connected with a structured decision making process. Besides this call of duties, each individual is in the position to voluntarily activate the community, do things online, and stimulate actions by other community members.

Sometimes the collective action crosses the community boundaries to enter other organizational settings or communities: *"I posted a picture of one of Grillo's show really crowded using their same hashtag [that of a rival party]. This allowed me to cross the boundaries of the community."* [Subscriber in charge of a local Twitter account]. Any member may spread information outside community, but there are also some members with boundary-spanning roles. They use several technologies like blogs, social networking platforms, microblogging platforms, mailing lists, and websites. The final aim is that disseminating individual and collective action to a wider audience, also entering other communities whenever needed.

5 Enhanced Understanding of Online Collective Actions

To study the working dynamics of OCs we performed a retroduction process from the empirical evidences to the reality, using the concept of affordance to identify the generative mechanisms. The aim of the retroduction process was that of identifying the organizational affordances to determine the causal explanations existing within our data [16], in order to identify both the individual and collective mechanisms that sustain the collective action of an OC. We identified four affordances through this process, they are described in detail below:

- Circulating Information
- Connecting People
- Triggering Actions
- Crossing Boundaries.

With regard to *Circulating information*, we observed in the empirical domain that subscribers and non-members of the M5S use tools, such as Facebook, Twitter, Meetups, or forums, to share information and to take part in the discussion on topics of interest. Each of them can disseminate and circulate information according to the limits and boundaries of their role. It may be discovered in the real domain that such mechanism allows the OC to coordinate a variety of online tools, whose access is shaped by rules and by roles assigned or taken on by members to let information circulate among members.

As regards the affordance *Connecting People*, in the empirical domain there are evidences that members of M5S can easily reach each other. They can also reach members who are in different sections of the community or play different roles. The central staff of M5S partially maintains the network through the administration of M5S' own tools, at the same time leaving freedom for people to connect through other tools. Related to this, in the real domain organizational structures include the retention of an effective structure within internal IT-artifacts, maintaining flexibility by allowing the use of external and trivial services. Such a mechanism allows people to establish connections independently of their roles and positions in the network.

When referring to the affordance *Triggering Actions*, in the empirical domain it may be noticed that there is a large amount of activities within the M5S spread across various platforms and services, resulting in a web of activities within which actions are made. Actions are sometimes voluntary, and at other times stimulated by community members who play specific roles. When moving to the real domain, this affordance allows specific community members to call the rest of the community to action, for example to participate in discussions or decision making processes. Such a call to duties is performed through triggers that are activated by those members who embody specific roles, or are legitimated to do that by rules.

The last affordance, *Crossing Boundaries*, relates to the fact that discussions related to the M5S not only occur within their own OC, but in some cases reach a larger public outside of the OC sphere, through tools such as Facebook, Twitter, and forums, or through the actions of people, like the spokespersons, who play the boundary spanner role. This mechanism, moving into the real domain, allows the OC to manage boundary-crossing activities, by assigning roles to members who can perform the activity, by defining rules on how individuals should behave when crossing the borders, and by providing tools allowing circulating information to be addressed outside the community.

6 Discussion of Results

On the basis of a critical realist qualitative study, we analyzed the mechanisms that sustain the collective work of the M5S' OC. We identified four affordances, describing mechanisms that underpin OCs collective action. The contribution of our paper builds on the concept of affordance under a critical realist perspective within the domain of online communities. Our contributions provide value for each of these three different areas, which will be discussed in this section.

The four identified affordances explain how OCs sustain the dynamics of collective action. Although inspired by similar approaches by other scholars in this area [42, 43], our approach extends the conceptualization of affordances by including the specific organizational settings and the relevance for specific individuals to achieve specific goals through the use of technology. Strong et al.'s [43] extension of the concept of affordance to the organization level has been an important reference for our study.

Affordances have a relative nature [39]. Affordances are relative not only to the individual and the technology, but also to the individuals who actualize them [37, 40], implying that affordances actualized by some individuals might be of no use for other individuals. Hence, the affordances we have identified provide a fruitful starting point for research, by applying them to different empirical settings. Researchers could extend our theoretical contribution, on the one hand by identifying different affordances, and on the other hand by confronting different working dynamics of different OCs through comparative studies.

Thank to the adoption of a critical realist perspective, we were able to investigate the complexity of the interactions among people, technology, and organization inside OCs, while maintaining the dual perspective of seeing them intertwined and exploring the separation between them. Critical realism is a promising research approach in the IS area that makes it possible to discuss causality explanations within organization-related IT phenomena [29, 47–49]. The current literature on critical realism from an IS perspective focuses mainly on epistemological aspects and methodological principles [24, 29]. To date, only a few studies use critical realism to investigate empirical phenomena [25, 49].

7 Conclusions and Future Research

This paper contributes to the discourse on OCs by bringing in novel perspectives, describing the collective working dynamics of an OC through a set of affordances. Such an approach to the study of OCs targets the understanding of the practices and the dynamics that sustain collective action in OCs. Our work does not focus only on individuals, rules, or technology (like most previous studies do), but complements them by proposing causal explanations of the dynamics of online collective actions, identifying how people with individual goals play specific roles, using technologies with specific features, and following rules from a surrounding organizational environment. By so doing, we explore the intertwined interactions among these major components of an OC, in order to sustain and explain its working dynamics.

In summary, the paper unveils a more complex understanding of the OCs phenomenon, explaining how the different components (people, technology, and organization) interact within a specific mechanism (an affordance) to achieve a specific result. Furthermore, having identified four affordances, our work could inspire comparative studies to confront different affordances from different systems or contexts to further expand our knowledge on affordances.

Our results are promising for fruitful future research projects. First, the nature of our identified affordances should be further investigated to deepen our understanding of collective actions within OCs. On the side of the motivation of people joining OCs, one question that might be explored is how to balance activities related to triggering participation with activities related to voluntary participation to avoid negative influences (constraints) between them. More research is needed to better understand how crossing boundaries roles and rules may extend the information circulation from inside to outside the community. Secondly, we believe that our work can contribute as guidance on how to investigate IT and organization-related phenomena from the critical realist perspective, especially in the field of OCs. Finally, the situational nature of mechanisms [49] should be investigated: different combinations of the same mechanisms might lead to the same result, or the same combination of mechanisms might lead to different results.

References

1. Ren, Y., Harper, F.M., Drenner, S., Terveen, L., Kiesler, S., Riedl, J., Kraut, R.E.: Building member attachment in online communities: applying theories of group identity and interpersonal bonds. MIS Q. **36**, 841–864 (2012)
2. Preece, J.: Online Communities: Designing Usability and Supporting Sociability. Wiley, New York, NY, USA (2000)
3. Faraj, S., Jarvenpaa, S.L., Majchrzak, A.: Knowledge collaboration in online communities. Organ. Sci. **22**, 1224–1239 (2011)
4. Holmström, H., Henfridsson, O.: Improving packaged software through online community knowledge. Scand. J. Inf. Syst. **18**, 2–36 (2006)

5. Kankanhalli, A., Tan, B.C.Y., Wei, K.-K.: Contributing knowledge to electronic knowledge repositories: an empirical investigation. MIS Q. **29**, 113–143 (2005)
6. von Krogh, G.: Systems How does social software change knowledge management? Toward a strategic research agenda. J. Strateg. Inf. Syst. **21**, 154–164 (2012)
7. Ma, M., Agarwal, R.: Through a Glass darkly: information technology design, identity verification, and knowledge contribution in online communities. Inf. Syst. Res. **18**, 42–67 (2007)
8. Majchrzak, A., Wagner, C., Yates, D.: The impact of shaping on knowledge reuse for organizational improvement with Wikis. MIS Q. **37**, 455–469 (2013)
9. Butler, B., Sproull, L., Kiesler, S., Kraut, R.: Community effort in online groups: who does the work and why? Leadersh. Dist. **5**, 455–469 (2002)
10. von Krogh, G., Haefliger, S., Spaeth, S., Wallin, M.W.: Carrots and rainbows: motivation and social practice in open source software development. MIS Q. **36**, 649–676 (2012)
11. Wasko, M.M., Faraj, S.: Why should i share? examining social capital and knowledge contribution in electronic networks of practice. MIS Q. **29**, 35–57 (2005)
12. Fleming, L., Waguespack, D.M.: Brokerage, boundary spanning, and leadership in open innovation communities. Organ. Sci. **18**, 165–180 (2007)
13. Fulk, J., DeSanctis, G.: Electronic communication and changing organizational form. Organ. Sci. **6**, 337–349 (1995)
14. Murray, F., O'Mahony, S.: Exploring the foundations of cumulative innovation: implications for organization science. Organ. Sci. **18**, 1006–1021 (2007)
15. O'Mahony, S., Ferraro, F.: The emergence of governance in an open source community. Acad. Manag. J. **50**, 1079–1106 (2007)
16. Volkoff, O., Strong, D.M.: Critical realism and affordances: theorizing IT-associated organizational change processes. MIS Q. **37**, 819–834 (2013)
17. Leonardi, P.M.: Theoretical foundations for the study of sociomateriality. Inf. Organ. **23**, 59–76 (2013)
18. Resca, A., Tozzi, M.L.: Designing Organizational Systems. Springer, Berlin Heidelberg, Berlin, Heidelberg (2013)
19. Shirky, C.: Here Comes Everybody: The Power of Organizing Without Organizations. Penguin, USA (2008)
20. Ostrom, E.: Collective action and the evolution of social norms. J. Econ. Perspect. **14**, 137–158 (2000)
21. Olson, M.: The Logic of Collective Action. Harvard University Press (2009)
22. Orlikowski, W.J., Scott, S.V.: Sociomateriality: challenging the separation of technology. Work Org. Acad. Manag. Ann. **2**, 433–474 (2008)
23. Orlikowski, W.J.: Sociomaterial practices: exploring technology at work. Organ. Stud. **28**, 1435–1448 (2007)
24. Mingers, J., Mutch, A., Willcocks, L.: Critical realism in information systems research. MIS Q. **37**, 795–802 (2013)
25. Mutch, A.: Technology, organization, and structure—a morphogenetic approach. Organ. Sci. **21**, 507–520 (2010)
26. Kautz, K., Jensen, T.B.: Sociomateriality at the royal court of IS. Inf. Organ. **23**, 15–27 (2013)
27. Bhaskar, R.: A Realist Theory of Science. Hemel Hempstead, Harvester (1978)
28. Bhaskar, R.: The Possibility of Naturalism: A Philosophical Critique of the Contemporary Human Sciences. Harvester Press, Sussex, UK (1979)
29. Wynn, D.J., Williams, C.K.: Principles for conducting critical realist case study research in information systems. MIS Q. **36**, 787–810 (2012)
30. Kant, I.: Critica della Ragion Pura. UTET, Novara (1967)
31. Hedström, P., Swedberg, R.: Social mechanisms: an introductory essay. In: Hedström, P., Swedberg, R. (eds.) Social Mechanisms, pp. 1–31. Cambridge University Press, Cambridge, UK (1998)
32. Elster, J.: A Plea for Mechanisms. Social Mechanisms: an Analytical Approach to Social Theory. pp. 45–71 (1998)

33. Mahoney, J.: Beyond correlational analysis: recent innovations in theory and method. Sociol. Forum **16**, 575–593 (2001)
34. Hedström, P., Ylikoski, P.: Causal mechanisms in the social sciences. Annu. Rev. Soc. **36**, 49–67 (2010)
35. Gibson, J.J.: A Theory of Affordances. Perceiving, Acting and Knoweing: Toward an Ecological Psychology, pp. 67–82. Lawrence Erlbaum Associates, Hillsdale, NJ (1977)
36. Gibson, J.J.: The Ecological Approach to Visual Perception. Lawrence Erlbaum Associates, Hillsdale, NJ (1986)
37. Markus, L.M., Silver, M.S., Markus, M.L.: A foundation for the study of IT effects: a new look at desanctis and poole's concepts of structural features and spirit. J. Assoc. Inf. Syst. **9**, 609–632 (2008)
38. Chemero, A.: An outline of a theory of affordances. Ecol. Psychol. **15**, 181–195 (2003)
39. Pozzi, G., Pigni, F., Vitari, C.: Affordance theory in the IS discipline: a review and synthesis of the literature. In: Proceedings Twentieth Americas Conference on Information Systems. AIS, Savannah, US (2014)
40. Bernhard, E., Recker, J., Burton-Jones, A.: Understanding the actualization of affordances: a study in the process modeling context. In: ICIS 2013 Proceedings, Milan (2013)
41. Zammuto, R.F., Griffith, T.L., Majchrzak, A., Dougherty, D.J., Faraj, S., Dogherty, D.J.: Information technology and the changing fabric of organization. Organ. Sci. **18**, 749–762 (2007)
42. Seidel, S., Recker, J., Vom Brocke, J.: Sensemaking and sustainable practicing: functional affordances of information systems in green transformations. MIS Q. **37**, 1275–1299 (2013)
43. Strong, D.M., Johnson, S.A., Tulu, B., Trudel, J., Volkoff, O., Pelletier, L.R., Bar-On, I., Garber, L.: A theory of organization-EHR affordance actualization. J. Assoc. Inf. Syst. **15**, 53–85 (2014)
44. Leonardi, P.M.: When does technology use enable network change in organizations? a comparative study of feature use and shared affordances. MIS Q. **37**, 749–776 (2013)
45. Walsham, G.: Doing interpretive research. Eur. J. Inf. Syst. **15**, 320–330 (2006)
46. Federici, T., Braccini, A.M., Sæbø, Ø.: "Gentlemen, all aboard!" ICT and party politics: reflections from a Mass-eParticipation experience. Gov. Inf. Q. **32**, 287–298 (2015)
47. Smith, M.L.: Testable theory development for small-N studies. Int. J. Inf. Technol. Syst. Appr. **3**, 41–56 (2010)
48. Volkoff, O., Strong, D.M., Elmes, M.B.: Technological embeddedness and organizational change. Organ. Sci. **1**, 832–848 (2007)
49. Henfridsson, O., Bygstad, B.: The generative mechanisms of digital infrastructure evolution. MIS Q. **37**, 907–931 (2013)

A Definition of Community Crowdsourcing Engagement and Application

Cuong Nguyen, Nargess Tahmasbi, Triparna de Vreede,
Gert-Jan de Vreede, Onook Oh and Roni Reiter-Palmon

1 Introduction

Crowdsourcing refers to the use of technologies to gather the collective effort and wisdom from an undefined group of online users for organizational innovation and/or problem solving [30]. The idea of crowdsourcing has been quickly embraced and employed in practice [39] and in various disciplines or sectors such as medicine [42], journalism [20], art [16], finance [6], and government [7].

Crowdsourcing initiatives can exist in multiple forms, among which we particularly focus on community crowdsourcing in this paper. Community crowdsourcing is a form of crowdsourcing in which online participants collaborate to produce the final outcome [10]. This is different from crowdsourcing initiatives that function as online labour market place (e.g. freelancer.com) or innovation contests

C. Nguyen (✉)
Allrecipes.com, Seattle, WA, USA
e-mail: cdnguyen083@gmail.com

N. Tahmasbi · R. Reiter-Palmon
University of Nebraska at Omaha, Omaha, NE, USA
e-mail: nargess.tahmasbi@gmail.com

R. Reiter-Palmon
e-mail: rreiter-palmon@unomaha.edu

T. de Vreede · G.-J. de Vreede
University of South Florida, Tampa, FL, USA
e-mail: tdevreede@usf.edu

G.-J. de Vreede
e-mail: gdevreede@usf.edu

O. Oh
University of Colorado Denver, Denver, CO, USA
e-mail: onook.oh@ucdenver.edu

© Springer International Publishing Switzerland 2016
F. D'Ascenzo et al. (eds.), *Blurring the Boundaries Through Digital Innovation*,
Lecture Notes in Information Systems and Organisation 19,
DOI 10.1007/978-3-319-38974-5_22

(e.g. innocentive.com). Community crowdsourcing typically requires a large number of participants engaging in a discussion to make suggestions or propose solutions regarding an issue that they have a stake in. It has been used to involve citizens in debates regarding the development of their neighbourhood and cities or employees to discuss product and process innovations.

Regardless of the type of crowdsourcing, a key challenge to crowdsourcing implementation is to convince online users to participate and gradually make them more engaged in the crowdsourcing tasks [8, 13, 50]. While the issue is naturally important, actually addressing it is tricky, due to the ambiguity of what is meant by being "more engaged". A participant may contribute fifty contributions the first time (s)he accesses the crowdsourcing event and never come back, or contribute less but follow every development of the event till its end. Which case should we consider "more engaged"? Another example: how should we judge the relative engagement between the participants who express high interest in the crowd-sourcing tasks orally and make only one or two contributions, versus those who report moderate or even low interest, yet contribute a lot?

To address this problem, we need a clear definition of the "participant engagement" construct and a way to measure it. Achieving this goal has several benefits. First, it provides researchers with a dependent variable for crowdsourcing studies that focus on interventions and factors that drive participation. Second, it provides crowdsourcing providers a way to assess the relative performance of their crowdsourcing initiatives. Third, it benefits organizations that employ crowd-sourcing to support their decision making processes; the level of participant engagement may inform the governance of the crowdsourcing effort as it provides insights regarding the quality, comprehensiveness, and persistence of the partici-pants' involvement.

Unfortunately, despite a considerable number of studies on motivations to par-ticipate and contribute to crowdsourcing events [9, 11, 12, 28, 31, 34, 36, 41, 48, 50], the concept of engagement itself and how to evaluate it have not been explicitly and thoroughly investigated. Most research refers to it in general terms such as "participation" or "contribution" without a clear definition. Some of them, such as those by Borst [9] or Hristova et al. [28] equated it to the number of submissions, yet without explicit rationale on why it was the case.

To fill this gap in the crowdsourcing literature, this research in progress paper proposes a definition and measurement of participant engagement for community crowdsourcing. Towards this goal, the paper is structured as follows. First, we review how engagement has been defined and studied in different disciplines. Second, we develop a definition of participant engagement in the community crowdsourcing context. Third, we propose the Participant Engagement Index (PEI) as an operational instance of the construct in the context of MindMixer, a community crowdsourcing service provider. We further illustrate the PEI's utility through the analysis of field project data from MindMixer. We conclude the paper with a summary of the key contributions of this study.

2 Background

To define participant engagement for community crowdsourcing, we first examined how the term "engagement" had been defined in the literature in various disciplines. This section presents our findings from the literature in information systems, organizational behaviour, education, and marketing.

As crowdsourcing is an Internet phenomenon, we searched for the engagement definition in its broader field—information systems (IS). In the IS discipline, user engagement with technology has been considered an important issue, especially in the areas of e-commerce, gaming, and e-learning [4]. Notable works on user engagement conceptualization include those by [4, 43]. Both of the two research groups proposed that user engagement was a synthesis of multiple psychological and behavioural states. In particular, Attfield et al. [4] defined user engagement as "the emotional, cognitive and behavioural connection that exists, at any point in time and possibly over time, between a user and a resource". Similarly, O'Brien and Tom [43] proposed that user engagement was a set of attributes including "challenge, positive affect, endurability, aesthetic and sensory appeal, attention, feedback, variety/novelty, interactivity, and perceived user control". Employing this user engagement concept, Goh et al. [24] assessed user engagement as a composite construct of leisure, control and immersion upon their study on user engagement in mobile human computation games. However, in the context of online activities, user engagement appeared to be evaluated mainly through user behaviours. For example, Lehmann et al. [35] proposed different models of user engagement with web applications based on online behavioural metrics such as number of unique users, page views, length of visits and return rates. Similarly, Colbert and Boodoo [17] considered a website was more engaging than another one if users stayed longer and visited them more frequently than the other. In the e-learning context, Huang et al. [30] referred to "online participation" as the level of students' online involvement, which was quantified through the number of discussion board posts, file views, online session duration, and number of pages read. Studying active participation in online communities, Ludford et al. [37] differentiated level of participation by the numbers of posts that participants made on the forums.

In organizational behaviour research, work engagement (a.k.a. employee or job engagement) gained much attention from both researchers and practitioners [27, 38]. Arguably, the most popular definition of work engagement came from Schaufeli et al. [45], defining it as "a positive, fulfilling, work-related state of mind that is characterized by vigour, dedication, and absorption". In contrast, according to Macey and Schneider's [39, 40], the term was understood in a broader sense, either as a trait, or a state, or a behaviour. As a trait, work engagement was considered a permanent attribute of individuals who were emotionally positive, proactive, conscientious, and autotelic. As a state, strong work engagement was characterized by a high level of positive affectivity, job satisfaction, involvement, commitment and empowerment. Finally, work engagement could also be observed from the workers' proactive and innovative behaviours that generally went "beyond what is, within specific frames of reference, typically expected or required" [39].

In the education context, student engagement was considered an antidote to increasing dropout rates and declining student motivation for learning [2, 22, 44]. Hu and Kuh [29] defined student engagement from a behavioural perspective as "the quality of effort students themselves devote to educationally purposeful activities that contribute directly to desired outcomes". Adopting this standpoint, the National Survey of Student Engagement was developed to evaluate the students' level of involvement in school activities [33]. Nevertheless, other education researchers argued that the student engagement construct was not complete without including cognitive and affective elements [2, 5, 32]. For example, Appleton et al. [3] conceptualized student engagement as a multidimensional construct with four components: academic, behavioural, cognitive, and psychological. While endorsing the multidimensional nature of student engagement, Fredricks et al. [23] questioned the novelty of the construct. They noted a resemblance with other more established constructs such as attitudes [20, 49], values [19], motivation to learn [15], learning goals [1, 18], and intrinsic motivation [27].

Finally, in the marketing discipline, the term "customer engagement" (CE) has gained increasing popularity in the last decade [14]. Similar to other domains, there were different understandings of the term. In particular, Van Doorn et al. [47] introduced customer engagement behaviours (CEB) by defining it as "a customer's behavioural manifestations that have a brand or firm focus, beyond purchase, resulting from motivational drivers". However, Mollen and Wilson [42] suggested that, rather than being a behavioural manifestation, CE was close to "a cognitive and affective commitment to an active relationship with the brand".

3   Defining Participant Engagement in Community Crowdsourcing

The findings from these literatures show that engagement is a relatively new but important construct both from an academic and practice perspective. A high level of engagement is desirable for or equated with positive effects on key outcomes in the respective domains [2, 14, 26, 35]. However, conceptually speaking, engagement appears to be an umbrella of multiple separate constructs rather than a phenomenon on its own. Shared across disciplines is the agreement that engagement has been considered a set of positive behavioural, emotional, or cognitive attributes. As a result, there have been two general suggestions regarding the conceptualization of engagement. First, it should be evaluated as a multidimensional construct (e.g. [3]). That is, the measure of the construct should be a simultaneous evaluation of different dimensions that constitute engagement. Second, engagement should be defined and evaluated through one of its representative perspectives depending on the context of study [39]. We follow the second direction and approach engagement from the behavioural perspective because of three reasons. First, as crowdsourcing events are set to utilize online labour resources, it is essential that participants make tangible contributions to these events. If the participants report being highly engaged emotionally and cognitively, but do not convert this psychological engagement into actions, it will be of less interest to the crowdsourcing organizers. Second, besides being the most important engagement aspect, behavioural engagement is also the easiest to observe, especially in the crowdsourcing context. Characterized by the geographically distributed environment, it is more convenient for the crowdsourcing organizers to evaluate participant engagement through their actions than through other means (e.g. self-report). Third, as crowdsourcing is Internet-based, participants' online activities are fully recorded and can be analysed automatically. This condition allows crowdsourcing organizers to monitor behavioural engagement on daily basis and take action to boost their participant engagement in a timely manner.

To define behavioural engagement, two key challenges must be addressed. First, we need to know which behaviours represent engagement and which do not. Second, we need to know how to measure it. Thus, we examine how the issues have been addressed in a number of previous behavioural engagement definitions presented in the Table 1.

Based on the above two challenges, the engagement definition by Colbert and Boodoo [17] and Sundar et al. [46] is too broad. Macey and Schneider's [39] definition is challenging to operationalize because expectation is not a fixed benchmark [25]. Van Doorn et al.'s [47] definition has the same problem because it is difficult to know whether a behaviour is "resulting from motivational drivers". Arguably, Hu and Kuh's [29] definition of student engagement is the clearest on the criteria of what represent engagement behaviours. However, the definition is not very directive to measurement of the construct, as the term "quality of effort" is subject to different interpretations.

In our research, we define participant engagement in the community crowdsourcing context as *"the magnitude, temporal intensity, diversity, and recency of tangible effort online users voluntarily devote to what is requested in a community crowdsourcing initiative"*. We argue that this definition characterizes engaging behaviours and is instructive to the measurement of the construct. By this definition, engagement possesses some key attributes. First, it represents an effort, not a work

Table 1 Behavioural engagement definitions

Definition	Reference
Customer engagement—A customer's behavioural manifestations that have a brand or firm focus, beyond purchase, resulting from motivational drivers	[47]
Work engagement—Work engagement behaviours are those that go "beyond what is, within specific frames of reference, typically expected or required"	[39]
Student engagement—The quality of effort students themselves devote to educationally purposeful activities that contribute directly to desired outcomes	[29]
IT user engagement—the number of user actions	[17, 46]

outcome. It does not matter whether users' contributions are outstanding or mediocre; the emphasis is on the fact that they actually make an attempt to make a meaningful contribution. Second, it should be observable in some ways. The definition leaves out cases where participants express high interest in the community crowdsourcing event but do not make any tangible contributions to it. Third, engagement is voluntary. Participants should do the things they do out of their own will, not because they are forced. Finally, participant engagement is 'on-task'. Not everything a participant does represents participant engagement. Actions that are irrelevant to the task at hand are not considered as engagement. For example, when the task requests participants to envision the future of public transport in a city, user comments on how good their neighbours are should be considered off-task and not indicators of engagement.

Besides specifying the attributes that distinguish engaging behaviours from those that are not, we also specify how to determine which participants are more engaged than others. In particular, we propose to differentiate the quality of the engaging behaviours of different participants along four attributes—magnitude, temporal intensity, diversity, and recency.

Magnitude refers to the total amount of effort a single participant contributes to a community crowdsourcing event. Each contribution a participant makes requires a certain amount of effort from his/her end. Therefore, it is reasonable that the more contributions a participant makes, the more voluntary effort he/she puts into the event. The evaluation of participant engagement through the total amount of effort is in line with how the behavioural engagement has been judged in previous crowdsourcing motivation research (e.g. [9, 50]), as well as studies on engagement in online activities such as e-learning [30] and online communities [37].

Temporal intensity refers to the sustained nature of a participant's contributions over time. Our appreciation of the temporal intensity comes from two reasons. First, a community crowdsourcing initiative typically lasts for some months and involves multiple stages. Therefore, it is desirable that participants follow up during the course of the event, such as responding to the other participants' comments and feedback on their previously submitted ideas. In fact, research on open source software (OSS) projects, which bear similarities to community crowdsourcing, showed that 80 % of the OSS projects failed because the participants did not follow up [21]. Second, marketing research shows that keeping existing customers is cheaper than acquiring new ones, increases the chance of up-selling and cross-selling, and enhances a firm's popularity through word-of-mouth channel [46]. We expect that sustained engagement will bring about similar effects, such as increasing the likelihood that the participants will participate in other similar events, or be more willing to introduce the events to their friends.

In addition, when a community crowdsourcing event offers more than one way for participants to contribute, the *diversity* of participants' effort also needs to be taken into account. That is, participants that try various activities of the event are judged as more engaged than those that are less diverse in their contributions. The activity diversity is important because it differentiates participants who enjoy only some aspects of the crowdsourcing event with those who enjoy the whole event.

For example, participants who only contribute ideas are considered not as engaged as those who not only contribute ideas but also give their feedback on contributions of others.

Finally, in case of on-going community crowdsourcing events, engagement is also evaluated in relation to the current date of the event through the *recency* dimension. That is, the closer the participant's contributions are to the current date of the event, the more engaged (s)he is judged to be. Our consideration of the recency of participant contributions is inspired by findings in marketing research. Marketing researchers showed that recency, or the length of time since the last purchase, was the most powerful predictor of the next purchase [51]. We expect a similar effect in community crowdsourcing. The more recent a participant's contributions are, the more likely it is that the participant will contributing in the near future. Also, imagine two crowdsourcing events that have comparable levels of participant contributions, both in terms of magnitude, temporal intensity, and diversity. In the first event the majority of contributions took place several months ago while in the second event the majority of contributions happened during the last several weeks. It would be reasonable to declare that the second event *currently* enjoys a higher level of engagement.

The engagement of a participant can now be measured as the multiplication of the measures along the four dimensions. Multiplication, rather than addition, is used to reflect the fact that the temporal intensity, diversity, and recency of participant behaviour further qualify the magnitude of his/her behaviour.

4 An Example of Measuring Participant Engagement in Community Crowdsourcing

To illustrate how the proposed participant engagement can be operationalized in a specific context, in this section we present the participant engagement index (PEI) that we developed to measure participant engagement on the community crowdsourcing platform MindMixer. MindMixer supports city halls and government offices to solve civic problems such as upgrading neighbourhood infrastructures, city hall budget plans, or improving government administrative operations. Upon the request of a client (i.e. city halls and government offices), MindMixer sets up a website and calls for online users' participation in online discussions on various topics requested by the client. Within a website (called a "project"), there may be multiple topics, which are issues for discussion or problems to solve.

As the first step to determine the PEI, we identify the *tangible effort online users voluntarily devote to what is requested in a community crowdsourcing initiative*. In the context of a MindMixer project, we can specify nine possible participants actions (i.e. behaviours or contributions): submitting an idea, submitting a comment, taking a poll, taking a survey, sharing a photo, rating an idea, sharing topics to friends, and referring the event to friends. Next, we measured the effort a participant exerted on these nine activities along the four dimensions (i.e. magnitude, temporal intensity, diversity, and recency) which are operationalized as the four sub-indices below:

Participant Activity Engagement (PAE): the PAE index reflects the magnitude of a participant's effort. It captures the number of times a participant performs any of the nine desired actions e.g. the number of idea submissions. Moreover, depending on the nature of the discussion topics, some activities may be perceived more significant than others. For example, in a brainstorming topic, submitting ideas may be considered more important than rating an idea, while in evaluation topics the contrary is true. Therefore, each action is also assigned a weight, or activity value to denote the relative significance of the action. The general formula to calculate PAE is presented below:

$PAE = \sum_{i=1}^{9} an_i av_i$ where an_i = number of times action i is performed (in a week) and av_i = activity value of the action i

Participant Intensity Engagement (PIE): We evaluate this temporal intensity through the PIE index, which has two components:

The frequency aspect of the temporal intensity (Intensity Frequency): Participants can contribute one day a week, or two days a week, or all seven days of a week—this is represented by intensity frequency. Higher the number of days a contribution was made, the higher the engagement is judged. This differentiation is denoted by the intensity frequency coefficient whose value is defined as follows in the MindMixer context: Contribute all 7 days—factor 1.25; 5–6 days—factor 1.00; 2–4 days—factor 0.75; 1 day—factor 0.50; 0 days—factor 0.

The repetition aspect of the temporal intensity (Intensity Repetition): For the days that the participant has contributed during the week, his or her contributions can range from once a day to several times a day. It is represented by intensity repetition coefficient. When participants contribute more than once a day, they are assigned higher weights. In the MindMixer context, the intensity repetition coefficient is specified as: Contributes once a day—factor 1.00; Contributes more than once a day—factor 1.25.

The PIE is calculated as the product of the intensity frequency and intensity repetition. For example, a participant who contributed 3 days during the examined week, and contributed more than once in any of these 3 days, has a PIE of 0.75 (Intensity Frequency) × 1.25 (Intensity Repetition) = 0.94.

Participant Diversity Engagement (PDE): The diversity dimension is operationalized as the PDE index. In the context of MindMixer projects, the PDE values are determined as being equal to 1 if the participant performs only 1 activity type during the examined week, equal to 1.25 if the participant performs 2 to 6 of the possible activity types, and equal to 1.5 if the participant performs 7 or more.

For example, a participant who contributed two ideas, five comments, and rated seven ideas, has a PDE of 1.25 because (s)he performed three different activity types.

Participant Recency Engagement (PRE): The recency dimension is operationalized as the PRE coefficient, which assigns more weight for more recent contributions for a period of four weeks, in one week increments. Specifically, the contributions made within the first week before the current date are assigned the PRE score of 1.00; within the second week before the current date—0.75; Third week—0.50; Fourth week—0.25.

Participant Engagement Index (PEI): Finally, the PEI score is the product of its four sub-indices. In the MindMixer context, the PEI is examined for a 4-week period. First, weekly PEIs are calculated for each week and then the PEI for the whole 4-week duration is taken as the average of the weekly PEIs. The formula for the PEI calculation is presented below:

Weekly PEI Score = Weekly PAE Score × Weekly PIE Score × Weekly PDE Score × Weekly PRE Score

4-week PEI = Average of the weekly PEI scores for the past four weeks

Note that the 4-week PEI gives the engagement level of an individual participant in a community crowdsourcing project. To evaluate the participant engagement at the higher levels, such as topics, or projects, we take the sum of the individual PEIs from all the participants at the corresponding level e.g. adding all PEIs from the participants in a specific project to get the Project PEI. We rely on two assumptions to calculate the Project PEI and Topic PEI as such. First, the level of engagement, conceived as tangible and voluntary effort, is additive. That is, the engagement level of two participants is equal to the sum of the engagement levels of each of them. Second, besides individual engagement, a project or topic is considered more engaging if it can attract more participants.

5 An Illustration of PEI Utility

Our measure of engagement can be applied for different purposes. For example, it can be used as a yardstick for comparing the engagement levels of different projects at a particular point in time. To illustrate, the PEI was calculated for a particular date for a set of 6 MindMixer projects, thus giving insight in the engagement each project experienced over the past 4 weeks from that date. The results are depicted in Table 2. By calculating the Project PEI this way, historical data can be gathered that

Table 2 Illustrative PEI scores

Project	Project PEI
EnvisionSacramento	59.4
YourVoiceVegas	16.0
LexEngage	15.9
EngageOakland	11.1
SpeakUpSierraVista	9.1
EngageOrlando	2.1

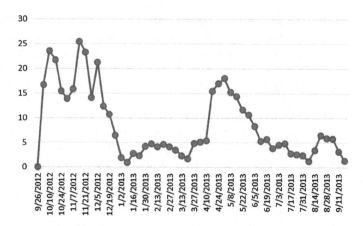

Fig. 1 Lifetime PEI for continuous engagement monitoring

will assist in benchmarking certain engagement thresholds, while controlling for the number of active participants.

The PEI can also be used to monitor the changes in engagement level of a project, topic, or a participant over time. The PEI during the life of a project can be obtained by applying the formula on each 4-week period of a project lifetime. Continuous monitoring of engagement in a project can help to find the rise and falls in the level of engagement and further track the causes of those changes. An example the lifetime PEI of a MindMixer project is given in Fig. 1.

Finally, the PEI can also be used as a dependent variable to study the effect of various factors on engagement. For example, we examined the impact of feedback from project owners (in the form of comments from an admin user on a participant's idea) on participant engagement. For this analysis, we analysed 387 MindMixer projects, 56 of which had some level of feedback from project owners while the remaining did not. We calculated each project's engagement based on an aggregation of all individual PEI scores in the project. Using a non-parametric rank-ordered ANOVA test, we found that there was a significant difference in the project PEI for projects with feedback (Mean rank = 222.07) and projects without feedback (Mean rank = 189.25) conditions (p = 0.042). Similar analyses on the topic level and participant level show that problem owner feedback has a significant positive effect on participant engagement.

6   Conclusions and Expected Contributions

Participant engagement is a critical determinant of crowdsourcing success. Yet, the conceptualization and measurement of the construct have not been sufficiently addressed in the crowdsourcing research community. We contribute to the literature by proposing a behavioural view of community crowdsourcing participant engagement. In particular, we propose to judge engagement by the quality of *tangible* and *volunteer* effort participants contribute to the crowdsourcing event. We argue that engagement judged from the behavioural viewpoint is of most relevance to crowdsourcing providers in the crowd-sourcing context. Further, while it may seem straightforward to gauge a participant's effort by their number of contributions to the crowdsourcing event, we argue for a more complex assessment of the quality of crowdsourcing engaging behaviours. That is, besides the *magnitude* of the effort, we also need to be attentive to its *temporal intensity*, *diversity*, and *recency*. The strengths of this complex view of behavioural engagement, besides being relevant to the crowdsourcing context, also lie in the fact that they can be captured quantitatively and easily through current web-logging metrics. We demonstrate this feasibility by describing the Participant Engagement Index (PEI) to measure the participant engagement in the specific context of MindMixer. While the PEI is tailor-made to the MindMixer, its development is suggestive to how to operationalize the participant engagement construct in other crowdsourcing instances. In addition, we illustrate the utility of a behavioural participant engagement index, either as an objective and quantitative indicator of participant engagement, or as a dependent variable for exploratory and confirmatory studies.

Our continued research activities include the following: First, we are validating the generalizability of the engagement definition and measurement in other community crowdsourcing contexts. Second, we are investigating the sensitivity of each PEI dimension separately. Finally, we are exploring whether there are additional dimensions that are required to characterize the quality of participant effort beyond the four dimensions discussed in this research in progress paper.

Acknowledgments Funding for this research was provided by the National Science Foundation Grant #1322285.

References

1. Ames, C.: Classrooms: goals, structures, and student motivation. J. Educ. Psychol. **84**, 261–271 (1992)
2. Appleton, J.J., Christenson, S.L., Furlong, M.J.: Student engagement with school: critical conceptual and methodological issues of the construct. Psychol. Schools **45**(5), 369–386 (2008)
3. Appleton, J.J., Christenson, S.L., Kim, D., Reschly, A.L.: Measuring cognitive and psychological engagement: validation of the student engagement instrument. J. Sch. Psychol. **44**(5), 427–445 (2006)
4. Attfield, S., Kazai, G., Lalmas, M., Piwowarski, B.: Towards a science of user engagement. In: Paper presented at UMWA 2011, Workshop on User Modelling for Web Applications, Hong Kong, China, 9–12 (2011)
5. Baumeister, R.F., Leary, M.R.: The need to belong: desire for interpersonal attachments as a fundamental human motivation. Psychol. Bull. **117**, 497–529 (1995)

6. Belleamme, P., Lambert, T., Schwienbacher, A.: Crowdfunding: Tapping the right crowd. In: Proceedings of the International Conference of the French Finance Association (AFFI) (2010)
7. Bommert, B.: Collaborative innovation in the public sector. Int. Public Manage. Rev. **11**(1), 15–33 (2010)
8. Bonabeau, E.: Decision 2.0: the power of collective intelligence. MIT Sloan Manage. Rev. **50** (2), 44–52 (2009)
9. Borst: Understanding crowdsourcing: effects of motivation and rewards on participation and performance in voluntary online activities. Ph.D. thesis, Erasmus University Rotterdam (2010)
10. Boudreau, K., Lakhani, K.: How to manage outside innovation. MIT Sloan Manage. Rev. **50** (4), 69–76 (2009)
11. Brabham, D.C.: Moving the crowd at threadless: motivations for participation in a crowdsourcing application. Inform. Commun. Soc. **13**(8), 1122–1145 (2010)
12. Brabham, D.C.: Motivations for participation in a crowdsourcing application to improve public engagement in transit planning. J. Appl. Commun. Res. **40**(3), 307–328 (2012)
13. Brabham, D.C.: Crowdsourcing as a model for problem solving: an introduction and cases, convergence. Int. J. Res. New Media Technol. **14**(1), 75–90 (2008)
14. Brodie, R.J., Hollebeek, L.D., Jurić, B., Ilić, A.: Customer engagement conceptual domain, fundamental propositions, and implications for research. J. Serv. Res. **14**(3), 252–271 (2011)
15. Brophy, J.E.: Socializing students' motivation to learn. In: Maehr, M.L., Kleiber, D. (eds.) Advances in Motivation and Achievement: Enhancing motivation, pp. 181–210. JAI Press, Greenwich, CT (1987)
16. Butler, B., Sproull, L., Kiesler, S., Kraut, R.: Community effort in online groups: who does the work and why. In: Weisband, S., Atwater, L. (eds.) Leadership at a distance. Lawrence Erlbaum Publishers, Mahwah, NJ, pp. 171–194 (2002)
17. Colbert, M., Boodoo, A.: Does' Letting go of the words' increase engagement: a traffic study. In: Proceedings of the 2011 Annual Conference Extended Abstracts on Human Factors in Computing Systems, pp. 655–667 (2011)
18. Dweck, C., Leggett, E.L.: A social-cognitive approach to motivation and personality. Psychol. Rev. **95**, 256–273 (1988)
19. Eccles (Parsons), J.S., Adler, T.F., Futterman, R., Goff, S.B., Kaczala, C.M., Meece, J.L., et al.: Expectations, values and academic behaviours. In: Spence, J.T. (ed.) Achievement and achievement motivation. W.H. Freeman, San Francisco, pp. 75–146 (1983)
20. Epstein, J.L., McPartland, J.M.: The concept and measurement of the quality of school life. Am. Educ. Res. J. **13**, 15–30 (1976)
21. Fang, Y., Neufeld, D.: Understanding sustained participation in open source software projects. J. Manage. Inform. Syst. **25**(4), 9–50 (2009)
22. Fitt, V.A.: Crowdsourcing the news: news organization liability for iReporters. William Mitchell Law Rev. **37**(4), 1839–1867 (2011)
23. Fredericks, J.A., Blumenfeld, P.C., Paris, A.H.: School engagement: Potential of the concept, state of the evidence. Rev. Educ. Res. **74**, 59–109 (2004)
24. Fredricks, J.A., Eccles, J.S.: Children's competence and value beliefs from childhood to adolescence: growth trajectories in two "male-typed" domains. J. Dev. Psychol. **38**, 519–533 (2002)
25. Goh, D., Razikin, K., Lee, C. S., Chua, A.: Investigating user perceptions of engagement and information quality in mobile human computation games. In: Proceedings of the 12th ACM/IEEE-CS Joint Conference on Digital Libraries, pp. 391–392 (2012)
26. Griffin, M.A., Parker, S.K., Neal, A.: Is behavioural engagement a distinct and useful construct. Indus. Organ. Psychol. **1**(1), 48–51 (2008)
27. Harter, J.K., Schmidt, F.L., Hayes, T.L.: Business-unit-level relationship between employee satisfaction, employee engagement, and business outcomes: a meta-analysis. J. Appl. Psychol. **87**, 268–279 (2002)

28. Hassenzahl, M., Tractinsky, N.: User experience-a research agenda. Behav. Inform. Technol. **25**(2), 91–97 (2006)
29. Howe, J.: The Rise of Crowdsourcing. Wired, (2006) Retrieved April 30 2012 from: http://www.wired.com/wired/archive/14.06/crowds.html
30. Hristova, D., Mashhadi, A., Quattrone, G., Capra, L.: Mapping community engagement with urban crowd-sourcing. In: Proceedings of When the City Meets the Citizen Workshop, Dublin, Ireland, vol. 4 (2012)
31. Hu, S., Kuh, G.D.: Being (dis) engaged in educationally purposeful activities: the influences of student and institutional characteristics. Res. High. Educ. **43**(5), 555–575 (2002)
32. Kaufmann, N., Schulze, T., Veit, D.: More than fun and money. Worker Motivation in Crowdsourcing-A Study on Mechanical Turk. In: AMCIS, vol. 11, pp. 1–11 (2011)
33. Koda, T., Maes, P.: Agents with faces: the effect of personification. In: 5th IEEE International Workshop on Robot and Human Communication, 1996, pp. 189–194 (1996)
34. Kuh, G.D.: The National Survey of Student Engagement: Conceptual framework and Overview of Psychometric Properties. Indiana University Center for Postsecondary Research, Bloomington, IN, pp. 1–26 (2001)
35. Lakhani, K.R., Wolf, R.G.: Why hackers do what they do: understanding motivation and effort in free/open source software projects. Perspect. Free Open Source Softw. **1**, 3–22 (2005)
36. Lehmann, J., Lalmas, M., Yom-Tov, E., Dupret, G.: Models of user engagement. In: User Modeling, Adaptation, and Personalization, pp. 164–175. Springer Berlin Heidelberg (2012)
37. Leimeister, J.M., Huber, M., Bretschneider, U., Krcmar, H.: Leveraging crowdsourcing: activation-supporting components for IT-based ideas competition. J. Manage. Inform. Syst. **26**(1), 197–224 (2009)
38. Lührs, R., Albrecht, S., Lübcke, M., Hohberg, B.: How to grow? online consultation about growth in the city of hamburg: methods, techniques, success factors. In: Traunmüller, R. (ed.) Electronic Government (EGOV 2003), pp. 79–84, LNCS 2739. Springer, Berlin, Germany (2003)
39. Macey, W.H., Schneider, B.: Engaged in engagement: i am delighted i did it. Indus. Organ. Psychol. **1**(1), 76–83 (2008)
40. Macey, W.H., Schneider, B.: The meaning of employee engagement. Indus. Organ. Psychol. **1**(1), 3–30 (2008)
41. Massolution: Crowdsourcing Industry Report-Enterprise Crowdsourcing: Market, Provider and Worker Trends, (2012) Retrieved 10/28/2013 from: http://www.crowdsourcing.org/editorial/enterprise-crowdsourcing-research-report-by-massolution/11736 (Last accessed 4/17/2014)
42. Morgan, J., Wang, R.: Tournaments for ideas. Calif. Manage. Rev. **52**(2) (2010)
43. Norman T.C, Bountra C., Edwards A.M., Yamamoto K.R., Friend S.H.: Leveraging crowdsourcing to facilitate the discovery of new medicines. Sci. Trans. Med. **3**(88) (2011)
44. O'Brien, H.L., Toms, E.G.: What is user engagement? A conceptual framework for defining user engagement with technology. J. Am. Soc. Inform. Sci. Technol. **59**(6), 938–955 (2008)
45. Pope, D.: Doing School: How We are Creating a Generation of Stressed-Out, Materialistic, and Miseducated Students. Yale University Press, New Haven, CT (2002)
46. Reichheld, F.F., Schefter, P.: E-loyalty. Harvard Bus. Rev. **78**(4), 105–113 (2000)
47. Schaufeli, W.B., Salanova, M., González-Romá, V., Bakker, A.B.: The measurement of engagement and burnout: a two sample confirmatory factor analytic approach. J. Happiness Stud. **3**(1), 71–92 (2002)
48. Sundar, S.S., Xu, Q., Bellur, S., Oh, J., Jia, H.: Beyond pointing and clicking: how do newer interaction modalities affect user engagement? In: Proceedings of the 2011 Annual Conference Extended Abstracts on Human Factors in Computing Systems, pp. 1477–1482 (2011)
49. Van Doorn, J., Lemon, K.N., Mittal, V., Nass, S., Pick, D., Pirner, P., Verhoef, P.C.: Customer engagement behaviour: theoretical foundations and research directions. J. Serv. Res. **13**(3), 253–266 (2010)

50. Wagner, C., Prasarnphanich, P.: Innovating collaborative content creation: the role of altruism and wiki technology. In: The 40th Annual Hawaii International Conference on System Sciences (2007)
51. Wei, J.T., Lin, S.Y., Wu, H.H.: A review of the application of RFM model. Afr. J. Bus. Manage. **4**(19), 4199–4206 (2010)

What Do Local Governments Discuss in Social Media? An Empirical Analysis of the Italian Municipalities

Benedetta Gesuele, Concetta Metallo and Rocco Agrifoglio

1 Introduction

The social media, such as Facebook and Twitter, represent the last step in Internet development using by municipalities. These systems promote inter-connectivity between government and citizens, companies, employees, and others, representing innovative methods to informally communicate [1] and to support traditional communication channels (e.g., official webpage) [2]. The social media can be considered as the best expression of Web 2.0, term coined by O'Really in 2005 to indicate a second generation of web based applications. The Web 2.0 applications have become an important tool to increase the public transparency and accountability [3], key drivers for good governance in the public sector. Social media facilitate access to information, openness, the engagement of citizens, and they have been seen as effective tools to promote public goals [4–6].

This study takes a first step toward understanding of the social media adoption, such as Facebook in particular, by Italian municipalities because their rising adoption and the small amount of academic research on the topic. In fact, Norris and Reddick's [7] survey on social media adoption of local governments (e.g., Facebook, Twitter, and YouTube) in the United States highlighted an amazing adoption rates, two-thirds of local governments had adopted at least one social

B. Gesuele (✉)
Department of Law and Economics, Pegaso University, Naples, Italy
e-mail: benedettagesuele@gmail.com

C. Metallo
Department of Sciences and Technology, Parthenope University, Naples, Italy
e-mail: concetta.metallo@uniparthenope.it

R. Agrifoglio
Department of Management, Accounting and Economics,
Parthenope University, Naples, Italy
e-mail: rocco.agrifoglio@uniparthenope.it

© Springer International Publishing Switzerland 2016
F. D'Ascenzo et al. (eds.), *Blurring the Boundaries Through Digital Innovation*,
Lecture Notes in Information Systems and Organisation 19,
DOI 10.1007/978-3-319-38974-5_23

media. Bonsón and colleagues' research [3] on the use of Web 2.0 and social media tools in European Union (EU) local governments has shown that most local governments are using social media. However, research on social media in the local governments is still at its early stages and there is still need for empirical research on this topic [3, 8, 9].

The Italian context is an interesting field of investigation of this phenomena because in Italy is recognized the importance of mandatory e-disclosure through municipality's website (with legislative decrees 150/2009 and 33/2013). Despite this, voluntary e-disclosure through social media is becoming more and more established.

Therefore, this study aims to contribute to this research gap by investigating how municipalities are using Facebook to communicate with citizens and what are the main topics discussed. Using content analysis and posts categorization on the Facebook pages, we analyze topics of municipality posts to understand the communicative practices and types of use by municipalities.

The structure of this paper is as follows. In the next section we introduce the literature review on social media usage by municipalities, and then we deepen the role of social media as communication channels (Sect. 3). In Sect. 4, we describe the research methodology and the results of the analysis. Finally, in Sect. 5 we present the discussion and conclusions.

2 Literature Review

Social media refers to "a group of Internet-based applications that build on the ideological and technological foundations of Web 2.0, and that allow the creation and exchange of User Generated Content" [10, p. 61]. In practice, Web 2.0 is the technical platform in which social media applications are built to create and exchange user-generated content [5].

To date the number of users has quickly increased and social media became more relevant for public administrations for promoting interactions between government and citizens, for disseminating government information, enabling stakeholders to engage in governance. Corresponding to the increased popularity of social media into the governmental, there has been a significant growth of studies investigating the social media's impact on e-government (for a review see Magro [11]).

Klang and Nolin [12] investigated several Swedish social media policies produced by municipalities in order to recommend practical guidelines for improving transparency and interaction through social media. Kavanaugh and colleagues [13] analyzed social media use by local governments for managing crisis situations from the routine (e.g., traffic, weather crises) to the critical (e.g., earthquakes, floods). Feeney and Welch [14] investigated whether different e-participation technologies and the intensity of e-participation technology use are associated with managers' perceptions of outcomes in the local governments. Mossberger and colleagues [15] analyzed the use of social media and other interactive tools in the 75 largest US cities between 2009 and 2011, constructing an index of interactivity. Oliveira and Welch [6] have shown patterns of social media application for particular purposes, highlighting that social media tools are not a monolithic group. Ma [16] examined the diffusion of police microblogging and its determinants in Chinese municipal police bureaus through the perspective of organizational innovation diffusion. Findings have shown that government size, Internet penetration rate, regional diffusion effects and upper-tier pressure are positively and significantly associated with the adoption and earliness of police microblogging. Picazo-Vela and colleagues [5] showed the perceptions of risks, benefits and strategic guidelines about social media applications in the Mexican public sector. Mishaal and Abu-Shanab [2] proposed a framework for measuring communication success over social networks such as Facebook. Zheng and Zheng [17], through a content analysis, investigated performance of information and interactions in selected Chines government microblog accounts as innovations in the public sector. Sobaci and Karkin [9] investigated the impact of Twitter in Turkey on transparent, participatory and citizen-oriented local public services, showing the role of Twitter for offering better public services. Lovari and Parisi [18] focused on the motivations to become Facebook fan of a municipality in Italian context, and on the variety of digital practices carried out by citizens to communicate and relate with this type of public administrations. Chun et al. [19] explored how successfully local governments utilize Facebook for managing their external communication with citizens. Bonsón and colleagues [20] analyzed the impact of media and content types on stakeholders' engagement on Western European local governments' Facebook pages. Findings highlighted that local governments' preferences to different media and content types seem to depend on the institutional context. Guttormsen and Sæbø [21] classified municipalities' social media usage into six thematic areas. The explanatory potential is illustrated by conducting a qualitative case study in which a local municipality's use of Facebook is analyzed based on the suggested thematic areas.

3 The Social Media Adoption in the Public Sector as Communication Tools

Many scholars pointed the opportunities provided by social media for government such as improvement of the transparency and accountability [1, 3, 4], through dissemination information to the citizens [19, 22], improvement of policy making [3], by increasing opportunities to participate and collaborate in decision making or voting [22] improvement of public services [20], providing, for example, feedback about services and design contents [5]. Through social media citizens leave their passive role and become users able to interact with government [3].

The major benefit for government using social media is that they enable to disclosure information about their services and activities, and otherwise by municipality official web page, they can arrive to bigger number of people [23].

Mishaal and Abu-Shanab [2] proposed a framework for exploring the communication success using social media by municipalities. The framework is based on transparency, such as information disclosure checked by stakeholder; participation, such as capacity of government that allows to citizens to express their idea; collaboration, such as the high level of engagement between citizens and government.

Sobaci and Karkin [9] argued that local governments could have several benefits tanking social media usage, such as the improvement of the public services. Trough social media, local government can arrive at different goals, as collected the different point of view of their stakeholders (citizens, employers, and beneficiaries), and broadcast documents and news (draft, regulation, announce and accounting statement). In line with Sobaci and Karkin [9], Bonsón and colleagues [3] highlighted that social media are new communication tools to disclosure information about local service and for improving policy making and knowledge management in municipalities.

In particular, benefits for municipalities from the use of social media can be [3]: facilitate the mass distribution of the content of the official website, allowing users to redistribute these contents in their own blogs or social networks; open corporate dialogue where not only local government but also citizens would have the opportunity of publishing their own points of view on the material distributed.

There are some studies that analyzed how municipalities use social media (such as Facebook or Twitter) as new communication channels between government and citizens, suggesting categories under which the posts' topics, message contents, or tweets published by governments can be categorized [9, 17, 20].

For example, Zheng and Zheng [17] highlighted that social media usage by government can be aimed for information and interaction, proposing three categories under which the message contents can be coded: government internal activities; public services and social news. In particular, social media usage for information refers to disseminating information for improving government transparency and delivering public services. Social media usage for interaction refers to interacting with various stakeholders for promoting participation in decision-making and improving collaboration. In their categorization, government internal activities refer to content related to government meetings, event, and leaders' activities, mostly for self-promotion. Public services refer to weather forecast, healthy advices, and transportation status. Social news usually broadcasts general events and news.

Sobaci and Karkin [9] classified, using content analysis and tweet categorization, the tweets of mayors in Turkey in 11 categories based on their topics: information and news sharing, location and activity sharing, personal messages, direct communication with citizens, communication with elected and appointed, better public services, self promotion, invitation to events, personal opinion and perspective sharing, promoting participation and the unknown.

Bonsón et al. [20] coded posts of Western European local governments' Facebook pages in sixteen categories, based on the lists of local services elaborated by Torres and Pina [24] and subsequently adapted by Martí et al. [25]: public works and town planning; environment; attention to the citizen; citizen participation; social services; citizen protection and security; public transport; employment and training schemes; health; education; cultural activities and sports; housing; governance issues; financial reporting; marketing/city promotion/tourism; and others.

Hofmann et al. [23, 26] analyzed the official Facebook sites of German local government using a content analysis to categorize topics of the posts. The coding scheme for governments' post in Facebook proposed is: up-to-date provision of information, allowing real-time communication; marketing, for advertise their e-government services; co-design, collecting feedback and ideas by citizens; f-transaction, such as starting a government service on Facebook and subsequently redirect on the official government website.

4 Research Method and Data Analysis

We analysed the Facebook sites of Italian local governments aimed to explore how the latter use social media in the external communication strategies. Data was collected from official Facebook fan page of 9 largest municipalities located in different Regions of the Italian peninsula. Among them, 3 cities (Venice, Pavia, and Forlì) are located in Northern Italy, 3 cities (Pescara, Frosinone, and Lucca) in Central Italy, and the last 3 (Naples, Bari, and Palermo) in Southern Italy.

Data was collected with reference to considered period from December 1, 2014–May 31, 2015, while data coding took place in June 2015. In particular, we collected all posts of the 9 selected cities and then performed data by using a qualitative data analysis software, such as NVivo. NVivo was recognized as a particularly suitable software to aid qualitative data management and analysis for social research [27].

Firstly, data was manually codified for assigning topic tags to the posts and comments uploaded on Facebook sites. In particular, we evaluated about the 5 % of total posts and comments of the 9 selected cities that were commented on most often. Then, we automatically performed data in restrictive way by using the topic tags previously created. Table 1 contains the aggregated results for the 9 selected cities.

Table 1 shows that the municipality of Bari's Facebook site contains 1405 posts and comments, of which 554 (39.43 %) were codified by using 33 topic tags. The municipality of Forlì's Facebook site contains 593 posts and comments, of which 103 (17.37 %) were codified by using 25 topic tags. Moreover, the municipality of Frosinone's Facebook site contains 3701 posts and comments, of which 1496

Table 1 Descriptive analysis of post properties

Local government	Posts and comments in total	Topic tags	Codified post and comments	% of codified post and comments
Municipality of Bari	1405	33	554	39.43
Municipality of Forlì	593	25	103	17.37
Municipality of Frosinone	3701	32	1496	40.42
Municipality of Lucca	1632	40	274	16.79
Municipality of Naples	1309	33	248	18.95
Municipality of Palermo	2795	37	506	18.10
Municipality of Pavia	407	28	91	22.36
Municipality of Pescara	1605	28	293	18.26
Municipality of Venice	1017	36	413	40.61
Total	14,464	–	3978	27.50

(40.42 %) were codified by using 32 topic tags. Also, The municipality of Lucca's Facebook site contains 1632 posts and comments, of which 274 (16.79 %) were codified by using 40 topic tags. Table 1 also shows that 1309 posts and comments were uploaded on the municipality of Naples' Facebook site, pf which 248 (18.95 %) were codified by using 33 topic tags. Moreover, Table 1 also shows that the 2795 posts and comments were uploaded on the municipality of Palermo's Facebook site, of which 506 (18.10 %) were codified by using 37 topic tags. The municipality of Pavia's Facebook site, instead, contains 407 posts and comments, of which 91 (22.36 %) were codified by using 28 topic tags. Moreover, the municipality of Pescara's Facebook site, instead, contains 605 posts and comments, of which 293 (18.26 %) were codified by using 28 topic tags. Finally, 1017 posts and comments were uploaded on the municipality of Venice's Facebook fan page, of which 413 (40.61 %) were codified by using 36 topic tags. Overall, we collected 14464 posts and comments on the Facebook sites of sampled cities, of which 3978 (27.50 %) were codified.

Based on the prior literature [9, 23], we then classified the codified posts and comments into 4 categories, such as co-design, local events, local public services, and provision of information. Co-design refers to "the participation of citizens in participatory mechanisms such as municipality councils or city council meetings or in meetings where citizens can directly ask questions about local issues to a mayor

Table 2 List of categories for municipalities

Category/municipality	A: co-design	B: local events	C: local public services	D: provision of information	Total for municipality
Municipality of Bari	67	45	27	415	554
Municipality of Forlì	8	16	24	55	103
Municipality of Frosinone	27	728	41	700	1496
Municipality of Lucca	14	48	87	125	274
Municipality of Naples	49	14	60	125	248
Municipality of Palermo	48	53	128	277	506
Municipality of Pavia	18	13	26	34	91
Municipality of Pescara	13	16	22	242	293
Municipality of Venice	14	116	72	211	413
Total for category	258	1049	487	2184	3978

or a minister or an MP in order to debate about local services and policies" [9, p. 421]. Local events, instead, contains posts and comments that inform citizens about "artistic, cultural or sportive events organized by the municipality or other public institutions" [9, p. 421]. Local public services contains posts and comments related to local government activities aimed to improve the public services provided to citizens, such as transport, environment, security, energy, welfare, sport, etc. Finally, provision of information contains posts and comments by which local governments provide to citizens current information and news considered important for citizens, such as weather forecast, traffic information, contracts and tenders, etc. [9, 23]. Table 2 shows the 4 aggregated categories of codified posts and comments for each municipalities.

Table 2 shows that Italian local municipalities uploaded posts and comments related to provision of information (2184; 54.91 %), local events (1049; 26.37 %), local public services (487; 12.24 %), and co-design (258; 6.48 %) categories. Apart the municipality of Frosinone, all posts and comments uploaded on the Facebook sites of municipalities contain are mainly related to provision of information category. Indeed, the Facebook site of the municipality of Frosinone mainly contains information related to local event (728), rather than provision of information (700).

Finally, we also reported the list of most cited words. Table 3 contains the most 35 cited words and the weighted percentage for each of them.

Table 3 The most cited words

No.	Word	Weighted percentage (%)	No.	Word	Weighted percentage (%)
1	Comune (municipality)	0.85	19	Presentazione (presentation)	0.08
2	Città (city)	0.29	20	Teatro (theatre)	0.08
3	Sindaco (mayor)	0.21	21	Pubblico (public)	0.08
4	Comunale council	0.17	22	Programma (programme)	0.08
5	Piazza (square)	0.15	23	Nuovo (new)	0.08
6	Cittadini (citizens)	0.13	24	Servizi (services)	0.07
7	Stato (status)	0.13	25	Consiglio council	0.07
8	Essere (to be)	0.12	26	Territorio (territory)	0.07
9	Presso (at)	0.11	27	Conferenza (conference)	0.07
10	Progetto (project)	0.11	28	Scuole (school)	0.07
11	Servizio (service)	0.10	29	Presidente head	0.07
12	Parte (part)	0.10	30	Attività (activity)	0.07
13	Lavori (works)	0.10	31	Possibile (possible)	0.07
14	Youtube (youtube)	0.10	32	Giunta (board)	0.06
15	Giorni (days)	0.09	33	Tempo (time)	0.06
16	Lavoro (job)	0.09	34	Persone (people)	0.06
17	Corso (main street)	0.09	35	Mostra (exihibit)	0.06
18	Palazzo (palace)	0.08	–	–	–

5   Discussion and Conclusions

The aim of this work was to investigate what municipalities communicate through social media. Previous research mainly focused on the analysis of how local governments utilize social media for managing their external communication with citizens. To date, while we known as social media are used for communication, little is yet known about the communication topics between local governments and citizens in social networking sites. Using a qualitative methodology, this paper explored the social media usage by Italian local governments aimed to understanding the topics that are most discussed in online social networks, such as Facebook. In particular, data sampling concerns 9 of the bigger Italian municipalities (more than 50,000 people living) that are situated in the Northern (Venice, Pavia, and Forlì), Central (Pescara, Frosinone, and Lucca), and Southern Italy (Naples, Bari, and Palermo). Considering the Italian context, where the importance of mandatory e-disclosure through municipality's website is recognized (with legislative decrees 150/2009 and 33/2013), the implementation of voluntary e-disclosure tools, such as social media, become more and more established because in this way the municipalities can create stronger trust relationship.

Using a qualitative data analysis method, data was performed to understanding what Italian municipalities communicate with citizens in official Facebook sites. Firstly, results have shown that the main communication topics between Italian local governments and citizens are provision of information, local events, local public services, and co-design. These result is compliant with previous research that are investigated the social media usage by local governments [9, 23]. However, in respect of previous research, a smaller number of topics discussed by Italian local governments and citizens is emerged. Italian local governments have paid more attention to current information and news, such as weather forecast, traffic information, contracts and tenders, etc., as well as to information about social and cultural events organized by the municipality or other public institutions. On the contrary, less importance has been given to local public services and co-design. In this regard, communication topics about the improvement of local public services and the participation of citizens in participatory mechanisms of municipalities were recognized as less critical than the previous ones.

This study presents several limitations. One limitation stems from the sample, some cities are difficult to compare because are different in terms of size, economic figures, citizens, etc. This could affect the consistency of the findings. Moreover, despite findings of this research, data analysis is yet not complete to date. In the next phase, we would use another method like Social network analysis in order to know the link among different words and also the distance. In this case, it should be possible to know 'the strength of weak ties' [28] among concepts.

References

1. Jaeger, P.T., Bertot J.C., Shilton K.: Information policy and social media: framing government—citizen web 2.0 interactions. Web 2.0 Technologies and Democratic Governance, pp. 11–25. Springer, New York (2012)
2. Mishaal, D.A., Abu-Shanab, E.: The effect of using social media in governments: framework of communication success (2015)
3. Bonsón, E., Torres, L., Rayo, S., Flores, F.: Local e-government 2.0: social Media and corporate transparency in municipalities. Gov. Inf. Q. 29(12), 123–132 (2012)
4. Bertot, J.C., Jaeger, P.T., Hansen, D.: The impact of polices on government social media usage: issues, challenges, and recommendations. Gov. Inf. Q. 29(1), 30–40 (2012)
5. Picazo-Vela, S., Gutierrez-Martinez, I., Luna-Reyes, L.F.: Understanding risks, benefits, and strategic alternatives of social media applications in the public sector. Gov. Inf. Q. 29(4), 504–511 (2012)
6. Oliveira, G.H.M., Welch, E.W.: Social media use in local government: linkage of technology, task, and organizational context. Gov. Inf. Q. 30(4), 397–405 (2013)
7. Norris, D.F., Reddick, C.G.: Local e-government in the United States: transformation or incremental change? Public Adm. Rev. 73(1), 165–175 (2013)

8. Sandoval-Almazan, R., Gil-Garcia, J.R., Luna-Reyes, L.F., Luna-Reyes, D., Diaz-Murillo, G.: The use of Web 2.0 on Mexican state websites: a three-year assessment. Electron. J. E-gov. **9**(2), 107–121 (2011)
9. Sobaci, M.Z., Karkin, N.: The use of twitter by mayors in Turkey: tweets for better public services? Gov. Inf. Q. **30**(4), 417–425 (2013)
10. Kaplan, A.M., Haenlein, M.: Users of the world, unite! the challenges and opportunities of social media. Bus. Horiz. **53**(1), 59–68 (2010)
11. Magro, M.J.: A review of social media use in e-government. Adm. Sci. **2**, 148–161 (2012)
12. Klang, M., Nolin, J.: Disciplining social media: an analysis of social media policies in 26 Swedish municipalities. First Monday **16**, 8 (2011)
13. Kavanaugh, A.L., Fox, E.A., Sheetz, S.D., Yang, S., Li, L.T., Shoemaker, D.J., Xie, L.: Social media use by government: from the routine to the critical. Gov. Inf. Q. **29**(4), 480–491 (2012)
14. Feeney, M.K., Welch, E.W.: Electronic participation technologies and perceived outcomes for local government managers. Public Manag. Rev. **14**(6), 815–833 (2012)
15. Mossberger, K., Wu, Y., Crawford, J.: Connecting citizens and local governments? Social media and interactivity in major US cities. Gov. Inf. Q. **30**(4), 351–358 (2013)
16. Ma, L.: The diffusion of government microblogging: evidence from Chinese municipal police bureaus. Public Manag. Rev. **15**(2), 288–309 (2013)
17. Zheng, L., Zheng, T.: Innovation through social media in the public sector: information and interactions. Gov. Inf. Q. **31**(S), 106–117 (2014)
18. Lovari, A., Parisi, L.: Listening to digital publics. investigating citizens' voices and engagement within Italian municipalities' facebook pages. Public Relat. Rev. **41**(2), 205–213 (2015)
19. Chun, S.A., Shulman, S., Sandoval, R., Hovy, E.: Government 2.0: making connections between citizens, data and government. Inf. Polity **15**(1), 1 (2010)
20. Bonsón, E., Royo, S., Ratkai, M.: Citizens' engagement on local governments' facebook sites. An empirical analysis: the impact of different media and content types in Western Europe. Gov. Inf. Q. **32**(1), 52–62 (2015)
21. Guttormsen, C., Sæbø, Ø.: Municipalities 'like' facebook: the use of social media in local municipalities. In: Organizational Change and Information Systems, pp. 157–166. Springer Berlin Heidelberg (2013)
22. Cromer, C.: Understanding web 2.0's influences on public e-services: a protection motivation perspective. Innovation **12**(2), 192–205 (2010)
23. Hofmann, S., Beverungen, D., Räckers, M., Becker, J.: What makes local governments' online communications successful? Insights from a multi-method analysis of Facebook. Gov. Inf. Q. **30**(4), 387–396 (2013)
24. Torres, L., Pina, V.: Public–private partnership and private finance initiatives in the EU and Spanish local governments. Eur. Account. Rev. **10**(3), 601–619 (2001)
25. Martí, C., Royo, S., Acerete, B.: The effect of new legislation on the disclosure of performance indicators: the case of spanish local governments. Int. J. Public Adm. **35**(13), 873–885 (2012)
26. Hofmann, S., Rackers, M., Beverungen, D., Becker, J.: Old blunders in new media? How local governments communicate with citizens in online social networks. In: Proceedings of the System Sciences (HICSS), 2013 46th Hawaii International Conference on, 2023–2032. IEEE (2013)
27. Johnston, L.: Software and method: reflections on teaching and using QSR NVivo in doctoral research. Int. J. Soc. Res. Methodol. **9**(5), 379–391 (2006)
28. Granovetter, M.: Economic action and social structure: the problem of embeddedness. Am. J. Sociol. **91**, 481–510 (1985)

Encouraging Vaccination Behavior Through Online Social Media

David J. Langley, Remco Wijn, Sacha Epskamp and Riet van Bork

1 Introduction

The overall prevalence of the human papillomavirus (HPV) that causes cervical cancer [1] was estimated 9.2 % in Europe [2] and 26.8 % in the US [3]. This makes HPV one of top ranking sexual transmitted diseases, not only in Western countries but around the world. For this reason, in many Western countries young girls are currently being vaccinated to protect them from the effects of this virus. However, societal penetration of this inoculation is much lower than other vaccinations, which has caused substantial concern and debate. For example, in the Netherlands most vaccination programs achieve a penetration of more than 90 % but the HPV-vaccination remained at around 50 % in its first year, 2009 [4], and has still not reached 60 %.

Peoples' understanding of health-related issues, and their health-related choices are increasingly influenced by information distributed via the internet and online social media (OSM) [5–7]. OSM have proven to be highly effective at influencing

D.J. Langley (✉) · R. Wijn
TNO Netherlands Organisation for Applied Scientific Research,
Groningen, The Netherlands
e-mail: david.langley@tno.nl

R. Wijn
e-mail: remco.wijn@tno.nl

D.J. Langley
University of Groningen, Groningen, The Netherlands

S. Epskamp · R. van Bork
University of Amsterdam, Amsterdam, The Netherlands
e-mail: s.epskamp@uva.nl

R. van Bork
e-mail: r.vanbork@uva.nl

© Springer International Publishing Switzerland 2016   307
F. D'Ascenzo et al. (eds.), *Blurring the Boundaries Through Digital Innovation*,
Lecture Notes in Information Systems and Organisation 19,
DOI 10.1007/978-3-319-38974-5_24

public opinion by promoting a critical position with respect to the government's vaccination policy [8]. Consequently, anti-vaccination reporting—for example, via the internet and OSM, by worried parents, the alternative medical community and others—has become an important factor explaining the low level of public acceptance of vaccinations [9–12].

The Information Systems community is ideally suited to offer new insights about the role of the social internet on vaccination decisions. We define online social media (OSM) as having unique user profiles, user-generated digital content, and relational connections. OSM include online blogs and microblogs, social network applications, and online forums [13]. In many countries, OSM have quickly become a dominant arena for consumers and citizens to express their views openly and learn from others' views. Social influence thus becomes an important mechanism in OSM [14, 15]. OSM have been shown to play a role in influencing health-related opinions and behaviors [16, 17], and they have indeed been implicated in the low uptake of the HPV vaccination [9]. What has not yet been shown is evidence that the same OSM are also suitable for promoting the scientific or government's position and thereby balancing the debate in controversial issues [18].

In this paper, we attempt to develop knowledge as a basis for offering more guidance about whether and which interventions can or should be used online to actively support offline vaccination behavior, once negative information is spread via OSM. Specifically, in this paper we explore the suitability of OSM as a means of intervening in the public's decision making process. We do this by analyzing the effect of different cues to action communicated via online discussion forums on the behavioral intention to receive the vaccination against HPV. To this end, we invited parents of daughters due to be called up to receive their vaccination, to participate in an online discussion forum where they could discuss their stand on their daughter's getting or not getting a vaccination to protect them against HPV. We presented cues to action on the forums, in direct response to an anti-vaccination opinion, such that they promoted vaccination in different ways. After their active participation on the forums, we measured the participants' attitude towards the vaccination.

In the following sections we describe our model development, the method using an online discussion forum, data collection, results and we conclude with a discussion of the initial findings and their relevance for health communication via OSM.

2 Model Development

Health decisions, such as a decision to get vaccinated, are assumed to depend on a complexity of cognitions and attitudes. The Health Belief Model (HBM) [19, 20] specifies the most elemental of these cognitions and attitudes and was constructed to explain which beliefs should be targeted in communication campaigns to cause positive health behaviors. Four constructs are proposed to vary across individuals and to be predictive of adopting health-related behaviors, including receiving vaccinations. First, individuals should believe they are susceptible to a particular negative health outcome. Second, individuals should believe that this negative health outcome is severe or threatening. Third, the proposed solution should be effective and prevent the negative health outcome. Fourth, is the role of a cue to action. This cue is necessary for prompting engagement in health-promoting behaviors. Cues to action include internal cues, such as pain or discomfort, or external cues, such as media campaigns, or conversations with others. The intensity of cues needed to prompt action is moderated by an individual's perceived susceptibility, seriousness, benefits, and barriers [19].

Since Rosenstock put forward his original version of the HBM, it has been noted that the cue to action is the most underdeveloped and least researched element of the HBM [21]. This paper tries to fill this void. Additionally, we posit that health choices are not taken in social isolation. As with many important decisions, others may play a role in the decision making process. One of the key mechanisms at work on OSM is the strong influence on individuals that can be exerted via peer connections [14, 22]. That is, individuals with close interpersonal bonds tend to influence each other [23–25]. In the case of health decisions, however, peers are often not health experts. Also, the formal authority enjoyed by health professionals, or governmental health officials could have a different influence than the interpersonal trust between people who interact in an online community [26]. This leads to the question whether individuals will be persuaded to a greater extent in their health decisions by their peers than by health professionals, or governmental health officials, if at all.

A second mechanism which has received attention in the psychology and communication literature, is the role of different types of persuasive message in changing individuals' behavior. A distinction is made with respect to approach and avoidance tendencies toward some behavior and persuasive strategies that fit those tendencies [27]. Alpha strategies to promote a vaccination focus on "approach" by promoting gains, or putting forth reasons why someone should do something. In contrast, omega strategies focus on reducing resistance or "avoidance" by side-stepping or by directly or indirectly addressing resistance that can hold someone back from performing some behavior. Thus, for instance, when persuading an individual to get inoculated one could name all the reasons for doing it (e.g., reducing chances of illness, reducing chances to infect others, etc.), add incentives, or increase the credibility of the source of a persuasive message. These are alpha strategies. On the other hand, one could also focus on devaluing the reasons against getting the jab (e.g., it does not hurt so much, it does not make you ill, etc.). This is an omega strategy.

Thus far, in the case of the HPV inoculation efforts that the Dutch government has undertaken, it seems that most focus has been on alpha strategies. That is, inoculation advocates have persistently framed their message using positive persuasion (e.g., "The jab helps to prevent HPV"), and they have boosted their credibility (e.g., "you can trust us, we are scientists"). However, to date no efforts seem to have focused on omega strategies. We expect that this mechanism—the nature of the persuasive message, either alpha or omega—will also moderate the effect of cues to action on the intention to vaccinate. The model is shown in Fig. 1.

Fig. 1 The Health Belief
Model [19, 20] adapted to
include influence effects via
online social media (OSM)

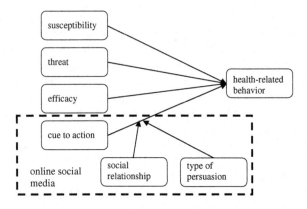

3 Method

3.1 Participants and Design

A total of 184 participants (67 % women; age: M = 43.07, SD = 5.37), recruited
via a leading marketing research firm, took part in our experiment in exchange for
special credits redeemable for products by the recruitment organization. All participants were parents of daughters born in 2001, 2002 or 2003 who would be
invited by the responsible government health agency to get their HPV inoculation
in the next cohorts. Participants were randomly assigned to the conditions of a 2
(source: peer vs. governmental organization) × 4 (influence strategy: source
credibility, self-belief, direct challenge, indirect challenge) between-subjects design.
The first two influence strategies are alpha strategies, approaching the vaccination
issue in a positive way, and the latter two are omega strategies, devaluing the
reasons against getting the vaccination. In our design, the parents took part in
discussion forums where they were exposed to the conditions, and they subsequently filled in questionnaires where we measured the effects of the conditions on
the dependent variables, vaccination attitudes and intention, as well as other relevant questions.

3.2 Procedure and Data Collection

Participants were invited by the recruitment organization to participate in an online
discussion group to discuss raising adolescents and related issues. We informed
participants that we were interested to know how parents discuss issues on OSM
and how they value communicating about parenting issues with peer-parents. We
asked them to log in on a specified date and time and to be available to participate in
the experiment for 50 min. Besides the topic of interest to our study, we added two
irrelevant topics of discussion so that the participants would not be aware what the

experiment was about. This was to reduce bias on their responses to the HPV vaccination. Each participant was made to believe that the focus was on raising adolescents and related issues, and that parents would be asked to complete questionnaires on one of three topics, energy drinks, HPV vaccination and cyber bullying.

At first log in, participants first read and agreed with the informed consent information. We emphasized that all communications were anonymous and would only be used for scientific analysis and that their reactions would not be individually retraceable. Participants read that they would take part in an internet discussion forum, about topics of interest to parents of growing children who will soon be going to high school. They were told there were three topics for discussion, each lasting between one and 15 min after which they would answer questions pertaining to one of the topics.

After clicking on the link to the forum, the participants saw the first topic on energy drinks, and could join the discussion. We used this first topic for people to get acquainted to the internet forum and to each other. The second topic introduced the HPV issue. The discussion was started by the host, as follows: "The government health service offers all girls in the Netherlands the opportunity to be vaccinated against the HPV virus, which can cause cervical cancer. Some people are for and some against this vaccination. What will you do? Share your opinion below and click on 'add message'".[1]

The first reaction, posted by a confederate, reflected often used criticism by anti-vaccination lobbyists [9], stressing strong side effects and the lobbying by pharmaceutical firms. Following this the next post in the timeline was from another confederate and communicated a pro-vaccination opinion. Depending on the condition the participant was assigned to this post was either from a peer (i.e., starting with the introduction: "I am the parent of two daughters") or a government official (i.e., starting with the introduction: "I am a spokesperson for the government health service") and was followed by a pro-vaccination comment along the lines of one of four persuasion strategies: persuasion by indirect challenge, persuasion by direct challenge, persuasion by self-belief, and persuasion by source credibility. For this topic, we manipulated the forum so that parents could not read each other's messages so that the only influence would be from the confederates. Once the participant had posted their opinion, we asked them to go on to the third topic, cyber bullying.

After all three discussions, the participants filled out a questionnaire, taken from van Keulen et al. [4]. This questionnaire contained our dependent variables on attitudes and planned behavior regarding the HPV inoculation for their daughters and other questions relating to the HBM [19]. Specifically, we asked one question pertaining to the intention of getting the vaccination (i.e., Do you intend to have your daughter vaccinated against HPV?), four questions measuring valence of the vaccination (e.g., I find vaccinating my daughter very positive/negative; $\alpha = 0.98$),

---

[1]Literal texts have been translated from Dutch.

one question measuring how they viewed their daughter's chances of getting cervical cancer (i.e., I feel that the chance of my daughter getting cervical cancer later in life is very small/big"), one question measuring anticipatory regret of getting cervical cancer when not vaccinated, one question measuring anticipatory regret of suffering side effects after vaccination, four items measuring participants' trust in institutions (viz., science, healthcare, government, pharmaceutical industry; $\alpha = 0.91$), one item measured trust in other parents and one item measured trust in vaccination critics in relation to HPV, seven items measuring belief in counterarguments of vaccination critics (e.g., too little is known about side effect to vaccinate all young girls in The Netherlands; $\alpha = 0.83$), two questions measuring assumed positive effects of the HPV vaccination (e.g., when my daughter will receive the vaccination I think she will not get cervical cancer; $\alpha = 0.80$), five questions measuring assumed negative effects of the HPV vaccination (e.g., when my daughter will receive the vaccination I think she will become infertile; $\alpha = 0.61$). Finally, we asked what they thought their partner's, daughter's, parents', close friends', doctor's, health institutions', government's and other parents' opinions regarding the vaccination were. We also asked to what extent they valued these individuals' or institutions' opinions. For each set of these two questions—the other's opinion and the value attached to this opinion—we calculated the product to come to a measure of influence of this other individual or institution. All items were measured on Likert-type 5-point scales.

All participants were debriefed after filling in the questionnaire, whereby they received clear information about the experimental design, the scientific evidence for the efficacy of the vaccination and for its safety. This information was taken from the relevant government agency's promotional material regarding the HPV vaccination. All answered supplementary questions showing that they understood that the anti-vaccination message was fake, that no serious side effects are known and that the government's scientifically based policy is that all girls receive the vaccination.[2]

3.3 Analysis

We analyzed our data in two ways. First, we tested our hypotheses regarding the effect of a cue to action (viz., the source of communication and persuasion strategies) on attitudes and the intention to get the vaccination using multivariate analyses of variance (MANOVA). Second, we employed a new network modelling method [28] to explore the relations between the variables measured. Specifically, this method was used to explore whether other variables than those already

---

[2]The research ethics committee of the Netherlands Organisation for Applied Scientific Research was consulted during the design of this study.

described in the HBM contribute to the decision making process regarding HPV vaccinations.

A 2 × 2 multivariate analysis of variance (MANOVA) did not yield statistically significant main effects of communication source (peer vs. organization) or persuasion strategy (alpha vs. omega), or an interaction effect of these factors on the perceived valence of HPV vaccinations and the intention to get the vaccination, all $Fs < 2.15$, $ps > 0.19$. The absence of significant effects means we are unable to reject the null hypothesis that a cue to action does not influence the decision making process. There are several explanations for this lack of effect. First, our manipulation may not have been strong enough. They consisted of only a few lines of text and tried to offer a nuanced perspective. Related to this, possibly the specific medium used (i.e., an online forum) does not lend itself well for nuanced positions. Often the focus of individuals is on finding and scrutinizing information that confirms ones original beliefs and sharing these beliefs back with the online community. A simple, nuanced message may have been too subtle to resort any effect. In any case, from the current findings no conclusions on the effect of our cue to action can be drawn.

Our second goal of the present research was to explore the relations between the variables measured, and to investigate relations beyond those already described in Health Belief Models. To estimate the network structure, we fitted a sparse Gaussian Graphical Model (GGM) [29] following [30] as is done in recent psychological literature (e.g. [31, 32]). In a GGM, variables are indicated by nodes that are connected by an edge if two variables are not independent after partialling out shared variance with all other variables in the dataset [33]. The edges are parametrized as partial correlation coefficients; a partial correlation coefficient of zero indicates that two nodes are independent after conditioning on all other variables and thus feature no edge in the network.

To relax the assumption of multivariate normality, we employed the nonparanormal transformation [34], using the huge package [35]. Subsequently, to control for spurious connections due to sampling error, we employed the least absolute shrinkage and selection operator (LASSO) [36] regularization technique as suggested by [30]. We used the graphical LASSO [37, 38], which is a fast variant of the LASSO aimed at estimating the GGM. The graphical LASSO uses a shrinkage parameter to reduce the overall strength of parameter estimates and setting many parameter values to be exactly equal to zero, thus simplifying the model. We set this shrinkage parameter to minimize the extended Bayesian Information Criterium (EBIC) [39], which has been established to accurately recover the network structure [40]. GGM estimation, using the graphical LASSO in combination with EBIC, has been implemented in version 1.3.1 of the qgraph package for R [28, 41].

The network was drawn using qgraph [28, 41] version 1.3.1, in which edges are colored according to the strength of the partial correlations; positive partial correlations are displayed as green edges, negative partial correlations as red edges and the stronger the absolute value of the partial correlation the wider and more saturated the edge. For each node, the partial correlations between that node and all other nodes are directly related to the multiple regression coefficients of one variable when regressed on all other variables in the dataset [42]. As such, the strength of partial correlations—the width and saturation of the edge—can be interpreted as predictive quality between two nodes. If node A is strongly connected with node B then node A predicts node B well and vice versa. A path in the network, such as node A is connected to node B and node B is connected to node C, can be interpreted as a mediation effect of node B on the predictive quality between node A and C.

4 Results

Results of the network analysis are shown in Fig. 2, and offer new insights into the potential for OSM to be used as a channel for influencing health-related behavior. In particular, we highlight four specific findings from this explorative study: the nature of social influence, (a) from family, and (b) from peers, (c) the effects of the different influence strategies as online cues to action, and (d) the relevance of the HBM for the OSM setting.

First, we can see the influence of close family members by assessing the position of the participants' daughter and partner. Clustered with the intention to vaccinate are valence (the vaccination is a good/bad thing), and belief in the effectiveness of

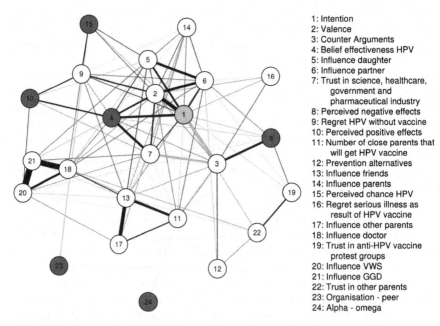

1: Intention
2: Valence
3: Counter Arguments
4: Belief effectiveness HPV
5: Influence daughter
6: Influence partner
7: Trust in science, healthcare, government and pharmaceutical industry
8: Perceived negative effects
9: Regret HPV without vaccine
10: Perceived positive effects
11: Number of close parents that will get HPV vaccine
12: Prevention alternatives
13: Influence friends
14: Influence parents
15: Perceived chance HPV
16: Regret serious illness as result of HPV vaccine
17: Influence other parents
18: Influence doctor
19: Trust in anti-HPV vaccine protest groups
20: Influence VWS
21: Influence GGD
22: Trust in other parents
23: Organisation - peer
24: Alpha - omega

Fig. 2 Network analysis (Qgraph) output for the adapted Health Belief Model (HBM), showing partial correlations between constructs. Traditional HBM constructs are shaded

the vaccination. The variables "influence of the daughter" and "influence of the partner" are most strongly connected to this cluster of intention to vaccinate, valence and belief in the effectiveness of the vaccination.. This reflects the strong direct relationships—partial correlations—between opinions within the nuclear family, and shows that the family plays a more important role than others, such as friends, in vaccination decision making. The participants' parents also have a significant, albeit weaker, influence. Interestingly, our results highlight a difference between the influences between the participant and their daughter or partner. The daughter's opinion is predominantly related to the participant's intention to vaccinate, and less so to their valence with respect to the vaccination. The partner's influence is the other way around: predominantly related to the valence, and less so directly to intention. This means that partners are more likely to agree with each other about the vaccination being a good or bad thing, but that the opinion of the daughter who is to be vaccinated about whether to get the jab has most influence on that decision.

Second, we see that the influence of non-family is less related to the participants' intention or valence, including that of their friends, other (offline) parents they know, and online peers that they may not know. Even though the other parents joining in on the internet forum remained anonymous, their influence is highly similar to that of friends and offline peers, whom the respondents know well. This provides evidence for the immediate, and natural, relationships, and group feelings, that people develop via OSM. However, in our setting, the online peers do not play the moderating role that other authors have described [43]. Our manipulation of peer vs government spokesperson show no direct relationship to the participants' intention or valence with respect to the vaccination.

Third, the influence of the different cues to action (27 and 28 in Fig. 2) is negligible.

Fourth, our analysis reveals insights into the applicability of the HBM in relation to vaccination decisions, in the OSM setting. By looking at the position of the HBM elements in Fig. 2 (shaded), we see mixed findings. The efficacy construct—node 4 in Fig. 2—is particularly strong in driving intention and valence with respect to the vaccination, but the other HBM constructs do not have such an effect in our study.

5 Discussion

When people make vaccination-related choices, they are influenced by various factors as described by the HBM, including their perceived susceptibility to the virus, the threat the virus poses to their health, their perception of the efficacy of the vaccination, and also the cues to action which they receive [19]. Increasingly, the internet and OSM are subjecting individuals to many conflicting opinions, confounding official government messages with opinions from anti-vaccination groups, the alternative medical community and others [9]. As a result, decision-making becomes more complex. This explorative study attempts to offer new insights about the role of OSM on vaccination decisions, and in particular about whether OSM also offer a suitable mechanism for promoting the government's position on a vaccination program, and thereby reducing the effect of the critics.

In total, 184 parents of girls soon to be called up to receive the HPV vaccination took part in OSM discussion forums and communicated their opinions on three topics relating to their children, including the vaccination. In a carefully designed protocol, they were subjected to eight different conditions (between subjects) attempting to stimulate them to get their daughters vaccinated. Using a network modelling technique [28] we explored the influences on the participants' intentions to vaccinate, focusing on elements of the HBM. We find that opinions relating to the vaccination within the nuclear family have the strongest relationships, suggesting that influences via OSM may need to concentrate not just on one decision-maker, but on the interdependent family members. We find a strong direct link from the daughter's opinion to the focal parent's intention to vaccinate which may reflect the low power-distance culture in the Netherlands (c.f. [44]). The parent's opinion about the vaccination (valence) is less strongly related to that of the daughter, but whether they agree or not, the daughter's opinion is highly influential on the decision whether or not to vaccinate. The partner's opinion, on the other hand, predominantly influences the participant's own opinion (valence). In contrast, parents' friends and peers have a far weaker effect on the decision to vaccinate, whereby there appears to be almost no difference in influence between a person's close friends, the other parents they know in their social environment, and people they interact with via OSM. This suggests an important role for OSM in carrying mechanisms of influence, although in our study all these peer effects are minimal.

A key question in this study is if the HBM applies in the online setting. Our exploratory findings suggest that the elements of the HBM work differently via OSM, whereby perceived efficacy is highly influential and cues to action appear to have little influence. We also see that trust in authority remains influential, despite the claims for bottom-up empowerment which some authors make in relation to OSM.

We see three main avenues for continuing this study. First, in the current paper we have only analyzed the data from the questionnaire which was administered directly after the participants had taken part in the discussion forums. We may enrich our findings by also carrying out a content analysis of the comments made during the forum discussions. Second, health-related decisions can be complex and require a great deal of thought, and this is certainly the case for new vaccinations of children. In this study, we investigate the possibilities of using OSM as a means to 'nudge' parents to become more positive towards the HPV vaccination, in a single session on an OSM. Further research may uncover stronger influence effects if they assess the effect of a series of nudges, as these can be expected to build up to a stronger effect on attitudes and behaviors [45]. Finally, based on the influence approaches posited by Knowles and Linn [27], and on competing theories of influence from peers versus authority figures [22, 26], we investigated influence via eight specific conditions. Although preliminary results do not show strong effects from these conditions, further research may including other online influence attempts by health professionals to uncover more successful influence effects.

References

1. Bosch, F.X., Lorincz, A., Munoz, N., Meijer, C.J.L.M., Shah, K.V.: The causal relation between human papillomavirus and cervical cancer. J. Clin. Pathol. **55**(4), 244–265 (2002)
2. Clifford, G.M., Gallus, S., Herrero, R., Munoz, N., Snijders, P.J.F., Vaccarella, S., Franceschi, S.: Worldwide distribution of human papillomavirus types in cytologically normal women in the international agency for research on cancer HPV prevalence surveys: a pooled analysis. Lancet **366**(9490), 991–998 (2005)
3. Dunne, E.F., Unger, E.R., Sternberg, M., McQuillan, G., Swan, D.C., Patel, S.S., Markowitz, L.E.: Prevalence of HPV infection among females in the United States. J. Am. Med. Assoc. **297**(8), 813–819 (2007)
4. van Keulen, H.M., Otten, W., Ruiter, R.A., Fekkes, M., van Steenbergen, J., Dusseldorp, E., Paulussen, T.W.: Determinants of HPV vaccination intentions among Dutch girls and their mothers: a cross-sectional study. BMC Public Health **13**(1), 111 (2013)
5. Fox, S.: Pew internet and american life project: the engaged E-patient population. http://www.pewinternet.org/Reports/2008/The-Engaged-Epatient-Population.aspx (2008)
6. Betsch, C., Sachse, K.: Dr. Jekyll or Mr. Hyde? (How) the internet influences vaccination decisions: Recent evidence and tentative guidelines for online vaccine communication. Vaccine **30**(25), 3723–3726 (2012)
7. Grajales III, F.J., Sheps, S., Ho, K., Novak-Lauscher, H., Eysenbach, G.: Social media: a review and tutorial of applications in medicine and health care. J. Med. Internet Res. **16**(2), e13 (2014)
8. Campbell, E., Salathé, M.: Complex social contagion makes networks more vulnerable to disease outbreaks. arXiv:1211.0518 (2012)
9. Kata, A.: Anti-vaccine activists, Web 2.0, and the postmodern paradigm–An overview of tactics and tropes used online by the anti-vaccination movement. Vaccine **30**(25), 3778–3789 (2012)
10. Nan, X., Madden, K.: HPV vaccine information in the blogosphere: how positive and negative blogs influence vaccine-related risk perceptions. Attitudes Behav. Intentions Health Commun. **27**, 829–836 (2012)
11. Nicholson, M.S., Leask, J.: Lessons from an online debate about measles–mumps–rubella (MMR) immunization. Vaccine **30**(25), 3806–3812 (2012)
12. Zimmerman, R.K., Wolfe, R.M., Fox, D.E., Fox, J.R., Nowalk, M.P., Troy, J.A., Sharp, L.K.: Vaccine criticism on the world wide web. J. Med. Internet Res. **7**(2), e17 (2005)
13. Kaplan, A.M., Haenlein, M.: Users of the world, unite! The challenges and opportunities of social media. Bus. Horiz. **53**(1), 59–68 (2010)
14. Stieglitz, S., Dang-Xuan, L.: Emotions and information diffusion in social media—sentiment of microblogs and sharing behavior. J. Manag. Inf. Syst. **29**(4), 217–248 (2013)
15. Matook, S., Brown, S.A., Rolf, J.: Forming an intention to act on recommendations given via online social networks. Eur. J. Inf. Syst. **24**(1), 76–92 (2015)
16. Fichman, R.G., Kohli, R., Krishnan, R.: The role of information systems in healthcare: current research and future trends. Inf. Syst. Res. **22**(3), 419–428 (2011)
17. Yan, L., Tan, Y.: Feeling blue? Go online: an empirical study of social support among patients. Inf. Syst. Res. **25**(4), 690–709 (2014)
18. Keelan, J., Pavri, V., Balakrishnan, R., Wilson, K.: An analysis of the human papilloma virus vaccine debate on myspace blogs. Vaccine **28**(6), 1535–1540 (2010)
19. Rosenstock, I.M.: Historical origins of the health belief model. Health Educ. Monogr. **2**, 328–335 (1974)
20. Janz, N.K., Becker, M.H.: The health belief model: a decade later. Health Educ. Q. **11**, 1–47 (1984)
21. Carpenter, C.J.: A meta-analysis of the effectiveness of health belief model variables in predicting behavior. Health Commun. **25**(8), 661–669 (2010)

22. Watts, D.J., Dodds, P.S: Influentials, networks, and public opinion formation, J. Consum. Res. (2007)
23. Sassenberg, K., Boos, M.: Attitude change in computer-mediated communication: effects of anonymity and category norms. Group Processes Intergroup Relat. 6(4), 405–422 (2003)
24. Pornpitakpan, C.: The persuasiveness of source credibility: a critical review of five decades' evidence. J. Appl. Soc. Psychol. 34(2), 243–281 (2004)
25. Cialdini, R.B., Goldstein, N.J.: Social influence: compliance and conformity. Annu. Rev. Psychol. 55, 591–621 (2004)
26. Anagnostopoulos, A., Brova, G., Terzi, E.: Peer and authority pressure in information-propagation models. In: Machine Learning and Knowledge Discovery in Databases, pp. 76–91. Springer: Berlin (2011)
27. Knowles, E.S., Linn, J.A.: Approach-avoidance model of persuasion: alpha and omega strategies for change. Resist. Persuasion, 117–148 (2004)
28. Epskamp, S., Cramer, A.O., Waldorp, L.J., Schmittmann, V.D., Borsboom, D.: Qgraph: Network visualizations of relationships in psychometric data. J. Stat. Softw. 48(4), 1–18 (2012)
29. Lauritzen, S.L.: Graphical Models. Oxford University Press (1996)
30. Costantini, G., Epskamp, S., Borsboom, D., Perugini, M., Mõttus, R., Waldorp, L.J., Cramer, A.O.: State of the aRt personality research: a tutorial on network analysis of personality data in R. J. Res. Pers. 54, 13–29 (2015)
31. Fried, E.I., Bockting, C., Arjadi, R., Borsboom, D., Amshoff, M., Cramer, A.O.J., Epskamp, S., Tuerlinckx, F., Carr, D., Stroebe, M.: From loss to loneliness: the relationship between depressive symptoms and bereavement. J. Abnorm. Psychol. (in press)
32. McNally, R.J., Robinaugh, D.J., Wu, G.W.Y., Wang, L., Deserno, M., Borsboom, D.: Mental disorders as causal systems: a network approach to posttraumatic stress disorder. Clin. Psychol. Sci. (2014)
33. Epskamp, S., Maris, G., Waldorp, L., Borsboom, D.: Network psychometrics. In: P. Irwing, D. Hughes, T. Booth (eds.), Handbook of psychometrics. Wiley, New York (in press)
34. Liu, H., Lafferty, J., Wasserman, L.: The nonparanormal: semiparametric estimation of high dimensional undirected graphs. J. Mach. Learn. Res. 10, 2295–2328 (2009)
35. Zhao, T., Liu, H., Roeder, K., Lafferty J., Wasserman, L.: Huge: high-dimensional undirected graph estimation. R package version 1.2.6. http://CRAN.R-project.org/package=huge (2014)
36. Tibshirani, R.: Regression shrinkage and selection via the lasso. J. R. Stat. Soc. Ser. B (Methodol.), 267–288 (1996)
37. Friedman, J., Hastie, T., Tibshirani, R.: Sparse inverse covariance estimation with the graphical lasso. Biostatistics 9, 432–441 (2008)
38. Witten, D.M., Friedman, J.H., Simon, N.: New insights and faster computations for the graphical lasso. J. Comput. Graph. Stat. 20, 892–900 (2011)
39. Chen, J., Chen, Z.: Extended Bayesian information criteria for model selection with large model spaces. Biometrika 95, 759–771 (2008)
40. Borkulo, C.D. van, Borsboom, D., Epskamp, S., Blanken, T.F., Boschloo, L., Schoevers, R.A., Waldorp, L.J.: A new method for constructing networks from binary data. Nat. Sci. Rep. 4 (2014)
41. Epskamp, S., Costantini, G., Cramer, A.O.J., Waldorp, L.J., Schmittmann, V.D., Borsboom, D.: qgraph: graph plotting methods, psychometric data visualization and graphical model estimation. R package version 1.3.1.http://CRAN.R-project.org/package=qgraph (2015)
42. Pourahmadi, M.: Covariance estimation: the GLM and regularization perspectives. Stat. Sci. 26, 369–387 (2011)
43. Park, C., Lee, T.M.: Information direction, website reputation and eWOM effect: a moderating role of product type. J. Bus. Res. 62(1), 61–67 (2009)
44. Hofstede, G.: Cultures and Organizations, pp. 159–166. London: McGraw-Hill (1991)
45. Johnson, E.J., Shu, S.B., Dellaert, B.G., Fox, C., Goldstein, D.G., Häubl, G., Larrick, R.P., Payne, J.W., Peters, E., Schkade, D., Wansink, B., Weber, E.U.: Beyond nudges: tools of a choice architecture. Mark. Lett. 23(2), 487–504 (2012)

Author Index

© Springer International Publishing Switzerland 2016   319
F. D'Ascenzo et al. (eds.), *Blurring the Boundaries Through Digital Innovation*,
Lecture Notes in Information Systems and Organisation 19,
DOI 10.1007/978-3-319-38974-5

Printed in the United States
By Bookmasters